changing the way the world learns℠

To get extra value from this book for no additional cost, go to:

http://www.thomson.com/wadsworth.html

thomson.com is the World Wide Web site for Wadsworth/ITP and is your direct source to dozens of on-line resources. *thomson.com* helps you find out about supplements, experiment with demonstration software, search for a job, and send e-mail to many of our authors. You can even preview new publications and exciting new technologies.

thomson.com: *It's where you'll find us in the future.*

■ The Wadsworth Advisory Panel for the Commuter Student

JESSE DE ANDA
Supervisor of Admissions and Recruitment
Mesa Community College
Mesa, Arizona

ANN GARVEY
Director of Student Life
Normandale Community College
Bloomington, Minnesota

DIANA GOULD
Associate to the Vice President, Student Affairs
Director of Enrollment Services
Youngstown State University
Youngstown, Ohio

ALAN PAPPAS
Coordinator of Career and Job Placement
and Cooperative Education
Santa Fe Community College
Gainesville, Florida

ANN PROVIS
Director, Freshman Year Experience
Mississippi Gulf Coast Community College
Perkinson, Mississippi

Selling this complimentary examination copy is unauthorized.
In past years, the sale of complimentary copies has been a
prime contributor to rising textbook prices for your students.
Help us keep textbooks affordable—
please don't sell these books!

the commuter student

being your best at college & life

Carl Wahlstrom
GENESEE COMMUNITY COLLEGE

Brian K. Williams

STUDENT PHOTOGRAPHS BY MICHAEL GARRETT / GENESEE COMMUNITY COLLEGE

 Wadsworth Publishing Company

I(T)P® An International Thomson Publishing Company

Belmont, CA · Albany, NY · Bonn · Boston · Cincinnati · Detroit · London · Madrid
Melbourne · Mexico City · New York · Paris · Singapore · Tokyo · Toronto · Washington

Publisher: *Gary Carlson*

Editorial Assistant: *Ryan Vesely*

Director of Marketing: *Lauren Ward*

Marketing Manager: *Chaun Hightower*

Marketing Assistant: *Tami Strang*

Senior Project Editor: *Jerry Holloway*

Production Management: *Stacey C. Sawyer,*
*   Sawyer & Williams, Incline Village, NV*

Interior Design: *Seventeenth Street Studios, Oakland, CA*

Print Buyer: *Barbara Britton*

Permissions Editor: *Robert Kauser*

Copy Editor: *Stacey C. Sawyer*

Cover Design: *Seventeenth Street Studios*

Cover Photos: *Background: Telegraph Colour Library-FPG.*
In boxes from left: Tom Stewart/The Stock Market; Simon
Wilkinson/Image Bank; John Henley/The Stock Market.

Compositor: *Seventeenth Street Studios*

Printer: *Bawden Printing*

COPYRIGHT © 1997
By Wadsworth Publishing Company
A Division of International Thomson Publishing Inc.

I(T)P® The ITP logo is a registered trademark under license.

Printed in the United States of America.
1 2 3 4 5 6 7 8 9 10

All rights reserved. No part of this work covered by the copyright
hereon may be reproduced or used in any form or by an
means—graphic, electronic, or mechanical, including photocopying, recording, taping, or information storage and retrieval
system—without the written permission of the publisher.

ISBN 0-534-53289-6

For more information, contact Wadsworth Publishing Company:

Wadsworth Publishing Company
10 Davis Drive
Belmont, California 94002 USA
International Thomson Publishing

International Thomson Publishing
  Europe
Berkshire House 168-173
High Holborn
London, WC1V 7AA, England

Thomas Nelson Australia
102 Dodds Street
South Melbourne 3205
Victoria, Australia

Nelson Canada
1120 Birchmount Road
Scarborough, Ontario
Canada M1K 5G4

International Thomson Editores
Campos Eliseos 385, Piso 7
Col. Polanco
11560 México D.F. México

International Thomson Publishing GmbH
Königswinterer Strasse 418
53227 Bonn, Germany

International Thomson Publishing Asia
221 Henderson Road
#05-10 Henderson Building
Singapore 0315

International Thomson Publishing Japan
Hirakawacho Kyowa Building, eF
2-2-1 Hirakawacho
Chiyoda-ku, Tokyo 102, Japan

brief contents

about the authors

CARL WAHLSTROM is Professor of Intermediate Studies and Sociology at Genesee Community College, Batavia, New York. He has been the  recipient of the State University of New York Chancellor's Award for Excellence in Teaching, the National Freshman Advocate Award, and several other teaching honors. He is past president of the New York College Learning Skills Association and a member of the State University of New York College Transition Course Development Council.

Besides developing and teaching First-Year Experience courses, he has taught courses in human development, learning strategy, sociology, psychology, and human relations. He has a B.S. in Sociology and an M.S. Ed. in Counselor Education from SUNY Brockport and an M.A. in Sociology from the University of Bridgeport.

He lives with his wife, Nancy, an employee benefits consultant, in the Finger Lakes area of New York. He enjoys running, skiing, tennis, boating, mountain biking, karate, motorcycling, music, travel, and getting together with friends and students.

BRIAN K. WILLIAMS has a B.A. in English and M.A. in Communication from Stanford University. He has been Managing Editor for college  textbook publisher Harper & Row/Canfield Press in San Francisco; Editor-in-Chief for trade book publisher J. P. Tarcher in Los Angeles; Publications & Communications Manager for the University of California, Systemwide Administration, in Berkeley; and an independent writer and book producer based in San Francisco and in Incline Village (Lake Tahoe), Nevada.

He has co-authored 16 books, including such best-selling college texts as *Computers and Data Processing* with H. L. Capron, *Microcomputing: Annual Edition* with Tim and Linda O'Leary, *Invitation to Health* with Dianne Hales, and *Using Information Technology* with Stacey Sawyer and Sarah Hutchinson.

He is married to author/editor and book producer Stacey Sawyer, and the two have a passion for travel and for experimenting with various cuisines. He enjoys reading four daily newspapers and numerous magazines and books, hiking in the Sierra, playing blues on the guitar, and getting together with his family.

To Instructors Everywhere: Are We Ready for the Paradigm Shift?

by John E. Roueche, Ph.D.

*Director, Community College
Leadership Program
The University of Texas at Austin*

We college instructors are experiencing an amazing paradigm shift during the closing days of the 20th Century. The dramatic fact is, simply, . . . *students aren't what they used to be!*

The 300-year-old image of a college student in North America—that of someone who lives in a campus residence hall, pursues a degree full time, and graduates according to the schedule in the college catalog—is no longer realistic. In its place we are seeing a greatly different picture, one that has been coming into focus only during the last few years:

- Four-fifths of all students live off campus, over half attend college part time, and a huge number are likely to spend 5 hours or more a week just commuting to class.

- Today most students enrolling in the freshman classes of North American colleges are significantly older—by 10 years or more—than first-year college students of even 5 years ago.

- They are often employed, working 20 hours or more a week, which puts strenuous demands on their time and energy.

- They are more apt to have significant family responsibilities—to be single parents or the primary wage earners in their households.

- More than ever before, they are increasingly likely to be the first in their families to attend college—meaning they are less likely to have role models to mentor them in their new experience.

- Often they feel themselves rusty from having been away from the classroom for several years or they have a history of marginal academic performance, so that they have serious doubts about how successful they can be.

■ And, needless to say, any or all of these attributes can significantly increase the time required to achieve their academic goals.

How are colleges handling this paradigm shift? Many are discovering that they must look with new eyes at the realities the new crop of students is bringing to higher education. They are finding ways to become more accessible, to make allowances for different experiences, to deliver education within varying time frames, to help students balance college with their work and family commitments.

This book parallels these new attempts to engage and meet the needs of today's students. Here students will find answers to the major questions they ask, descriptions of the common challenges and opportunities they will face, and useful strategies they can employ to address them. They will become more proficient at using a variety of important tools as they work through lessons and activities—tools they will find as valuable outside college as inside. The authors have created an excellent learning resource, expertly crafted from their collective experiences and ideas. You and your students will benefit greatly from their many years of experience in helping today's students succeed in college.

—John E. Roueche

Sid W. Richardson Regents Chair
The University of Texas at Austin

preface to the instructor

Q: *"What, in brief, is this book about?"*

A: *"This book is specifically intended for the 80% of college students who are <u>commuters</u>. It shows <u>how you can learn to be the best in college—and thereby learn to be the best in life</u>."*

—The Authors

THE AUDIENCE FOR THIS BOOK

THE COMMUTER STUDENT: *Being Your Best at College & Life* is intended for use in colleges that are heavily or exclusively attended by commuter students—students enrolled in a one-term College Success or First-Year Experience course. Offered in community colleges, vocational-technical schools, four-year colleges, and universities, this course is designed to help students master the academic and personal skills needed to succeed in higher education.

THE PROMISES OF THIS BOOK

The key features of *THE COMMUTER STUDENT* are as follows.

1. *The book is intended specifically for commuter students.*

2. *The principal theme is that the skills mastered for success in college are the skills needed for success in life.*

3. *Our book presents a concise version of essential material.*

4. *The book presents a highly interactive approach to teaching and learning.*

   Extra feature: We offer two special sections in the body of the book, **"Productivity Tools for Your Future"** and **"Survival Skills for Commuters."**

   We elaborate on these features on the following pages.

KEY FEATURE #1: OUR BOOK IS INTENDED SPECIFICALLY FOR COMMUTER STUDENTS. This book is *designed for students who are attending college in commuter areas.* Whether they do so by car or by public transportation, commuter students often differ greatly from the stereotype of a college student—that is, the 18- to 24-year-old, nonworking, full-time student living in a college residence hall and participating in extracurricular activities. Although some commuters may fit this profile (but not live on campus, of course), we assume that many, perhaps most, readers of this book do not. Rather they are students . . .

who live outside the boundaries of the campus,

who commute by car or public transportation to school,

who may attend college part time (as half of students do),

who may work (perhaps full time) while attending school,

who may be older than their classmates (many older than 24),

who may be parents (and worry about day care),

who may participate little in campus activities,

who have many time demands.

At various points in the book we try to address all these concerns.

KEY FEATURE #2: OUR PRINCIPAL THEME IS THAT THE SKILLS MASTERED FOR SUCCESS IN COLLEGE ARE THE SKILLS NEEDED FOR SUCCESS IN LIFE. This book provides a *practical philosophy based on action.* This book is designed to help students *be the best*—that is, achieve mastery—in two areas:

■ *Be the best in college:* We show readers how to master the academic and personal skills needed to succeed in college—how to manage their time, improve their

memory, handle money, deal with relationships, and so on.

■ *Be the best in life:* We point out how the skills one needs for success in college are the same skills one needs for success in life—in work, in relationships, in stress management, in finances, and so on. We pay great attention to the connection between higher education and the rest of one's life.

KEY FEATURE #3: OUR BOOK PRESENTS A CONCISE VERSION OF ESSENTIAL MATERIAL. *THE COMMUTER STUDENT is a concise version of material presented elsewhere.* Much of this book was adapted from *Learning Success: Being Your Best at College & Life* by Carl Wahlstrom and Brian K. Williams. Because it contains fewer pages, *THE COMMUTER STUDENT* is designed to serve the needs of schools that offer a shorter version of the College Success course (such as those offered for less than three credit hours). It is also intended to address the needs of commuter students who are more apt to have to combine school and commuting, school and work, and school and family obligations.

Principal differences with the more comprehensive *Learning Success* text are that this book reduces total text—for example, material on reading, oral presentation, health, and relationships. In addition, the book was redesigned so that less space is given over to artwork.

THE COMMUTER STUDENT covers both *academic success strategies* and *personal success strategies* in just 13 chapters. Special-interest bonus material is covered within regular chapters. Specifically:

■ *Academic success strategies—covered in nine chapters:* We cover making the transition to college, goal-setting, campus resources, time and memory management, learning from lectures and readings, test taking, and researching and writing papers.

- *Personal success strategies—covered in four chapters:* We cover stress, relationships, money, and work (majors/careers). (Instructors of abbreviated courses may wish to skip these topics.)

- *Bonus material—covered within regular chapters:* Instead of having a full chapter for each special-interest topic, we discuss all such "bonus material" within the confines of regular material. *Values clarification*, for instance, is discussed in Chapter 2, "Succeeding." *Multicultural diversity* is covered in Chapter 3, "Resources." *Learning styles* are considered in Chap. 5, "Memory." *Math confidence* is discussed in Chap. 7, "Reading."

KEY FEATURE #4: OUR BOOK PRESENTS A HIGHLY INTERACTIVE APPROACH TO TEACHING AND LEARNING. *THE COMMUTER STUDENT* takes a very focused approach in presenting material—*heavy use of interactive features, techniques to reinforce learning,* and *flexible organization for instructors.* Here's how:

- *Heavy use of interactive features:* Recognizing that most first-year classes are interactive ones, we provide a number of features that ask the student to become actively engaged with the material:

(1) *Personal Explorations,* or learning exercises for individuals, are activities that ask students to examine their feelings and behaviors with regard to particular matters. There are 29 such Personal Explorations in the book.

(2) *Classroom Activities* are collaborative exercises that instructors may elect to assign, in or outside of the classroom. There are 50 such Classroom Activities in this book, grouped at the end of each chapter.

(3) *The Examined Life: Assignments for Journal Entries* is a regular end-of-chapter feature that asks students to explore their own thoughts with regard to something that is meaningful to them in the chapter they have just read.

(4) *Essentials for Time & Life Management* is a six-step strategy that shows students how to set daily tasks from life goals.

- *Techniques to reinforce student learning:* To help students in acquiring knowledge and developing critical thinking, we offer the following to provide learning reinforcement:

(1) *Interesting writing*, studies show, significantly improves students' ability to retain information. Thus, we have employed a number of journalistic devices—such as the personal anecdote, the colorful fact, the apt direct quote—to make the material as interesting as possible.

(2) *Brief interviews with 27 students* of different majors, ages, and ethnic backgrounds help students make a meaningful personal connection to the book.

(3) *Key terms are marked by an underscore and definitions are printed in boldface* in order to help readers avoid any confusion about what terms are important and what they actually mean.

(4) *Section "previews"* offer additional reinforcement. These are the "abstracts" presented at the beginning of each section, which enable the reader to preview, and later review, the material that follows.

(5) *Material is presented in "bite-size" portions.* Major ideas are presented in bite-size form, with generous use of advance organizers, bulleted lists, and new paragraphing when a new idea is introduced.

(6) *Sentences are kept short*—the majority not exceeding 22 – 25 words in length.

- *Flexible organization:* After the first two chapters, the remaining 11 chapters may be taught in any sequence, or omitted, at the instructor's discretion.

BONUS FEATURE: WE OFFER TWO SPECIAL SECTION—"PRODUCTIVITY TOOLS FOR YOUR FUTURE & "SURVIVAL SKILLS FOR COMMUTERS." The first special section, Productivity Tools for Your Future," which appears between Chapters 4 and 5, presents tools of the Information Age that students will find useful in college and essential in their careers. These include personal computers (including notebooks and subnotebooks), computer software (including spreadsheets and database managers), communications tools (such as fax machines and e-mail), online services, and Internet sites and browsers.

The second special section, "Survival Skills for Commuters," which appears between Chapters 9 and 10, offers many suggestions and tips associated with cars, driving, public transportation, and other aspects of commuting.

SUPPLEMENTS & SUPPORT

Several useful supplements accompany this text. They include the following:

INSTRUCTOR'S RESOURCE MANUAL. This supplement for *THE COMMUTER STUDENT* helps instructors teach the chapters of this text by making available additional activities and exercises, advice, teaching suggestions, and answers to questions students commonly ask.

THE WADSWORTH COLLEGE SUCCESS INSTRUCTOR'S COURSE GUIDE. Suitable for instructors of all types—in community colleges, vocational-technical schools, four-year colleges, and universities—*The Wadsworth College Success Course Guide* is a general resource designed to offer general assistance in the teaching the first-year experience course. Examples of subjects covered are how to build support for such course, how to administer it, and how to shape it for the future. Regarded as the most useful resource of its kind available in the market, it is available free to adopters of this text.

TEST PACKAGE. This collection of test and quiz items supports the main chapters of *THE COMMUTER STUDENT.*

TRAINING/WORKSHOPS. Wadsworth offers training and workshop opportunities of various kinds to instructors and/or coordinators of college success or study skills courses. Contact your local sales representative or Wadsworth's Customer Service Department at 1-800-245-6724.

FILMS & VIDEOS. Wadsworth's film and video policy is designed to help instructors enhance their course presentations. Ask your sales representative for more details.

NEWSLETTER. *The Keystone Newsletter* of the Wadsworth College Success Series enables instructors to share ideas with colleagues around the country.

CUSTOM PUBLISHING & BUNDLING OPTIONS. Wadsworth makes available several ways of customizing this text to specifically suit instructors' preferences. In addition, instructors may have local materials shrinkwrapped with *THE COMMUTER STUDENT.* For further information about content, binding options, quantities, and price, contact your local sales representative or Wadsworth's Customer Service Department at 1-800-245-6724.

FACILITATOR'S GUIDE. A special Facilitator's Guide will be available in late 1997 for a fee as a "train the trainer" package that can be used to conduct on-site training by local school personnel.

ACKNOWLEDGMENTS

Two names are on the front of this book, but there are a great many other talented people whose efforts helped to strengthen our own.

Foremost among the staff of Wadsworth Publishing Company were Susan Badger, Gary Carlson, Lauren Ward, Ryan Vesely, and Jerry Holloway, all of whom did a terrific job of supporting us. Susan, we really appreciate your continual presence; we've never seen the president of a publishing company take this kinds of hands-on interest, as you did, and we're very grateful. Gary, you were terrific in keeping this project on track and in handling all the interaction with reviewers; we discovered amazing things in our joint phone conferences as a result of your participation. Lauren, thanks for your warm support and for keeping the spirit of this book alive among the ITP staff. Ryan, it was wonderful the way you were able step into a vacuum and make happen all the necessary things that had to happen to help this book achieve publication. Jerry, you were super, as always; all the knowledge gained through those years of experience—your mastery of how to get things done—really paid off for us. Thanks a billion.

We are also grateful for the cheerfulness and efficiency of others in the Wadsworth editorial and marketing departments: Joe Fierst, Chaun Hightower, and Tami Strang. In addition, we want to express our special appreciation to Alan Venable and, especially, to Mike Alread. We also want to acknowledge the support of Pat Brewer, Kathy Head, Bob Kauser, Peggy Meehan, and Stephen Rapley. Thank you, everyone!

Outside of Wadsworth, we were ably assisted by a community of top-drawer publishing professionals. Directing the production of the entire enterprise, as well as doing the copyediting, was Stacey Sawyer—Brian's wife and an author herself and thus fully equipped to understand authors' travails. Stacey, once again you've pulled a book out under intolerable deadlines, and once again we're in your debt. Thanks for everything!

We also were extremely fortunate to be able to get the services of Seventeenth Street Studios and designer Randall Goodall, who created the cover. Seventeenth Street Studios also handled the composition, and we greatly appreciate their efforts.

Carl Wahlstrom would like to acknowledge the support and encouragement of many friends and associates, including and most importantly his best friend and wife, Nancy, for her continued support, patience, and understanding; Don Green for his tremendous support, suggestions, and direct input; Glenn DuBois for his caring about this project and student success; Meredith Altman, Charley Boyd, and Brenda Beal for encouragement and being part of the team; Stuart Steiner for his continued support; and Pamella Schmitt for helping with information on financial aid. Kudos once again go to Michael Garrett, whose photographic help and willingness to hit the road have helped to make this book once again a student-centered resource. Special thanks are due to the tremendous help from the faculty and staff at Rochester Institute of Technology, including J. Wixson Smith, Latty Goodwin, Maureen Berry, Enid Stevenson, Gail Gucker, Kris Mook, Jackie Czamske, Lorna Mittelman, Jo Cone, Ann Gleason, Audrey Debye, and Dottie Hicks. Carl would also like to thank all his friends and associates in the New York College Learning Skills Association. Last, but surely not least, he would like to express his gratitude to his students for providing him with a source of energy and warmth to help facilitate their growth and learning.

ACKNOWLEDGMENT OF THE WADSWORTH/ITP ADVISORY PANEL FOR THE COMMUTER STUDENT We are grateful to the members of the Wadsworth/ITP Advisory Panel for the Commuter Student for their consultations and for their comments on recent drafts of the manuscript: Jesse De Anda, Supervisor of Admissions and Recruitment, Mesa Community College, Mesa, Arizona; Ann

Garvey, Director of Student Life, Normandale Community College, Bloomington, Minnesota; Diana Gould, Associate to the Vice President, Student Affairs, and Director of Enrollment Services, Youngstown State University, Youngstown, Ohio; Alan Pappas, Coordinator of Career and Job Placement and Cooperative Education, Santa Fe Community College, Gainesville, Florida; and Ann Provis, Director, Freshman Year Experience, Mississippi Gulf Coast Community College, Perkinson, Mississippi.

WE WANT TO HEAR FROM YOU!

We welcome your response to this book, for we are truly trying to make it as useful as possible. Write to us in care of Director of College Success, Wadsworth Publishing Company, 10 Davis Drive, Belmont, CA 94002 (fax: 1-800-522-4923).

Or contact us directly as follows:

Prof. Carl Wahlstrom
Genesee Community College
One College Road
Batavia, NY 14020
Phone: 716-343-0055 ext. 6305
(Eastern Time)
Fax: 716-343-0433
E-mail: Wahlstrom@SGCCVA.SUNY
GENESEE.CC.NY.US
Wadsworth/ITP voice mail:
1-800-876-2350 ext. 339

Mr. Brian K. Williams
Box 10006, 771 Randall Avenue
Incline Village, NV 89450
Phone: 702-832-7336 (Pacific Time)
Fax: 702-832-3026
E-mail: 76570.1533
@COMPUSERVE.COM
Wadsworth/ITP voice mail:
1-800-876-2350 ext. 858

detailed contents

5 memory

6 lectures

11

relationships

12

money

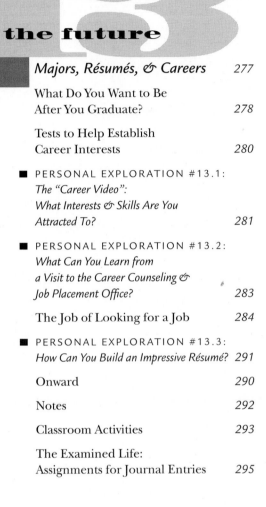

1
transitions

surviving as a commuter student

IN THIS CHAPTER: Commuter students often have different life circumstances than those who live on residential campuses. This chapter considers some of the challenges you will face. We consider the following:

■ *The commuter student—who are you?* Besides living off campus, commuter students often work, attend school part time, are older than classmates, and in other ways differ from traditional students.

■ *Seven challenges:* Among your challenges, you need to quickly adjust to the extra responsibilities of college, upgrade skills, learn to make campus friends, and so on.

■ *Your strengths:* You bring certain strengths to college that will help you achieve success.

Go to campus, go home.
Go to work, go unwind.
Throttle up, throttle down.
Your day consists of
independent sectors
separated by movement.
Commuter student:
This is your life.

T his is my life, too, so I can sympathize.

Hurtling along the highway, often before sunrise and after sunset, sometimes in rain or snow, I strive to connect the different parts of my day. The college I teach at in upstate New York is 60 miles from where I live, so for 2–½ hours out of every 24, Monday through Friday, I am in neither place. I am in between, in transit—a commuter.

Many people live this way, getting back and forth either by car or by public transportation—bus, train, subway, streetcar. In the New York, Chicago, and Washington, D.C. metropolitan areas, the average commute one way is about a half hour, and more than 10% of commuters take more than an hour. Nationwide the average work commute —again, one way—is now 22.3 minutes, and it's usually done by car. Moreover, because the suburbs accounted for 70% of all new jobs between 1980 and 1990, suburb-to-suburb travel is now the largest category, accounting for 44% of commuting. City-to-suburb commutes also have increased, from 9% to 12%.[1,2] But not only are most workers commuters, so are most students.

The Commuter College Student: Who Are You?

PREVIEW A great many commuter students don't fit the profile of the traditional student who lives on campus, is between 18 and 24 years old, attends college full time, and graduates in four years. Instead, they may be part time, older, working, and parents.

T oday about 80% of college undergraduates in the United States commute from housing beyond the borders of their campuses.[3,4] Almost half of students attend college part time, many of them older adults who are working at full-time jobs and engaged in raising families.[5] Only about two in five students complete a bachelor's degree within four years after entering college; some take as long as nine years to graduate.[6]

What is the significance of these numbers? It means that *MOST STUDENTS DO NOT FIT THE PICTURE OF THE COLLEGE STUDENT PORTRAYED ON TV OR IN THE NEWS-PAPERS.* That is, for the most part, a college student is NOT someone who lives on campus, is 17–22 years old, takes a full load of courses, doesn't work, and graduates in four years. Of course, some commuter students *do* fit this profile of what is considered a "traditional" college student, although they don't live in a campus residence, and this book is for them as well.

I am assuming, however, that you may not fit this description. Instead, you may share some or all of the following characteristics. You are a student . . .

who lives off campus, perhaps at home,

who gets back and forth by car or public transportation,

who may be going to college part time,

who may work—perhaps full time—while attending school,

" *As a commuter student, what things do you do to compensate for not living on campus?* "

Name: Nancy Willis

Major: Human Services

Family & work situation: Married, two children, two stepchildren; work part time in grocery store

Interests: Floral arranging, Girl Scouts, wood crafts, cooking

Answer to question: "I planned my schedule so I have free time between classes. This allows me to use the library, the Center for Academic Progress [learning center], and the computer lab. Also, it allows me time to get tutoring, if necessary."

who may be a parent (and worry about day care),

who may be older than the so-called norm for your college class,

who may be mostly on campus to take classes,

who may often take courses in the evening,

who has many time demands,

who may feel isolated.

Even if only one or two things on this list describe your situation, this book is for you. The fact that you are a commuter student means you have special needs different from those of many other students.

The rest of this chapter considers the challenges you face and the strengths you bring to meet those challenges.

Seven Challenges of the Commuter Student

PREVIEW As a commuter college student, you have seven challenges: (1) to quickly adjust to the extra responsibilities that college imposes compared to high school; (2) to begin upgrading academic skills, if necessary; (3) to learn to make friends on campus; (4) to learn to balance school, commuting, and work; (5) to help your family adjust to your new responsibilities; (6) to help your old friends understand your new commitments; and (7) to adjust to new personal challenges.

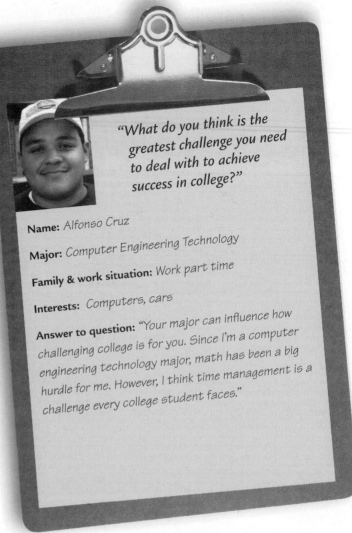

"What do you think is the greatest challenge you need to deal with to achieve success in college?"

Name: Alfonso Cruz

Major: Computer Engineering Technology

Family & work situation: Work part time

Interests: Computers, cars

Answer to question: "Your major can influence how challenging college is for you. Since I'm a computer engineering technology major, math has been a big hurdle for me. However, I think time management is a challenge every college student faces."

Going to college—any college—is "like moving to a foreign country," says Karen Leven Coburn, an associate dean of students at Washington University in St. Louis. "There's a new landscape, a new culture, and a new language. . . ."[7] No wonder it's been said that the first college year "is punctuated by feelings of panic and incompetence."

In this book, I'll do my best to help you try to minimize these feelings of anxiety and inadequacy. To achieve this, you need to meet the following challenges:

1. Quickly adjust to the extra responsibilities that college imposes—responsibilities you probably didn't have in high school. This is crucial.

2. Begin upgrading your academic skills, if necessary, so you can be competitive.

3. Learn to make friends on campus, which may take some extra effort.

4. Learn to balance school, commuting, and work.

5. Help your family adjust to your new responsibilities, if you're living at home.

6. Help your old friends—including boyfriends/girlfriends—understand your new commitments.

7. Adjust to new personal challenges.

Let us consider these.

CHALLENGE #1: ADJUSTING TO THE EXTRA RESPONSIBILITY OF COLLEGE COMPARED TO HIGH SCHOOL. Regardless of the kind of college they're attending, many first-year students have one difficulty in common. This difficulty is: *getting used to the fact that college is not high school.*

High school is required of all students; college is not. High schools have homerooms; colleges do not. In high school, you have the same daily class schedule; in college, the schedule can vary every day. In high school, text-books are given to you; in college, you buy your own. In high school, teachers take class attendance; in college, they often do not. High schools require a doctor's note saying you were ill if you miss a class; colleges usually don't. High schools emphasize teachers teaching; colleges emphasize learners learning. Finally, the biggest difference is: *college requires you devote a lot more time to studying than high school did.*

In short, in going from high school to college, you are going from a system with many rules to one with fewer rules. You are going from an educational structure that often restricts freedom to one that allows a good deal of freedom.

But this new environment has a condition attached to it: You're going from an environment with fewer demands to one with LOTS OF demands—and you're expected to take more responsibility for your actions. In particular, this will mean learning to manage your time in a different way.

CHALLENGE #2: UPGRADING YOUR ACADEMIC SKILLS.

Are you up for college-level work? It's possible you went to a high school that didn't really prepare you for college, and that's not your fault. However, it's certainly not the college instructor's fault if you find it a struggle to keep up in his or her courses. It's up to you to catch up on the necessary skills.

What kind of skills are we talking about? Many students find high school didn't give them the foundation they need in reading, writing, and math. I offer suggestions for reading textbooks and writing papers later in this book. However, your college offers special courses—developmental reading, writing, and mathematics classes—that are designed to help students do college-level work. You can discuss with your academic advisor (as I describe in Chapter 3) which

classes might be best for you. This might be determined in part by college entrance exams.

Taking developmental classes is not something to feel ashamed or resentful of. Maybe you had the misfortune to have had a substandard high-school education. However, you now have the *good* fortune to be able to do something about it. Indeed, one of the great things about the educational systems of North America is that (unlike those in many other countries) they offer lots of second chances. Developmental classes can be your second chance.

You can also think about developmental education this way: All kinds of people find later on in life that they've suddenly developed an interest in an activity—job hunting, public speaking, management, investing, painting, golf, computer operation, a foreign language—for which they've had little previous training. So they do the obvious thing: They go to some sort of school to learn the basics that they missed earlier. That's what you would be doing with developmental courses.

In any case, it's not up to your instructors to reach down and give you an "A" because you have the best of intentions to do well but may have been disadvantaged by a poor academic background. It's up to you to reach up and earn that "A" by powering up your academic skills.

CHALLENGE #3: MAKING FRIENDS ON THE COMMUTER CAMPUS.

When you go to college as a commuter student, you may find yourself surrounded by people you don't know, many of whom are quite different from you. Yet even while in the midst of masses of people, you may often feel alone.

Making friends is easier for students who live on residential campuses—those with on-campus dormitories, residence halls, and live-in fraternities and sororities. This is because students continually cross paths when they're not in class, as in dormitory hallways and dining areas.

At commuter schools, however, many students simply leave campus after class. Outside of class, they may be reluctant to speak with fellow students, join clubs, or go to social functions. As a result, in one survey, 76% of college presidents stated that students' lack of participation in campus events was one of the most serious problems affecting student life.[8]

Even if students spend some time in the library or in the cafeteria, they may not find it easy to connect with other students. They may resist reaching out to other people because they worry that others will reject them for being supposedly unattractive, uninteresting, unintelligent, uncool, or unlike them. Connecting with others requires overcoming shyness and becoming somewhat assertive. (For example, you might try introducing yourself to someone that you find yourself walking out the door with when leaving a class.) I describe assertiveness in Chapter 11, "Relationships."

Maybe you feel you already have sufficient friends outside of college. However, getting to know other college students—and instructors and advisors—is important if only for one reason: *They help you stay in school.*

Who are you going to borrow notes from if you miss a class? (Another student.) Who are you going to talk to for clarification on an assignment? (The instructor.) Who's going to explain what sequence of courses you need to take?

(Your advisor.) Who's going to offer ideas for handling common problems—dealing with families, outside jobs, day care, getting college loans, and so on? (Others on campus.) Who's going to boost your spirits and say, "You can do it!" (Other students like you.) Making connections is important. *Overcoming isolation makes you feel like you belong and helps motivate you to do college work.*

The proof of this is shown in a 1996 study by the University of California at Los Angeles, which found that although more people are going to college, fewer are graduating. The reason? More students commute to school and work off campus. "Staying home detracts from your ability to finish," says UCLA education professor Alexander Astin, the principal author of the study. "You get less committed. It's less a change from your high school years."[9]

I describe ways to connect with others on campus in other chapters in this book.

CHALLENGE #4: BALANCING SCHOOL, COMMUTING, & WORK. Let's assume, for the moment, that you are going to college full time, taking a full load of courses. If that's the case, you should be aware that *classes and studying alone can take more time than a full-time job!* This is because of the rule of thumb—which does not apply in most high schools but certainly applies in college—that *YOU SHOULD ALLOW AT LEAST 2 HOURS OF STUDYING FOR EVERY HOUR YOU SPEND IN CLASS.*

Thus, if you take a full-time course load of 16 units (credits), which represents 16 hours a week of going to class, you should assume you need to put in an *additional* 32 hours of studying a week—reading textbooks, reviewing lecture notes, writing papers, and so on. The 16 hours of class time and 32 hours of study time, then, would total 48 hours a week—*more* than the standard 40-hours-a-week job.

Perhaps you are going to college part time rather than full time. Many commuter students do, as I mentioned. However, even if you're taking just one course (of 5 units, say), class time and study time might add up to 15 hours. This is a big chunk out of the week, if you have other demands on your time.

Regardless of the type of campus—urban, suburban, rural; residential or nonresidential—probably most college students feel continually starved for time. However, a great many readers of this book must allow time for two activities on top of doing their college work—*commuting* and *working*.

■ *Commuting:* How many hours a day will it take you to get from home or work to campus and back? (And how about any additional hours for picking up children or doing shopping, if necessary?) Some people may spend *2 hours or more a day* just riding or driving, as I do.

If you take public transportation, it's possible you can use some of the commuting time for studying—if you don't have to stand up, aren't too tired, and are able to concentrate.

If you drive, most of your attention necessarily has to be on your driving, unless you're riding with someone else.

Thus, unless you're willing to be a bit creative (as I'll discuss), commuting can be lost time—gone, useless—except perhaps for allowing you to let your mind wander and relax mentally.

■ *Working:* Many commuter students have to work while going to college. Some, in fact, work full time or work at more than one job. As I mentioned, working can handicap your ability to get ahead in school. This is not only because it takes time away from the books but also because it drains you of energy you could certainly use later while studying.

Perhaps you're fortunate enough to have a job (or jobs) in which you can find time to study, if your employer allows it. Being a weekend or night-shift security guard, for example, or the person who hands out towels at a gym may provide long, uninterrupted moments that you can use for yourself.

On the other hand, a job, no matter how energy- and time-demanding, could fit right in with your future plans. Working as a clerk in a television station, for instance, may help illuminate for you exactly what you have to do academically to get the before-the-camera TV career you want. Alternatively, the job you hold may be exactly on the career path you want, and the purpose of college is to give you the courses or degrees that will advance you along it.

Is there any way you can use commuting or work time for study purposes? Depending on your situation, you can carry 3-by-5-inch note cards that can help you memorize important terms, formulas, names, dates, and so on. Or, if you have a Walkman-type portable audiotape player or a tape deck in your car, you can listen to tapes on school-related subjects. In Chapter 4, "Time," I describe these and other study tips in detail.

CHALLENGE #5: HELP YOUR FAMILY ADJUST TO YOUR COLLEGE RESPONSIBILITIES. Since, by definition, commuter students don't live in campus student housing, where do they live? Some share apartments or houses off campus with others their own age. However, many live with their families. There are (at least) two variations here:

■ *Living with parents or other older adults:* Many urban students of traditional student age—that is, 17–24—continue to live with their parents. Or they live with the same adults—such as grandparents or aunts or uncles—that they lived with while in high school.

Unlike students who move out to live on campus, students who live at home experience the same family pressures they always have. Thus, for example, they may be expected to continue doing housekeeping chores, shopping and cooking, and babysitting of younger brothers and sisters. They may even be expected to follow curfew rules imposed on them in high school, such as being home by 10:00 o'clock every night.

In addition, they are exposed to the usual household conflicts and crises, such as problems about money or a family member's alcohol abuse. On top of the family demands, of course, they now have the new demands associated with attending college.

Are the people in your household proud and supportive of your desire to go to college? Some families see the student as fulfilling their own dreams for a better life, although this can put extra pressure on the student to succeed. However, it is often the case—particularly for students who are the first in their families to attempt higher education—that other members of the household will be resentful and jealous. Indeed, they may actively work *against* your college career, usually under the guise that you're not "pulling your own weight" (by doing chores or earning extra money).

- *Living with spouses and children:* Older students may not live with their parents (although some do), but they may live with a spouse or lover and/or with children. The time demands of college can force all kinds of changes in the nature of the relationship.

Spouses or lovers may resent the loss of attention or of having to take on extra burdens. If you've cut back on work hours, they may worry about less money coming in (even though your college skills will probably lead to a higher income later). Or they may be jealous that you are taking advantage of opportunities that weren't available to them.

Children, too, may be upset that the parent is able to spend less time with them. And they may insist on getting attention during times you need to be studying.

Whatever the nature of your household and whatever your age, whether 18, 28, 38, or 48, you need to try to enlist your family members as allies in your pursuit of a college education. Make them aware that you'll have to devote more time to school than you've had to in the past. Post your class schedule and study schedule in a prominent place at

home (such as on the refrigerator door). Indicate that your study time is sacred by, for example, hanging a DO NOT DISTURB sign near your study place when you sit down to hit the books. Tell them that you'll now have to use evenings and weekends for studying rather than for your former activities. Above all, you need to explain the reasons why you're going to college in the first place, reasons that I'll help you identify in Chapter 2, "Succeeding." They may appreciate what you're doing, for example, if you can show them that the more education you have, the more money you're apt to make.

CHALLENGE #6: HELP FRIENDS UNDERSTAND YOUR NEW COMMITMENTS. Whenever we try something new, there are often old friends and acquaintances who are disturbed by the change. If you're promoted to a higher position at work, for instance, your former co-workers may no longer feel able to kid around with you the same way (since you're now their boss).

Similarly, if you're serious about college, you may encounter the same kind of strain in your relationships with your old friends who are not going to college. This can happen in two ways:

- **Strains on friendships:** In high school, your studies were probably not so demanding, and it was easy for you to simply hang out with friends, go to parties, or go out every night. Now you won't have this much free time, but your old friends who are not in college may not appreciate this. Indeed, if you say "I've got to go home and study," they may even scorn you as pretending to be better than they are. Your friends may feel you're rejecting them, and their natural response is to act resentful.

- **Strains on relationships:** Telling a boyfriend or girlfriend (or a spouse) that you can't spend as much time together can cause similar reactions. However, they may express their concerns in a different way than your other friends. They may say, "So you no longer think I'm good enough for you, now that you're in college!" Or they may go a step further and worry that you'll meet "someone better" at college and start a new relationship.

The opinion of friends and lovers may be very important to you. You might try to explain to them that you hope college will help you achieve a fuller life but that you don't want to give up everything that's good about your life so far. At bottom, though, you need to decide just how important college is to you. This comes down to the strength of your *motivation*, a matter discussed in Chapter 2.

CHALLENGE #7: ADJUST TO NEW PERSONAL CHALLENGES.

By now it may be clear that the first year of college is not just the "thirteenth grade" of high school. There really are significant differences, but they mainly come down to *you*—your attitude, your motivation, your determination.

Reality check: What do you think the dropout rate is for first-year college students? That is, what percentage fail to return to the same college the second year?

Answer: More than one in four students (26.9%), according to a report of 2564 colleges. For community colleges, 44.3% of first-year students did not return the second year.[10]

Now, this doesn't mean that all these dropouts *flunked* out. Some may have simply transferred to another college. Others may have dropped out because of lack of money. Still, one reason for the great number of dropouts, it is speculated, is that college enrollment has skyrocketed and so there are "more people going to college who aren't prepared academically to deal with the work."[11]

Aside from lack of money, people who end up leaving school do so for the following reasons:[12]

- **They are underprepared academically, which leads to frustration:** Some students are underprepared—in reading, writing, and math skills, for instance—and find themselves in college courses that are too difficult for them. (Then they may be angry and resentful because they think someone has somehow set them up or sold them a bill of goods.) *It's important to know that your college offers all kinds of academic support services—for example, math tutoring. But it's best not to wait until you're in trouble to find them.*

  If you sense even in the first couple of weeks of your first term that you're slipping, tell the instructor of the class for which you are reading this book. Or go to the student counseling center. Be honest also about telling your academic advisor if you're worried about being in over your head.

- **They are overprepared academically, which leads to boredom:** Some first-year students complain that their courses repeat work they already covered in high school. This is why good academic advising by a counselor is important.

- **They perceive college as being not useful:** First-year students who don't think their college work will be useful beyond the classroom are high candidates for dropping out. This may be particularly so for first-year students who have not chosen a major. However, it also happens to those who do have career goals but who consider general-education requirements (normally a big part of the first year) irrelevant.

One of the important lessons of this book is that the techniques you learn for success in college—regardless of the courses you take—are the same techniques that will help you attain success in life. From this point of view, then, college *is* useful.

- **They have unrealistic expectations about college:** Some first-year students don't have realistic expectations about themselves and college. For example, some come to college expecting great things to happen without much investment on their part. Thus, they devote little effort in making higher education work for them.

- **They are uncertain about their major or career:** It's okay to come into college undecided about your major or career. Indeed, college is a great place to explore these possibilities. Even so, you should be aware that indecision about these important goals is a reason for dropping out.

- **They don't have a personal support system:** Most first-year students have to start from scratch building a personal support system. This means making friends with other students, counselors, and professors or otherwise finding support. As I mentioned, this may take more effort on a commuter campus than on a residential campus. Nevertheless, whoever you are, a support system *is* available.

In general, all these difficulties can be boiled down to three matters:

- *Motivation*
- *Support*
- *Skills achievement*

These are your major challenges during this coming year. This book gives a lot of attention to these issues.

Survival Skills: What Strengths Do You Bring to College?

PREVIEW Four qualities are helpful for achieving success in college—and in life: (1) Sense of personal control and responsibility. (2) Optimism. (3) Creativity. (4) Ability to take psychological risks.

f you've been a commuter for a while, you've probably developed some survival skills. If you travel by public transportation, for instance, you've learned to be watchful for small signs to avoid unpleasantness, such as being alert to certain kinds of people or behavior. You've learned flexibility and patience, as when dealing with interruptions in public transit schedules. The trick now is to adapt these survival skills to to surviving in college.

People who are successful in college—and in other pursuits in life—have the following qualities:

- Sense of personal control and responsibility
- Optimism
- Creativity
- Ability to take psychological risks.

Let's take a look at these.

SENSE OF PERSONAL CONTROL & RESPONSIBILITY. How much personal control do you feel you have over your destiny? **The term *locus of control* refers to your beliefs about the relationship between your behavior and the occurrence of rewards and punishment.** (*Locus* is pronounced "*loh*-kuss.")

People's beliefs may fall on a continuum, or range, from external locus of control to internal locus of control:

■ **External:** *Do you believe strongly in the influences of chance or fate or the power of others?* **People who believe their rewards and punishments are controlled mainly by outside forces or other people are said to have an _external locus of control_.**

■ **Internal:** *Do you believe that "I am the captain of my fate, the master of my soul"?* **People who believe their rewards and punishments are due to their own behavior, character, or efforts are said to have an _internal locus of control_.**[13]

You may wish to try the following activity to see what your locus of control is.

PERSONAL EXPLORATION #1.1

WHO'S IN CHARGE HERE?

Are you in charge of your fate, or is a great deal of it influenced by outside forces? Answer the following questions to see where you stand.

1. Do you believe that most problems will solve themselves if you just don't fool with them?
   ❏ Yes   ❏ No

2. Do you believe that you can stop yourself from catching a cold?
   ❏ Yes   ❏ No

3. Are some people just born lucky?
   ❏ Yes   ❏ No

4. Most of the time do you feel that getting good grades means a great deal to you?   ❏ Yes   ❏ No

5. Are you often blamed for things that just aren't your fault?
   ❏ Yes   ❏ No

6. Do you believe that if somebody studies hard enough he or she can pass any subject?
   ❏ Yes   ❏ No

7. Do you feel that most of the time it doesn't pay to try hard because things never turn out right anyway?   ❏ Yes   ❏ No

8. Do you feel that if things start out well in the morning, it's going to be a good day no matter what you do?   ❏ Yes   ❏ No

9. Do you feel that most of the time parents listen to what their children have to say?
   ❏ Yes   ❏ No

10. Do you believe that wishing can make good things happen?
    ❏ Yes   ❏ No

11. When you get punished, does it usually seem it's for no good reason at all?   ❏ Yes   ❏ No

12. Most of the time, do you find it hard to change a friend's opinion?
    ❏ Yes   ❏ No

13. Do you think cheering more than luck helps a team win?
    ❏ Yes   ❏ No

14. Did you feel that it was nearly impossible for you to change your parents' minds about anything?
    ❏ Yes   ❏ No

15. Do you believe that parents should allow children to make most of their own decisions?
    ❏ Yes   ❏ No

16. Do you feel that when you do something wrong, there's very little you can do to make it right?
    ❏ Yes   ❏ No

17. Do you believe that most people are just born good at sports?
    ❏ Yes   ❏ No

18. Are most other people your age stronger than you are?
    ❏ Yes   ❏ No

19. Do you feel that one of the best ways to handle most problems is just not to think about them?
    ❏ Yes   ❏ No

20. Do you feel that you have a lot of choice in deciding who your friends are?   ❏ Yes   ❏ No

21. If you find a four-leaf clover, do you believe that it might bring you good luck?   ❏ Yes   ❏ No

22. Did you often feel that whether or not you did your homework had much to do with the kind of grades you got?   ❏ Yes   ❏ No

23. Do you feel that when a person your age is angry with you, there's little you can do to stop him or her?   ❏ Yes   ❏ No

(continued on next page)

24. Have you ever had a good-luck charm? ❏ Yes ❏ No

25. Do you believe that whether or not people like you depends on how you act? ❏ Yes ❏ No

26. Did your parents usually help you if you asked them to? ❏ Yes ❏ No

27. Have you ever felt that when people were angry with you, it was usually for no reason at all? ❏ Yes ❏ No

28. Most of the time, do you feel that you can change what might happen tomorrow by what you do today? ❏ Yes ❏ No

29. Do you believe that when bad things are going to happen, they are just going to happen no matter what you try and do to stop them? ❏ Yes ❏ No

30. Do you think that people can get their own way if they just keep trying? ❏ Yes ❏ No

31. Most of the time, do you find it useless to try to get your own way at home? ❏ Yes ❏ No

32. Do you feel that when good things happen, they happen because of hard work? ❏ Yes ❏ No

33. Do you feel that when somebody your age wants to be your enemy, there's little you can do to change matters? ❏ Yes ❏ No

34. Do you feel it's easy to get friends to do what you want them to do? ❏ Yes ❏ No

35. Do you usually feel that you have little to say about what you get to eat at home? ❏ Yes ❏ No

36. Do you feel that when someone doesn't like you, there's little you can do about it? ❏ Yes ❏ No

37. Did you usually feel it was almost useless to try in school because most other children were just plain smarter than you were? ❏ Yes ❏ No

38. Are you the kind of person who believes that planning ahead makes things turn out better? ❏ Yes ❏ No

39. Most of the time, do you feel that you have little to say about what your family decides to do? ❏ Yes ❏ No

40. Do you think it's better to be smart than to be lucky? ❏ Yes ❏ No

■ SCORING

Place a check mark to the right of each item in the key when your answer agrees with the answer that is shown. Add the check marks to determine your total score.

1. Yes ❏	2. No ❏	3. Yes ❏
4. No ❏	5. Yes ❏	6. No ❏
7. Yes ❏	8. Yes ❏	9. No ❏
10. Yes ❏	11. Yes ❏	12. Yes ❏
13. No ❏	14. Yes ❏	15. No ❏
16. Yes ❏	17. Yes ❏	18. Yes ❏
19. Yes ❏	20. No ❏	21. Yes ❏
22. No ❏	23. Yes ❏	24. Yes ❏
25. No ❏	26. No ❏	27. Yes ❏
28. No ❏	29. Yes ❏	30. No ❏
31. Yes ❏	32. No ❏	33. Yes ❏
34. No ❏	35. Yes ❏	36. Yes ❏
37. Yes ❏	38. No ❏	39. Yes ❏
40. No ❏		

Total score: _____

■ INTERPRETATION

Low scorers (0–8):
Nearly one student in three receives a score of 0 to 8. These students largely see themselves as responsible for the rewards they obtain or do not obtain in life.

Average scorers (9–16):
Most students receive from 9 to 16 points. These students view themselves as partially in control of their lives. Perhaps they view themselves as in control academically but not socially, or vice versa.

High scorers (17–40):
Nearly 15% of students receive scores of 17 or higher. These students view life largely as a game of chance. They see success as a matter of luck or a product of the kindness of others.

Studies have shown that people who have an internal locus of control—that is, low (not high) scores in the Personal Exploration—are able to achieve more in school.[14] They are also able to delay gratification, are more independent, and are better able to cope with various stresses.[15] Some people may have both an internal and external locus of control, depending on their situation. For instance, they may feel they can control their lives at home but not in the workplace.

OPTIMISM. "Mom, where are all the jerks today?" asks the young girl as she and her mother are driving along. "Oh," says the mother, slightly surprised. "They're only on the road when your father drives."

Psychotherapist Alan McGinnis tells this story to make a point: "If you expect the world to be peopled with idiots and jerks, they start popping up."[16]

For city dwellers, it may be easy to think they are surrounded by jerks, idiots, and worse. Even so, are you an optimist? Or are you what some people like to call a "realist," when they actually mean a pessimist?

Perhaps optimism is related to matters of personal control. Pessimists may be overwhelmed by their problems, whereas optimists are challenged by them, according to McGinnis, author of *The Power of Optimism.*[17] Optimists "think of themselves as problem-solvers, as trouble-shooters," he says. This does not mean they see everything through rose-colored glasses. Rather they have several qualities that help them have a positive attitude while still remaining realistic and tough-minded. *(See ■ Panel 1.1.)*

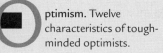

PANEL 1.1

Optimism. Twelve characteristics of tough-minded optimists.

OPTIMISTS . . .

1. Are seldom surprised by trouble.

2. Look for partial solutions.

3. Believe they have control over their future.

4. Allow for regular renewal.

5. Interrupt their negative trains of thought.

6. Heighten their powers of appreciation.

7. Use their imaginations to rehearse success.

8. Are cheerful even when they can't be happy.

9. Believe they have an almost unlimited capacity for stretching.

10. Build lots of love into their lives.

11. Like to swap good news.

12. Accept what cannot be changed.

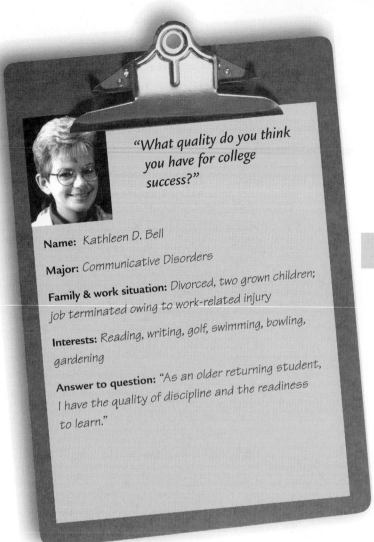

"What quality do you think you have for college success?"

Name: Kathleen D. Bell

Major: Communicative Disorders

Family & work situation: Divorced, two grown children; job terminated owing to work-related injury

Interests: Reading, writing, golf, swimming, bowling, gardening

Answer to question: "As an older returning student, I have the quality of discipline and the readiness to learn."

CREATIVITY. The capacity for creativity and spontaneity, said psychologist Abraham Maslow, is an important attribute of the psychologically healthy person. This attribute is not limited to some supposed *artistic* class of people; it is built into all of us. ___Creativity___ **refers to the human capacity to express ourselves in original or imaginative ways.** It may also be thought of as the process of discovery. As Nobel Prize–winning physician Albert Szent-Györgyi expressed it, "Discovery consists of looking at the same thing as everyone else and thinking something different."[18]

Being creative means having to resist pressure to be in step with the world. It means looking for several answers, not the "one right answer," as is true of math problems. As Roger von Oech, founder of a creativity consulting company, puts it: "Life is ambiguous; there are many right answers—all depending on what you are looking for."[19] It means forgetting about reaching a specific goal, because the creative process can't be forced. One should, in von Oech's phrase, think of the mind as "a compost heap, not a computer," and use a notebook to collect ideas.

ABILITY TO TAKE PSYCHOLOGICAL RISKS.
What is risk-taking? We are not endorsing the kind of risk-taking that might jeopardize your health (seen on the highway every day, such as fast driving). I am principally concerned with situations in which what is at risk is mainly your *pride*. That is, the main consequences of failure are personal embarrassment or disappointment. This kind of risk-taking—*having the courage to feel the fear and then proceeding anyway*—is a requirement for psychological health.

Consider failure: None of us is immune to it. Some of us are shattered but bounce back quickly. Others of us take longer to recover, especially if the failure has changed our lives in a significant way. But what *is* failure, exactly? Carole Hyatt and Linda Gottleib, authors of *When Smart People Fail*, point out that the word has two meanings:

■ *Failure can be an event:* First, "failure" is a term for an event, such as failing a test or not getting a job. This kind of failure you may not be able to do anything about.

■ *Failure can be a judgment about yourself:* Second, "failure" is a *judgment you make about yourself*—"so that 'failure' may also mean not living up to your own expectations."[20]

This kind of failure is a matter you can do something about. For instance, you can use your own inner voice—your "self-talk"—to put a different interpretation on the event that is more favorable to you. (For example, "I didn't get the job because I'm better at dealing with people than at typing.")

One characteristic of many peak performers, according to psychologist Charles Garfield, is that they continually *reinvent* themselves. Doing this requires constantly taking psychological chances. The late jazz musician Miles Davis, for example, was always changing his musical direction in order to stay fresh and vital. Novelist James Michener takes himself on a new adventure of travel and research with every book he writes.[21] These are examples of psychological risk-taking that lead toward success.

Onward

PREVIEW College is about deciding what you want your life to be and how to achieve it.

"Get a life!" everyone says.

But what, exactly, is "a life," anyway? And how do you "get" it?

We pass this way only once. The calendar leaves fall away. And then it's over.

Some things just happen to us, but a lot of things we choose. How many people, though, wake up at the age of 60 or 70 and say: "I missed the boat; there were better things I could have chosen to do"?

Over a lifetime everyone acquires a few regrets. But the things that people regret the most, according to a survey of elderly people by Cornell University researchers, is not what they *have done* so much as what they *haven't done*. And chief among the regrets are (1) *missed educational opportunities* and (2) *failure to "seize the moment."*[22]

You are at a time and place to seize some splendid opportunities. College allows you to begin examining the choices available to you—about what you want your life to be. We're talking about the main event here, the Big Enchilada—deciding what is *truly* important to you.

NOTES

1. Tyson, R. (1996, August 16). Travel time: For many, it's a longer, busier road. *USA Today*, p. 8A.

2. Tyson, R. 1996, August 16). Suburbs: Cities replaced as main work destinations. *USA Today*, p. 8A.

3. Jacoby, B. (1989). *The student-as-commuter: Developing a comprehensive institutional response.* ASHE-ERIC Higher Education Report No. 7. Washington, D.C.: George Washington University, School of Education and Human Development.

4. Stewart, S. S., & Rue, P. (1983). Commuter students: Definition and distribution. In Stewart, S. S. (Ed.). *Commuter students: Enhancing their educational experiences.* San Francisco: Jossey-Bass.

5. Gardner, L. F. (1994). *Redesigning higher education: Producing dramatic gains in student learning.* ASHE-ERIC Higher Education Report No. 7. Washington, D.C.: George Washington University, School of Education and Human Development.

6. Astin, A. W., et al., study at University of California at Los Angeles. Reported in: Henry, T. (1996, October 14). More in college; fewer graduate. *USA Today*, p. 1D.

7. Coburn, K. L. Quoted in: Kutner, L. (1992, September 3). For college freshmen, the first of breadth of freedom can hold a difficult and frightening lessen. *New York Times*, p. B4.

8. Boyer, E. L. (1990). *Campus life: In search of community.* Princeton, NJ: Carnegie Foundation for the Advancement of Teaching.

9. Astin, 1996.

10. Study of American College Testing, Iowa City, IA, reported in: Henry, T. (1996, July 11). College dropout rate hits all-time high. *USA Today*, p. 1A.

11. Saterfiel, T. Quoted in: Henry, 1996.

12. Levitz, R., & Noel, L. (1989). Connecting students to institutions: Keys to retention and success. Pp. 65–81 in Upcraft, M. L., & Gardner, J. N., & Associates (Eds.). *The freshman year experience: Helping students survive and succeed in college.* San Francisco: Jossey-Bass.

13. Rotter, J. B. (1966). Generalized expectancies for internal versus external control of reinforcement. *Psychological Monographs, 80* (Whole No. 603).

14. Findley, M. J., & Cooper, H. M. (1983). Locus of control and academic achievement: A literature review. *Journal of Personality & Social Psychology, 44,* 419–27.

15. Lefcourt, H. M. (1982). *Locus of control: Current trends in theory and research.* Hillsdale, NJ: Erlbaum.

16. McGinnis, A. Quoted in: Maushard, M. (1990, October 22). How to get happy: What makes optimists tick. *San Francisco Chronicle,* p. B5. Reprinted from *Baltimore Evening Sun.*

17. McGinnis, A. L. (1990). *The power of optimism.* San Francisco: Harper & Row.

18. Szent-Györgyi, A. Quoted in: von Oech, R. (1983). *A whack on the side of the head,* Menlo Park, CA: Creative Think, p. 7.

19. von Oech, 1983, p. 21.

20. Hyatt, C., & Gottlieb, L. (1987). *When smart people fail.* New York: Simon and Schuster, p. 20.

21. Garfield, C. Quoted in: Rozak, M. (1989, August). The mid-life fitness peak. *Psychology Today,* pp. 32–33.

22. Anonymous. (1995, April). What's your biggest regret in life? *Health,* p. 14.

CLASSROOM ACTIVITIES

Some of the most powerful learning occurs during small-group discussion and projects. (A small group consists of about three to six students.) Thus, this book offers frequent suggestions for group activities. Here's the first group.

1. ***Going to college—another "rite of passage."*** Have students form into small groups in the classrooom, far enough apart so they won't disturb other groups. Students within each group should take turns introducing themselves and saying a few words about their backgrounds.

   They should then describe some rites of passage they have been through. A *rite of passage* involves physical or emotional changes in one's life, changes in how others view you, new behaviors you take on, and new responsibilities. It is often accompanied by stress. College is clearly a rite of passage. Other examples are changing from a child to an adolescent, joining a particular group of friends or gang, getting married, earning one's first paycheck.

   One person in each group should act as recorder or secretary and make a list of the different rites of passage discussed. He or she should then copy the list onto the classroom blackboard.

   The class at large should consider the lists developed by each group. Questions for discussion: What are the similarities? the differences? Were any possibilities overlooked? What are different ways of dealing with rites of passage (anger, avoidance, feelings of fight-or-flight, and so on). Which of these ways are most appropriate? How do the past rites of passage compare to the first week of college?

2. ***Who's in charge?*** Ask students to meet with others in a small group and to review their answers to Personal Exploration #1.1, "Who's in Charge Here?"

   Questions for discussion: What is *one area* in which you feel you can influence and control people and events? Discuss this area and the feelings of mastery and power it gives you. Discuss whether you think this control and influence could be applied to your academic work in college.

3. ***What are your positive qualities?*** Ask students to make lists of all the things they like about themselves. Suggest they recall instances in which they really felt good about who they were and what they were doing.

   Then have students meet in small groups and discuss some of these qualities. Ask them to compare them to the qualities for success described earlier.

Instruct students to find something that they like about each person in the group and compliment that person. Because they may not know others in the group very well, they may want to make the compliments about the person's looks, clothes, or jewelry. Ask them to try to think of other things to compliment as well, such as posture, manner of speaking, or quality of ideas expressed.

Questions for discussion: How do you feel about being complimented? Do you tend to discount a compliment because of feelings of weak self-esteem? Do you tend to brag about yourself—also because of low self-esteem? Discuss whether your parents or others who raised you frequently praised you or frequently criticized or punished you. Do you think their general behavior toward you affected your positive or negative view of yourself?

THE EXAMINED LIFE:
ASSIGNMENTS FOR JOURNAL ENTRIES

"The unexamined life is not worth living," the great Greek philosopher Socrates believed. If ever there was a time to examine your life, it is now, during the first year of college.

As you read this book, you should be considering such basic questions as:

1. Why am I choosing the direction I've chosen?

2. How do I feel about the things I've seen, read, or heard?

3. What do I think of this idea, that person, those beliefs?

4. How can I *make use* of the experiences I'm experiencing?

The place to express these thoughts and to keep track of the progress you are making is in a *journal*. By writing in a journal, you come to a better understanding of yourself.

At the end of each chapter, we will indicate some suggestions or assignments for journal entries. We also provide lines to write them on.

Here is the first group of journal entry suggestions.

JOURNAL ENTRY #1.1: WHAT ARE YOUR STRONGEST MOTIVATIONS FOR COLLEGE? List your two *strongest* motivations for attending college.

_____

_____

_____

_____

_____

_____

_____

_____

_____

_____

JOURNAL ENTRY #1.2: WHAT ARE OTHER MOTIVATIONS FOR COLLEGE? What are some other motivations for attending college—reasons that are less strong but that motivate you nonetheless?

_____

_____

_____

_____

_____

_____

_____

_____

JOURNAL ENTRY #1.3: WHAT KINDS OF THINGS MAY CAUSE DIFFICULTY?

What kinds of things might cause you difficulty or create problems that may threaten your college success?

_____

_____

_____

_____

_____

_____

_____

_____

_____

_____

_____

JOURNAL ENTRY #1.4: HOW CAN YOU DEAL WITH DIFFICULTIES?

How can you effectively deal with the difficulties listed in entry #1.3?

_____

_____

_____

_____

_____

_____

_____

JOURNAL ENTRY #1.5: WHAT SUPPORT DO YOU HAVE FOR COLLEGE?

What kinds of support do you have that will help you succeed in college?

_____

_____

_____

_____

_____

_____

_____

_____

_____

2 succeeding

making the commuter college experience work for you

IN THIS CHAPTER: If the first year of college is "punctuated by feelings of panic and incompetence," as one observer put it, that's normal. This chapter begins to address those feelings. We consider the following subjects:

■ **The "why" of college:** Why are you here? We explore this most fundamental question.

■ **The fears of college:** What are your fears about college? You're not alone. They are probably mostly the same fears everyone else has—and they can be lessened.

■ **How college can better your life:** Compared to high-school graduates, college graduates usually make more money. They also experience gratifying personal growth during college. Finally, they probably have a better chance to discover what makes them happy.

■ **Life goals and college goals:** We look at six steps for translating your life goals into college goals and daily tasks.

"Motivation depends not only on what you want to do," says a Columbia University psychiatry professor, "but what you think you'll have to give up to do it." [1]

As you may already be finding out, going to college means giving up some things. Some recreational activities, for instance. Or pay from a full-time job. Or time with your friends or family. Is college worth it? The extent to which you can answer "yes" indicates the strength of your motivation.

Motivation is everything. A college is not a jail. You can walk away from it at any time. And no doubt there will be times when you will *want* to. So what, ultimately, is going to make you determined not only to stay in but to do your best while you're there? The answer depends on how you deal with two important questions:

1. *Why are you here?*

2. *What is your fear?*

Why Are You Here? Values & Your Reasons for College

PREVIEW Your reasons for going to college reflect your values. Values, the truest expression of who you are, are principles by which you lead your life. A value has three characteristics: (1) It is an important attitude. (2) It is matter on which you take action. (3) It should be consciously chosen.

Being in college, some students say, makes them feel as though they exist in suspension, postponing real life.

But life cannot be postponed. It is lived today—not held off until the weekend, or vacations, or graduation. Or until you're in a relationship or settled in a career. Or until your children leave home or you retire.

Real life starts when you open your eyes in the morning, when you decide—that is, *choose*—what you will do today. And what you choose to do reflects your values.

WHAT VALUES ARE. Your values are the truest expression of who you are. **A** *value* **is a principle by which you lead your life. It is an important belief or attitude that you think "ought to be" (or "ought not to be"). Moreover, it is a belief that you feel strongly enough about to take action on and that has been consciously chosen.**

There are three important parts here:

1. *A value is an important attitude:* A value is an important attitude or belief that you hold. Examples: "College should help me get a good job." "Fairness means hiring acccording to ability, not family background." "Murder is wrong except in self-defense." "It's worth trying my hardest to get an 'A.'" ("Chocolate is better than vanilla" is a preference, generally not a value.)

2. *A value is a matter on which you take action:* You can *think* whatever you want, but if you don't back up your thought with some sort of action, it cannot be considered a value. If you watch someone cheat on an exam, but you don't do anything about it, your attitude that "cheating is wrong" is, for all practical purposes, not really a value.

3. *A value should be consciously chosen:* Values are not very strong if they are not truly your own. Many first-year students hold ideas or opinions received from their parents or friends—ideas about which they may not have given much thought, such as religious beliefs. For an idea to be a value rather than just a belief, you have to have thought enough about it to consider accepting or rejecting it. You have to have made it yours. You can't just say "That's the way it is."

YOUR VALUES ABOUT COLLEGE. What kind of values do you hold? These are not frivolous matters, since they have a great bearing on how you view the whole subject of higher education. In order to see how your values affected your actions about going to college, try Personal Exploration #2.1.[2]

PERSONAL EXPLORATION #2.1

YOUR VALUES ABOUT HIGHER EDUCATION

Take at least 10–15 minutes for this activity. The purpose is to see how your values and family background affected your actions in going to college.

■ A. FAMILY MATTERS

1. College is not a tradition in my family. (Family includes not only parents and grandparents or guardians but also uncles, aunts, and brothers and sisters.)

   ____ True ____ False
   ____ Somewhat true

2. My father/guardian completed (check one): ____ grade school ____ high school ____ college ____ graduate or professional school ____ other (identify)

   _____

3. My father/guardian (check one):
   ____ supports
   ____ does not support
   my decision to go to this college.

4. My mother/guardian completed (check one): ____ grade school ____ high school ____ college ____ graduate or professional school ____ other (identify)

   _____
   _____

5. My mother/guardian (check one):
   ____ supports
   ____ does not support
   my decision to go to this college.

6. My spouse/boyfriend/ girlfriend (check one):
   ____ supports
   ____ does not support
   my decision to go to this college.

7. My spouse/boyfriend/girlfriend completed (check one):
   ____ grade school
   ____ high school ____ college
   ____ graduate or professional school ____ other (identify)

   _____
   _____

■ B. COLLEGE & FREE CHOICE

1. Regarding the influence of my parents/guardians or others, I'd say my going to college was the following (check one): (a) ____ It was mainly my decision but a little bit others' decision. (b) ____ It was mainly others' decision but a little bit my decision. (c) ____ It was about equally both mine and others' decisions. (d) ____ It was never talked about; it was just assumed I'd go.

2. If I wasn't going to college, I would do the following instead:

   _____
   _____
   _____
   _____
   _____
   _____
   _____
   _____
   _____
   _____
   _____

3. If I had the money and could do anything I wanted to this year, I would rather be doing the following:

   _____
   _____
   _____
   _____
   _____
   _____
   _____
   _____
   _____
   _____
   _____

4. Looking over my last three responses, I feel that I am going to college because of the following (check one): (a) ____ I am choosing to go and want to go. (b) ____ I don't really choose to go and don't really want to go, but others want me to. (c) ____ I don't feel I have a choice, but I want to go anyway. (d) ____ I don't know, I'm confused.

(continued on next page)

■ C. PUBLIC REASONS, PERSONAL REASONS

1. When people ask me why I chose this college, I tell them the following. (List three or four reasons.)

   a. _____
   _____

   b. _____
   _____

   c. _____
   _____

   d. _____
   _____

2. When people ask me why I am interested in a particular major or field of study (or why I am undecided), I tell them the following. (List three or four reasons.)

   a. _____
   _____

   b. _____
   _____

   c. _____
   _____

   d. _____
   _____

3. The reasons I chose (if I chose) the particular major or field of study mentioned in C.2 that I *don't* tell people about are as follows. (Examples: "My parents want me to do it." "I'm afraid I lack the talent or brains to do something else I might like better." "It's a matter of conscience.")

   a. _____
   _____

   b. _____
   _____

■ D. REASONS FOR GOING TO COLLEGE

The following is a list of reasons for attending college. Rank them in order of importance to you, with 1 meaning most important, 2 of secondary importance, 3 of third in importance, and so on.

My reasons for going to college are . . .

a. ___ To please my parents.

b. ___ To have fun.

c. ___ To get a degree.

d. ___ To prepare for a career.

e. ___ To make friends.

f. ___ To better support my family/help my children.

g. ___ To avoid having to work for a while.

h. ___ To find a girlfriend/boyfriend/mate.

i. ___ To raise my economic level/get a better job.

j. ___ To explore new ideas and experiences.

k. ___ To acquire knowledge.

l. ___ To gain maturity.

m. ___ To learn how to solve problems.

n. ___ To learn how to learn.

o. ___ To gain prestige.

p. ___ To become a better citizen.

■ E. IDENTIFYING YOUR VALUES REGARDING HIGHER EDUCATION

Look back over this Personal Exploration. Identify the top three values that influenced your decision to attend the college you are in. Write a brief essay in the following space. In the essay explain how each of the three values led you to a take a particular kind of action in choosing the present college.

_____
_____
_____
_____
_____
_____
_____
_____
_____
_____
_____
_____
_____
_____
_____
_____
_____
_____
_____
_____
_____
_____
_____
_____
_____

Adopting the attitude that you will try to do your best in college will also help you outside of college. Doing the best at whatever is the primary focus of your time and interests will give you a better chance of building the kind of life you want to live.

What Is Your Fear? Anxiety as a Positive & Negative Motivator

PREVIEW Anxiety can motivate you to do well, but too much anxiety can motivate you to withdraw from competition. It's important to identify fears about college so they won't become motivators for dropping out. Common fears include fear of flunking out, of the pressure, of loneliness, of not finding one's way around, of running out of money.

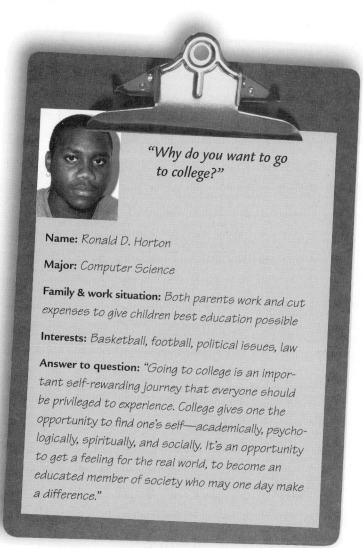

"Why do you want to go to college?"

Name: Ronald D. Horton

Major: Computer Science

Family & work situation: Both parents work and cut expenses to give children best education possible

Interests: Basketball, football, political issues, law

Answer to question: "Going to college is an important self-rewarding journey that everyone should be privileged to experience. College gives one the opportunity to find one's self—academically, psychologically, spiritually, and socially. It's an opportunity to get a feeling for the real world, to become an educated member of society who may one day make a difference."

As you know from playing videogames or sports, a certain amount of anxiety can actually motivate you to accomplish positive results. Anxiety about losing a game (or the will to win) makes you alert, focuses the mind, and induces you to try and do well. Similarly, some fear of losing the game of college can motivate you to do your best.

Too much anxiety, however, can motivate you to perform negatively. That is, you may be so overwhelmed by fear that you want to withdraw from the competition. This can and does happen to lots of students in college—but it need not happen to you.

YOUR VALUES ABOUT BEING THE BEST. Most of us discover early on that we can't be the best at everything. However, *it's important to try to be the best at the PRIMARY THINGS WE DO*—otherwise, why do them? For instance, you might devote your best hours or your most hours to being a parent, or a salesperson, or an athlete. If this is the major focus of your time and energy, why do a mediocre job of it? *WHY NOT BE THE BEST?*

To some extent, the desire to do well means competing with others to see who's the best. However, it's more important that you decide to achieve your *personal best*. Compared to some other people, you may not be a great basketball player, musician, mathematician, or whatever. But you can try to be the best that *you* can be in these endeavors. That is the paramount value.

IDENTIFYING YOUR FEARS. Concerns and fears about college are actually *normal*. However, it's important to identify them so that you can take steps to deal with them. Take a few minutes to stop at this point and try Personal Exploration #2.2. Do this before you read the next section.

GOING TO COLLEGE: WHAT IS YOUR FEAR?

Identifying your fears about college is the first step in fighting them.

WHAT TO DO

For each of the following statements, circle the number below corresponding to how much you agree or disagree:

1 = strongly disagree
2 = somewhat disagree
3 = neither disagree nor agree
4 = somewhat agree
5 = strongly agree

I am afraid that . . .

1. College will be too difficult for me.   1 2 3 4 5

2. I will get homesick.   1 2 3 4 5

3. I might flunk out.   1 2 3 4 5

4. I won't be able to handle the amount of school work.   1 2 3 4 5

5. My study habits won't be good enough to succeed.   1 2 3 4 5

6. I'll get lost on campus.   1 2 3 4 5

7. I'll be a disappointment to people important to me, such as my parents, family, or children.   1 2 3 4 5

8. I won't have enough money and will have to drop out.   1 2 3 4 5

9. I won't be able to handle working and/or family responsibilities and college at the same time.   1 2 3 4 5

10. I will get depressed.   1 2 3 4 5

11. I won't be able to manage my time being on my own.   1 2 3 4 5

12. I'll oversleep or otherwise won't be able to get to class on time.   1 2 3 4 5

13. I won't be able to maintain the grade average I want.   1 2 3 4 5

14. The college will find out that I'm basically incompetent and will kick me out.   1 2 3 4 5

15. I won't be able to compete with other students.   1 2 3 4 5

16. I won't make any friends.   1 2 3 4 5

17. I won't be able to overcome my shyness.   1 2 3 4 5

18. I'll have problems with my housemates or family.   1 2 3 4 5

19. I won't be able to handle writing/spelling or math.   1 2 3 4 5

20. My professors will find out I'm inadequate.   1 2 3 4 5

21. There will be no one to help me.   1 2 3 4 5

22. I'll choose the wrong major.   1 2 3 4 5

23. I'll have to cheat in order to survive the tough academic environment.   1 2 3 4 5

24. My family or my job will complicate things, and I won't be able to keep up.   1 2 3 4 5

25. Other (write in):

_____
_____
_____
_____
_____
_____

1 2 3 4 5

Add the number of points: _____

MEANING OF YOUR SCORE

100–125 *High*

You are very fearful or very concerned about your college experience. Although these concerns are not unusual, it would be a good idea to check into some college resources to assist you in dealing with your worries. Such resources include career and personal counseling, the college's learning center, and the financial aid office.

75–99 *Average*

You are somewhat fearful or somewhat concerned about your college experience. Welcome! Join the crowd! Your concerns are typical and are shared by the majority of college students. To assist you in addressing these issues, you may wish to identify the appropriate college resources—counseling center, learning center, financial aid—for assistance.

74 or less *Low*

You have few fears, perhaps are even laid back. Even so, it would be useful to identify college support services (such as counseling or learning center) in case you ever need them.

INTERPRETATION

We all tend to think that any one worry we have is unique, that it is ours alone, that no one else ever experiences it with the intensity that we do. This is not true! Indeed, the fears and concerns listed above are quite common. So also is the reluctance to seek help, to get support. But seeking support is probably what will help you overcome the fear. Resources such as counseling and financial aid are described in Chapter 3.

COMMON FEARS OF COLLEGE STUDENTS.
What are common fears of college students?[3,4] They include the following:

Fear of flunking out—this may be the biggest.

Fear of the pressure—of the work and responsibility, of not being able to compete.

Fear of loneliness, of not finding supportive friends.

Fear of not finding one's way around.

Fear of running out of money.

Then there are all the specific fears —about being on one's own, about not having a good time, even about oversleeping. Many commuter students express concerns about not being able to balance their college work and their family and/or job responsibilities.

With the help of this book and this course, however, you can get beyond those fears and make college the success you want it to be.

Now let's consider how going to college could change your life for the better—the benefits it will produce that will help you get past your fears and keep on going for college success.

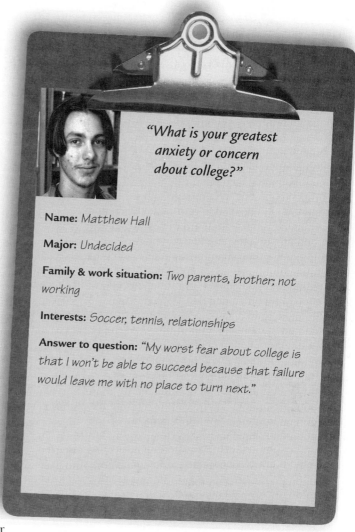

"What is your greatest anxiety or concern about college?"

Name: *Matthew Hall*

Major: *Undecided*

Family & work situation: *Two parents, brother; not working*

Interests: *Soccer, tennis, relationships*

Answer to question: *"My worst fear about college is that I won't be able to succeed because that failure would leave me with no place to turn next."*

How Could College Make a Difference in Your Life?

PREVIEW College graduates usually make more money, are more knowledgeable and competent, and experience more personal growth. These factors may contribute to an increase in happiness.

Suppose you were to decide right now not to continue on in college. What would you be missing if you didn't finish?
Let's take a look.

INCREASED INCOME. With the widespread competitive and technological changes of the last few years, it has become clear that the rewards go to those with skill and education. There is all kinds of supporting evidence. Some examples:

■ *The more education, the more income:* The more education people have, the higher their income, according to studies by Princeton University economists Orley Ashenfelter and Alan Kreuger. From grade school through graduate school, every year spent in school adds 16% to the average person's lifetime earnings. This means that a two-year or community college degree, for instance, can be expected to increase an individual's earnings by about *one-third*. A four-year college degree would increase them by almost *two-thirds*.[5]

■ *Widening gap:* The gap between high-school graduates and college graduates has widened over the years. In 1979, for example, a male college graduate earned 49% more than a man with a high-school diploma. In 1992, the average male college graduate was earning 83% more than his high-school graduate counterpart. "Well-educated and skilled workers are prospering," says Robert Reich, U.S. Secretary of Labor, while "those without education or skills drift further and further from the economic mainstream."[6] In 1993, young college graduates earned a whopping 75% more than comparable high-school graduates.[7]

■ *Growth in employer demands:* In the 1990s jobs requiring college degrees will grow 1.5% per year, according to the head of one economic advisory firm. For high-school degrees, the demand will grow only 0.6% per year.[8]

■ *Lifetime earnings:* According to the U.S. Census Bureau, a high-school graduate can expect to earn $821,000 over the course of a working life. By contrast, a college graduate with a bachelor's degree can expect to earn $1.4 million. And a person with a professional degree can expect to receive more than $3 million.[9]

Although a college degree won't *guarantee* you higher earnings, it provides better odds than just a high-school degree. Moreover, going to college will probably help you develop additional "street smarts"—that is, flexibility—so that whatever happens in the job market you'll be better apt to land on your feet.

INCREASED PERSONAL DEVELOPMENT. Money, however, is not the only reason for going to college. Higher education can also provide some of the most significant experiences possible in life—those having to do with personal growth and change.

The very fact that college serves up unfamiliar challenges and pressures can help you develop better adjustment skills, such as those of time management. The competition of different values and ideas—religious, political, and so on—can help you evaluate, modify, and strengthen your belief system.

Some of the positive changes that studies show are characteristic of college graduates are as follows.[10]

■ *Increase in knowledge, competence, and self-esteem:* The college experience increases people's knowledge of content, as you might expect, extending their range of competencies and providing them with a greater range of work skills. It also helps them develop their reasoning abilities. Finally, it increases their self-esteem.

■ *Increase in personal range:* College helps people to develop their capacity for self-discovery and to widen their view of the world. They become more tolerant, more independent, more appreciative of culture and art, more politically sophisticated, and more future-oriented. Finally, they adopt better health habits, become better parents, and become better consumers and citizens.

INCREASED HAPPINESS. Is there a relationship between educational level and happiness? A lot depends on what is meant by "happiness," which is hard to measure. Still, wealthy people tend to be happier than poor people, points out one psychologist. "Does that mean that money buys happiness," he asks, "or that happy people are likely to succeed at their jobs and become wealthy?"[11]

Whatever the case, better educated people do make more money, as we have shown. They also have the opportunity to explore their personal growth and development in a way that less educated people cannot. This gives them a chance to discover what makes them happy.

How College Work Can Improve Your Career Skills

PREVIEW The four principal ways of learning in college are via lectures, readings, writing, and laboratories. The skills you develop to master these learning activities can be used not only to improve your grades but also to further your career in the work world.

Let's get down to basics: How is knowledge transferred to you in college? Can you apply the methods of learning in college courses—whatever the subject—to help you be successful in your career *after* college? The answer is: Absolutely!

THE FOUR PRINCIPAL WAYS OF INSTRUCTION. Although systems of higher education in other countries operate somewhat differently, in the colleges, universities, and technical institutes of the U.S.A. and Canada most first-year students acquire knowledge in four principal ways—by lectures, reading, writing, and laboratories. Let's consider these:

- **Lectures:** Students attend lectures by instructors and are tested throughout the school term on how much they remember.

  Relevance to your career: When you are out of school and go to work in the business or nonbusiness world, this method of imparting information will be called a "presentation," "meeting," or "company training program." And the "test" constitutes how well you recall and handle the information in order to do your job. (Sometimes there's an actual test, as in government civil service, to see if you qualify for promotion.)

- **Readings:** Students are given reading assignments in textbooks and other writings and are tested to see how much they recall. Quite often lectures and readings make up the only teaching methods in a course.

  Relevance to your career: In the work world, comparable ways of communicating information are through reports, memos, letters, instruction manuals, newsletters, trade journals, and books. Here, too, the "test" constitutes how well you interpret and use the information to do your work.

- **Writing:** Students are given assignments in which they are asked to research information and write it into a term paper. Generally, you need not recall this information for a test. However, you must manage your time so that you can produce a good paper, which is usually an important part of the course grade.

  Relevance to your career: In the work world, a research paper is called a "report," "memo," "proposal," or "written analysis." Police officers, nurses, salespeople, lawyers, managers, and teachers all write reports. How well you pull together facts and present them can have a tremendous impact on how you influence other people. This factor in turn affects how you are able to do your job.

- **Laboratories:** Laboratories are practice sessions. You use knowledge gained from readings, and sometimes lectures, to practice using the material, and you are graded on your progress. For example, in computer science or office technology, you may take a lab that gives you hands-on instruction in word processing. In learning to speak Japanese, you may go a lab to listen to, and practice repeating, language tapes. In chemistry, you may do experiments with various chemicals on a laboratory workbench.

  Relevance to your career: In the world of work, your job itself is the laboratory. Your promotions and career success depend on how well you pull together and practice everything you've learned to do the job.

There are also other instructional techniques. Instead of lectures, you may have *seminars,* or discussion groups, but you'll likely still be tested on the material presented in them. Instead of readings, you may have to *watch films, slides, or videotapes* or *listen to audiotapes,* on which you may be tested. Instead of term papers or laboratories, you may be assigned *projects.* For example, in psychology or geology, you may be asked to do a field trip and take notes. In music or engineering drawing, you may be asked to create something. Still, most of these alternative methods of instruction make use of whatever skills you bring to bear in lectures, reading, writing, and laboratory work.

HOW LEARNING IN COLLEGE CAN HELP YOUR CAREER.

I have pointed out that each of these instructional methods or situations has counterparts in the world of work. This is a very important matter. Whenever you begin to think that whatever you're doing in college is irrelevant to real life—and I have no doubt you *will* think this from time to time—remember that the *time-management methods* by which you learn are *necessary skills for success in the work environment.*

If you know how to take efficient notes of lectures, for example, you can do the same for meetings. If you know how to extract material from a textbook, you can do the same for a report. If you know how to research a paper, you can easily adapt to finding your way around a computer network such as the Internet. Moreover, these and other learning skills will be valuable all your life because they are transferable skills between jobs, between industries, and between the for-profit (business) and nonprofit (education and government) sectors of the economy. They are also valuable in nonwork areas, as in volunteer activities.

In sum: If you master the skills for acquiring knowledge in college, these skills will serve you well in helping you live the way you want to live professionally and personally.

Setting College Goals from Life Goals

PREVIEW The six-step strategy called "Essentials for Time & Life Management" describes how to set daily tasks from life goals. The first step is to determine your ultimate goals.

We make decisions all the time. *Taking* action is making a decision. So is *not taking* action. There's nothing wrong with inaction and aimlessness, if that's what you want to do, but realize that aimlessness is a choice like any other. Most first-year students find out, however, that college works better if they have a program of aims. The following pages tell you how to set up such a program.

ESSENTIALS FOR TIME & LIFE MANAGEMENT: SETTING DAILY TASKS FROM LIFE GOALS.

Essentials for Time & Life Management is a six-step program for translating your life goals into daily tasks. *(See* ■ *Panel 2.1.)* The idea is to make your most important desires and values a *motivational force* for helping you manage your time every day.

In Chapter 4, you will see how you can apply these steps and employ them as strategies for time management. Here let us do just the first step.

STEP 1: WHY AM I IN COLLEGE?

Why are you here? Even if you haven't picked a major yet—even if you're still a "searcher," which is perfectly all right—it's important to at least *think* about your long-range goals, your *life goals.*

These goals should be more than just "I want to get a college education" or "I want a degree so I can make a lot of money." You need ultimate goals but not goals that are too general. Better to state the goals not in terms of surpassing

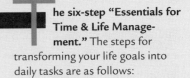he six-step **"Essentials for Time & Life Management."** The steps for transforming your life goals into daily tasks are as follows:

- ■ *Step 1:* The planning process starts when you answer the question "Why am I in college?"—that is, define your life goals or long-range goals.

- ■ *Step 2:* You then proceed to "What are my plans?"—setting your intermediate-range goals.

- ■ *Step 3:* This leads to "What are my actions?"—the steps you will take to achieve your goals.

- ■ *Step 4:* "What is my master timetable?" In this step you set your schedule for the semester or quarter.

- ■ *Step 5:* "What is my weekly timetable?" This is the schedule you follow from week to week.

- ■ *Step 6:* "What is on the To Do list today?" This is the errand list or "things to do" list that is no different from the To Do list that millions of people make every day.

other people—for there will always be people yet to be surpassed—but rather in terms of fulfilling your own potential. These goals should express *your* most important desires and values—not necessarily what your family wants you to do or what you think society expects of you. Some examples of life goals are shown in the list on the next page (See ■ *Panel 2.2.*)

PANEL 2.2 Examples of life goals.

Heroes: To follow in the footsteps of . . . (name a hero or heroine). (*Example:* an entertainer, political figure, someone you know—a teacher, a successful relative or family friend.)

Sacrifice: What is worth sacrificing for and what the sacrifice is. (*Examples:* giving up making a lot of money in order to help people; giving up close family life in order to travel the world.)

Values: What you hold to be most important and dear to you.

Love: How you would express it and to whom.

Family: What its importance is to you at present and in the future.

Security: What the least security is you would settle for financially, emotionally.

Principles: What you would stand up for and base your life on.

Creativity: What things you would like to create.

Curiosity: What questions you want to satisfy.

Personal challenges: What abilities you need to prove about yourself.

Death: What you hope to accomplish in the face of your own mortality.

As I mentioned, because college is not an easy experience, in order to pull yourself through some difficult times, you will need to know *why* you are doing all this. Now, then, is the time to set down your long-range goals. See Personal Exploration #2.3 below.

PERSONAL EXPLORATION #2.3

WHAT ARE YOUR LONG-RANGE GOALS?

Look back over your lists of reasons for attending college. Do they include what might be considered *life goals*—things you hope college will help you achieve, say, 10 years from now? If not, add some life goals to the list below.

The top five goals I hope college will help me reach are . . .

1._____

_____

2._____

_____

3._____

_____

4._____

_____

5._____

_____

Onward

PREVIEW The secret of college success is discipline. The stronger your motivation for going to college, the more you're apt to develop the discipline that will help you prevail.

The secret of college success is actually quite simple. In a word, it is *discipline*—using self-control to manage your time and master your tasks.

Discipline means showing up for every class on time. It means taking notes of lectures and frequently reviewing those notes so you understand them. It means doing assigned readings not just once but as often as is required to memorize the material. It means devoting two hours to study for every hour of class. It means taking developmental classes, if necessary, to improve your reading, writing, and math skills. It means dealing with objections of family and friends about your spending time on your studies.

At the heart of discipline is the answer to the question, *Why do you want to go to college?* The clearer your purpose, the higher your resolve, and the greater your chances for success.

NOTES

1. Person, E. S. Quoted in: Anonymous (1990, September). Motivation. *Self*, p. 215.

2. Adapted from Friday, R. A. (1088). *Create your college success: Activities and exercises for students.* Belmont, CA: Wadsworth, pp. 116–19.

3. Carter, C. (1990). *Majoring in the rest of your life: Career secrets for college students.* New York: Noonday Press, pp. 61–62.

4. Rotter, J. B. (1966). Generalized expectancies for internal versus external control of reinforcement. *Psychological Monographs, 80* (Whole No. 603).

5. Passell, P. (1992, August 19). Twins study shows school is sound investment. *New York Times*, p. A14.

6. Reich, R., interviewed in Belton, B. (1994, September 2). Reich: College education a buffer against recession. *USA Today*, p. 3B.

7. Shilling, A. G. (1991, December 10). Good news: more productivity; bad news: high unemployment. *Wall Street Journal*, p. A14.

8. Wessel, D. (1994, September 26). For college graduates, a heartening word. *Wall Street Journal*, p. A1.

9. U.S. Bureau of the Census. Cited in: Healy, M. (1994, July 22). Time (in school) is money. *USA Today*, p. 1D.

10. Katz, J. (Ed.) (1968). *No time for youth: Growth and constraint in college students.* San Francisco: Jossey-Bass.

11. Kalat, J. W. (1990). *Psychology* (2nd ed.). Belmont, CA: Wadsworth, p. 440.

CLASSROOM ACTIVITIES

1. *How do your values compare?* Ask each student in the class to take out a sheet of paper and make a list of 20 matters he or she considers important—their values. Then ask them to reduce their lists to their five most important values.

   Have the class assemble in small groups of three to five people, and instruct each group to appoint one person as a recorder or secretary. Groups members should go through and discuss their lists and agree (if possible) on what the top five values are for the group. The secretary should then write this list on the classroom blackboard.

   Questions for classroom-wide discussion: What are the similarities and differences of values among the groups? How do individual student values compare to those on the group lists? To what extent did their group influence their choices? Did students in a group find it difficult to come to agreement and, if so, why? If you had only a month or year to live, how would that fact influence your choices?

2. *What are your values about higher education?* Have students review their answers to Personal Exploration #2.1, "Your Values About Higher Education." The purpose of that survey was to see how their values and

family background affected their actions about going to college.

In a small group (three to five people), students are to discuss some of the answers. Questions for discussion: What role did your family or people close to you have in your decision to go to college? What would you do (or rather do, if you had the money) if you weren't going to college? What top three values influenced you to go to college?

3. *Why are you here? Your reasons for attending college.* Have students form into small groups (three to five people each). Ask them to discuss some of the reasons for attending college. Are there any public reasons that students express to people that they feel shaky about? Are there any private reasons that they care to bring out that might benefit from group discussion?

4. *What are your fears? Your greatest concerns and anxieties.* Have students take a few minutes to list, on a half sheet of paper or 3×5 card, their greatest concerns and anxieties. Some of them may be about college, of course, but some may be about other matters (which their attendance at college may affect or aggravate). Important: Students *should not* sign their names to the cards.

Collect the lists and shuffle them. Call upon students to come to the front of the class, pick a list at random, and copy the material on the blackboard. One area of the board should be saved; you, the instructor, will write down common themes here.

Questions for discussion: What are common themes or overlapping issues? What are your reactions to the most common themes? What techniques or resources do you have to cope with these concerns?

5. *What are your long-range goals?* Ask students to form into small groups and to take turns describing their life goals, referring to their answers to Personal Exploration #2.3, "What Are Your Long-Range Goals?"

Questions for discussion: How do your goals compare to, or differ from, those of others? How will going to college help you reach these goals?

Question for classroom-wide discussion: How do the goals in your group compare with those of other small groups in your class?

JOURNAL ENTRY #2.1: WHY ARE YOU HERE?
This is the most important question you can answer about college. Write at least 25 words about this matter.

_____

_____

_____

_____

_____

_____

_____

_____

_____

_____

JOURNAL ENTRY #2.2: WHAT IS YOUR FEAR?
This is the probably the second most important question you can answer about college. Write at least 25 words about your two or three principal fears.

_____

_____

_____

_____

_____

_____

_____

_____

_____

JOURNAL ENTRY #2.3: WHAT ARE YOUR STRENGTHS? Write about what you consider your strengths that will help see you through.

_____

_____

_____

_____

_____

_____

_____

_____

_____

_____

_____

_____

_____

_____

_____

_____

_____

_____

_____

3 resources

getting help, finding opportunities, benefiting from diversity

HELP!

That's a word we've all used at some point. Or certainly wanted to.

Often help is easy to ask for and easy to get. ("Am I in the right line?") At other times, however, *Help!* may be the silent cry of a student overwhelmed by confusion, loneliness, test anxiety, family problems, or money worries. Is help available for these sorts of matters? The answer is: You bet!

Unfortunately, sometimes people with a problem can't imagine there's a way out. People may feel pressured to mask their feelings, to wear an "Everything's cool" expression. But sometimes things are *not* cool. That's why I've put this chapter early in the book. Its purpose is to show what kind of assistance is available *before* you need it.

In addition, I wanted to give you the chance to find out what a gold mine college is outside of the classroom. Often commuter students think, "I don't have time for extracurricular stuff! Besides, what good could it possibly do me?" However, many college graduates treasure lifelong friendships—and helpful career connections—they made while in school. Many also still practice athletic, musical, and other skills they developed at that time. To help you do the same, we will look at opportunities college gives you to make these connections.

Finally, people in the 21st century will be exposed to far more cultural diversity than was true in the past. Thus, we will look at ways you can use college to learn to get along with people different from you. By "different" I mean different in all ways—in dress, gender, age, religion, skin color, nationality, sexual preference, cultural tastes, and so on.

A Look Around the Campus

PREVIEW Finding out about campus services resembles looking over an unfamiliar neighborhood. The orientation program and campus tour for new students is a good way to start. Helpful publications include the college catalog, campus map, student handbook, campus newspaper and bulletins, course lists and instructor evaluations, brochures and posters. Areas of assistance include academic help; physical, emotional, and spiritual help; other college help; activities and campus life; and community services.

What do you usually do first after getting off a bus or parking your car in an unfamiliar neighborhood?

You take a quick look around.

You check out the area to get a sense of the layout of things. You scan the environment to see if everything looks all right. You get a picture of what your options are.

That's what we're going to do in this chapter—take a quick look around the campus, so you can see what your options are. We will see how you can check out various campus facilities to find out what services and opportunities are available to help you survive, enjoy, and profit from college.

THE ORIENTATION PROGRAM & CAMPUS TOUR. Many colleges offer an orientation program and tour of the campus for new students. However, some facilities and services may be left off the tour (because of time). Or you may not find some of them personally interesting or currently valuable to you. Still, if you have a chance to take the tour, I urge you to do so. You may sometime need to know where to go to get permission to skip a course or get into one already started. Or you may need to get information on how to resolve a tenant—landlord hassle or other problem.

Obviously, if you've already had a campus tour or orientation, you're ahead of the game.

PUBLICATIONS: INSTRUCTION MANUALS FOR COLLEGE. Many jobs have instruction manuals, briefing books, and similar publications to help employees understand what they are supposed to do. College has them too, as follows:

- *College catalog:* Publications are a great way to learn about all aspects of campus life. Probably the most valuable is the college catalog, which is the playbook or rule book for the game of higher education. **The *college catalog* contains requirements for graduation, requirements for degree programs, and course descriptions.** It also may contain a history of the school, information about faculty members, and various programs and services. In addition, it may contain information about financial aid.

  The college catalog is most likely available in the Admissions Office, Counseling Office, or campus bookstore.

- *Campus calendar:* **Of particular value is the *campus calendar*, which lists the deadlines and dates for various programs.** You'll particularly want to note the last days to enroll in a new course and to drop a course without penalty. The campus calendar may be included in the college catalog.

- *Campus map:* Many college catalogs include a map of the campus, but if yours does not, pick up one. You might wish to have a one-page map anyway because it's easier to carry around.

- *Student handbook:* Some colleges publish a *student handbook*, **which summarizes many of the college's policies and regulations.** This may duplicate information in the catalog but be written so as to be more accessible to students.

- *College newspaper and campus bulletins:* **The *college newspaper* is a student-run news publication that is published on some campuses.** The college newspaper may be the single best source of ongoing information. Depending on the campus, it may be published daily, twice a week, weekly, or every two weeks. Because its readership is the entire college community—students, staff, faculty, and possibly townspeople—the news may cover topics of broad interest. In addition, some colleges publish a special "Orientation Edition" of the paper as a service to new students.

  On some campuses, there may also be a student bulletin. **The *student bulletin*, or *campus bulletin*, is helpful in keeping you informed of campus activities and events,** as well as other matters. This periodical, appearing occasionally throughout the term, may be published by the student government or by an office of the administration.

- *Course lists and instructor evaluations:* **The *course list* is simply a list of the courses being taught in the current school term.** Published before each new term, the course list states what courses are being taught. The list states on what days at what times courses are given, for how many units, and by what instructor.

  Sometimes the instructor is simply listed as "Staff." This may mean he or she is a teaching assistant (often a graduate student). Or it may mean that the instructor was simply unassigned at the time the course list was printed. Call the department if you want to know who the instructor is.

  On some campuses, students publish instructor evaluations. *Instructor evaluations* **consider how fairly instructors grade and how effectively they present their lectures.** If your campus does not have such evaluations, you may be able to sit in on a potential instructor's class. You can also talk with other students there to get a feel for his or her style and ability. In addition, you can find out what degrees an instructor has and from what institutions, usually by looking in the college catalog.

- *Brochures, flyers, and posters:* Especially during orientation or when registering, you may find yourself flooded with brochures. You may also see flyers and posters on campus bulletin boards.

  Some of these may be on serious and important personal subjects. Examples are security and night escorts to parked cars, alcohol and other drug abuse, and date rape. Some may be on campus events and club offerings. Some may simply list apartments to share or rides wanted. Some may list upcoming concerts, political rallies, or film festivals.

  Most of this kind of information has to do with the informal or extracurricular side of your college experience. Much of this is as important as the purely academic part. Indeed, many prospective employers look at this extracurricular side to see how well rounded a student's educational experience has been.

  To begin to get familiar with the college catalog, do Personal Exploration #3.1 (opposite page).

SOME PARTICULARLY IMPORTANT PLACES TO KNOW ABOUT. There are three places on campus that, in my opinion, a newcomer should get to know right away:

- *The library:* Most new students don't understand how to use the library and are unaware of the scope of its services. When it comes to writing papers, this is the place to know about.

- *The learning center:* This is the place for learning specific subjects or skills (for example, word processing or math help). You can also get tutoring in most subjects here. The learning center is an invaluable resource.

- *The career counseling center:* If you're undecided about your major, the career counseling center is the place to go. This can save you from going down a lot of

blind alleys. Even students who have already chosen a major can benefit from this place, which can help them focus their efforts.

FIVE ADDITIONAL IMPORTANT SERVICES OR CENTERS. There are five additional areas of services or centers, as I will describe in this chapter.

- *Academic help:* Examples are instructors, academic advisors and counselors, librarians, and tutors.

- *Physical, emotional, and spiritual help:* Examples are health and fitness professionals, counselors, psychotherapists, security personnel, and chaplains. In addition, there are probably support groups (as for adult returning students or single parents, for example).

- *Other help:* Examples are financial affairs, housing office, career counseling and placement, child care, and legal services. There may also be various community services, such as on-campus post office and bank.

- *Activities and campus life:* Examples are athletics, clubs, bands and other musical groups, and fraternities and sororities (often nonresidential).

- *Multicultural centers:* Examples are centers for racial and ethnic groups, women, international students, gays and lesbians, adult returning students, single-parent students, and students with disabilities.

LEARNING TO USE YOUR COLLEGE CATALOG

Obtain a copy of your college catalog. Fill in the answers in the following lines.

A. GENERAL

1. How many undergraduate students are enrolled?_____

2. When was the college founded?_____

3. What is the mission, orientation, or specialization of the college? (Examples: liberal arts, religious values, teacher training.)

   _____
   _____
   _____
   _____

4. How is the institution organized? (Example: schools, with divisions and departments.)

   _____
   _____
   _____

5. What are three graduate or professional programs offered by the college, if any, that interest you? (Examples: teacher certification, business, law.)

   _____
   _____
   _____

6. What are some other campuses or sites the college has, including extension divisions, if any?

   _____
   _____
   _____

7. Look at the lists of majors and minors offered by the college. Which three majors might interest you?

   _____
   _____
   _____

   Which three minors might interest you?

   _____
   _____
   _____

8. Is it possible to graduate with more than one major? If so, which two might interest you?

   _____
   _____
   _____
   _____

B. THE CAMPUS CALENDAR

1. *Cut-off dates:* What is the last date this semester on which you may … (specify month and day)

   Add a course?_____

   Drop a course?_____

   Drop a course and receive partial tuition refund?_____

   Ask for a grade of "Incomplete," if offered?_____

   Withdraw from a course?_____

2. *Holidays:* On what holidays is the college closed this semester?

   _____
   _____
   _____
   _____

3. *Registration:* What are the dates for registration for next semester?

   _____
   _____

4. *Exams:* When are final exams scheduled for this semester?

   _____
   _____

5. *Class end and start dates:*

   What is the last day of classes for this semester?_____

   What is the first day of classes for next semester?_____

C. TUITION & FINANCIAL AID

1. What is the annual tuition for in-state students at the college? _____ For out-of-state students? _____

2. What financial aid is available? (Examples: loans, scholarships, work/study.)

   _____
   _____
   _____

D. GRADES

1. Grades instructors give (such as A, B, C, D, F) and what they mean:

   _____
   _____
   _____

2. Meaning of "Pass/fail," if offered:

   _____
   _____
   _____

3. Meaning of "Incomplete," if offered:

   _____
   _____
   _____

4. Meaning of "Audit":

   _____
   _____
   _____

5. What minimum grade-point average do you need to maintain in order to be considered in satisfactory academic standing?

   _____
   _____

6. What happens if you fall below that minimum?

   _____
   _____
   _____

E. CREDITS

1. What is the definition of a credit (or unit)?

   _____
   _____
   _____

2. Does your college give credit for advanced courses taken in high school? _____ For courses taken at other colleges? _____

   For some life experience outside of college? _____

   (continued on next page)

■ F. GRADE-POINT AVERAGE & GRADUATION REQUIREMENTS

1. Explain the formula for computing students' grade-point average:

_____
_____
_____
_____

2. List the courses you are taking this semester or quarter and the number of credits (units) for each.

_____
_____
_____
_____
_____
_____

For each course assign a hypothetical grade according to the following formula: A = 4.0, B = 3.0, C = 2.0, D = 1.0, F = 0.0. Then compute the grade points earned for each course. (Example for one course: "First-Year Experience, 3 credits, grade of A = 4.0; 4.0 x 3 credits = 12 grade points.")

Now add up your grade points earned for all courses. Finally, divide them by the total number of credits (units) attempted to derive your hypothetical grade-point average for the semester or quarter.

_____
_____
_____
_____
_____
_____

3. What minimum grade-point average is required for graduation?

_____

4. Besides completing a major, what are the other requirements for graduation?

_____
_____
_____
_____
_____
_____

■ G. MISCONDUCT

1. *Academic matters:* How does the college deal with cheating and plagiarism? (Plagiarism is passing off someone else's work as your own, as when writing a paper.)

_____
_____

2. *Nonacademic matters:* How does the college deal with nonacademic matters such as sexual harassment, drunkenness, property damage, or off-campus arrests?

_____
_____
_____
_____
_____
_____
_____

■ H. SPECIAL PROGRAMS

1. *Academic honors:* What forms of recognition does the college offer for academic excellence? What are the standards for achieving such honors? (Examples: honors programs, dean's list, Phi Beta Kappa, scholarships.)

_____
_____
_____
_____

2. *Other special programs:* What other special programs are offered, and what are the criteria for participation? (Examples: study-abroad programs, internships.)

_____
_____
_____
_____
_____
_____
_____
_____

Academic Help

PREVIEW People who can assist you with academic problems are academic advisors, instructors, librarians and media center staff, and tutors and study-skills staff. Other academic services include the computer center, music practice rooms, and the Dean of Students office. Academic advising—which is principally about degrees, majors, and courses—is extremely important because it affects your college, career, and life plans.

Some day you may return to college as a retired person and *actually take some courses for the fun of it.* Older people often do this. I assume, however, that you are the type of student for whom "fun" is not the main priority of the college experience. That is, you are here on the serious mission of getting a degree.

Obtaining a college degree—whether associate's, bachelor's, master's, or other—is the goal, of course, of the academic part of college. The degree signifies that you have passed certain courses with a minimum grade. Completing the courses means that you have passed tests, written research papers, done projects, and so on. To accomplish all these, you must have attended classes, listened to lectures, gone to the library, and read a lot. Hopefully, while you're having to jump through all these hoops, learning is also taking place.

POSSIBLE ACADEMIC DIFFICULTIES. The problem with accomplishing these tasks is that there are many places where hangups can occur—and where you might need some help. Here are some possibilities: You can't get the classes you want. You wonder if you can waive some prerequisites. You don't know what you still need to do to graduate. You're having trouble with your writing, math, or study skills. You're sick and can't finish your courses. You don't know how to compute your grade-point average. You need recommendations for an employer or a graduate school.

Knowing how to find help, get good advice, and cut through bureaucratic red tape aren't skills that become obsolete after college. They are part and parcel of being A Person Who Can Get Things Done, which is what we all wish to be. Learning how to find your way around the college academic system, then, is training for life. Outside college, these skills are called *networking* and *troubleshooting*—and they are invaluable in helping you get where you want to go.

To get help or advice in college, you may need to consult the following academic services or people:

- Academic advisors
- Instructors
- Librarians and media-center staff
- Tutors and study-skills staff
- Some other academic services
- When all other help fails: the Dean of Students office

ACADEMIC ADVISORS. What people will you deal with the most for academic matters? Probably your instructors. But there is another individual who, in the grand scheme of things, could be *more* important: your academic advisor. Why? "For most freshmen, the first year of college is both exciting and crisis oriented," say one pair of writers. "New students are unfamiliar with college resources, their major field, the faculty, course work, academic expectations, and career applications of their major." [1] Thus, *academic advising is important because it affects your planning for college and beyond that for your career and for your life.*

The *academic advisor* **counsels students about their academic program.** The academic advisor is either a full-time administrative employee or a faculty member, often in the field in which you'll major. What does he or she do that I think is so important? There are two principal activities:

- *Gives information about degrees, majors, and courses:* The academic advisor explains to you what courses are required in your degree program. The *degree program* **consists of all the courses you must take to obtain a college degree in a specific field.**

  Courses will be of two types:

(1) *General education courses* are those specified in the college catalog that all students have to take to obtain a degree. Examples are a choice of some courses in social science (as in sociology, political science) or in humanities (as in English, philosophy).

(2) *Courses in your major* will be those offered, from another list, that are needed for you to complete your major. **Your major is your field of specialization.** Perhaps a third of the courses you need to graduate will be in this category. Some colleges also require a <u>*minor*</u>, **a smaller field of specialization**, which will entail fewer courses.

Both general-education courses and the courses for your major are identified on a *curriculum worksheet*, available to you and your advisor. **The *curriculum worksheet* lists all the courses required for the major and the semesters in which it is recommended you take them.** It may also list additional courses you might have to take if you transfer from a community college to a university. The accompanying example shows a curriculum worksheet for Hotel Technology: Hospitality Management. (See ■ Panel 3.1.)

▮ *Provides information, advice, and support in general:* Academic advisors are usually also available to talk about other matters important to you. These include difficulty keeping up with course work, uncertainty about your major, worries about fair treatment by an instructor, and personal stresses. If an advisor does not feel capable of helping you directly, he or she can certainly suggest where to turn. (You may be directed to a counselor, who is different from an advisor.)

■ Here's an important fact: *poor academic advising is a major reason students drop out of college.*[2] Conversely, students who receive good academic advising are not only more apt to graduate but also are happier while in college. For students in community colleges planning to go on to a university, seeing an academic advisor can save them headaches later. This is because different colleges and universities sometimes have different transfer requirements. Thus, it's possible to end up spending extra semesters taking courses at the junior or senior level that you could have completed earlier. An academic advisor can help you avoid such time wasters.

When you enter college, an academic advisor will be assigned to you. Later, if you change majors or if you go

PANEL 3.1

A curriculum worksheet. This example, which shows the courses required and their recommended order, is for a major in Hotel Technology: Hospitality Management.

HOTEL TECHNOLOGY: HOSPITALITY MGT.
DEGREE: A.A.S.

HOTEL TECHNOLOGY: HOSPITALITY MANAGEMENT
SEMESTER COURSE PLANNING WORKSHEET

SUGGESTED FIRST SEMESTER	CREDITS	SUGGESTED SECOND SEMESTER	CREDITS
		ENG 105 or ENG 102	3
ENG 101 (By Placement)	3	ACC 104	3
ACC 101	3	HOS 102	3
TUR 101	3	HUR 101	3
HOS 103	3	BUS 102	3
BUS 101	3	HEALTH/PHYS.ED./REC.	1
	15		16

SUGGESTED THIRD SEMESTER	CREDITS	SUGGESTED FOURTH SEMESTER	CREDITS
		BUS 217	3
TUR 205	3	HOS 202	3
BUS 201	3	LIBERAL ARTS ELECTIVE	3
BUS 104	3	TUR 210	3
BUS 205	3	SOC 101 or ECO 101	3
SPE 108	1	SCIENCE ELECTIVE	3
HEALTH/PHYS.ED./REC.	1		18
	16		

GENERAL CURRICULUM INFORMATION

TRANSFER TO A FOUR-YEAR SCHOOL - Certain additional courses may be required such as ACC102, ECO105 or MAT129. Please see the transfer advisor in the Career Development Center.

ENGLISH (By Placement) - Satisfactory completion of the writing skills exam is a prerequisite for ENG101. Students who do not satisfactorily complete the writing exam must register for ENG100 prior to completing their 6 hour English sequence.

HEALTH/PHYSICAL EDUCATION REQUIREMENT - Select from any Health, Physical Education or Recreation course for two credits.

LIBERAL ARTS ELECTIVE - Selection must be made from courses listed on the reverse side of this worksheet. Please note that performance classes may not be used to fulfill liberal arts elective, i.e., MUS112-114 and THE116-118.

READING PROFICIENCY REQUIREMENT - All students will be required to demonstrate proficiency in reading through testing prior to earning a degree or certificate. Students who do not meet the required standard will be expected to begin remediation immediately.

MATH PROFICIENCY - All students will be required to demonstrate proficiency in basic algebra prior to earning a degree by either satisfactory completion of MAT092 (algebra) or passing a placement exam.

COOPERATIVE EDUCATION - A cooperative placement is required after completion of thirty (30) hours of course work.

DEGREE REQUIREMENTS for HOTEL TEC:HOSPITALITY MGT
ADVISING GUIDE FOR: HOSPITALITY MANAGEMENT   CURR: 575   DEGREE: AAS

REQUIREMENTS		CREDITS
1) COMMUNICATIONS		
ENG101 ENGLISH COMM 1		3
ENG102 ENGLISH COMM 2 OR ENG105 WRITING IN HUMANI		3
		6
2) HUMANITIES		
SPE108 PUBLIC SPEAKING		3
		3
3) SOCIAL SCIENCES		
SOC101 INTRO SOCIOLOGY OR ECO101 MICROECONOMICS		3
HUR101 HUMAN RELATIONS 1		3
		3
4) SCIENCE		
SCIELE SCIENCE ELECTIVE(S)		3
(Select From - AST***,BIO***,CHE***,PHY***,SCI***)		6
5) BUSINESS		
ACC101 ACCOUNTING 1		3
ACC104 HOSP MGMT ACCOUNT		3
BUS101 PRIN OF BUSINESS		3
BUS102 PRIN OF MARKET		3
BUS104 MANAGEMENT PRINC		3
BUS205 BUSINESS LAW 1		3
BUS201 PROF SALES		3
BUS217 CO-OP EDUCATION		3
TUR101 INTRO TO TOURISM		3
HOS103 HOTEL OPERATIONS		3
HOS102 FOOD SYSTEMS		3
HOS202 RESORT DEVEL&MGT		3
TUR205 GEO OF TOURISM		3
TUR210 TOURISM ISSUES		3
		42
6) HEALTH/PE/REC		
HPEELE HEALTH/PE/REC ELECTIVE(S)		2
(Select From - HED***,PED***,REC***)		2
7) LIBERAL ARTS		
LIBELE LIBERAL ARTS ELECTIVE(S)		3
(Select From - ANT***,ART101,ART103,ART104,ART105,ART110,		3
ART111,ART114,ART125,ART126,ART132,AST***,BIO***,		
CHE***,ECO***,ENG102,ENG105,ENG106,ENG214,FRE***,HIS***,		
HUM***,HUR101,HUR102,HUS101,LIT***,MAT***,MUS101,MUS102,		
MUS103,MUS110,MUS111,MUS190,MUS191,MUS192,MUS193,MUS194,		
MUS195,MUS196,MUS199,MUS201,MUS202,PHI***,PHY***,POS***,		
PSY***,SOC***,SPA***,SPE103,SPE108,SPE109,THE101,THE103,		
THE190,THE191,THE192,THE193,THE194,THE202,THE204,THE212,		
THE221)		

.. READING and MATH Proficiency Required ..
Minimum QPI: 2.00

Total Degree Credits   65

from being "Undecided" or "Unde-clared" to declaring your major, you may change advisors.

On some campuses, touch-screen kiosks are available to provide students with some academic functions. However, students should see their academic advisor *at least* once a semester or quarter. You should also see him or her whenever you have any questions or important decisions to make about your college career. *(See ■ Panel 3.2.)*

INSTRUCTORS. You will have many instructors, and they can be valuable resources to you. College instructors and high-school teachers have different kinds of training and different emphases on teaching, as follows.

- ■ *Training in teaching:* You may have been bored by some of your high-school teachers, but, believe it or not, all such teachers have actually had training in how to teach. College instructors, on the other hand, often have not, unless they are former high-school teachers. (Some graduate students are required to take a course in teaching.)

- ■ *Years of study:* Most high-school teachers have earned a teaching credential on top of a bachelor's degree (B.A. or B.S.), representing a minimum of four to five years of schooling.

  Full-time college instructors usually have at least a master's degree (M.A. or M.S.), which represents one or two years of study after the bachelor's degree. Many professors—those you might address as "Doctor"—have a *doctorate* or Ph.D. or Ed.D. degree. (Ph.D. stands for "Doctor of Philosophy," although the degree is given for all subject areas in addition to philosophy. Ed.D. stands for "Doctor of Education.") To earn this degree, instructors must take additional courses and spend several years researching and writing a doctoral dissertation. This dissertation is a book-length investigation of a specific subject.

  Part-time college instructors may also have master's or doctoral degrees. Or they may be graduate students (called *teaching assistants,* or "T.A.'s"). Or they

PANEL 3.2 •

Using your advisor for college success.

Like everything else in college, you get out of academic advising what you put into it. Here are some tips for using your advisor to make college work best for you:

Be aware of the advising period—see the catalog: The college requires students at least once a semester or quarter to see their advisors about which courses they will take the next term. The period for doing this, often about two weeks, is usually listed on the academic calendar in the college catalog and is announced in the campus newspaper and elsewhere. *Put the dates of the advising period on your personal calendar and be sure to make an appointment to see your advisor.*

See your advisor more than once a term to establish a relationship: Your advisor is not just a bureaucrat who has to sign off on your courses and should not be treated as such. See him or her at least one other time during the semester or quarter to discuss problems and progress. Ask about interesting courses, interesting professors, any possible changes in major, and difficult courses and how to handle them. Discuss any personal problems affecting your life and work. *In short, if possible, make your advisor a mentor—a person you can trust.*

If your advisor isn't right for you, find another one: If you feel your advisor is distant, uncaring, arrogant, ignorant, or otherwise unsuitable, don't hesitate to make a change. You have this right, although you have to be your own advocate here. *To make a change, ask another instructor or staff person to be your advisor.* Depending on the arrangements on your campus, you may get another advisor by going to the Advisement Center, the Registrar, the Office of Student Services, or the Dean of Students.

may be people from another campus or the nonacademic world (called *adjunct professors*) teaching special courses. Their years of study may be about the same as those of most high-school teachers. (These instructors may be addressed as "Mr." or "Ms." or "Professor.")

- **_Mission—teaching or research?_** High-school teachers teach—that's their principal job. That's also the principal mission of _some_, but not all, college instructors. It depends on what kind of institution of higher learning you're attending.

For example, professors in two-year colleges—community colleges or junior colleges—are hired mainly to teach. A full-time instructor may teach four or five courses a week. The same is true in vocational-technical schools.

However, the teaching demands for professors in four-year colleges may not be so explicit. Teaching may indeed be the main mission of an instructor at a private liberal-arts college or even at some state universities. (These are institutions that grant bachelor's and master's degrees and sometimes doctorates.) However, for the really large and/or top-flight state or private universities, teaching is _not_ the main emphasis for professors. Rather, research, writing, and publishing are.

The biggest difference between taking courses in high school and in college is: _more is expected of you in college._ College, after all, is designed more to treat you as an adult. Thus, you have more adult freedoms than were probably allowed you in high school. For example, many instructors do not take daily attendance. Moreover, they may not check your assignments on a daily basis. Thus, you are expected to do more of your work on your own.

Still, instructors are among the academic resources available to you. All college faculty members are required to be in their offices during certain hours. (Hours are posted on their office doors and/or are available as course handouts or through the department secretary.) In addition, many are available for questions a minute or so after class. You may also be able to make appointments with them at other times. (Be sure to make a note of the time of the appointment. Telephone the instructor if you can't keep it.)

The instructor is the one to see if you have a question or problem about the course you are taking. These include which books to buy, what readings a test will cover, anything you don't understand about an assignment or a test question. Don't be afraid to ask. And if you begin to have trouble in a course, don't wait until the test. See your instructor as soon as possible.

LIBRARIANS & MEDIA-CENTER STAFF. Perhaps you think the library is just a quiet place with books and magazines where you can go to study. Actually, there is more to it than that. _One of the first things you should do in college is find out how to use the library._ Often the library has a room or section in it called the _media center._

The library is one of the most important buildings on campus. Don't be intimidated by all the staff, books, and machines (computer terminals, microfilm readers). Instead, I suggest doing the following:

- **_Tour the facilities:_** Go to the library/media center and simply walk around every place you are allowed to go. _Actively_ scan the titles on the shelves, looking for books or magazines you're interested in. _Actively_ take note of the desks and study areas available, picking out a couple of spots you might favor using later. _Actively_ read the directions on how to use machines, such as computers, microfilm readers, and copiers.

- **_Ask how to use the facilities:_** Have you ever noticed how some people are so concerned with how they look to others that they never ask directions? Some drivers, for instance, would rather "figure it out for themselves" than stop and ask someone on the street how to get somewhere.

If you're the kind of person who's reluctant to seek help, here's a good exercise. Ask the librarians or media-center staff for a _demonstration_ on how to use the facilities to do research. Sometimes there is a standard guided tour. Ask how to use the computer-based catalog for books and periodicals and how to use microfilm equipment. Ask how to play videotapes or audiotapes in the media center. Ask about other research libraries and facilities on campus. Especially be sure to ask about how the interlibrary loan system works and how quickly you can get a book you need from another library in the state.

■ We take a look at libraries and media centers in more detail in Chapter 9, "Communication."

TUTORS & STUDY-SKILLS STAFF. *This is an important, probably underused resource.* Most colleges offer courses or services for improving your reading, writing, math, or study skills. The place for doing this may be located in a learning center. **A *learning center*, or *learning lab*, is a special center where you go to learn a specific subject or skill.** Sometimes learning centers are located in a special building on campus. Sometimes they are attached to various departments, such as foreign-language departments. For example, some foreign-language learning centers have computer terminals or booths with television monitors and earphones for practice purposes.

In addition, you can arrange through the learning center or through academic departments (ask the department secretary) for tutoring help. **A *tutor* is essentially a private teacher or coach.** This person will help you, through a series of regularly scheduled meetings, to improve a particular skill.

SOME OTHER ACADEMIC SERVICES. Other on-campus resources are available to help you with your academic work, ranging from photocopiers to music practice rooms. For example, your campus may have several art resources: museums, art galleries, archives, and special libraries.

Some campuses have computers or a lab in which you may use a personal computer. Computers are useful for such tasks as writing papers (word processing), doing calculations (using spreadsheets), doing computer graphics, and the like. Courses that teach valuable computer skills, such as word processing,

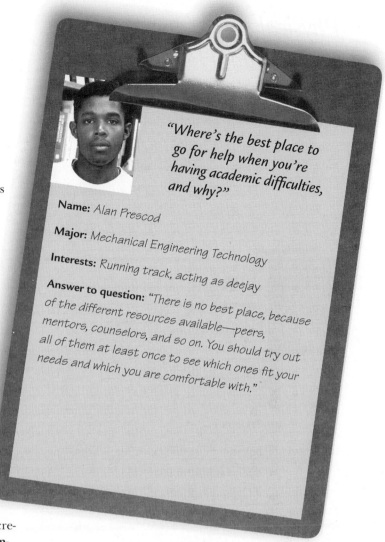

"Where's the best place to go for help when you're having academic difficulties, and why?"

Name: Alan Prescod

Major: Mechanical Engineering Technology

Interests: Running track, acting as deejay

Answer to question: "There is no best place, because of the different resources available—peers, mentors, counselors, and so on. You should try out all of them at least once to see which ones fit your needs and which you are comfortable with."

are offered through the computer center or academic courses.

These days its also important to find out what options the college offers in independent study and distance learning. For instance, you may be able to take courses offered via television (telecourses) or via computer connected to the Internet.

WHEN ALL OTHER HELP FAILS: THE DEAN OF STUDENTS OFFICE. If you can't seem to find help for whatever your difficulty is, try the Dean of Students office. It is the *job* of the staff here to see that you are taken care of in college. If they can't handle the problem themselves, they will find someone who will.

Physical, Emotional, & Spiritual Help

PREVIEW People to help you take care of your physical, emotional, and spiritual well-being are found in several places. They include the health service, counseling center, security office, chapel, wellness/fitness services, and on-campus and off-campus support groups.

The academic help I described has to do with taking care of your mind. Now let's consider the services offered to take care of your body, heart, and spirit.

The basic facilities and services are:

- Health service
- Counseling center
- Security
- Chapels and religious services
- Wellness/fitness services
- Support groups

HEALTH SERVICE. Most colleges have some sort of health or medical service. Treatment is often free or low-cost for minor problems.

If you go to a commuter college, the health service may be just a nurse's office. The college assumes that most students' health care will be handled by community hospitals and other resources. However, you can at least get first aid, aspirin, and advice and referrals.

The health service is a good place to go to if you need help with physical problems, of course. In addition, it can help with anxiety, birth-control information, sexually transmitted diseases, and alcohol or other drug problems.

COUNSELING CENTER: PSYCHOLOGICAL SERVICES. We all have lots of stresses in our lives, and going to college unquestionably adds to them. If you're sleeping through classes because you dread the subject or are panicky with test anxiety, *don't hesitate to seek help at the counseling center.* Certainly if you feel you're on the verge of flunking for whatever reason, get to the center as quickly as you can. Such counseling is often free or low-cost.

In addition, problems arise that may not have much to do with the academic side of college. These include love relationships and problems with parents and self-esteem, "Who am I?" identity concerns, pregnancy, and worries about sexually transmitted diseases. Most psychological counselors are familiar with these problems and can help.

Psychological distress is as real as physical distress and should not be ignored. Some students worry that it is not cool or it will be seen as an admission of weakness to seek counseling help. Nothing could be further from the truth. People who are unwilling to admit they need help often find their problems "leak out" in other ways. These could include oversleeping, alcohol or other types of drug abuse, or anger toward family members. By refusing to get help, they compound their problems until they need help even more. Believe me, I speak from experience on this because, besides teaching first-year college experience courses, I also work as a counselor.

SECURITY: CAMPUS POLICE. Campus security personnel or police may be most visible in their roles of enforcing parking control—a problem on every commuter college campus. However, they do far more than that.

Afraid to walk across campus to your car after a night class? Call campus security to ask for an escort. It's done all the time on many urban campuses. Locked out of your car or locker? Call the campus police. Lost your watch, been hassled by a drunk, or found yourself dealing with someone who's been raped? Such problems are the reasons why, unfortunately, campus security exists. *(See* ■ *Panel 3.3)*

Tips for staying safe.

Safety is a major issue on many commuter campuses. At your college, you may see posters, brochures, and newspaper articles concerned with such matters as use of nighttime escorts to parked cars. The basic piece of advice is: Use common sense about your safety; be alert for trouble. Other safety tips are as follows:

WHEN WALKING, TRAVELING, OR OUT IN PUBLIC:

1. At night or early morning, don't walk alone or jog alone. Stay with groups. Take advantage of campus escort services. Travel in well-populated, well-lighted areas.

2. Don't show money or valuables in public. Discreetly tuck away your cash after using an automated teller machine.

3. On foot: Walk rapidly and look as though you're going somewhere; don't dawdle. If someone makes signs of wanting to talk to you, just keep on going. It's less important that you be polite than that you be safe.

4. In a car: Make sure all doors are locked. Don't open them for anyone you don't know.

5. Don't leave backpacks, purses, or briefcases unattended.

WHEN IN YOUR RESIDENCE:

1. Lock your residence doors at all times.

2. Don't let strangers into your residence. Ask any stranger the name of the person he or she wants to see.

IF YOU SENSE YOU MIGHT BE ATTACKED:

1. If you are facing an armed criminal, the risk of injury may be minimized by cooperating with his or her demands. Avoid any sudden movements and give the criminal what he or she wants.

2. If you sense your life is in immediate danger, use any defense you can think of: screaming, kicking, running. Your objective is to get away.

3. In a violent crime, it is generally ineffective for the victim to cry or plead with the attacker. Such actions tend to reinforce the attacker's feeling of power over the victim.

CHAPELS & RELIGIOUS SERVICES. Some campuses have chapels that students may attend for religious services. Even nonreligious students are welcome to go in during quiet times just to meditate. Or they may wish to talk about personal or spiritual problems with the chaplain.

In addition, many campuses have organizations serving students of different religious affiliations. Examples are the Newman Club for those of the Catholic faith and Hillel House for those of the Jewish faith.

WELLNESS/FITNESS SERVICES: ATHLETIC & FITNESS CENTERS. If you think gymnasiums, field houses, and athletic centers are just for athletes (as I did in my first year), think again. They are supposed to be available for all students, including physically challenged students.

You can use not only lockers, showers, and spas but also pools, fitness centers, weight equipment, racquetball courts, and basketball courts. If your campus is anything like mine, you'll see scores of students jogging or playing or working out every day. And many of them did not take up such activities until they got to college.

SUPPORT GROUPS. Most colleges offer some sort of connection to support groups of all kinds. There are, for example, support groups for people having difficulties with weight, alcohol, drugs, gambling, incest, spouse abuse, or similar personal problems. There are also support groups or "affinity" groups. They may exist for women, men, physically challenged, gays, ethnic and racial minorities, returning students, foreign students, and so on. The counseling center can probably connect you with a support group of interest to you. Or you may see meeting announcements in campus publications.

Other Kinds of Assistance

PREVIEW Questions about your academic record can be resolved at the registrar's office. Other assistance is available to help with financial aid, housing, transportation, check cashing, job placement, career counseling, day care, and legal services. Alumni organizations can also be interesting resources. Finally, a variety of services not found on campus are available in the community.

Going to a college campus is almost like going to a one-industry town, with the main industry in this case being education. Fortunately, the town's administrators also care about students. Thus, they have set up services to deal with those of your needs that are not academic, physical, emotional, or spiritual.

Among the departments and services available are the following:

- Registrar
- Financial aid
- Housing
- Transportation
- Cashier/Business office
- Job placement
- Career counseling
- Child care
- Legal services
- Community services

REGISTRAR. The *registrar* **is responsible for keeping all academic records.** This is the office you need to seek out if you have questions about whether a grade was recorded correctly. The people there can also answer your inquiries about transcripts, graduation, or transfer from or to another college.

FINANCIAL AID. This is one of the most important offices in the college. If you're putting yourself through school or your family can't support you entirely, you need to get to know this office. Just as its title indicates, **the *financial aid office* is concerned with finding financial aid for students.** Such help can consist of low-interest loans, scholarships, part-time work, and other arrangements.

The workings of financial aid are discussed in Chapter 12, "Money."

HOUSING. No doubt you already have a roof over your head for this semester or quarter. If you're living in a campus residence hall, you probably got there through the housing office when you accepted your admission. Most urban students live off campus or at home.

The campus *housing office* helps students find housing. It also provides listings of off-campus rooms, apartments, and houses for rent in the community. Because landlords probably must meet standards for safety and cleanliness, the housing office may be a better source than advertisements for rentals.

TRANSPORTATION. The transportation office may be part of campus security or the campus police. **The *transportation office* issues permits for parking on campus and gives out information on public transportation and car pools.**

CASHIER/BUSINESS OFFICE. **The *cashier's office* or *business office* is where you go to pay college fees or tuition.** On some campuses you may also be able to cash checks here.

JOB PLACEMENT. **The *job placement office*, or *employment office*, provides job listings from campus or other employers looking for student help.** Many of the jobs are part time. They may range from waiting tables, to handing out equipment in the chemistry lab, to working behind a counter in a store.

CAREER COUNSELING. The *career counseling center* **is the place to find help if you're having trouble deciding on career goals or a major.** (It may also be called the *career development center* or the *career center.*) We consider the process of selecting a major and a career in Chapter 13, "Work."

CHILD CARE. Many commuter colleges offer child-care or day-care facilities for children of adult students. The centers are usually staffed by professional child-care specialists. They may be assisted by student interns or helpers studying child-related disciplines, such as education or psychology. Because perhaps as many as a quarter of commuter students are parents, child care is an important resource.

LEGAL SERVICES. Some urban colleges and universities have a legal-services office to provide information and counseling to students. Naturally, I hope you'll never have to use it. Still, it's good to know where to call if problems such as landlord–tenant disputes, auto accidents, drunk driving, or employment discrimination arise.

COMMUNITY SERVICES. You'll probably want such services as a post office, copy centers, automated teller machines, eating places, and service stations. These may exist right on campus, at least at larger colleges. If not, you may be able to find them close by the campus or in the community that you commute from. You may also be able to find help in consumer organizations, political and environmental organizations, city recreation departments, and YMCAs and YWCAs. Finally, you may need to find such services as off-campus counseling, child care, and legal assistance.

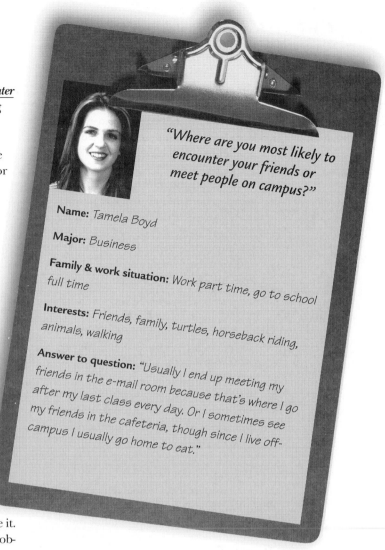

"Where are you most likely to encounter your friends or meet people on campus?"

Name: *Tamela Boyd*

Major: *Business*

Family & work situation: *Work part time, go to school full time*

Interests: *Friends, family, turtles, horseback riding, animals, walking*

Answer to question: *"Usually I end up meeting my friends in the e-mail room because that's where I go after my last class every day. Or I sometimes see my friends in the cafeteria, though since I live off-campus I usually go home to eat."*

Activities & Campus Life

PREVIEW A great deal of student life centers on the student union, the bookstore, and clubs and activities.

f colleges consisted only of lecture halls, laboratories, and libraries, they wouldn't be much fun. Much of the fun and energy on a college campus come from the places that are student-centered. These include the student union, the bookstore, and other centers of student life.

STUDENT UNION. This is often the "crossroads of the campus," the place where you go to hang out after class, to find your friends. **The *student union*, often called the *student center* or *campus center*, is different on every campus. However, it most certainly includes a cafeteria or dining hall and probably some recreation areas.** Recreation may include television rooms, Ping-Pong tables, pool tables, and video games. There may also be a bookstore, study lounges, a post office, convenience store, and bank or automated teller machine. Here's where you will find bulletin boards advertising everything from films to shared rides.

BOOKSTORE. Often located in the student center, the campus bookstore's main purpose is to make textbooks and educational supplies available for students. Beyond that, it may carry anything from candy, coffee mugs, and college sweatshirts to general-interest books and personal computers. The bookstore also often sells the *college catalog* and the *course list* (if these are not free).

In most college bookstores, you can find textbooks for the courses you're taking by looking for the course number on the shelves. Three tips I give my students regarding textbooks are:

- *Check out the books for your courses:* If ever there was a way of getting a preview of your academic work, it is here. Want to know how hard that course in physics or German is going to be? Go to the bookstore and take a look through the textbooks.

- *Buy the books early:* Many students do a lot of course adding and dropping at the beginning of the school term. Thus, they may wait to buy their textbooks until they are sure of what their classes are. Big mistake. Books may be sold out by the time they make up their minds, and new ones may take weeks to arrive. Better to buy the texts, but don't write in them. Hang on to your receipts so that you can return the books later and get your money back.

- *Buy the right edition:* As material becomes outdated, publishers change the editions of their books. If you buy a used version of the assigned text, make sure you get the most recent edition. An out-of-date edition (even for a history book) won't have all the facts you need to know. Moreover, the tests that instructors give are usually tied to the most recent edition of the text.

In some communities, off-campus bookstores also carry textbooks, both new and used.

STUDENT LIFE. "The most important determinant of college impact is living on campus," says one report, "an experience that opens students to other forces for change."[3] As I mentioned earlier, however, 80% of American undergraduates commute to campus (you presumably being one of them). How, then, are you going to get the benefit of going to college besides that of just going to class? The answer is simple: *You have to want to.* You have to be motivated so that, after class is over, you don't just automatically head for the parking lot or the bus stop. You have to find at least *one single thing besides your classes* that is as important enough to make you want to come to and stay on campus.

Whatever your background, there is probably some club, association, or activity on or near the campus that will interest you. Through these you can continue to develop talents discovered before college, such as in music or sports. You can also use them to develop new talents and interests, such as those in theater, politics, or camping.

You can join groups not only simply to have fun but also for two other important reasons. The first is to make friends. The second is to get some experience related to your major. For instance, if you major in journalism, you'll certainly want to work in whatever media are available on campus—newspaper, radio, film, television. The same is true with other majors. This is not just "pretend" stuff. It is valid experience that you'll want to put on your career résumé when you go job hunting later.

The College Multicultural "Salad Bowl": Diversity of Genders, Ages, Cultures, Races, & So On

PREVIEW Because of the changing "melting pot," global economy, and electronic communications, you will live in a world that is increasingly culturally and racially diverse. College gives you the opportunity to learn to live with diversity in gender and sexual orientation, age, race and culture, and disabilities.

We are in the midst of three developments that ensure the future will not look the same as the past:

■ *Changing "melting pot" (or "salad bowl"):* By the year 2000, it is estimated that white males will make up less than 10% of newcomers to the American workforce. Most new workers will be women, minorities, and recent immigrants.[4] America has always been considered a "melting pot"—or maybe "salad bowl" is a better description—of different races and cultures. However, it seems we will become more so in the near future.

■ *Changing world economy:* The American economy is becoming more a part of the world economy. "We are in an unprecedented period of accelerated changes," point out futurists John Naisbitt and Patricia Aburdene. Perhaps the most breathtaking, they say, "is the swiftness of our rush to all the world's becoming a single economy."[5] The American economy is now completely intertwined with the other economies of the world—and therefore with the world's people.

■ *Changing electronic communications:* Electronic communications systems—telephones, television, fax machines, computers—are providing a wired and wireless universe that is bringing the cultures of the world closer together.

For example, 24 million people in North America alone already communicate with each other through the Internet. The *Internet* is a global computer-linked network tying together thousands of smaller computer networks.

Many people are not prepared for these changes. Fortunately, many colleges are *multicultural*, **or culturally and racially diverse places.** *Diversity* **means variety—in race, gender, ethnicity, age, physical abilities, and sexual orientation.** College gives you the opportunity to learn to study, work, interact, and get along with people different from you. In this way you prepare yourself for life in the 21st century.

In this section, we look at the following kinds of diversity:

■ Gender and sexual orientation

■ Age

■ Race and culture

■ Disabilities

GENDER & SEXUAL ORIENTATION. After steady increases over two decades, college enrollments of women now exceed those of men. In 1970 women made up 42% of college enrollment. By 1990 that figure had risen to 55%. Why the dramatic change? One reason, perhaps, is the surge of interest among older women who postponed or never considered college and now are enrolling. Indeed, 49% of women in college are more than 24 years old, compared with 24% of men.[6]

Women have reasons to feel proud of their accomplishments. They get higher grades on average than men do, are awarded more scholarships, and complete bachelor's degrees at a faster pace.[7] However, traditionally they also suffer lower pay and slower advancements after college. Still, with so many women in college, the increased numbers of female graduates could put pressure on employers to change.

Colleges have experienced considerable pressures to develop policies for countering sex stereotypes, sexism, and sexual harassment:

- **Stereotype:** A *stereotype* **is an expected or exaggerated expectation about a category of people, which may be completely inaccurate when applied to individuals.** For example, a stereotype is that men are better than women in math and science, or women are better than men in cooking.

- **Sexism:** *Sexism* **is discrimination against individuals based on their gender.** An example is instructors who call more often on men than women (as is frequently the case) to answer questions in class.

- **Sexual harassment:** *Sexual harassment* **consists of sexually oriented behaviors that adversely affect someone's academic or employment status or performance.** Examples are requests for sexual favors, unwelcome sexual advances, or demeaning sexist remarks.

Colleges and universities have also been trying to improve the climate for homosexuals, or gays and lesbians, on their campuses. In recent times, surveys have found freshmen more accepting of gay rights. For example, in 1987 60% of male freshmen said there should be laws prohibiting homosexuality. Four years later only 33% of them still supported such laws.[8]

Most students keep their views on homosexuality to themselves. However, in some localities, homophobia still exists and may be expressed in active ways. *Homophobia* **is fear of, or resistance to, the idea of homosexuality or of homosexuals.** Students may express their opposition by harassing gay rights activists or even physically assaulting students whose sexual orientation they do not accept.

AGE. About 17 million Americans are taking college courses. However, only 6 million are so-called *traditional students*—**that is, between 18 and 24 years old.**[9] The

dramatic shift from students in their late teens and early 20s occurred because of the rising number of nontraditional students. *Nontraditional students*—**sometimes called adult students or returning students—are those who are older than 24.** As mentioned, nearly half the women and a quarter of the men attending college are over 24. Many of these also attend part time. (Actually, about half of college students, regardless of age, are enrolled part time.) On many commuter campuses, the average age of students is about 30.

Who are these nontraditional students? There is no easy way to catalog them. Large numbers are women entering the labor force, displaced workers trying to upgrade their skills, and baby boomers switching careers. Some are managers taking courses to gain advancement, others are people seeking intellectual stimulation. Some are retirees: In a recent year, 320,000 Americans age 50 and over were enrolled in college courses.[10]

Whatever their reasons, nontraditional students often bring a high level of motivation, much life experience, and a willingness to work hard. They also bring a number of concerns. They worry that their skills are rusty, that they won't be able to keep up with younger students. They worry that their memory is not as good, that their energy level is not as high. Single parents worry that they won't be able to juggle school and their other responsibilities. Fortunately, most campuses have someone whose job it is to support adult students. There are also a number of other strategies that adult learners can employ. (*See* ■ *Panel 3.4.*)

Strategies for adult learners.

Some strategies for students who are over age 24 or attending college part time:

Ask for support: Get your family involved by showing them your textbooks and giving them a tour of the campus. Hang your grades on the refrigerator right alongside those of the kids. Or get support from friends (such as other adult students), a counselor, or an instructor. See if the college sponsors an adult support group.

Get financial aid: See Chapter 12, on money. You may be able to get loans, scholarships, or fellowships.

Enroll parttime: Going part time will ease the stresses on your time and finances. Start with just one course to test the waters.

Arrange for child care: If you have young children, you'll need child care not only for when you're away at class but also when you're home doing homework.

Learn time-management skills: See the other chapters in this book, particularly Chapter 4, on how to manage your time.

Get academic support: If you're worried about being rusty, look for review courses, one-on-one free tutoring, and similar support services.

Avoid grade pressure: Unless you're trying to get into a top graduate school, don't put yourself under undue pressure for grades. Just do the best you can in the time you have to devote to school.

Have fun: College should also be enjoyable for itself, not just a means to a better life. If you can't spare much time for campus activities, at least spend some time with other nontraditional students. Some campuses, for example, even have a "resumers lounge." Or experiment with your image, dressing in ways (hip? professional? sexy?) that will allow you to reinvent yourself a bit.

Form or join a returning students group: Get together with others in your classes who seem to be in similar circumstances for study and other mutual support.

RACE & CULTURE. Past generations of the dominant culture in the United States felt threatened by the arrival of Irish, Italians, Germans, Eastern Europeans, Catholics, and Jews. (And some people are still uncomfortable with them today.) Now the groups considered prominent racial minorities are people of African, Hispanic, and Asian descent or Native American and Alaskan Native. Indeed, four of these groups (African-Americans, Hispanic-Americans, Native Americans, and Alaskan Natives) presently make up 20% of Americans. By the year 2000 they are expected to make up nearly a third of the college population.

Let us briefly consider some of these groups.

■ *African-Americans:* The largest nonwhite minority, African-Americans make up 12% of the population of the United States, comprising 30 million people. By almost any measure, African-Americans continue to face disadvantages resulting from the burden of slavery and three centuries of racial discrimination. Indeed, one survey found that 80% of African-Americans who responded reported some form of racial discrimination during their college years.[11]

Gains in civil rights and voting rights during the 1960s increased the number of African-Americans in elective office sixtyfold during the last 30 years. Outlawing discrimination in education and employment has helped establish a third of African-Americans in the middle class (up 10% from the 1960s). Still, unemployment rates for African-Americans continue to be double those of whites. Moreover, they continue to suffer disproportionately from serious health problems, crime, and poverty.

Many African-Americans go to school in the large system of black colleges and universities. Still, perhaps 80% of African-American students attend institutions of higher education in which the majority of students are white.[12]

■ *Hispanic-Americans:* People from Spanish-speaking cultures make up the second largest minority group in the United

States (at 9% of the population, or 22 million). They make up more than 10% of the population of Colorado, Florida, and New York. They constitute nearly a fifth of Arizona, a quarter of California and Texas, and more than a third of New Mexico.

Two-thirds of Hispanics are Mexican-Americans, who, after African-Americans, represent the second largest disadvantaged minority group. Puerto Ricans and Cubans are the next largest groups of Hispanics, followed by others from Caribbean, Central American, and South American countries.

- *Asian-Americans:* There are 28 separate groups of Asian-Americans, according to census studies, ranging from Chinese to Japanese to Pacific Islanders. Asian-Americans are the fastest-growing minority in the United States, with 40% living in California and most of the rest in Hawaii and New York.[13] The two largest groups are Chinese and Filipino who, along with the Japanese, are descendants of earlier tides of immigration. However, the fastest-growing groups of recent years have been those from Vietnam, India, Korea, Cambodia (Kampuchea), and Laos. Asian-Americans continue to suffer discrimination, as reflected in lower income levels compared to whites.

- *Other races, cultures, religions:* Of course there are many other groups of ethnic and religious minorities. Indeed, many of them—blacks, Jews, Roman Catholics, and others—have established their own colleges to serve their special needs.

Those with the longest history of habitation in the United States are those considered native—Indians, Alaskans, and Hawaiians. In 1990, there were nearly 2 million Native Americans and Alaskan Natives, according to the U.S. census. Since 1968, 24 colleges have been established in the United States that are owned and operated by Native Americans.[14]

The dominant religion in the U.S. is Protestant. Nevertheless, there are numerous minority religions: Catholic, Jewish, Muslim, Buddhist, Hindu, and so

on. And, of course, many people have no formal religion or no religion at all.

- *International students:* Many campuses are enriched by the presence of international students. These are foreign visitors who have come to the United States to pursue a course of study. Some of them may find themselves especially welcomed. Others, however, may find that their skin color, dress, or accent exposes them to no less bias than American-born minorities experience. Some Americans worry that, with so much overseas talent in science and engineering programs, we are offering a kind of foreign aid. In fact, however, over half of all foreign graduate students in science and engineering choose to remain here after completing their schooling. Thus, they form an important part of our high-tech work force.[15]

DISABILITY. Nearly one in eleven first-year college students reports some kind of physical disability.[16] **A *physical disability* is a health-related condition that prevents a person from participating fully in daily activities,** including school and work. Because of the 1990 Americans With Disabilities Act, colleges have had to change policies to accommodate students with disabilities. For instance, the law bars discrimination against the disabled in public accommodations and transportation. This means that new and renovated buildings and buses must be accessible to people with handicaps.

People with disabilities include not only those who are physically handicapped (for example, wheelchair-users) or the visually or hearing impaired. They also include those with any type of learning disability. For example, people with dyslexia have difficulty reading. In any case, people with disabilities resent words that suggest they're sick, pitiful, childlike, or dependent or, conversely, objects of admiration. They also object to politically correct euphemisms such as the "differently abled," "the vertically challenged," or the "handi-capable."[17]

Onward

PREVIEW Don't always pretend "everything's cool" when it's not.

It's clear that all kinds of support is available to you in college. The main thing is to decide that *you are not alone* and go after it. I recall when I was in college I tried to project an aura of "Everything's cool." But sometimes everything *wasn't* cool. Thus, when the pressures of college life begin to be overwhelming, that's the time to take another look at this chapter. I think you'll find it will lead you to some solutions.

The principal lesson of this chapter has a great deal of value outside college. That lesson is: *find out everything you can about the organization you're in.* The more you understand about the departments and processes of your work world, for instance, the better you'll be able to take control of your own life within it. The same is true with the world outside of work.

NOTES

1. Kramer, G. L., & Spencer, R. W. Academic advising. P. 97 in Upcraft, M. L., Gardner, J. N., & Associates (Eds.). (1990). *The freshman year experience: Helping students survive and succeed in college.* San Francisco: Jossey-Bass.

2. Crockett, D. S. Academic advising. Pp. 244–63 in Noel, L., Levitiz, R., & Saluri, D., & Associates (Eds.). (1985). *Increasing student retention.* San Francisco: Jossey-Bass.

3. Gamson, Z. F. (1991). Why is college so influential? The continuing search for answers. Change, 23(6), 50–53.

4. Hudson Institute, Workforce 2000, U.S. Bureau of Labor Statistics, in Anonymous (1988, July). Jobs for women in the nineties, *Ms*, p. 77.

5. Naisbitt, J., & Aburdene, P. (1990). *Megatrends 2000.* New York: Morrow, p. 19.

6. Freedberg, L. (1993, November 12). Women outnumber men at college. *San Francisco Chronicle*, pp. A1, A9.

7. Adelman, C., U.S. Department of Education. *Women at thirtysomething.* Cited in: Stipp, D. (1992, September 11). The gender gap. *Wall Street Journal.*

8. Cage, M. C. (1993, March 10). Openly gay students face harassment and physical assaults on some campuses. *Chronicle of Higher Education*, pp. A22–A24.

9. Freedberg, L. (1992, June 28). The new face of higher education. *This World, San Francisco Chronicle*, p. 9.

10. Beck, B. (1991, November 11). School day for seniors. *Newsweek*, pp. 60–65.

11. Simpson, J. C. (1987, April 3). Campus barrier? Black college students are viewed as victims of a subtle racism. *Wall Street Journal.*

12. Evans, G. (1986, April 30). Black students who attend white colleges face contradictions in their campus life. *Chronicle of Higher Education*, pp. 17–49.

13. Barringer, F. (1991, June 12). Immigration brings new diversity Asian population in the U.S. *New York Times*, pp. A1, D25.

14. Marriott, M. (1992, February 26). Indians turning to tribal colleges for opportunity and cultural values. *New York Times*, p. A13.

15. Kotkin, J. (1993, February 24). Enrolling foreign students will strengthen America's place in the global economy. *Chronicle of Higher Education*, pp. B1–B2.

16. Jaschik, S. (1993, February 3). Backed by 1990 law, people with disabilities press demands on colleges. *Chronicle of Higher Education*, p. A26.

17. Shapiro, J. P. (1993). *No pity: People with disabilities forging a new civil rights movement.* New York: Times Books.

CLASSROOM ACTIVITIES

1. *What are you unsure about?* Ask students to write down on a piece of paper some aspect of college they're not quite clear on. Also have them list some resources they might be interested in. They may include matters related to grades, majors, and graduation. They may also include nonacademic matters that will help them benefit from their college experience.

In a small-group setting (in a group of three to six students), have students discuss anything they're still unsure or confused about. Also have them discuss those matters they would like to investigate further.

Which things that came out of each small group's discussion are particularly interesting or noteworthy? Have the group designate someone to describe them to the class as a whole.

2. **How do you make friends on campus?** Because commuter students often have so many other commitments, making friends on campus may be a low priority. Yet studies show that having friends on campus is important for making students stay in school. The goal of this activity is to help students become acquainted with others, with the goal of developing possible friendships.

Have everyone in the class write down on a piece of paper five ways they can think of to meet people on campus. Also have them describe the primary hindrance to making friends. (Examples: shyness, not enough time.) Call on people to discuss their thoughts and suggestions.

3. **What off-campus resources does your community offer?** When considering the topic of helpful resources, many students consider only those available on campus. The advantage of commuting from somewhere else, however, is that one may have access to additional resources not found at the college.

Have students list as many off-campus and community resources they can think of that might assist them while in college. Call on people to discuss their ideas.

4. **What is real diversity?** In class discussion, ask students to explain why diversity is important.

Questions for discussion: Is diversity more than just having numerous people from various minority backgrounds working for a company or attending a college? Is diversity really about how a person thinks and feels about others? How realistic are the mass media in portraying minorities? Give examples. Have there been times in your life when you have been a victim of prejudice and discrimination? Is society becoming more or less tolerant and accepting of diversity? What examples of tolerance and diversity in this country would you be proud to show a foreign visitor?

JOURNAL ENTRY #3.1: WHAT PROBLEM MIGHT YOU NEED HELP SOLVING? What problem can you think of that might occur during your college career for which you might need help? It could be lack of money, conflicts in a personal relationship, dealing with child care, or difficulty in keeping up with a course. What kind of assistance could you get to ease the problem?

_____

_____

_____

_____

_____

_____

_____

_____

_____

JOURNAL ENTRY #3.2: FINDING IMPORTANT COLLEGE SERVICES. Find the following places, and write down the location and the telephone number for contacting them. (If these places do not exist on your campus, indicate *None* in the space.) Unless your instructor asks you to turn this in, post the list over your desk or near your bed.

Services	Building name & room number	Telephone
Learning/ tutoring center	_____	
Library/ media center	_____	
Your academic advisor	_____	
Dean of students	_____	
Health service or infirmary	_____	
Counseling center	_____	

Security or campus police	_____	
Chapel	_____	
Registrar	_____	
Financial aid office	_____	
Housing office	_____	
Transportation office	_____	
Cashier/ business office	_____	
Job placement center	_____	
Career counseling center	_____	
Child care	_____	
Legal services	_____	
Student union or center	_____	
Bookstore	_____	

JOURNAL ENTRY #3.3: WHAT'S AN IMPORTANT EXTRACURRICULAR ACTIVITY? If any extracurricular activity *could be considered as important as your major*, what would it be? How would you go about becoming involved, if you haven't done so already?

_____

_____

_____

_____

_____

_____

_____

_____

_____

JOURNAL ENTRY #3.4: GETTING TO KNOW AN INSTRUCTOR You never know when you will need the help of an instructor—to explain a homework problem, to clarify an exam question, to give you a reference, or just be a good friend.

Select an instructor, such as one from a course you are now taking or from a field you are considering majoring in, or your faculty advisor. Telephone that instructor, explain you are doing a class assignment, and ask if he or she can spare 10 minutes for a brief interview. Make an appointment to meet.

1. Name of instructor being interviewed:

_____

_____

_____

2. Department in which instructor teaches (example: Sociology):

_____

_____

_____

3. What is your particular discipline? (Example: First-Year Experience, Sociology.)

_____

_____

_____

_____

_____

4. What is your area of specialization or research?

_____

_____

_____

_____

_____

5. What are your other interests or hobbies?

_____

_____

_____

_____

_____

6. Why did you choose to teach in this particular discipline?

_____

_____

_____

_____

_____

7. What kind of undergraduate and graduate degrees do you have and where did you receive them from?

_____

_____

_____

_____

8. Why did you decide to teach at this college?

_____

_____

_____

_____

9. *Ask a question of your own.* (Example: "What do you think are the characteristics of a good student?")

Your question:

_____

_____

_____

_____

_____

The instructor's answer:

_____

_____

_____

_____

_____

Thank the instructor for giving you his or her time.

JOURNAL ENTRY #3.5: WHAT IS YOUR CULTURAL HERITAGE? Many people have never taken the time to learn about their cultural heritage. Using library research and interviews with family members and relatives, answer the following questions:

1. What factors brought your family to this country?

_____

_____

_____

_____

_____

2. What are the unique characteristics of your cultural background?

_____

_____

_____

_____

_____

3. How has your family's living in North America changed the influences of your cultural heritage?

_____

_____

_____

_____

_____

4. What would you like others to know about your cultural background that you feel they don't understand?

_____

_____

_____

_____

_____

4

time

translating your life goals into task management

IN THIS CHAPTER: One of the most important skills you can have is the ability to manage your time in order to fulfill your goals. We consider these subjects:

■ *Setting priorities:* How to set daily tasks from your life goals.

■ *Beating time wasters:* How to avoid procrastinations and distractions and gain The Extra Edge.

Do you have a long commute? Are you working one or more jobs? Do you have family responsibilities?

These are only a handful of reasons why you may already be constantly pressed for time—and why going to college will only add to the pressure.

The general universal advice given on all campuses is:

Students are expected to devote at least 2 hours of study for every hour of class.

By "study," I mean reviewing notes, reading assignments, writing papers—all the activity known as "homework." Some classes may require less than 2 hours, but some might require *more*. Indeed, some might require 3 or 4 hours of study for every hour in class, if you find the subject hard going. (No one said that life is fair.)

Thus, suppose you have 16 hours of class time, a standard full-time course load in the semester system. If to this you add 32 hours of study time, then *at least* 48 hours a week should be devoted to college work. (This is still short of the workload of some business executives, who work 50 or 60 hours a week.)

How are you going to handle your classes and studying *on top of* commuting, working, family responsibilities, and so on?

Going to college means learning two skills basic to mastering our system of higher education:

- *Knowing how to manage your time*—discussed in this chapter;

- *Knowing how to use your memory*—discussed in the next chapter.

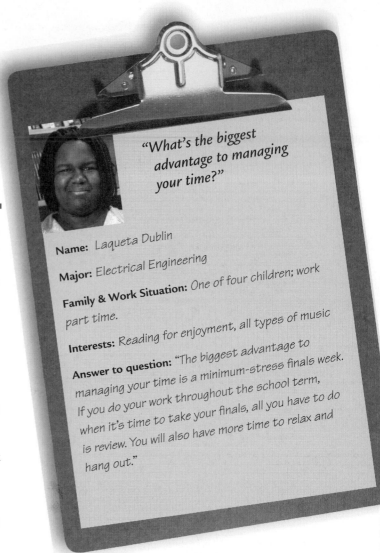

"What's the biggest advantage to managing your time?"

Name: Laqueta Dublin

Major: Electrical Engineering

Family & Work Situation: One of four children; work part time.

Interests: Reading for enjoyment, all types of music

Answer to question: "The biggest advantage to managing your time is a minimum-stress finals week. If you do your work throughout the school term, when it's time to take your finals, all you have to do is review. You will also have more time to relax and hang out."

How to Improve Your Time Management

PREVIEW The six-step "Essentials for Time & Life Management" plan describes how to set daily tasks from your life goals. The steps are: (1) Determine your ultimate goals. (2) Identify your plans for achieving them. (3) State the actions needed to realize your plans. (4) Lay out your master timetable for the school term. (5) Set your weekly timetable. (6) Do a daily or weekly To Do list with reminders and priorities.

You may hear a fellow student say offhandedly, "Yeah, I got an A in the course. But it was easy—I hardly had to study at all."

Don't believe it.

Sure, I guess there really are some people who can get by this way (or courses that are really that easy). However, most people who talk like that just want to look as though they are brainy enough not to need to study. In general, though, the reality is that either they *are* studying a lot or they are *not* getting top grades.

Here is clearly an area in which you have to be tough-minded: Most of the time, studying *is* hard work. It *does* take time. It *does* take personal commitment. Most students *don't* like to do it. Studying *isn't* usually something to look forward to (although learning and exploring may be fun).

You need not feel upset or guilty about this. Accept that studying is not always something you're going to do because you feel like it. Then you can begin to organize your time so that you can always get enough studying done.

THE SIX-STEP PROGRAM OF ESSENTIALS FOR TIME & LIFE MANAGEMENT. Essentials for Time & Life Management, as I stated in Chapter 2, is a six-step program for translating your life goals into daily tasks. (*See* ■ *Panel 4.1.*) The idea is to make your most important desires and values a *motivational force* for helping you manage your time every day.

The steps are as follows:

■ *Step 1:* The planning process starts when you answer the question "Why am I in college?"—that is, define your life goals or long-range goals.

■ *Step 2:* You then proceed to "What are my plans?"—setting your intermediate-range goals.

■ *Step 3:* This leads to "What are my actions?"—the steps you will take to achieve your goals.

■ *Step 4:* "What is my master timetable?" In this step you set your schedule for the semester or quarter.

The six-step program of "Essentials for Time & Life Management." Steps for transforming your life goals into daily tasks.

What you want college to help you do in life

1. Why am I in college? (Long-range goals)

2. What are my plans? (Intermediate-range goals)

3. What are my actions? (Steps to implement goals)

4. What is my master timetable?

5. What is my weekly timetable?

6. What is on today's To Do list?

How you make it happen

■ *Step 5:* "What is my weekly timetable?" This is the schedule you follow from week to week.

■ *Step 6:* "What is on today's To Do list?" This is the errand list or "things to do" list that is no different from the To Do list that millions of people make every day.

It's possible you already know your life goals and how they translate into a college major and required courses. In that case, you may be interested only in how to get through the present quarter or semester most efficiently. If so, you will want to skip Steps 1–3 and go directly to Step 4 (or even Step 6). Alternatively, you may simply not feel like doing Steps 1–3 right now. At some point, however, you will have to, because they have everything to do with why you're in college in the first place.

Now let's look at the six-step program of "Essentials for Time & Life Management" in detail.

STEP 1: WHY AM I IN HIGHER EDUCATION? You already answered this question in Personal Exploration #2.3 in Chapter 2, when you defined your long-range goals. Repeat them in Personal Exploration #4.1. If you've changed your mind about a few matters since then, that's fine. Just modify them in the space below.

STEP 2: WHAT ARE MY PLANS? Maybe you don't know what you want to be, but you know that you want to explore areas that express your values:

- to help people,
- to make good products,
- to create,
- to educate,
- to exercise your curiosity,
- to entertain,
- . . . or whatever.

Or maybe you already know what you want to be: a journalist, an engineer, an actor, a nurse, a teacher, a lawyer, a businessperson. In any event, now you need a plan, a rough strategy, of how to achieve or figure out your life goals.

PERSONAL EXPLORATION #4.1

WHAT ARE YOUR LONG-RANGE GOALS?

The top five goals I hope college will help me reach are . . .

1. _____

2. _____

3. _____

4. _____

5. _____

We're talking here about career choices and your major field. "So soon?" you may say. "I just got here!" Nevertheless, you at least need to decide what you *don't* want to do. For example, a major in engineering, medicine, music, or mathematics requires a sequence of courses that begins in the first year of college. If you think you might want to pursue these or similar fields, you need to be thinking about it now. Otherwise, you'll be required to make up courses later.

In making a plan, you need to take your thoughts about your life goals or long-range goals and then do the following things:

- *Decide on a major field (if only tentatively) and two or more alternatives:* Looking at the college catalog, state what major will probably help you realize your life goals. Also state two or more alternative majors you think you would enjoy pursuing.

- *Think of obstacles:* You need to think of the possible problems that may have to be overcome. Money possibly running out? Job and family responsibilities? Uncertainty about whether you're suited for this path? (Lack of motivation can be a killer.) Deficient math or language or other skills necessary for that major? Lack of confidence that you're "college material"?

- *Think of reinforcements:* Think of what you have going for you that will help you accomplish your goals. Burning desire? Sheer determination? Family support? Personal curiosity? Relevant training in high school? Frustration with present job? Ability to get along with people? Acquaintance with someone in the field who can help you? It helps to have positive reinforcement over the long haul.

To begin this process, do Personal Exploration #4.2.

PERSONAL EXPLORATION #4.2

WHAT ARE YOUR PLANS? INTERMEDIATE-RANGE GOALS

The point of this exercise is not to lock in your decisions. You can remain as flexible as you want for the next several months, if you like. The point is to get you thinking about your future and what you're doing in college—even if you're still undecided about your major.

▨ WHAT TO DO: DETERMINING YOUR INTERMEDIATE-RANGE GOALS

Look at the five goals you expressed in Personal Exploration #4.1. Now determine how these goals can be expressed relating to college.

Example: Suppose your life goals or long-range goals include:

1. "To enter a profession that lets me help people."

2. "To find out how I can become a world traveler."

3. "To explore my interest in health and science."

4. "To meet interesting people."

You might list possible majors in Health, Nursing, and International Relations. In addition, you might list nonacademic activities—for instance, "Join International Club." "Go to a meeting of Premed Society" (for premedical students).

Decide on Three or More Alternative Majors: Determine which major fields seem of particular interest to you. You can simply do this out of your head. However, it's better if you look through the college catalog.

Three possible majors that might help me fulfill my life goals are the following:

1. _____

   _____

2. _____

   _____

3. _____

   _____

Decide on Nonacademic Activities Supporting Your Goals: Determine what kind of extracurricular activities interest you. Again, you can make this up out of your head, or you can consult the college catalog or people in the campus community.

(continued on next page)

Five possible areas of extracurricular activities that might help me advance my college goals are the following:

1. _____
    _____

2. _____
    _____

3. _____
    _____

4. _____
    _____

5. _____
    _____

Identify Possible Obstacles: List the kinds of possible problems you may have to overcome in your college career.

Examples: Possible money problems. Conflict with job and family responsibilities. Temptation to pursue too active a social life. Uncertainty about a major. Lack of preparation in mathematics.

The five following obstacles could hinder me in pursuing my college career:

1. _____
    _____

2. _____
    _____

3. _____
    _____

4. _____
    _____

5. _____
    _____

Identify Reinforcements: List the kinds of things you have in your life that will support you in the achievement of your college goals when the going gets rough.

Examples: Support of your parents, husband/wife, or boyfriend/girlfriend. Personal curiosity. Knowing someone in a career you're considering. History of enjoying similar fields or activities in high school.

The five following facts or ideas could help sustain me in pursuing my college career:

1. _____
    _____

2. _____
    _____

3. _____
    _____

4. _____
    _____

5. _____
    _____

STEP 3: WHAT ARE MY ACTIONS? Step 2 provides you with the general guidelines for your college career. Step 3 is one of *action*. You have a plan for college; now you have to act on it. (Or why bother doing the preceding steps?)

Let me say a few words on behalf of taking action. *If you don't feel as if you're a terrific student or time manager, just fake it.*

Seriously.

Even if you haven't done well in school in the past, pretend now that you're the ultimate student. Be a phony and "play at" being a scholar. Feign at being organized. Simulate being a good time manager.

There's a reason for all this. If you *act* like the person you want to become, you will *become* that person. This is true whether it's being less shy, having a more optimistic outlook, having more self-esteem, or being a better student. After you have gotten used to your new role, the feelings of discomfort that "this isn't natural for me" will subside. *You are more apt to ACT your way into a new way of thinking than to think your way into it.*[7]

If you don't believe this, just consider that people act their way into behavior change all the time. People may not feel as if they can handle the responsibilities of a promotion or a new job beforehand, but they usually do. Being a parent looks pretty awesome when you're holding a newborn baby, but most people in the world get used to it. I've taught a number of students at a nearby prison who had dropped out of high school, got into all kinds of trouble, and ended up behind bars. Yet they then earned bachelor's and master's degrees. You too, then, can remake your behavior—and consequently remake your thinking.

As part of taking action, you need to look at what areas need to be improved in order for you to excel. Are your math, reading, or writing skills a bit shaky? Take advantage of the (often free) assistance of the college and get tutorial help. This is not something to be embarrassed about. Lots of people find they need practice of this sort to upgrade their skills.

In Personal Exploration #4.3 you will need to accomplish the following:

■ **Determine the courses needed to accomplish your goals:** You need to know what courses you will probably take in what semester or quarter in order to make progress. Generally you can tell the courses you need to take for a particular major by looking in the college catalog. (Look for language such as the following: "Students seeking the bachelor of arts degree in Journalism must complete at least 128 credits, 40 of which will be in courses numbered 300 or higher . . ." Or, "The requirements for the degree of Associate in Applied Science in Criminal Justice are . . .")

Laying out course sequences will take some time. But, believe me, *students who don't do such planning could find themselves out of step on some course requirements. This could require extra semesters or quarters later on.* Such slippage is especially a hazard in colleges suffering from budget cutbacks, where it may be difficult to get the courses you want.

■ **Determine what extracurricular activities to pursue:** If you're commuting long distances, working, or have family responsibilities, you may think "I don't have time for fun and games outside of school!" You may be right—in which case, you should simply skip this part.

But wait a minute. Suppose the kind of "extracurricular activity" is exactly what could help you survive in college. Suppose you were to take an hour or two

a week to meet with other people like yourself for friendship, support, and sharing of experience. You might be an adult returning student, parent, part-timer, foreign student, gay, black, Hispanic, Asian, or whatever. On most campuses there is likely to be a way for you to connect with these groups.

Alternatively, suppose the "extracurricular activity" could advance your career. You might consider looking into the computer club, law club (for prospective paralegals or lawyers), or the like. Or suppose you want to just work out at the gym, look into sharing rides, find new day care, or fulfill a similar need. Whatever it is, write it down here.

■ **Determine how to overcome obstacles, if possible:** Money worries? Family problems? Work conflicts? See if you can identify some solutions or avenues that might lead to solutions (such as checking the Financial Aid Office).

■ **Get advice about your tentative plans, then revise them:** Take your plans (including your list of obstacles) to your academic advisor and discuss them with him or her. In addition, I strongly recommend taking them to a counselor in the career counseling center. Since all this advice is free (or included in your student fees or tuition), you might want to take advantage of it. You will end up with a reality-based plan that may help save you a semester or two of misdirection.

To identify your courses of action, do Personal Exploration #4.3 on pages 68–69.

WHAT ARE YOUR ACTIONS? STEPS TO IMPLEMENT YOUR PLANS

This activity may take some time—perhaps an hour or so. However, *it is one of the most important Personal Explorations in this book*—maybe *the* most important.

■ WHAT TO DO

Here you list the *details* of how you will carry out your college plans. These include identifying courses to take, activities to pursue, and strategies for overcoming obstacles and getting appropriate advice.

Identify Courses to Take: Use the space below and/or a separate sheet of paper. List what courses (including prerequisites) you might need to take to realize your college degree and to fulfill your major and alternative majors. Indicate what years or semesters you will need to take them. These courses will be listed for the degree requirements in your college catalog. You may use a curriculum worksheet to complete this, like that shown in Panel 3.1 on page 42.

The courses I will need to take to obtain my degree or degrees are as follows:

_____
_____
_____
_____
_____
_____
_____
_____
_____
_____
_____
_____
_____
_____
_____
_____

_____
_____
_____
_____
_____
_____
_____
_____
_____
_____
_____
_____
_____
_____
_____
_____
_____
_____
_____
_____
_____
_____
_____
_____
_____
_____
_____
_____
_____
_____
_____

(Continue on a separate sheet of paper, if necessary.)

Identify Nonacademic Activities to Pursue: In the space below, list the nonacademic activities you want to try to pursue.

Examples: You might wish to connect with other adult returning students, parents, part-timers, foreign students, gay students, blacks, Hispanics, Asians, or whatever. Or you might want to work out at the gym, play music, or practice a language.

The nonacademic activities I wish to pursue, and arrangements I will have to make, are as follows:

1. _____
   _____
   _____
   _____

2. _____
   _____
   _____
   _____

3. _____
   _____
   _____
   _____

4. _____
   _____
   _____
   _____

5. _____
   _____
   _____
   _____

(continued on the next page)

Identify Strategies for Overcoming Obstacles: If you're worrying about obstacles, now is the time to begin to deal with them. In the space below, indicate the steps you will take.

Examples: For "Possible money problems," you might state you will look into financial aid. For "Family conflicts," you might look into child-care possibilities.

The possible obstacles I need to overcome, and the steps I will take to begin to overcome them, are as follows:

1. _____
   _____
   _____
   _____
   _____
   _____
   _____

2. _____
   _____
   _____
   _____
   _____
   _____
   _____

3. _____
   _____
   _____
   _____
   _____
   _____
   _____

4. _____
   _____
   _____
   _____
   _____
   _____

5. _____
   _____
   _____
   _____
   _____

Get Advice About Your Plans: This section takes very little time, but it may involve using the telephone and then following up with a personal visit. The point of the activity is to identify and then follow through on courses of action you need to take.

Examples: With your list of prospective majors and course sequences in hand, call your academic advisor. Make an appointment to meet and discuss your concerns. If you're thinking about joining the student newspaper, call to find out what you have to do. If you're worried that money might be a problem, call the Financial Aid Office to discuss it. (Some kinds of action need not involve a telephone. For example, you could tell your family members that you need to sit down and talk about child-care arrangements and study time.)

Here are the telephone numbers I need to call, or people I need to see and when, about a certain matter. The date following signifies when I took the action.

1. PERSON TO CONTACT (AND PHONE NUMBER) AND MATTER TO BE DISCUSSED
   _____
   _____
   _____
   _____

   ACTION WAS TAKEN ON (DATE)
   _____
   _____

2. PERSON TO CONTACT (AND PHONE NUMBER) AND MATTER TO BE DISCUSSED
   _____
   _____
   _____
   _____

   ACTION WAS TAKEN ON (DATE)
   _____
   _____

3. PERSON TO CONTACT (AND PHONE NUMBER) AND MATTER TO BE DISCUSSED
   _____
   _____
   _____
   _____

   ACTION WAS TAKEN ON (DATE)
   _____
   _____

4. PERSON TO CONTACT (AND PHONE NUMBER) AND MATTER TO BE DISCUSSED
   _____
   _____
   _____
   _____

   ACTION WAS TAKEN ON (DATE)
   _____
   _____

5. PERSON TO CONTACT (AND PHONE NUMBER) AND MATTER TO BE DISCUSSED
   _____
   _____
   _____
   _____

   ACTION WAS TAKEN ON (DATE)
   _____
   _____

Once you've determined your line-up of courses for the next few years, you need to block out your master timetable for the term you're now in. The reason for this is so you can establish your *priorities.*

To make a master timetable for the semester or quarter, do the following:

■ *Obtain a month-at-a-glance calendar with lots of writing room:* You should use the blank calendar shown on pages 71–72. (Or buy a month-at-a-glance calendar covering all the weeks in the school term.) When filled in with due dates and appointments, this will become your master timetable for the term.

■ *Obtain your college academic calendar:* The college or university's academic calendar may be printed in the college catalog. The academic calendar tells you school holidays, registration dates, and deadlines for meeting various college requirements. It usually also indicates when final exam week takes place.

■ *Obtain the course outline for each course:* **The course outline or course information sheet is known as the** *syllabus* **("sill-uh-bus"). The syllabus tells you midterm and final exam dates, quiz dates (if any), and due dates for term papers or projects.** The syllabus is given to you by your instructor, usually on the first day of class.

Now go through the college calendar and all your course outlines. Transfer to your master timetable calendar all class times, important dates, and deadlines. These include pertinent due dates, dates for the beginning and end of the term, and college holidays. Also add other dates and hours you know about. Examples are those for part-time jobs, medical and dental appointments, parent-teacher

PANEL 4.2

The master timetable. This illustration shows an example of one month of a student's semester or quarter. Note it shows key events such as deadlines, appointments, and holidays.

			November			
Sunday	Monday	Tuesday	Wednesday	Thursday	Friday	Saturday
			1 Parent-Teacher Conf. 3 p.m.	2	3 Poli Sci test	4
5	6 English essay	7	8 Dentist 3 p.m.	9	10	11 Sue's Party 8 p.m.
12	13	14 Math test	15	16	17 Poli Sci test	18
19 Band in Park 3 p.m.	20 English essay	21	22	23	24 ←— Holidays	25 —→
26	27 Poli Sci paper due	28 Math test	29	30 Thanksgiving		

conferences, and birthdays. *(See* ■ *Panel 4.2.)* Leave enough space for any given day so that you can add other entries later, if necessary.

To begin making up your own master timetable for the present semester or quarter, do the following Personal Exploration.

PERSONAL EXPLORATION #4.4

YOUR MASTER TIMETABLE FOR THIS TERM

Make up your own master timetable for the present school term, using a blank calendar. *(See* ■ *Panel 4.3.)*

Blank calendar for the school term.

Sunday	Monday	Tuesday	Wednesday	Thursday	Friday	Saturday

Sunday	Monday	Tuesday	Wednesday	Thursday	Friday	Saturday

Sunday	Monday	Tuesday	Wednesday	Thursday	Friday	Saturday

Sunday	Monday	Tuesday	Wednesday	Thursday	Friday	Saturday

Now we get down to the business end of the Essentials for Time & Life Management: making up a weekly timetable. (*See* ■ *Panel 4.4.*) *The main point of creating a weekly timetable is to schedule your study time.*

Some first-year students aren't sure what I mean by "study time." They think of it as something they do a day or two before a test. By *study time* I mean *everything connected to the process of learning.* This means preparing for tests, certainly, but also reading textbook chapters and other required readings, doing library research, writing papers, and so on. Studying is *homework*, and it's an ongoing process.

PANEL 4.4

The weekly timetable. This illustration shows an example of the important activities in a student's weekly schedule. The most important purpose of this schedule is to program in study time. Some students, however, may wish to program in other fixed activities. Examples are workouts, church attendance, household responsibilities, and travel time to school.

	Monday	Tuesday	Wednesday	Thursday	Friday	Saturday	Sunday
7 a.m.						Work	
8		Work		Work		Work	
9	English	Work	English	Work	English	Work	
10	Study	Work	Study	Work	Study	Work	
11	Study	Work	Study	Work	Study	Work	
Noon		Commuter Club		Adult Student Group		Work	Study
1 p.m.	Psych	Study	Psych	Study	Psych	Work	Study
2	Study	Math	Study	Math	Study	Work	Study
3	Study	Study	Study	Study	Study	Work	
4							
5				Work	Work		Study
6	Work	Work	Work	Work	Work		Study
7	Work	Work	Work	Work	Work		Study
8	Work	Work	Work	Work	Work		
9	Work	Work	Work	Work	Work		
10							
11							

By actually creating a weekly timetable to schedule their study time, students are putting themselves on notice that they take their studying *seriously*. They are telling themselves their study time is as important as their classes, job, sports practice, band rehearsal, family meals, or other activities with fixed times.

They are also alerting others that they are serious, too. Some students post their weekly schedule on their bedroom doors, if they're living at home. (Thus, if someone drops into your room to talk, you can point to the schedule and say, "Unfortunately, I have to study now. Can I talk to you in another half hour?")

If you don't schedule your study time, you may well study only when something else isn't going on. Or you will study late at night, when your energy level is down. Or you will postpone studying until the night before a test.

The weekly master plan should include those activities that happen at fixed, predictable times. These are your classes, work, regularly scheduled student activities—and your regularly scheduled studying times. As mentioned, studying time should amount to about 2 hours of studying for every hour of class time, perhaps more.

If you want, you can add meals, exercise, church, and commuting or transportation times. However, I believe that the fewer things you have on your calendar, the more you'll pay attention to the things that *are* there. Otherwise, you may get to feeling overregulated. You shouldn't schedule break times, for instance; you'll be able to judge for yourself the best times to stop for a breather. (I describe extended study time and breaks later in the chapter.)

To begin making up your own weekly timetable for this semester or quarter, do Personal Exploration #4.5. This may be three-hole-punched and carried in your notebook and/or prominently posted near your principal study place.

PERSONAL EXPLORATION #4.5

YOUR WEEKLY TIMETABLE FOR THIS TERM

Make up your own timetable that indicates your recurring responsibilities every week in this term. (*See* ■ *Panel 4.5.*)

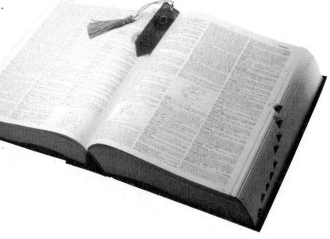

B lank timetable
for the week.

	Monday	Tuesday	Wednesday	Thursday	Friday	Saturday	Sunday
7 a.m.							
8							
9							
10							
11							
Noon							
1 p.m.							
2							
3							
4							
5							
6							
7							
8							
9							
10							
11							

STEP 6: WHAT IS MY DAILY "TO DO" LIST?

The final step is just like the informal "To Do" lists that many people have, whether students or nonstudents. (*See Panel ■ 4.6.*)

The To Do list can be made up every week or every evening, after referring to your master timetable and weekly timetable. The To Do list can be written on a notepad or on a 3 × 5 card. Either way, it should be easy to carry around so that you can cross things off or make additions. You can be as general or as detailed as you want with this list, but the main purpose of a To Do list is twofold:

Reminders: Remind yourself to do things you might otherwise forget. Examples are doctor's appointments, things to shop for, and books to return to the library. Don't forget to write down promises you made to people (such as to get them a phone number or a photocopy of your lecture notes).

■ ***Priorities:*** Set priorities for what you will do with your day. It may be unnecessary to list your scheduled classes, since you will probably go to them anyway. You might want to list an hour for exercise, if you're planning on it. (It's important to exercise at least three times a week for 20 minutes or more, if you can.) You may wish to list laundry, shopping, and so on.

However, *the most important thing you can do is to set priorities for what you're going to study that day.* Thus, your To Do list should have items such as "For Tues.— Read econ chapter 13" and "Wed. p.m.— Start library research for psych paper."

■ Most managers and administrators find a To Do list essential to avoid being overwhelmed by the information overload of their jobs. Since you, too, are on the verge of drowning in information and deadlines, you'll no doubt find the To Do list a helpful tool. Clearly also the To Do list is another application that you can carry over from your educational experience to the world outside of college.

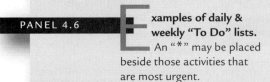

PANEL 4.6

Examples of daily & weekly "To Do" lists. An "*" may be placed beside those activities that are most urgent.

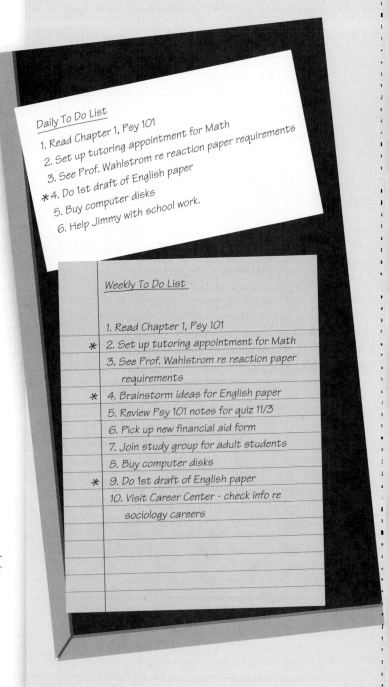

Daily To Do List
1. Read Chapter 1, Psy 101
2. Set up tutoring appointment for Math
3. See Prof. Wahlstrom re reaction paper requirements
*4. Do 1st draft of English paper
5. Buy computer disks
6. Help Jimmy with school work.

Weekly To Do List

1. Read Chapter 1, Psy 101
* 2. Set up tutoring appointment for Math
3. See Prof. Wahlstrom re reaction paper requirements
* 4. Brainstorm ideas for English paper
5. Review Psy 101 notes for quiz 11/3
6. Pick up new financial aid form
7. Join study group for adult students
8. Buy computer disks
* 9. Do 1st draft of English paper
10. Visit Career Center - check info re sociology careers

PERSONAL EXPLORATION #4.6

YOUR "TO DO" LIST FOR THIS WEEK

O n a separate piece of paper make up your own weekly To Do list for the present week.

Battling the Killer Time Wasters

PREVIEW There are four principal strategies to prevent wasting time. (1) Schedule study sessions that actually work. Study during the best times of day, don't schedule overly long sessions, allow short breaks, reward yourself afterward. (2) Fight procrastination. Concentrate on boring assignments intensively for short periods; study with a friend or in a study group. Break long tasks into smaller ones, tackle difficult tasks first, and meet unsettling tasks head on. (3) Fight distractions. Establish regular study sites, set up a good study environment, combat electronic and telephone distractions, and learn to handle people distractions. (4) Gain The Extra Edge. Use waiting and commuting time for studying, use spare time for thinking, listen to tapes of lectures.

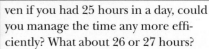

E ven if you had 25 hours in a day, could you manage the time any more efficiently? What about 26 or 27 hours?

Everyone gets the same ration, a disappointingly small 24 hours a day. Although some people are indeed smarter, usually the ones who excel at school and at work simply *use* their time better. If you try Personal Exploration #4.7 on the next page—"How Do You Spend Your Time?"— for a week, you can begin to see where your time goes.

CONSIDERING WHERE THE TIME GOES. You have 168 hours in a week (7 days of 24 hours each equals 168 hours). Let's see where the time is apt to go.

- *Sleeping:* Everyone needs between 6 and 9 hours of sleep a night. (If you short yourself on sleep, you may find the "sleep deficit" causes you to fall asleep in class. But it's possible you may be able to make it up by, for example, napping on the bus.)

- *Showering, dressing, grooming:* This might take 30–60 minutes a day. It depends on how long you shower, whether you shave or not, if you put on makeup at home or on the bus, and so on.

- *Eating:* This might take at least an hour a day, perhaps 14–21 hours in a week. If you skip breakfast and even lunch, you still probably have at least a snack or two throughout the day. Dinner might just be a quick visit to Burger King or microwaving a prefab dinner pulled from the freezer. Or it might mean shopping for, preparing, cooking, eating, and cleaning up after a full-scale meal for your family. (And making lunches for others for the next day.) In any case, you'd be surprised the amount of time eating takes out of your week.

- *Commuting, travel time, errands:* Travel time—between home and campus, between campus and job, and so on— might take an hour or more a day, perhaps 10–16 hours a week. In 1990, the average commute to work by car was 10.4 miles and 19.7 minutes.[1] Often, however, travel time can take much longer.

HOW DO YOU SPEND YOUR TIME?

The purpose of this activity is to enable you to see where your time goes. Honesty is important. The idea is to figure out how much time you *do* spend on studying. Then you can determine if you could spend *more* time.

KEEPING A LOG OF YOUR TIME

Record how many hours you spend each day on the following activities. (There are 168 hours in a week.)

	MON	TUES	WED	THUR	FRI	SAT	SUN
1. Sleeping							
2. Showering, dressing, and so on							
3. Eating							
4. Communing to and from class, work, and so on							
5. Going to classes							
6. Working							
7. Watching television							
8. Leisure activities (such as movies, dating, parties)							
9. Other scheduled matters— church, tutoring, volunteering							
10. Other (such as "hanging out," "partying," "child care")							
11. Studying							
TOTAL HOURS							

YOUR INTERPRETATION

We put "Studying" at the bottom of the list so you can see how other activities in your life impinge on it.

Now consider the following:

1. Do you feel you are in control of your time? _____

2. Are you satisfied with the way you spend your time? _____

3. On what three activities do you spend the most time?

4. Do you feel you're giving enough time to studying? _____

5. If you had to give more time to studying, what two or three activities could you give up or cut down on?

When computing travel time, you have to remember to include time waiting at bus or subway stops, hunting up parking places, and walking from bus stop or car to classes. You also have to total all the time involved in getting yourself not only to campus, job, and home but also, for example, in picking up children from day care, shopping, and running errands.

■ *Classes and work:* Figuring out the amount of time you spend in class is easy. If you're enrolled in three courses, totaling 9 semester units, you should be spending 9 hours a week in class.

If you work while going to school, you can probably easily figure out the hours your job requires each week. (Two exceptions are if you're subject to unpredictable overtime hours or if you're working as a temp for a temporary-employment agency.)

■ *Studying:* As mentioned, on average you should devote 2 hours of studying outside of class for every hour you are sitting in class. With three courses requiring 9 hours a week in the classroom, for example, you should be spending 18 hours a week doing homework.

Add up the hours in these categories for the week, then subtract them from 168. What's left over is the time you have left for *everything else*. And I mean EVERYTHING: "hanging out," watching television, dating or parties, sports, church, playing with or helping children, doing household chores (if not included above), and so on.

Does it seem, then, that you're suddenly going to have to be more efficient about how you manage your time? What follows are some suggestions for battling the killer time wasters.

SCHEDULE STUDY SESSIONS THAT ACTUALLY WORK. As I've said, creating a schedule for studying *and sticking with it* are terribly important. Indeed, this is probably the single most valuable piece of advice anyone can give you.

There are, however, certain things to consider when you sit down to block out the master timetable that includes your study time:

■ *Make study times during your best time of day:* Are you a "morning person" or a "night person"? That is, are you most alert before breakfast or most able to concentrate in the evening when it's quiet? When possible, schedule some of your study time for the times of day when you do your best work. These are particularly good times for doing difficult assignments, such as writing research papers.

■ *Don't schedule overly long sessions:* Imagine how you're going to feel at the start of a day in which you've scheduled 10 hours for studying. You'll probably take your time getting to work and won't do more than 7–9 hours of actual studying that day anyway.

To avoid setting yourself up for failure, I suggest programming *no more than* 8 hours of studying in a day. Also, divide that time block into two 4-hour sessions separated by perhaps a couple of hours of time off. (Actually, many students will find they just can't stand 8 hours of studying in a single day.) And if you do schedule long blocks of study time, mix the subjects you're working on so you'll have some variety. The point, after all, is not how *long* you study but how *effectively* you study.

Perhaps an even better strategy, however, is to schedule *several short sessions* rather than a handful of long sessions.

■ *Allow for 5- to 10-minute study breaks:* Some people are like long-distance runners and do better by studying for long sessions—for example, 50 minutes followed by a 10-minute break. Others (myself included) are like sprinters and perform better by studying for 25 minutes followed by a 5-minute break.

Of course, you don't have to go exactly by the clock, but you should definitely permit yourself frequent, regularly scheduled breaks. Taken at regular intervals, breaks actually produce efficiencies. They enable you to concentrate better while studying, reduce fatigue, motivate you to keep going, and allow material to sink in while you're resting.

Breaks should be small ways of *pleasuring yourself*—going for a soft drink, taking a walk outside, glancing through the newspaper. I don't recommend getting on the phone, picking up your guitar, or dropping in on a friend, however, unless you can keep it short. You don't want the diversion to be so good that it wrecks your study routine.

■ **Reward yourself when you're done studying:** The end of the course is weeks away, the attainment of a degree months or years. What's going to keep you going in the meantime?

You need to give yourself as many immediate rewards as you can for studying, things to look forward to when you finish. Examples are a snack, phone talk with a friend, some music or TV time. Parts of your college career will be a grind, but you don't want it to be *just* a grind. Rewards are important.

If, after scheduling in your study time, you find it still isn't enough, you need to see where you can make adjustments. Can you reduce the number of courses? Work fewer hours? Get help with chores from family members? Whatever, the main thing is to make your scheduled study time effective when you're doing it.

FIGHT PROCRASTINATION! All of us put off doing things sometimes, but *procrastination* **is defined as putting off things intentionally and habitually.** This continual delay in doing your work can manifest itself in many small ways: You can't seem to get up when the alarm clock goes off. You're always a measly 5 or 10 minutes late getting to your desk. You take time "warming up" by sharpening pencils, adjusting the room temperature, getting coffee, and so on. You find you always need to get organized—pull your notes and books together and find the place where you left off. You wander away from your work to take phone calls. You knock off early at the slightest convincing excuse.

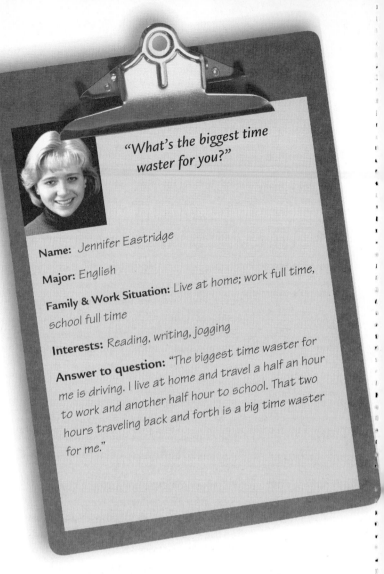

"What's the biggest time waster for you?"

Name: Jennifer Eastridge

Major: English

Family & Work Situation: Live at home; work full time, school full time

Interests: Reading, writing, jogging

Answer to question: "The biggest time waster for me is driving. I live at home and travel a half an hour to work and another half hour to school. That two hours traveling back and forth is a big time waster for me."

Procrastination can result when your prospective task is *boring, long, difficult,* or *emotionally unsettling* to you. You need to look hard to see if one of these reasons applies, then fight back by applying the appropriate strategies:

■ **Fight boring assignments with short concentrations of effort:** If the task is boring, you need to concentrate on seeing how fast you can get a portion of it done. That is, you need to concentrate on the benefits of completing it in a short time rather than on the character of the task itself.

Thus, you can say to yourself, "I'm going to work on this for 15 minutes without stopping, applying my full concentration. Then I'm going to move along to something else." You can stand anything for 15 minutes, right? And this task may seem more acceptable if it's not seen as several hours of work—especially if you plan a mini-reward for yourself (getting a soft drink, say) at the end of that time.

■ *Fight delaying tactics by studying with a friend or joining a study group:* Some students find that it helps to get together with a friend in the same course to study boring—or even nonboring—subjects. By exchanging ideas about the subject matter, you may find the time goes faster.

An extremely valuable aid to learning is the *study group*, **in which a group of classmates get together to share notes and ideas.** In a study group you can clarify lecture notes, quiz each other about ideas, and get different points of view about an instructor's objectives. Being in a group also helps to raise everyone's morale. It makes you realize that you are not alone.

■ *Fight long assignments by breaking them into smaller tasks:* Most people have a difficult time tackling large projects, such as research papers. Indeed, most of us tend to take on simple, routine tasks first, saving the longer ones for later when we'll supposedly "have more time." [2] Thus, we often delay so long getting going on large assignments that we can't do an effective job when we finally do turn to them.

The way to avoid this difficulty is to break the large assignments into smaller tasks. You then schedule each of these tasks individually over several days or weeks. (That's how this book got written—in small amounts over several months.) For example, when reading a chapter on a difficult subject, read just five or seven pages at a time.

■ *Fight difficult tasks by tackling them first and by making sure you understand them:* If you have one particular area of study that's difficult or unpleasant, *do that one first,* when your energy level is higher and you can concentrate best. For instance, if you find math problems or language learning more difficult than reading a sociology text, tackle them first. The easiest tasks, such as list-making

and copying-type chores, can be done late in the day, when you're tired.

If a task seems difficult, you may also take it as a warning signal: maybe there's something about it you don't understand. Are the directions clear? Is the material over your head? If either of these conditions is true, *run, do not walk,* to your instructor. Ask for clarification, if directions are the problem. Be frank with the instructor if you think the material (statistics? grammar? lab experiments?) is hard to comprehend or perform. It may be that what you need is to quickly get yourself the help of a tutor.

I cannot stress enough the importance of taking your own worries seriously if you find that what you're studying is too difficult. However, if you can deal with this before the semester or quarter is too far along, you'll probably be all right.

■ *Fight emotionally unsettling tasks by getting allies:* You may not be able to predict what some of these are. Let me just say, however, that I've seen students blow an assignment or a course because something about it was emotionally disagreeable or frightening.

Maybe, for instance, it's some aspect of *shyness,* so that you find making an oral presentation nearly unbearable. (Shyness, incidentally, is an extremely common condition, one afflicting 4 out of 10 people.) [3] Maybe it's some deep embarrassment about your writing or language skills. Maybe you think "I'm no good at math." Maybe you're queasy about doing biology lab experiments. Maybe there's a former boyfriend/girlfriend in the class whose presence is upsetting you. Maybe the instructor turns you off in some way.

These and most similar situations can be helped, but *you have to reach out and get the help.* If you don't feel you can take the problem up with your instructor, then *immediately* go to the student counseling center. Counseling and tutoring are open to you, normally without any additional charge, as part of the support system available to students. But try not to wait until you're overwhelmed.

FIGHT DISTRACTIONS! A phone call comes in while you're studying, and 25 minutes later you finish the conversation. Are you later going to tell yourself that you actually studied during your scheduled study time? Or are you going to pretend that you'll simply make up the work some other time?

There are many such possible intrusions, but it's important that you not delude yourself—that you not play games with your study time. The following are some strategies for preventing or handling various common distractions:

■ *Establish a couple of places where all you do is study:* You see students studying just about everywhere, which is fine. However, it's important that *you establish a couple of places for regular studying* and, if possible, do nothing else there. Many students study at the library or at a desk in their room. Unless you can't avoid it, don't routinely study on your bed, where you might fall asleep. Avoid studying at the kitchen table, where you may be inspired to eat. Don't work in the student lounge in front of the TV. If you use your study places only for studying, they will become associated just with that and will reinforce good study behavior.[4]

■ *Establish a good study environment:* For your principal study site, the best arrangement is a separate room, such as a spare room, that you treat as your home office. Otherwise, use a corner of your bedroom. Turn a desk or table to the wall to provide you with as much privacy as possible from others sharing the room.

Make this spot as comfortable and organized as you can. Make sure you have the right temperature, good lighting, and a comfortable chair. The desk should have room on it for a computer or a typewriter, as well as reading/writing space. Books and supplies should be within reach. Having a personalized bulletin board is useful. Adult returning students in particular may have to be somewhat assertive with others in their household about their need for a quiet space.

If your living area is too distracting, you can do as many students do and make the campus library your primary study place. Some libraries have small tables tucked away in quiet areas. Moreover, the entire atmosphere of quiet is supportive to studying.

■ *Fight electronic distractions:* Electronic equipment has completely taken over many households. If the noise becomes too overwhelming and you can't get it turned down by common agreement, go elsewhere. Plan to do your studying in the library or other quiet place such as a laundry room.

I realize this is a tricky matter, because so many students think that they can study better with television or music as background noise. Indeed, it may be possible to study to certain kinds of music, such as classical music. However, the evidence suggests that the best studying is done when it's quiet.

■ *Fight telephone distractions:* Of course you don't have to make any outgoing calls during your scheduled study times, and you should resist doing so. As for incoming calls, there are four things you can do:

(1) Be disciplined and don't answer the phone at all. (What kind of power is it that the telephone has over us? When it rings, do we *have* to pick it up?)

(2) Answer the phone, but tell the caller you'll have to call back because "I have something important going on here."

(3) Tell whoever answers the phone to take a message for you. You can then call back on your 5-minute study break, if you can manage to keep the conversation short. Even better, you can call back after you're done studying.

(4) Let an answering machine collect your calls, then call back later. Whatever tactic you use, the idea is to minimize the interruption, of course.

I personally suggest letting another person or a machine take the calls. You're then like business people who have answering machines or secretaries hold their calls while they're doing important work, then return them all at once later.

■ **Fight people distractions:** People interruptions can be a real problem, and eventually you have to learn to "Just say no." You shouldn't be complaining or accusatory, but polite and direct. There's a piece of advice that says, *Don't complain, don't explain, just declare.* So when interrupted, you just declare: "Sidney, this is interesting, but I have to study right now. Can we talk later?"

Early on you need to develop some understanding with your housemates or family members about your study requirements. Show them your study schedule. Tell them that when you're at your desk you're supposed to be doing your college work. Ask them for their assistance in helping you accomplish this. One writer says that a student he knows always wears a colorful hat when he wants to study. "When his wife and children see the hat, they respect his wish to be left alone."[5] You can also hang a DO NOT DISTURB sign on your door while studying.

• • • • • • • • • • • • • • • • • • • •

"There's a piece of advice that says, Don't complain, don't explain, just declare."

• • • • • • • • • • • • • • • • • • • •

What if you're a parent and have nowhere to put a young child (not even in front of a television set or in a room full of toys)? In that case, just plan on doing the kind of studying that is not too demanding, expecting to be interrupted. Or use your study breaks to play with the child. Or take a few minutes to play attentively with the child before you hit the books, then say you have work to do. As long as the child feels he or she is getting *some* of your attention, you can still get some things done.

Of course, you can't control everything. Things will come up that will cut into your study time, as in the electricity going off or the flu wiping you out. That's why it's important to think of your scheduled study sessions as your main, inviolable study times. In addition, however, you need to be willing to study at various other, "fill-in" times. Let me explain how this works.

GAINING THE EXTRA EDGE. We often read of the superstar athlete who spends many extra hours shooting baskets or sinking putts. Or we hear of the superstar performer who endlessly rehearses a song or an acting part. These people don't have The Extra Edge just because of talent. (There's *lots* of talent around, but few superstars.) They have put in the additional hours because they are in a highly competitive business and they want to perfect their craft. Students are in the same situation.

What do you think when you walk across campus and see students studying in a bookstore line or at the bus stop? Perhaps you could think of them as doing just what the superstar basketball player shooting extra hoops does. *They are making use of the time-spaces in their day to gain The Extra Edge.*

Here are some techniques that can boost your performance:

- **Always carry some school work and use waiting time:** Your day is made up of intervals that can be used—waiting for class to start, waiting for meals, waiting for the bus, waiting for appointments. These 5- or 10- or 20-minute periods can add up to a lot of time during the day. The temptation is to use this time just to "space out" or to read a newspaper. However, it can also be used to look over class notes, do some course-related reading, or review reading notes.

  Make a point of carrying 3×5 cards. These cards can contain important facts, names, definitions, formulas, and lists that you can pull out and memorize.

  Students learning a foreign language often carry *flash cards*, with foreign words on one side and the English meaning on the other. **Flash cards are cards bearing words, numbers, or pictures that are briefly displayed as a learning aid. One side of the card asks a question, the other side provides the answer.** Flash cards are also sold in college bookstores for other subjects, such as biology, to help you learn definitions. You can make up flash cards of your own for many courses.

  The 5-minute mini-study session is far more beneficial than might first seem. The way to better memorizing is simply to *practice practice practice*, or *rehearse rehearse rehearse*. Just as the superstars do.

- **Use your spare time for thinking:** What do you think about when you're walking to class, waiting for the bus, or inching along in traffic? It could be about anything, of course. (Many people think about relationships or sex.) However, there are three ways your mind can be made to be productive:

(1) Try to recall points in a lecture that day.

(2) Try to recall points in something you've read.

(3) Think of ideas to go into a paper you're working on.

  Again, the point of this use of idle time is to try to involve yourself with your college work. This is equivalent to foot-ball players working plays in their heads or singers doing different kinds of phrasing in their minds. The superstars are always working at their jobs.

- **Make tapes of lectures and listen to them:** This advice is particularly suitable for students with a tape deck in the car or those with a portable tape player who ride the bus. At the end of a long day you might just want to space out to music. But what about at the beginning of the day, when you're fresh?

  Making tapes of lectures is no substitute for taking notes. But listening to the tapes can provide you with *additional reinforcement*. This is especially the case if the lecture is densely packed with information, as, say, a history or biology lecture might be.

  Special note: Be sure to ask your instructors for permission to tape them. Some are uncomfortable having tape recorders in their classes. Some institutions, in fact, *require* that you get the permission of instructors.

Onward

PREVIEW Avoiding cramming is important, since it usually only produces stress without the grades to show for it.

Perhaps you have a sneaky suspicion that all this time-management stuff really isn't necessary. After all, maybe in high school you put off a lot of studying, then at the last minute stayed up late *cramming*—studying with great intensity. Indeed, maybe you know that lots of college students seem to use this method.

Unfortunately, as a regular study technique, cramming leaves a lot to be desired. In fact, you'll probably find yourself greatly stressed without retaining much and without the grades to show for it. This is because in college there is so much more to learn.

In this chapter you looked at one of the two important techniques for being successful in college—time (and task) management. In the next chapter we'll consider the second one—*memorization*.

NOTES

1. Samuelson, R. J. (1996, July 1). The endless road 'crisis.' *Newsweek*, p. 47.

2. Lakein, A. (1973). *How to get control of your time and your life*. New York: Peter H. Wyden.

3. Zimbardo, P. G. (1977). *Shyness: What it is, what to do about it*. Reading, MA: Addison-Wesley, p. 14.

4. Beneke, W. M., & Harris, M. B. (1972). Teaching self-control of study behavior. *Behavior Research & Therapy, 10,* 35–41.

5. Ellis, D. (1991). *Becoming a master student* (6th ed.). Rapid City, SD: College Survival, Inc., p. 53.

1. ***What is happiness? Educating yourself for the way you want to live.*** Students are in college, presumably, in the pursuit of their ultimate happiness—or at least in pursuit of something that will make them happier than they are now. But what, in fact, *is* happiness?

   Ask students to take 5 minutes to write what they think happiness is and what would make them happy. Then have them discuss what happiness is. Discussion questions: What is the way you want to live? How will education help you accomplish it? How does your definition of happiness differ from others' definitions? Could you be happy under others' terms? Could you be happy doing something your family doesn't approve of?

2. ***Getting together a study group.*** Research shows that students who study in groups often get the highest grades. The reasons are many: Students in a group fight isolation by being members of a social circle, give each other support and encouragement, and help each other work through lecture notes and readings and prepare for exams. This activity shows students how to organize and perform in a study group.

   Organize students into groups of three to five (preferably a group that they've not been part of before). Have students introduce themselves to each other, then consider the following questions, which have to do with this chapter. What are the biggest problems you have in studying? What are your principal distractions or time wasters? What time-spaces in your day could you use for mini-studying? What are the principal questions that will be asked about this chapter on the next exam? How do you feel about continuing this study group through the term for this course? What are some of your other, more difficult courses for which a study group would be helpful? Who would you ask to join in forming one?

3. ***What are your killer time wasters?*** Ask students to make lists of their biggest time wasters. Get suggestions from the class and write them on the board. Poll the class to see how many students share each area listed, and write the number down. Ask students to discuss what they might do to make more effective use of their time.

JOURNAL ENTRY #4.1: HOW'S YOUR MOTIVATION? How strongly motivated are you to pursue your life and college goals? What activities would you be willing to give up to achieve them?

_____

_____

_____

_____

_____

_____

_____

JOURNAL ENTRY #4.2: HOW DO YOU WASTE TIME? Do you find, after keeping a record of your time usage for two or three days, that you waste time in certain specific ways? Do these time-wasting ways serve some other purposes in your life, such as alleviating stress or furthering friendships? Give some thought to how these needs might be addressed in some other ways so that you can save more time for college academic work.

_____

_____

_____

_____

_____

_____

_____

JOURNAL ENTRY #4.3: WHAT CAN YOU DO TO MANAGE YOUR TIME BETTER? Just as business and professional people often look for ways to improve their time-management skills, so can students. What kinds of things did you note in this chapter that might help you manage your time better?

_____

_____

_____

_____

_____

_____

_____

_____

JOURNAL ENTRY #4.4: ARE YOU INTO PARTYING? Some students get so deeply into "partying" that they find it has a major impact on their time. Often the kind of escape sought in partying is brought about by the stresses of the constant academic demands of college. Is this a possible area of concern for you?

_____

_____

_____

_____

_____

_____

_____

special section: productivity tools for your future

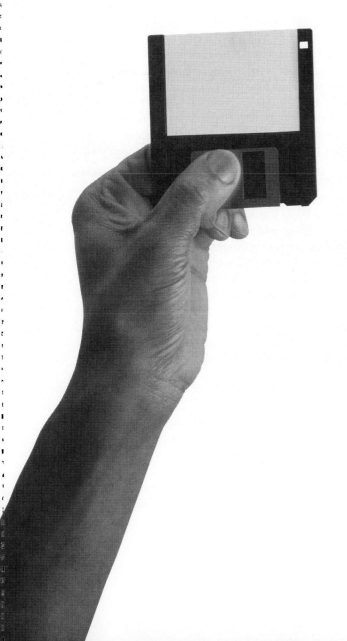

Just a few short years ago, a monumental watershed occurred: the Industrial Age gave way to the Information Age.

"In 1991 companies for the first time spent more on computing and communications gear," says one report, "than on industrial, mining, farm, and construction machines. Info tech is now as vital . . . as the air we breathe."[1]

"Info tech"—information technology—has brought new kinds of productivity tools into the workplace: computers, fax machines, cellular phones, electronic mail, the Internet, the World Wide Web. Learning to use these kinds of tools can increase your productivity as a student at the same time it gives you skills that will help you advance your career.

This special section considers the following:

- Personal computers
- Computer software
- Communications tools

Personal Computers

Students who have a **personal computer (PC)** are certainly ahead of the game. However, if you don't have one or are unable to borrow one, many campuses make computers available to students, either at minimal cost or essentially for free as part of the regular student fees. For instance, computers may be available at the library or campus computer lab. Often they allow students to communicate over phone lines to people in other locations, including outside the country.

NOTE: If the system cannot accommodate a large number of students, all the computers may be in high demand come term-paper time. Clearly, having access to your own computer offers you convenience and a competitive advantage.

GETTING YOUR OWN PERSONAL COMPUTER: IBM-STYLE OR MACINTOSH?

In general, personal computers are of two types—*IBM-style* and *Macintosh-style*.

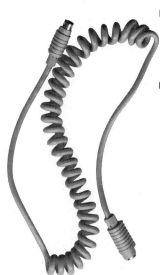

- *IBM-style:* The IBM-style (IBM-compatible) is the most popular personal computer in the world. Besides being sold by IBM, so-called "clones" (or copies) are made by AST, Compaq, DEC, Dell, Gateway, Hewlett-Packard, NCR, NEC, Packard-Bell, Radio Shack, Toshiba, and Zenith, to name some of the most reputable manufacturers.

- *Macintosh-style:* Macintoshes aren't as widespread, but they are generally easier to use than IBM or IBM-compatible PCs. Macintoshes are made by Apple Computer, and clones such as the PowerWave are made by Power Computing. (Other personal computers, such as the Apple II or Commodore, are not used in college.)

If all you need a computer for is to write term papers on, nearly any kind of machine, new or used, will do. Indeed, it's possible you may not even need a printer. The University of Michigan, for instance, offers "express stations" or "drive-up windows." These allow students to use a floppy disk or connect a computer to a student-use printer to print out their papers. Or, if a friend has a compatible computer, you can ask to borrow it and the printer for a short time to print your work.

What kind of system, IBM or Macintosh, is best for you? That may depend on your major. History, nursing, biology, English, speech communications, foreign language, physical education, and political science majors probably don't need a fancy computer system. For them an inexpensive IBM-style system may be just fine. Some business, engineering, architecture, and journalism majors, on the other hand, may need to acquire or have access to Macintosh systems, which may be pricier. For instance, an architecture major doing computer-aided design (CAD) projects or a journalism major doing desktop publishing may need reasonably powerful Mac systems.

If your major does not require a special computer system, a microcomputer can be acquired for relatively little. You can probably buy a used computer, with software thrown in, for under $500 and a printer for under $200.

DESKTOP PC OR PORTABLE?

Most students who buy computers get **desktop personal computers,** the larger models that sit on a desktop (and are awkward to move), because they are usually cheaper. However, many like **portable computers** because they can easily carry them around and work on them wherever it's convenient, such as in the campus library. (WARNING: Portable computers are as easily stolen as any purse or backpack. Thus, if you're out on the streets a lot, you might want to leave your portable at home most of the time.)

There are four categories of portables:

1. *Laptops*—8–20 pounds

2. *Notebooks*—4–7.5 pounds

3. *Subnotebooks*—2.5–4 pounds

4. *Handhelds (palmtops)*—1 pound or less

Portables, especially 7-pound notebooks and under-4-pound subnotebooks, represent the best intersection of power and convenience. The 8-pound-plus laptops probably have no advantages over the notebook size, except perhaps in price. The under-1-pound handhelds are too limited for regular student use; they have no floppy-disk drive, no hard-disk drive, and no easy way to swap files with other computers.

Look for a computer that fits your work style. For instance, you may want a portable if you spend a lot of time at the library or are able to study at work. If you do most of your work at home or in your room, you may find it more comfortable to have a desktop PC.

THE TRADE-OFF: MORE POWER OR LESS EXPENSE?

Buying a personal computer, like buying a car, often requires making a trade-off between *power* and *expense*.

The word *power* has different meanings when describing software and hardware:

■ *Powerful software:* Applied to software, "powerful" means that the program is *flexible*. That is, it can do many different things. For example, a word processing program that can print in different type styles (fonts) is more powerful than one that prints in only one style.

Although it may sound backward, you should select the software before the hardware. This is because you want to choose software that will perform the kind of work you want to do. First find the kind of programs you want—word processing, spreadsheets, communications, graphics, or whatever. Check out the hardware requirements for those programs. Then make sure you get a computer system that will run them.

■ *Powerful hardware:* Applied to hardware, "powerful" means that the equipment (1) is *fast* and (2) has *great capacity.*

A fast computer will process data more quickly than a slow one. With an older computer, for example, it may take few seconds to save (store on a floppy or hard disk) a 30-page term paper. On a newer machine, it might take less than a second.

A computer with great capacity can run complex software and process voluminous amounts of data. *This is an especially important matter if you want to be able to run newer forms of software, which tend to have extensive graphics.* Graphics tend to require a lot of memory, hard-disk storage, and screen display area.

(Translation of technobabble: **Memory** is the internal memory, often called "RAM," for Random Access Memory, that the computer uses for temporary storage in order to do quicker, more seamless processing. **Hard-disk,** or "hard-drive" storage, is your computer's filing cabinet, which allows you to permanently store all your data, as well as your software.)

Will computer use make up an essential part of your major, as it might if you are going into engineering, business, or graphic arts? If so, you may want to try to acquire powerful hardware and software.

CHECKLIST

Besides determining whether you want a desktop or a portable and what software you will need to be able to run, there are two other decisions to make before buying a computer:

■ *Is upgradability important?* The newest software being released is so powerful (meaning flexible) that it requires increasingly more powerful (faster, higher capacity) hardware. If you buy an older used computer, you probably will not be able to **upgrade** it. That is, you will be unable to buy internal parts, such as additional memory, that can run newer software.

This limitation is probably fine if you expect to be able to afford an all-new system in a couple of years (or to be working for an employer who will buy you one). If, however, you are buying new equipment right now, be sure to ask the salesperson how the hardware can be upgraded.

■ *Do I want a modem?* A **modem** is needed to send messages from one computer to another via a phone line. About 40% of personal computers these days have a modem. The speed at which a modem can transmit data is measured in Kbps (kilobits per second) rates. The faster the modem speed, the better. Try not to buy one lower than 28.8 Kbps.

What's the *minimum* hardware system you should get? Some technical details: Probably an IBM-compatible or Macintosh with 512K–640 kilobytes of memory and two floppy-disk drives or one floppy-disk and one hard-disk drive. However, 12 or 16 megabytes of memory is preferable if you're going to run many of today's programs. Dot-matrix printers are in widespread use on all campuses (24-pin printers are preferable to 9-pin). To be sure, the more expensive laser printers produce a better image. However, you can always use the dot-matrix for drafts and print out the final version on a campus student-use printer.

Some issues to consider in buying a portable computer are addressed in the accompanying checklist. *(See* ■ *Panel SS.1.)*

| PANEL SS.1 | **G**oing mobile: a buyer's checklist. Questions to consider when buying a notebook or subnotebook. |

1. Is the device lightweight enough so that you won't be tempted to leave it behind when you travel?

   ❑ Yes   ❑ No

2. Does it work with lightweight nickel-hydride batteries instead of heavier nickel-cadmium batteries?

   ❑ Yes   ❑ No

3. Is the battery life sufficient for you to finish the jobs you need to do, and is a hibernation mode available to conserve power?

   ❑ Yes   ❑ No

4. Can you type comfortably on the keyboard for a long stretch?

   ❑ Yes   ❑ No

5. Is the screen crisp, sharp, and readable in different levels of light?

   ❑ Yes   ❑ No

6. Does the system have enough storage for all your software and data?

   ❑ Yes   ❑ No

7. Can the system's hard disk and memory be upgraded to meet your needs?

   ❑ Yes   ❑ No

8. Does the system provide solid communications options, including a fast modem, so you can send files, retrieve data, and plug into a local area network?

   ❑ Yes   ❑ No

9. Can you get service and support on the road?

   ❑ Yes   ❑ No

WHERE TO BUY USED

Buying a used computer can save you a minimum of 50%, depending on the age of the system. If you don't need the latest software, this can often be the way to go. The most important thing is to buy *recognizable* brand names, examples being Apple and IBM or well-known IBM-compatibles: AST, Compaq, DEC, Dell, Gateway, Hewlett-Packard, NCR, NEC, Tandy, Toshiba, Zenith. Obscure or discontinued brands may not be repairable.

Among the sources for used computers are the following:

■ ***Retail sources:*** A look in the telephone-book Yellow Pages under "Computers, Used" will produce several leads. Authorized dealers (of IBM, Apple, Compaq, and so on) may shave prices on demonstration (demo) or training equipment. Also, colleges and universities may sell off their old equipment when it is being replaced.

- **Used-computer brokers:** There are a number of used-computer brokers, such as American Computer Exchange, Boston Computer Exchange, Damark, and National Computer Exchange.

- **Individuals:** Classified ads in local newspapers, shopper throwaways, and (in some localities) free computer newspapers/magazines provide listings of used computer equipment.

   One problem with buying from individuals is that they may not feel obligated to take the equipment back if something goes wrong. Thus, you should inspect the equipment carefully. *(See* ■ *Panel SS.2.)* For a small fee, a computer-repair shop can check out the hardware for damage.

How much should you pay for a used computer? This can be tricky. Some sellers may not be aware of the rapid depreciation of their equipment and price it too high. The best bet is to look through back issues of the classified ads for a couple of newspapers in your area until you have a sense of what equipment may be worth.

WHERE TO BUY NEW

Fierce price wars among microcomputer manufacturers and retailers have made hardware more affordable. One reason why IBM-compatibles have become so widespread is that non-IBM manufacturers early on were able to copy, or "clone," IBM machines and offer them at cut-rate prices. For a long time, Apple Macintoshes were considerably more expensive, but recently the company has allowed other computer makers to clone its machines, resulting in lower prices.

There are several sources for inexpensive new computers:

- **Student discount:** With a college ID card, you're probably entitled to student discounts (usually 10–20%) through the campus bookstore or college computer resellers. In addition, during the first few weeks of the term, many campuses offer special sales on computer equipment. Campus resellers also provide on-campus service and support and, says one expert, can help students meet the prevailing campus standards while satisfying their personal needs.[2]

PANEL SS.2

Tips for buying used computers. Buying from an individual means you have little recourse if something goes wrong. The following tips should help you to buy carefully.

- If possible, take someone who knows computers with you.
- Turn the computer on and off a few times to make sure there are no problems on startup.
- Use the computer and, if possible, try the software you want to use. Listen for strange sounds in the hard drive or the floppies.
- Turn the computer off and look for screen burn-in, a ghost image on the screen after the machine has been turned off. It can be a sign of misuse.
- Ask about the warranty. Some companies, including Apple and IBM, permit warranties to be transferred to new owners (effective from the date of the original purchase). A new owner can usually have the warranty extended by paying a fee.

SPECIAL SECTION: PRODUCTIVITY TOOLS

- **Computer superstores:** These are big chains such as Computer City, CompUSA, and Microage. Computers are also sold at department stores, warehouse stores (such as Costco and Price Club), Wal-Mart, Circuit City, Radio Shack, and similar outlets.

- **Mail-order houses:** Companies like Dell Computer Corp. and Gateway 2000 found they could sell computers inexpensively by mail order while offering customer support over the phone. Their success inspired IBM, Compaq, and others to plunge into the mail-order business.

   The price advantage of mail-order companies has eroded with the rise of computer superstores. Moreover, the lack of local repair and service support can be a major disadvantage. Still, if you're interested in this route, look for a copy of the phone-book-size magazine *Computer Shopper,* which carries ads from most mail-order vendors.

   When buying hardware, look to see if software, such as word processing or spreadsheet programs, comes "bundled" with it. *Bundled* means that software is included in the selling price of the hardware. This arrangement can be a real advantage, saving you several hundred dollars.

Computer Software

There are thousands of software programs, available on floppy disks, that will run on computer hardware. The best way to consider the kind of software that might be useful to you is to visualize yourself sitting at a desk in an old-fashioned office: You have a typewriter. You have a calendar, clock, and name-and-address file. You have a calculator. You have desk drawers full of files. You have a telephone. You have an In-box and an Out-box to which someone delivers and from which someone takes your interoffice and outside mail. Many of these items could also be found on a student's desk. How would a computer and software improve on this arrangement?

This section describes the following kinds of software:

- Word processing

- Desktop accessories and personal information managers

- Spreadsheets

- Database management systems

- Graphics

- Communications

- Integrated programs and suites

- Groupware

WORD PROCESSING

The typewriter, that long-lived machine, has gone to its reward. Today your choice is generally to buy (1) a *word processing typewriter,* (2) a *personal word processor,* or (3) *word processing software to run on your personal computer* and printer.

- **Word processing typewriter:** The **word processing typewriter** is like the old typewriter in that it can be made to type directly on paper. Yet it can also let you see and edit your words on a small display screen before they are printed on paper. It can automatically check your spelling. It can also store a few pages of text that you can retrieve and print later. This machine prints with a daisy wheel, the petals of which stamp characters directly onto the paper.

Priced at around $200, the word processing typewriter is probably fine if you do only short reports and routine correspondence. Models are available from Brother, Sears, and Sharp.

■ *Personal word processor:* The **personal word processor** is really a personal computer with a built-in word processing program, but it usually cannot run other types of programs. The machine is dedicated to creating, editing, and printing documents, and it can also store your written materials on diskettes. Display screens are usually easier to read than those on word processing typewriters.

Prices are higher than for typewriters, starting at about $300. Models are available from Brother, Panasonic, and AEG Olympia. Personal word processors are preferable if you do long reports.

■ *Word processing software to run on PC and printer:* Word processing typewriters and personal word processors don't run other kinds of software. The principal advantage of having a personal computer, on the other hand, is that you can run word processing software and also many other kinds of software.

Word processing software allows you to use computers to create, edit, revise, store, and print text material. Most current programs provide a number of menus, or lists of choices, for manipulating aspects of your document. Three common programs for IBM-style Windows computers are Microsoft Word, WordPerfect, and Ami Pro; for Macintoshes they are Word and MacWrite.

Word processing software allows personal computers to do what the other two types of machines do—namely, maneuver through a document with a cursor and *delete, insert,* and *replace* text, the principal correction activities. However, word processing software offers additional features that the other machines lack, such as Search, Replace, Block Move commands; spell checking; and thesaurus. *(See ■ Panel SS.3.)*

Opting for a personal computer for word processing means you have to make three decisions:

■ *Expense:* You have to be prepared to spend more than you would for a word processing typewriter or personal word processor. Personal computers start at $500, and a state-of-the-art system that includes software and printer may cost $3000–$4000.

■ *Software:* You have to determine what word processing software you want to use. For students, the easiest choice is to use that used by most other students, especially those in your major. That way you can easily borrow someone else's system if yours breaks down.

■ *Portability:* You have to make some decisions about portability and printers. A desktop machine is often cheaper than a laptop, but a laptop is more easily carried around. Printers are a problem, since (with some exceptions) they are not built into the computer—and, indeed, are often bigger than the computer itself. Transporting both a microcomputer and a printer can be cumbersome, although most people find they don't need to move a printer around. Some small, portable printers (about the size of a cigarette carton) are available, but they are slow to operate.

DESKTOP ACCESSORIES & PERSONAL INFORMATION MANAGERS

Is there any need to have an electronic version of the traditional appointment calendar, clock, and file of phone numbers and addresses? A lot of people with computers still use old-fashioned paper-and-pencil calendars and To Do lists. However, others find ready uses for the kind of software called *desktop accessories* or *personal information managers (PIMs).*

Features of a word processing program. Word processing software offers features such as the Search, Replace, and Block Move commands; spell checking; and thesaurus.

With a word processor, unlike with a typewriter, you can maneuver through a document and do the principal correction activities—*delete, insert,* and *replace*—with ease. In addition, word processing software offers these other features:

Search and replace: The *Search command* allows you to find any word or number that you know exists in your document. The *Replace command* allows you to automatically replace it with something else.

"Cut and paste" (block and move): Typewriter users were accustomed to using scissors and glue to "cut and paste" to move a paragraph or block of text from one place to another in a manuscript. With word processing, you can exercise the *Block command* to indicate the beginning and end of the portion of text you want to move. Then you can use the *Move command* to move it to another location in the document. (You can also use the *Copy command* to copy the block of text to a new location while also leaving the original block where it is.)

Report format: The *report format* is the layout of the printed page, including print columns, line spacing, justification, and headers or footers. It is easy to have one, two, or three columns of type on the page; to make the lines single-, double-, or triple-spaced (or all three within a document); or to have the text justified or unjustified.

Justify means to align text evenly between left and right margins, as, for example, is done with most newspaper columns. *Unjustify* means to not align the text evenly, as is done with the right side of many business letters ("ragged right").

A *header* is a small piece of text (such as a date) that is printed at the top of every page. A *footer* is the same thing printed at the bottom of every page.

You can also make format changes within a document, such as by centering or indenting headings or by emphasizing text with **boldface,** *italics,* or underlining.

Spelling and grammar checking, thesaurus, outlining, mail-merge: The principal word processing packages have some separate programs or functions that can really reduce your work.

Many writers automatically run their completed documents through a *spelling checker,* which tests for incorrectly spelled words. Another program is a *grammar checker,* which flags poor grammar, wordiness, incomplete sentences, and awkward phrases.

If you find yourself stuck for the right word while you're writing, you can call up an on-screen *thesaurus,* which will present you with the appropriate word or alternative words.

If you need assistance with organizing your thoughts, you might use an outline processor. An *outline processor* allows you to type in thoughts and then tag the topics with numbers and letters and organize them in outline form, with Roman numerals, letters, and numbers.

If you want to send out the same letter to different people, you can use the *mail-merge program* to print customized form letters, with different names, addresses, and salutations for each letter.

- *Desktop accessories:* A **desktop accessory,** or **desktop organizer,** is a software package that provides an electronic version of tools or objects commonly found on a desktop: calendar, clock, card file, calculator, and notepad. Some desktop-accessory programs come as standard equipment with some systems software (such as on Microsoft's Windows). Others, such as Borland's SideKick or Lotus Agenda, are available as separate programs to run in your computer at the same time you are running other software. Some are principally *scheduling and calendaring programs;* their main purpose is to enable you to do time and event scheduling.

  Suppose, for example, you are working on a word processing document and someone calls to schedule lunch next week. You can simply type a command that "pops up" your appointment calendar, type in the appointment, save the information, and then return to your interrupted work. Other features, such as a calculator keypad, a "scratch pad" for typing in notes to yourself, and a Rolodex-type address and phone directory (some with automatic telephone dialer), can be display on the screen when needed.

- *Personal information managers:* A more sophisticated program is the **personal information manager (PIM),** a combination word processor, database, and desktop accessory program that organizes a variety of information. Examples of PIMs are Ascend, CA-UpToDate, DayMaker Organizer, DateBook Pro, Dynodex, Instant Recall, Lotus Organizer, OnTime for Windows, and Personal Reminder System.

SPREADSHEET SOFTWARE

What is a spreadsheet? Traditionally, it was simply a grid of rows and columns, printed on special green paper, that was used by accountants and other financial types to produce financial projections and reports. A person making up a spreadsheet often spent long days and weekends at the office penciling tiny numbers into countless tiny rectangles. When one figure changed, all the rest of the numbers on the spreadsheet had to be recomputed—and ultimately there might be wastebaskets full of jettisoned worksheets.

In the late 1970s, someone got the idea of computerizing all this. The **electronic spreadsheet** allows users to create tables and financial schedules by entering data into rows and columns arranged as a grid on a display screen. The electronic spreadsheet quickly became the most popular small-business program. Today the principal spreadsheets are Excel, Lotus 1-2-3, and Quattro Pro. *(See ■ Panel SS.4.)*

DATABASE MANAGEMENT SYSTEMS

In its most general sense, a database is any electronically stored collection of data in a computer system. In its more specific sense, a **database** is a collection of interrelated files in a computer system. These computer-based files are organized so that those parts that have a common element can be retrieved easily. The software for maintaining a database is a **database manager** or **database management system (DBMS),** a program that controls the structure of a database and access to the data. *(See ■ Panel SS.5.)*

Today the principal database manager for computers running the DOS operating system is dBASE. The major ones that run under Microsoft Windows are Access and Paradox, followed by Filemaker Pro for Windows, FoxPro for Windows, Q&A for Windows, and Approach for Windows. A multimedia program called Instant Database allows users to attach sound, motion, and graphics to forms.

Databases have gotten easier to use, but they still can be difficult to set up. Even so, the trend is toward making such programs easier for both database creators and database users.

Characteristics of a spreadsheet program.

Spreadsheets can be used to display data in graphic form, such as in pie charts or bar charts, which are easier to read than columns of numbers. Spreadsheets can even be linked to more exciting graphics, such as digitized maps.

Columns, rows, and labels: *Column headings* appear across the top; *row headings* appear down the left side. Column and row headings are called *labels.* The label is usually any descriptive text, such as APRIL, PHONE, or GROSS SALES.

Cells, cell addresses, values, and spreadsheet cursor: The place where rows and columns intersect is called a *cell,* and its position is called a *cell address.* For example, "A1" is the cell address for the top left cell, where column A and row 1 intersect.

A number entered in a cell is called a *value.* The values are the actual numbers used in the spreadsheet—dollars, percentages, grade points, temperatures, or whatever. A *cell pointer* or *spreadsheet cursor* indicates where data is to be entered. The cell pointer can be moved around like a cursor in a word processing program.

Formulas and recalculation: Now we come to the reason the electronic spreadsheet has taken business organizations offices by storm. *Formulas* are instructions for calculations. For example, a formula might be SUM CELLS A5 TO A15, meaning "Sum (add) all the numbers in the cells with cell addresses A5 through A15."

After the values have been plugged into the spreadsheet, the formulas can be used to calculate outcomes. What is revolutionary, however, is the way the spreadsheet can easily do recalculation. *Recalculation* is the process of recomputing values *automatically,* either as an ongoing process as data is being entered or afterward, with the press of a key.

The "what-if?" world: The recalculation feature has opened up whole new possibilities for decision making. As a user, you can create a plan, put in formulas and numbers, and then ask yourself "What would happen if we change that detail?"—and immediately see the effect on the bottom line.

Characteristics of a database management system.

Organization of a database: A database is organized—from smallest to largest items—into *fields, records,* and *files.*

A *field* is a unit of data consisting of one or more characters. Examples of a field are your name, your address, or your driver's license number.

A *record* is a collection of related fields. An example of a record would be your name *and* address *and* driver's license number.

A *file* is a collection of related records. An example of a file could be one in your state's Department of Motor Vehicles. The file would include everyone who received a driver's license on the same day, including their names, addresses, and driver's license numbers.

Select and display: The beauty of database management programs is that you can locate records in the file quickly. For example, your college may maintain several records about you—one at the registrar's, one in financial aid, one in the housing department, and so on. Any of these records can be called up on a computer display screen for viewing and updating. Thus, if you move, your address field will need to be changed in all records. The database is quickly corrected by finding your name field. Once the record is displayed, the address field can be changed.

Sort: With a database management system you can easily change the order of records in a file. Normally, records are entered into a database in the order they occur, such as by the date a person registered to attend college. However, all these records can be sorted in different ways. For example, they can be rearranged by state, by age, or by Social Security number.

Calculate and format: Many database management programs contain built-in mathematical formulas. This feature can be used, for example, to find the grade-point averages for students in different majors or in different classes. Such information can then be organized into different formats and printed out.

GRAPHICS SOFTWARE

Computer graphics can be highly complicated, such as those used in special effects for movies. Here we are concerned with microcomputer applications useful for work and study—namely, *analytical graphics* and *presentation graphics*.

■ *Analytical graphics:* **Analytical graphics** are graphical forms that make numeric data easier to analyze than when it is in the form of rows and columns of numbers, as in electronic spreadsheets. The principal examples are bar charts, line charts, and pie charts.

Most analytical graphics are features of spreadsheet programs, such as Lotus 1-2-3. Whether viewed on a monitor or printed out, analytical graphics help make sales figures, economic trends, and the like easier to comprehend and analyze.

■ *Presentation graphics:* **Presentation graphics** are graphics used to communicate or make a presentation of data to others, such as clients or supervisors. Presentations may make use of analytical graphics, but they look much more sophisticated. They use different texturing patterns (speckled, solid, cross-hatched), color, and three-dimensionality. Examples of well-known graphics packages are Curtain Call, Free-lance Plus, Harvard Graphics, Hollywood, Persuasion, PowerPoint, and Presentation Graphics.

Some presentation graphics packages provide artwork ("clip art") that can be electronically cut and pasted into the graphics. These programs also allow you to use electronic painting and drawing tools for creating lines, rectangles, and just about any other shape. Depending on the system's capabilities, you can add text, animated sequences, and sound. With special equipment you can do graphic presentations on slides, transparencies, and videotape. With all these options the main problem may be simply restraining yourself.

COMMUNICATIONS SOFTWARE

Many microcomputer users feel they have all the productivity they need without ever having to hook up their machines to a telephone. However, having communications capabilities provides you with a great leap forward that vastly extends your range. This leap is made possible with communications software.

Communications software manages the transmission of data between computers. For most microcomputer users this sending and receiving of data is by way of a modem and a telephone line. As mentioned, a *modem* is an electronic device that allows computers to communicate with each other over telephone lines. When you buy a modem, you often get communications software with it. Popular microcomputer communications programs are Smartcom, Crosstalk, ProComm, PC-Dial, Blast, and PC Talk.

With communications software and a modem in your computer, you can connect with friends by e-mail (electronic mail), tap into so-called electronic bulletin-board systems (BBSs), and make use of the research possibilities of information services (America Online, CompuServe, Prodigy, Microsoft Network) and the Internet and World Wide Web. These are described in more detail in another few pages.

INTEGRATED PROGRAMS & SUITES

What if you want to take data from one program and use it in another—say, call up data from a database and use it in a spreadsheet? You can try using separate software packages, but one may not be designed to accept data from the other. **Integrated packages** combine the features of several applications programs into one software package. Usually these capabilities are the ones we have described: electronic spreadsheets, word processing, database management, graphics, and communications. Thus, if you were a sales manager, you could use a database to get various sales figures for different parts of the country. Then you could compare them using a spreadsheet and graphics program, write a memo about them using a word processing program, and send your memo to the sales representatives using communications software.

Examples of integrated packages are ClarisWorks, Eight-in-One, Lotus Works, Microsoft Works, PFS:First Choice, and WordPerfect Works. In general, integrated packages are less powerful than separate programs used alone, such as a word processing or spreadsheet program used by itself. Moreover, systems software such as Windows make integrated programs unnecessary, since the user can easily shift between applications programs that are *completely different*. Finally, integrated programs are largely being replaced by *software suites*.

Suites are applications—like spreadsheets, word processing, graphics, and communications—that are bundled together and sold for a fraction of what the programs would cost if bought individually. Examples of suites are Microsoft Office, Smart Suite, and Perfect Office.

Although cost is what makes suites attractive to many corporate customers, they have other benefits as well. Manufacturers have taken pains to integrate the "look and feel" of the separate programs within the suites to make them easier to use.

Communications Tools

The first wave of computing, 30 years ago, was driven by the huge computers known as mainframes. Twenty years later came the second wave, which produced the desktop personal computer. Now we are into the third wave, which is being driven by communications networks among computers. Communications technology, then, is vital to your future. The options include the following.

TELEPHONE-RELATED COMMUNICATIONS SERVICES

Services available through telephone connections, whether the conventional wired kind or the wireless cellular-phone type, include the following:

■ *Fax messages:* Asking "What is your fax number?" is about as common a question in the work world today as asking for someone's telephone number. **Fax** stands for "facsimile transmission" or reproduction. A fax may be sent by dedicated fax machine or by fax modem.

Dedicated fax machines are specialized devices that do nothing except send and receive documents over transmission lines from and to other fax machines. These are the stand-alone machines nowadays found everywhere, from offices to airports to instant-printing shops.

A **fax modem,** which is installed as a circuit board inside a computer's cabinet, is a modem with fax capability. It enables you to send signals directly from your computer to someone else's fax machine or fax modem.

■ *Voice mail:* Like a sophisticated telephone answering machine, **voice mail** digitizes incoming voice messages and stores them in the recipient's "voice mailbox" in digitized form. It then converts the digitized versions back to voice messages when they are retrieved.

Unlike conventional answering machines, voice-mail systems allow callers to direct their calls within an office by pressing numbers on their touch-tone phone. They also allow callers to deliver the same message to many people within an organization. They can forward calls to the recipient's home or hotel.

The main benefit is that voice mail helps eliminate "telephone tag." That is, two callers can continue to exchange messages even when they can't reach each other directly.

■ *E-mail:* **E-mail,** or **electronic mail,** links computers by wired or wireless connections and allows users, through their keyboards, to post messages and to read responses on their display screens. E-mail allows "callers," or users, to send messages to a single recipient's "mailbox," which is simply a file stored on the computer system. Or they can send the same message to multiple users on the same system.

As with voice mail, e-mail helps users avoid playing "telephone tag." It also offers confidentiality. Recipients cannot get into their "mailboxes" to pick up messages unless they enter a *password,* a secret word or numbers that limit access.

E-mail has jumped in use, especially in large organizations, where it helps to speed the exchange of memos and scheduling of appointments. Often a company will use its own specialized computer network. However, the Internet or outside online information services (described next) are also used. E-mail not only speeds communications, it can also reduce telephone, postage, and secretarial costs.

ONLINE INFORMATION SERVICES

An **online information service** provides access to all kinds of databases and electronic meeting places to subscribers equipped with telephone-linked microcomputers. Says one writer:

> *Online services are those interactive news and information retrieval sources that can make your computer behave more like a telephone; or a TV set; or a newspaper; or a video arcade, a stock brokerage firm, a bank, a travel agency, a weather bureau, a department store, a grocery store, a florist, a set of encyclopedias, a library, a bulletin board and more.*[3]

There are scores of online services, but perhaps the most prominent are those listed below. *(See* ■ *Panel SS.6.)* To use these services, you need a personal computer with hard disk, printer, and modem, plus communications software. Communications software is often sold with (is bundled with) modems. Popular information services such as America Online, CompuServe, Prodigy, and Microsoft Network (MSN) provide subscribers with their own software programs for going online.

PANEL SS.6

Online services. These are the principal mainstream online services. Prices are subject to change.

America Online (800-827-6364). $9.95/month for 5 hours, then $2.95/hour. Easy-to-use interface; ideal for hobbyists and families wanting low-cost access to online features.

CompuServe (800-848-8199). $4.95/month for 5 hours, then $2.95/hour. Easy-to-use interface; ideal for people wanting to combine academic or business with hobbyist and family-type activities.

Microsoft Network (MSN) (800-386-5550) $4.95/month for 3 hours, then $2.50/hour. Access is built in to the Windows 95 operating system, allowing users to connect with an easy mouse click; splashy graphics; still expanding offerings

Prodigy (800-776-3449). $9.95/month for 5 hours, then $2.95/hour.
The simplest online service, easy for beginners; rivaled only by CompuServe in number and variety of services.

Before you can use an online information service, you need to open an account with it, using a credit card. Billing policies resemble those used by cable-TV and telephone companies. As with cable TV, you may be charged a fee for basic service, with additional fees for specialized services. In addition, the online service may charge you for the time spent while on the line. Finally, you will also be charged by your telephone company for your time on the line, just as when making a regular phone call. However, most information services offer local access numbers. Thus, unless you live in a rural area, you will not be paying long-distance phone charges. All told, the typical user may pay $10–$20 a month to use an online service, although it's possible to run a bill of $100 or more. To keep costs down, many users go online only during off-hours (evenings and weekends), when the charges intended for business users are reduced.

As one of the hundreds of thousands of subscribers connected to an online service, you can have access to *e-mail, computer games* (both single-player and multi-player), *research, travel services,* and *shopping services.* The only restriction on the amount of research you can do online is the limit on whatever credit card you are charging your time to. Depending on the online service, you can avail yourself of several encyclopedias. Many online services store unabridged text from newspapers and magazines. CompuServe's Magazine Database Plus, for example, carries full-text articles from more than 90 general-interest publications (business, science, sports, and so on). Other features are book and movie/video news, contests, health reports, parenting advice, car-rental information, microwave cooking instructions, and on and on.

ELECTRONIC BULLETIN BOARD SYSTEMS

An **electronic bulletin board system (BBS)** is a centralized information source and message-switching system for a particular computer-linked interest group. Through a BBS users may "chat with" and share files with like-minded users.

There are thousands of BBSs worldwide. Many are free, some charge a nominal fee, and others may charge up to $10 an hour. The BBS is often an inexpensive way of learning to go online. If a BBS is local (or worldwide but locally accessed), as so many are, you pay only the cost of a local phone call. Bulletin boards that require a membership fee (charged to a credit card) generally give you a trial period to explore the BBS free of charge.

BBSs are basically of four types:

- *Large commercial BBSs:* All the major online services (America Online, CompuServe, Prodigy, MSN) operate bulletin boards. However, BBSs are only *one* of several services offered by commercial online services. And, of course, you are charged by the organization for using this particular feature.

- *Small local BBSs:* Small BBSs may be free or for-profit, but they are generally run by individuals, often out of their homes. BBS system operators are called *sysops.* Many bulletin boards are locally oriented or are devoted to a single hobby or theme. They are accessed through a local phone call.

  The best way to find BBSs in your area is to check with local computer publications (which may be free) or computer stores. Most of these are disappearing, evolving into Internet or Web BBSs.

- *Internet BBSs:* Worldwide BBSs are available, without the cost of long-distance dialing, through the Internet. You'll need to have access to the Internet through an Internet service provider that can help connect you ("telnet" you) to international BBSs.

- *World Wide Web BBSs:* The next generation is the Web BBS, which allows you to connect, for the price of a local phone call, to a BBS directly through that part of the Internet known as the World Wide Web. Web BBSs offer full-color graphics and (with your mouse) point-and-click ease.

The primary difference between a BBS and an online service is the single focus. "Typically, BBSs are targeted at a particular single-issue topic," says one expert, "and online services are kind of like department stores that have a thousand different topics that are being talked about."[4]

Using your computer's communications software, you dial up a bulletin board by pressing the numbers on your keyboard. You are then usually greeted by a welcome screen from the BBS that tells you what to do—what rules to follow and how to get help, if you need it.

As you move around the BBS, you will probably find a library of materials, such as computer games, that you can copy for your own use. You will also find places where other users have posted messages or where you can "chat" (type your messages and read theirs) with people who have similar interests. There seem to be no limits to the topics of electronic talk forums ("conferences" or "chat rooms") on bulletin boards. The participants range from bird watchers to socialists to Francophiles to Trekkies.

THE INTERNET

The computer, modem, and telephone line that explore online services and BBSs can also be used to connect with the global network of computers known as the Internet. The **Internet** is an international network connecting approximately 36,000 smaller networks.

Some principal services of the Internet are as follows:

- ***E-mail:*** Internet electronic mail is essentially like the e-mail in an office except that you can exchange messages all over the world. E-mail messages on the Internet can be transmitted from one user to another usually in a matter of seconds.

  Although Internet addresses may seem strange at first, they are not complicated. The Internet address for the President of the United States, for example, is *president@whitehouse.gov*. The first part is the user's name—in this case, *president*. (Yours might be your nickname, initials and last name, or some combination.) The second part is the computer network you use, which follows the @ (called "at") sign —in this case, *@whitehouse*. The third part, following a period, is the network's "domain"— in this case, *gov* for "government." Other domains are *com* (commercial organizations), *edu* (education), *mil* (military), *net* (network resources), and *org* (private organizations). A user of the online service America Online (AOL) would have an Internet e-mail address of *user@aol.com*.

- ***Information gathering:*** "Try as you may," says one writer, "you cannot imagine how much data is available on the Internet."[5] Besides hundreds of online databases from various universities and other research institutions and online library catalogs, here is a sampling:

The Library of Congress card catalog. The daily White House press releases. Weather maps and forecasts. Schedules of professional sports teams. Weekly Nielsen television ratings. Recipe archives. The Central Intelligence Agency world map. A ZIP Code guide. The National Family Database. Project Gutenberg (offering the complete text of many works of literature). The Alcoholism Research Data Base. Guitar chords. U.S. government addresses and phone (and fax) numbers. The Simpsons archive.[6]

- *Discussion and news groups:* One of the Internet's most interesting features are the news groups, or bulletin board discussion groups. For example, **Usenet** is a loose confederation of 5000 **newsgroups** or discussion groups on every conceivable subject. Users can post messages for others to read, then check back later to see what responses have appeared.

  Examples of topics offered by Usenet news groups are *misc.jobs.offered, rec.arts.startrek.info,* and *soc.culture.african.american.* The category called *alt* news groups offers more free-form topics, such as *alt.rock-n-roll.metal* or *alt.internet.services.*

- *World Wide Web:* The **World Wide Web (WWW,** or simply **"the Web")** is the Internet's most graphical and usable service. It resembles a huge encyclopedia filled with thousands of topics or sites (called "pages"), which have been created by computer users and businesses around the world. Each site has cross-reference links to other sites. Sites may theoretically be in *multimedia* form—meaning they can appear in text, graphical, sound, animation, or video form—although at present there are lots of pictures and text but little live, moving content. However, this is in the process of changing.

  In order to find your way through the dense data fields of the Web, you need a software program called a **browser.** Browsers allow you to use a mouse to click-and-jump through the various sites. Three important Web browsers are Netscape Navigator, Mosaic, and Internet Explorer.

  There are three principal ways of getting connected to the Internet:

- *School or work:* The people with the easiest access to Internet are those involved with universities and colleges, government agencies, and some commercial businesses. College students often get a free account through their institution. However, students and faculty living off-campus may not be able to use the connections of campus computers.

- *Commercial online services:* The large commercial online services—such as America Online, CompuServe, Prodigy, and Microsoft Network—offer access to the Internet.

- *Commercial access providers:* The commercial online serices may be the easiest path to the Internet, but they may charge more than independent access providers. These are companies that will provide public access to the Internet for a fee, from a few dollars an hour to thousands of dollars a year. The cheapest kind of access is the dial-up connection. Here the independent access provider charges a monthly and/or hourly fee for dialing into an intermediary source that then connects to the Internet.

  One thing to find out when you're looking into Internet connections is whether you will be getting e-mail only or full access. E-mail gives you virtually instantaneous worldwide communication. However, full access will allow you to acquire information, software, games, pictures, and other riches.

  A network information center called InterNIC has been set up to serve as a clearinghouse for Internet information. To find out more, call (800) 444-4345, or e-mail *info@internic.net.* For public access sites, ask about the PDIAL list.

NOTES

1. Stewart, T. A. (1994, April 4). The information age in charts. *Fortune,* pp. 75–79.

2. McGee, C. cited in Meers, T. (1993, September). College computing 101, *PC Novice,* pp. 18–22.

3. Branigan, M. (1992, January). The cost of using an online service. *PC Novice,* pp. 65–71.

4. Toplanski, M., quoted in Larson, J. (1993, March). Telecommunications and your computer. *PC Novice,* pp. 14–19.

5. Tetzeli, R. (1994, March 7). The Internet and your business. *Fortune,* pp. 86–96.

6. Landis, D. (1993, October 7). Exploring the online universe. *USA Today,* p. 4D.

5 memory

fundamentals of learning

IN THIS CHAPTER: You discover one of the most valuable tools you own—your memory—and how to use it effectively. We consider three subjects:

■ **The importance of managing memory:** Understanding the drawbacks of cramming, the differences between short-term and long-term memory, and the "forgetting curve."

■ **Your learning style:** Which senses you tend to favor for learning—sound, sight, touch, or all three.

■ **How to improve your memory:** How to give your memory an extra push—through overlearning, studying a little at a time frequently, avoiding interference, making material meaningful to you, using verbal memory aids, and using visual memory aids.

What would be your greatest wish to help you through college?

Maybe it would be for a photographic memory, a mind that could briefly look at something just once and later recall it in detail. Perhaps 5–10% of school-age children have this kind of memory—it's called *eidetic imagery*—but it seldom lasts into adulthood.[1] You can see, though, why a photographic memory would be so valuable. *If so much of college instruction consists of lectures and readings and of testing you on how much you remember from them, your ability to memorize great quantities of information becomes crucial.*

The Importance of Managing Long-Term Memory

PREVIEW So much of college teaching consists of lectures and reading, which require memorization for testing. "Cramming" for exams—massive memorization at the last minute—is not advisable because there is so much to learn in college. Memory is principally *immediate, short-term,* and *long-term.* Boosting your long-term memory is better than favoring your short-term memory because of the "forgetting curve," whereby information retention drops sharply after 24 hours.

How good is your memory? **_Memory_ is defined as a mental process that entails three main operations: recording, storage, and recall.** The main strategy at work seems to be *association*—one idea reminds you of another.[2] Actually, even though you may worry that you have a weak memory because you immediately forget people's names after being introduced to them at a party, it's probably just fine.

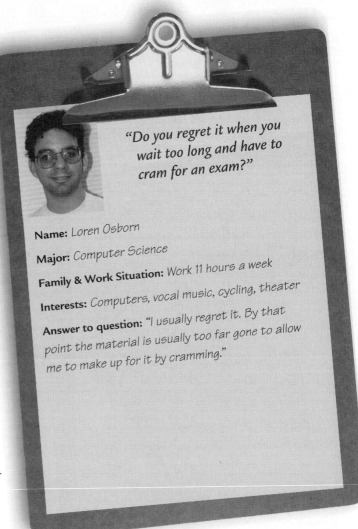

"Do you regret it when you wait too long and have to cram for an exam?"

Name: Loren Osborn

Major: Computer Science

Family & Work Situation: Work 11 hours a week

Interests: Computers, vocal music, cycling, theater

Answer to question: "I usually regret it. By that point the material is usually too far gone to allow me to make up for it by cramming."

"I CRAM, THEREFORE I AM." Your mind holds a wonderful mishmash of names, addresses, telephone numbers, pictures, familiar routes, words to songs, and thousands and thousands of other facts. How did you learn them—during several hours late one night or repeatedly over a long time? The answer is obvious.

When it comes to college, however, many students try to study for exams by doing a great deal of the work of a semester or quarter all in one night or in a couple of days. This is the time-honored memorizing marathon known as *cramming*. <u>Cramming</u> **is defined as preparing hastily for an examination.**

Many students have the notion that facts can be remembered best if they're *fresh*. There is indeed something to that, as I'll discuss. But does cramming work? Certainly it beats the alternative of not studying at all. Suppose, however, you crammed all night to memorize the lines of Hamlet. And suppose also that the next morning, instead of going to an examination room, you had to get up on a stage and recite the entire part. Could you do it? Probably not. Yet the quarter or semester's worth of material you have tried overnight to jam into your memory banks for a test may be even more comprehensive than all the lines Shakespeare wrote for his character.

In sum: Even if you found cramming a successful exam-preparation technique in high school, you should begin now to find other techniques for memorizing. In college there is simply too much to learn.

TYPES OF MEMORY: IMMEDIATE, SHORT-TERM, & LONG-TERM. To use your memory truly effectively to advance your college career—and your goals in life—it helps to know how it works. Memory is principally *immediate*, *short-term*, and *long-term*.

■ *Immediate perceptual memory:* <u>*Immediate perceptual memory*</u> **is defined as "a reflex memory in which an impression is immediately replaced by a new one."**[3] An example is in typing. As soon as a word is typed it is forgotten.

■ *Short-term memory:* <u>*Short-term memory*</u> **is defined by psychologists as recording seven elements for a maximum of 30 seconds.** This is about the number of elements and length of time required to look up a telephone number and dial it. Short-term memory has only limited capacity—for instance, about five to nine numbers for most people. To transfer such short-term information into your long-term memory requires reciting or other association techniques, as I'll discuss.

The details of short-term memories fade unless you rehearse them. Or unless some emotionally charged event happens at the same time.

■ *Long-term memory:* <u>*Long-term memory*</u> **entails remembering something for days, weeks, or years.** Long-term memory often requires that *some kind of change be made in your behavior* so that the information being learned makes a significant enough impression.

Remembering how to perform a musical piece, how to shoot a perfect free-throw, or how to do winning moves in chess require repetition. To achieve these things, you can't just "wing it" by learning something once. Of course, long-term memories also fade, but they do so more slowly.[4]

THE FORGETTING CURVE: FAST-FADING MEMORIES. To understand why, from the standpoint of college learning, long-term memory is so much more important, consider what psychologists call the *forgetting curve*. In one famous experiment long ago, Hermann Ebbinghaus found that, in memorizing nonsense syllables, *a great deal of information is forgotten just during the first 24 hours*, then it levels out.[5] Although fortunately you need not memorize nonsense syllables, the rate of forgetting also occurs rapidly for prose and poetry. (Poetry is easier to memorize than prose because it has built-in memory cues such as rhymes.) (*See* ■ *Panel 5.1, next page.*)

PANEL 5.1

The forgetting curve. Material is easily forgotten if you are exposed to it only once. The retention of information drops rapidly in the first 24 hours for nonsense syllables, which are not meaningful, and slightly less so for prose, which is meaning-ful. Poetry is remembered best because of helpful devices such as rhyming. Even so, only 40% of a poem is remembered after a month's time.

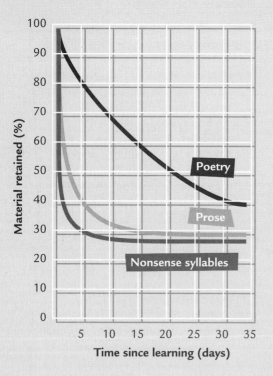

How good are people at remembering things in the normal course of events?

According to a survey from the National Institute for Development and Administration at the University of Texas, we remember only:

10% of what we read,
20% of what we hear,
30% of what we see,
50% of what we see and hear,
70% of what we say,
90% of what we do and say.[6]

Walter Pauk reports a study of people who read a textbook chapter in which it was found that they forgot:

46% of what they read after 1 day,
79% of what they read after 14 days,
81% of what they read after 28 days.[7]

As for remembering what one has heard, Pauk describes an experiment in which a group of psychologists who attended a seminar forgot over 91% of what they had heard after two weeks.[8]

If you were tested every other day on the lectures you attended and textbooks you read, memorizing wouldn't be much of a problem. But that's not the way it usually works, of course. Ordinarily an instructor will give you an exam halfway or a third of the way into the course. There may be another exam later, followed by a final exam at the end of the course. Each time you will be held accountable for several weeks' worth of lectures and readings.

Memory is also important in writing papers. If you start your research or writ-ing and then abandon it for a couple of weeks, it will take you some time to reconnect with your thoughts when you go back to it.

The Four Learning Styles: Which Fits You?

PREVIEW There are four types of learning styles, corresponding to the principal senses: auditory (hearing), visual (sight), kinesthetic (touch), and mixed modality (all three). You may favor one of these over the others.

Educators talk about differences in **_learning styles_—the ways in which people acquire knowledge.** Some students learn well by listening to lectures. Others learn better through reading, class discussion, hands-on experience, or researching a topic and writing about it. Thus, your particular learning style may make you more comfortable with some kinds of teaching and learning, and even with some kinds of subjects, than with others.

To find out the ways you learn best, try Personal Exploration #5.1.

PERSONAL EXPLORATION #5.1

HOW DO YOU LEARN BEST?

There are 12 incomplete sentences and three choices for completing each. Circle the answer that best corresponds to your style, as follows:

1 = the choice that is *least* like you.

2 = your second choice.

3 = the choice that is *most* like you.

1. When I want to learn something new, I usually . . .

   a. want someone to explain it to me.　　1 2 3

   b. want to read about it in a book or magazine.　　1 2 3

   c. want to try it out, take notes, or make a model of it.　　1 2 3

2. At a party, most of the time I like to . . .

   a. listen and talk to two or three people at once.　　1 2 3

   b. see how everyone looks and watch the people.　　1 2 3

   c. dance, play games, or take part in some activities.　　1 2 3

3. If I were helping with a musical show, I would most likely . . .

   a. write the music, sing the songs, or play the accompaniment.　　1 2 3

   b. design the costumes, paint the scenery, or work the lighting effects.　　1 2 3

   c. make the costumes, build the sets, or take an acting role.　　1 2 3

4. When I am angry, my first reaction is to . . .

   a. tell people off, laugh, joke, or talk it over with someone.　　1 2 3

   b. blame myself or someone else, daydream about taking revenge, or keep it inside　　1 2 3

   c. make a fist or tense my muscles, take it out on some thing else, hit or throw things.　　1 2 3

5. A happy event I would like to have is . . .

   a. hearing the thunderous applause for my speech or music.　　1 2 3

   b. photographing the prize picture of an exciting newspaper story.　　1 2 3

   c. achieving the fame of being first in a physical activity such as dancing, acting, surfing, or a sports event.　　1 2 3

6. I prefer a teacher to . . .

   a. use the lecture method, with informative explanations and discussions.　　1 2 3

   b. write on the chalkboard, use visual aids and assigned readings.　　1 2 3

   c. require posters, models, or in-service practice, and some activities in class.　　1 2 3

7. I know that I talk with . . .

   a. different tones of voice.　　1 2 3

   b. my eyes and facial expressions.　　1 2 3

   c. my hands and gestures.　　1 2 3

(continued on next pagee)

8. If I had to remember an event so I could record it later, I would choose to . . .

  a. tell it aloud to someone, or hear an audiotape recording or a song about it. 1 2 3

  b. see pictures of it, or read a description. 1 2 3

  c. replay it in some practice rehearsal, using movements such as dance, play acting, or drill. 1 2 3

9. When I cook something new, I like to . . .

  a. have someone tell me the directions, a friend or TV show. 1 2 3

  b. read the recipe and judge by how it looks. 1 2 3

  c. use many pots and dishes, stir often, and taste-test. 1 2 3

10. My emotions can often be interpreted from my . . .

  a. voice quality. 1 2 3

  b. facial expression. 1 2 3

  c. general body tone. 1 2 3

11. When driving, I . . .

  a. turn on the radio as soon as I enter the car. 1 2 3

  b. like quiet so I can concentrate. 1 2 3

  c. shift my body position frequently to avoid getting tired. 1 2 3

12. In my free time, I like to . . .

  a. listen to the radio, talk on the telephone, or attend a musical event. 1 2 3

  b. go to the movies, watch TV, or read a magazine or book. 1 2 3

  c. get some exercise, go for a walk, play games, or make things. 1 2 3

■ SCORING

Add up the points for all the "a's," then all the "b's," then all the "c's."

Total points for all "a's": _____

Total points for all "b's": _____

Total points for all "c's": _____

■ INTERPRETATION

If "a" has the highest score, that indicates your learning style preference is principally *auditory*.

If "b" has the highest score, your learning style preference is principally *visual*.

If "c" has the highest score, your learning style preference is *kinesthetic*.

If all scores are reasonably equal, that indicates your learning style preference is *mixed*.

See the text for explanations.

People have four ways in which they favor learning new material: *auditory, visual, kinesthetic,* and *mixed modality.*[9] Let's consider these.

AUDITORY LEARNING STYLE. Auditory has to do with listening and also speaking. _**Auditory learners**_ **use their voices and their ears as the primary means of learning.** They recall what they hear and what they themselves express verbally.

"When something is hard to understand, they want to talk it through," write professors Adele Ducharme and Luck Watford of Valdosta State University in Georgia. "When they're excited and enthusiastic about learning, they want to verbally express their response. . . .

These learners love class discussion, they grow by working and talking with others, and they appreciate a teacher taking time to explain something to them."[10]

If you're this type of person, it's important to know that such learners are easily distracted by sounds. Thus, it's a good idea that they *not* listen to the radio while studying, because they attend to all the sounds around them. An effective study technique, however, is to repeat something aloud several times because that helps them memorize it. These types of learners may do well in learning foreign languages, music, and other subjects that depend on a strong auditory sense.

VISUAL LEARNING STYLE. Visual, of course, refers to the sense of sight. *__Visual learners__* **like to see pictures of things described or words written down.** "They will seek out illustrations, diagrams, and charts to help them understand and remember information," say Ducharme and Watford. "They appreciate being able to follow what a teacher is presenting with material written on an overhead transparency or in a handout." For visual learners, an effective technique for reviewing and studying material is to read over their notes and recopy and reorganize information in outline form.

KINESTHETIC LEARNING STYLE. *Kinesthetic* (pronounced "kin-es-*thet*-ik") has to do with the sense of touch and of physical manipulation. *__Kinesthetic learner__*s **learn best when they touch and are physically involved in what they are studying.** These are the kind of people who fidget when they have to sit still and who express enthusiasm by jumping up and down. "These learners want to act out a situation, to make a product, to do a project, and in general to be busy with their learning," say Ducharme and Watford. "They find that when they physically do something, they understand it and they remember it."

MIXED-MODALITY LEARNING STYLE. Modality (pronounced "moh-*dal*-it-y") means style. As you might guess, *__mixed-modality learners__* **are able to function in any three of these learning styles or "modalities"— auditory, visual, and kinesthetic.** Clearly, these people are at an advantage because they can handle information in whatever way it is presented to them.

LEARNING STYLES, LECTURES, & READING. Lectures would seem to favor auditory learners. Textbooks would seem to favor visual learners. Lectures and readings are the two principal pipelines by which information is conveyed in college.

However, suppose one or both of these methods don't suit you? Since you don't usually have a choice about how a subject is taught, it's important to get comfortable with both methods. This means you need to be able to *extract* the most information out of a lecture or textbook—that is, take useful notes, for example—regardless of your learning preference and the instructor's style. Chapters 6 and 7 show how to do this.

How to Improve Your Memory Power

PREVIEW There are several principal strategies for converting short-term memory to long-term memory: (1) You can practice relaxation. (2) You can practice repeatedly, even overlearn material. (3) You can study a little at a time repeatedly (distributed practice) instead of cramming (massed practice). (4) You can avoid memory interference from studying similar material or being distracted. (5) You can make material personally meaningful to you. (6) You can use verbal memory aids—write out or organize information; use rhymes, phrases, and abbreviations; make up narrative stories. (7) You can use visual memory aids—make up a vivid picture or story of unusual images.

As should be clear by now, *success in college principally lies with a strategy in which you convert short-term memories into long-term memories.* Let me suggest a number of techniques for doing this.

1. RELAX & BE ATTENTIVE. You have certainly discovered that you easily recall those things that interest you—things to which you were *attentive*. *"Attention is conscious, not reflex,"* says one memory expert (the emphasis is hers). "It is indispensable to the controlled recording of information."[11]

The goal of improving your memory, then, is to improve your attention, as we explain in this section. The first means for doing this is through relaxation. Anxiety interferes with memorizing, distracting your recall abilities with negative worries. When you are relaxed, your mind captures information more easily.

Thus, when you sit down to read a textbook, write notes for a lecture, or take a test, take a few seconds to *become relaxed*. Close your eyes, take a deep breath, inhale, repeat. Say to yourself, "I plan to remember." If you're still tense, repeat this a few times.

The rule here, then, is: *Put yourself in a relaxed frame of mind when you're planning to absorb information you will have to remember later.*

2. PRACTICE REPEATEDLY—EVEN OVERLEARN MATERIAL. How well could you play a part in a play after two readings? five readings? fifteen? Clearly, you can't just speed-read or skim the script. You have to actively practice or rehearse the material. The more you rehearse, the better you retain information. Indeed, it has been found that *overlearning*—continued study even after you think you have learned the material—will help you really commit it to memory.[12] *Overlearning* **is defined as continued rehearsal of material after you first appeared to have mastered it.**[13]

A good way to learn is to repeatedly test your knowledge in order to rehearse it. Some textbooks come with self-testing study guides to help you do this, but you can also make up the questions yourself or form a study group with friends to trade questions and answers.

The more you rehearse, in fact, the better you may also *understand* the material.[14] This is because as you review your mind begins to concentrate on the most important features, thus helping your understanding.

The rule, then, is: *Study or practice repeatedly to fix material firmly in mind.* You can apply this rule to your social life, too. If you meet someone new at a party, for instance, you can repeat the person's name on being introduced, then say it again to yourself; then wait a minute and say it again.

3. STUDY A LITTLE AT A TIME FREQUENTLY: DISTRIBUTED PRACTICE VERSUS MASSED PRACTICE. Learning experts distinguish between two kinds of learning or practice techniques: massed practice and distributed practice.

- *Massed practice:* Massed practice is what students do when they are cramming. *Massed practice* **is putting all your studying into one long period of time**—for example, one study session of 8 hours in one day.

- *Distributed practice:* Distributed practice takes no more time than cramming. **With** *distributed practice* **you distribute the same number of hours over several days**—for example, four days of studying 2 hours a day.

Distributed practice has been found to be more effective for retaining information than mass practice, especially if the space between practice periods is reasonably long, such as 24 hours.[15] One reason is that studying something at different times links it to a wider variety of associations.[16]

The rule here, therefore, is: *Study or practice a little at a time frequently rather than a lot infrequently.* This rule suggests you can make use of the time-spaces in your day for studying. You can look over your notes or books or flash cards while on the bus, for example, or waiting for class to start. You can mentally rehearse lists while standing in line. It's like the difference between lifting weights once for 5 hours or five sessions of 1 hour each: the first way won't train you nearly as well as the second way.

4. AVOID INTERFERENCE. Learning some kinds of information will interfere with your ability to recall other kinds of information, especially if the subjects are similar. *Interference* **is the competition among related memories.** For example, if you tried to memorize the names of the bones in the feet and then memorize the names of the bones in the hand, one memory will interfere with the other. (*Proactive interference* is the disruption an older memory produces on a newer one. *Retroactive interference* is the disruption a newer memory produces on an older one.) And the more information you learn, such as lists of words, the more you may have trouble with new information on successive days, such as new lists of words.[17]

Interference can also come from other things, such as distractions from the people you share your living space with, background music, television, and so on. The notion of interference also suggests why you do better at recalling information when it is fresh in mind. In other words, though I don't recommend cramming for exams, I do recommend giving information a thorough last-minute review before you go into the test. A last-minute review puts the "frosting on the cake" of helping you absorb the material, but it's no substitute for studying the material earlier.

The lesson here is: *When you're trying to memorize material, don't study anything else that is too similar too soon.* This is why it is often a good idea to study before going to sleep: there is less chance of the new information getting competition from other information.[18] It also shows why it's a good idea to study similar material for different courses on different days.[19]

5. MAKE MATERIAL MEANINGFUL TO YOU: DEPTH OF PROCESSING. Information in memory may be stored at a superficial or at a deep level, depending on how well you understood it and how much you thought about it, according to the *depth-of-processing principle*.[20] **The *depth-of-processing principle* states that how shallowly or deeply you hold a thought depends on how much you think about it and how many associations you form with it.** The deeper the level of "processing" or thinking, the more you remember it.

This means that in memorizing something you shouldn't just mindlessly repeat the material; you are better able to remember it when you can make it meaningful.[21] It's important to somehow make the material your own—understand it, organize it, put it in your own words, develop emotional associations toward it, associate it with information you already know or events you have already experienced. For example, if you are trying to remember that business organizations have departments that perform five functions—accounting, marketing, production, personnel management, and research—you can look for relationships among them. Which departments do or do not apply to you? Which ones do your relatives work in? Indeed, one way to make material meaningful to you is to *organize* it in some way, which is why outlining your reading can be a useful tool.

To repeat, the rule here is: *Make learning personally meaningful to you.* This is also a trick you can use in your social life. If you meet someone new at a party, you can try to remember the new name by associating it with the face of someone else with that name. (When you meet someone named Kirk, remember that your uncle is named Kirk too, or think of actor Kirk Douglas or of *Star Trek*'s Captain Kirk.)

"What device or approach have you found most useful for helping you remember things you're trying to learn?"

Name: Laura Marsick

Major: General Studies

Family & Work Situation: Two parents, sister; work as lifeguard

Interests: Swimming, volleyball, music

Answer to question: "I find that making up little rhymes to remember things works best. If I can put material into a rhyme, I have a better chance of remembering it."

6. USE VERBAL MEMORY AIDS. One way to make information more meaningful, and so retain it better, is to use memory aids— and the more you are able to personalize them, the more successful they will be. Psychologists call memory aids *mnemonic* ("nee-*mahn*-ik") *devices,* **tactics for making things memorable by making them distinctive.**

Some verbal devices for enhancing memory are as follows:

- *Write out your information:* This advice may seem obvious. Still, the evidence is that if you write out a shopping list, for example, but lose it, you are more apt to remember the items than if you didn't write them out.[22] Clearly, this is a reason for taking notes during a lecture, quite apart from making a record: the very act of writing helps you retain information.

- *Organize your information:* People are better able to memorize material when they can organize it. This is one reason why imposing a ranking or hierarchy, such as an outline, on lecture notes or reading notes works so well, especially when the material is difficult.[23]

- *Use rhymes to remember important ideas:* You may have heard the spelling rule, "I before E except after C" (so that you'll be correct in spelling "receive," not "recieve"). This an example of the use of rhyme as a memory aid. Another is "Thirty days hath September, April, June, and November. . . ."

   Most of the time, of course, you'll have to make up your own rhymes. It doesn't matter how silly they are. Indeed, the sillier they are, the better you may be able to remember them.

- *Use phrases whose first letters represent ideas you want to remember:* Probably the first thing music students learn is "*Every Good Boy Does Fine*" to remember what notes designate the lines of the musical staff: *E G B D F.* This is an example of using a phrase in which the first letter of each word is a cue to help you recall abstract words beginning with the same letter.

   What kind of sentence would you make up to remember that business organizations have departments performing five functions—*Accounting, Marketing, Production, Personnel* management, and *Research?* (Maybe it would be, "*Any Man Playing Poker is Rich*"—this also plants a picture in your mind that will help your recall.)

- *Use a word whose first letters represent ideas you want to remember:* To remember the five business functions above, you could switch the words around and have the nonsense word *PRAMP* (to rhyme with "ramp," then think of, say, a wheelchair ramp or a ramp with a pea rolling down it), the letters of which stand for the first letters of the five functions.

   A common example of the use of this device is the name "Roy G. Biv," which students use to memorize the order of colors in the light spectrum: *r*ed, *o*range, *y*ellow, *g*reen, *b*lue, *i*ndigo, *v*iolet. Another is "Mark's Very Elegant Mother Just Sent Us Nine Puppies" for the order of the planets in our solar system: Mercury, Venus, Earth, Mars, Jupiter, Saturn, Uranus, Neptune, Pluto.

■ **Make up a narrative story that associates words:** In a technique known as the narrative story method, **it has been found that making up a narrative, or story, helps students recall unrelated lists of words by giving them meaning and linking them in a specific order.**[24]

Suppose you need to memorize the words *Rustler, Penthouse, Mountain, Sloth, Tavern, Fuzz, Gland, Antler, Pencil, Vitamin.* This is quite a mixed bag, but if you were taking a French class, you might have to memorize these words (in the foreign language). Here is the story that was constructed to help recall these unrelated words:

A Rustler *lived in a* Penthouse *on top of a* Mountain. *His specialty was the three-toed* Sloth. *He would take his captive animals to a* Tavern, *where he would remove* Fuzz *from their* Glands. *Unfortunately, all this exposure to sloth fuzz caused him to grow* Antlers. *So he gave up his profession and went to work in a* Pencil *factory. As a precaution he also took a lot of* Vitamin E.[25]

In using verbal memory tricks, then, the rule is: *Make up verbal cues that are meaningful to you to represent or associate ideas.* In social situations, as when you are introduced to several people simultaneously, you can try using some of these devices. For example, "LAP" might represent Larry, Ann, and Paul.

7. USE VISUAL MEMORY AIDS. Some psychologists theorize that using visual images creates a second set of cues in addition to verbal cues that can help memorization.[26] In other words, it helps if you can mentally "take photographs" of the material you are trying to retain.

There are two visual memory aids you may find useful—a single unusual visual image, or a series of visual images.

■ **Make up a vivid, unusual picture to associate ideas:** The stranger and more distinctive you can make your image, the more you are apt to be able to remember it.[27]

Thus, to remember the five business functions (research, accounting, marketing, personnel management, production), you might create a picture of a woman with a white laboratory coat (research) looking through a magnifying glass at a man a'counting money (accounting) while sitting in a food-market shopping cart (marketing) that is being pushed by someone wearing a letter sweater that says *Person L* (personnel) who is watching a lavish Hollywood spectacle—a production—on a movie screen (production). (If you wish, you could even draw a little sketch of this while you're trying to memorize it.)

■ **Make up a story of vivid images to associate ideas:** A visual trick called the method of loci (pronounced "loh-sigh" and meaning "method of places") is to memorize a series of places and then use a different vivid image to associate each place with an idea or a word you want to remember.[28]

For example, you might use buildings and objects along the route from your house to the campus, or from the parking lot to a classroom, each one associated with a specific word or idea. Again, the image associated with each location should be as distinctive as you can make it. To remember the information, you imagine yourself proceeding along this route, so that the various locations cue the various ideas. (The locations need not resemble the ideas. For example, you might associate a particular tree with a man in a white laboratory coat in its branches—research.)

In short, when using visual memory tricks, the rule is: *the more bizarre you make the picture, the more you are apt to remember it.*

MEMORIZING TECHNIQUES REVISITED. Get relaxed. Rehearse repeatedly. Study small amounts of information frequently. Avoid interference from similar material or distractions. Make material personally meaningful to you. Use distinctive verbal and visual memory cues.

Perhaps you've noticed something I'm doing in these pages: I am using the trick of repetition, telling you the principles of memorization three times. Does this help you retain the information? If not, stop here and look back through the preceding pages.

Onward

PREVIEW Rehearse it often, make it meaningful.

n this chapter I described the general strategies of memorization. In general, they may be summarized as two principles: (1) *Rehearse it often.* (2) *Make it meaningful to you.* In the upcoming chapters, I'll show you some refinements, such as how to apply these strategies to your reading assignments, lecture notes, and test taking.

NOTES

1. Haber, R. N. (1979). Twenty years of haunting eidetic imagery: Where's the ghost? *Behavioral & Brain Sciences, 2,* 583–629.

2. Lapp, D. C. (1992, December). (Nearly) total recall. *Stanford Magazine,* pp. 48–51.

3. Lapp, 1992, p. 48.

4. Crovitz, H. F., & Schiffman, H. (1974). Frequency of episodic memories as a function of their age. *Bulletin of the Psychonomic Society, 4,* 517–18.

5. Ebbinghaus, H. (1913). *Memory.* New York: Teachers College. (Original work published 1885.)

6. Survey by National Institute for Development and Administration, University of Texas. Cited in: Lapp, 1992.

7. Pauk, W. (1989). *How to study in college* (4th ed.). Boston: Houghton Mifflin, p. 92.

8. Pauk, 1989, p. 92.

9. Guild & Garger, 1986. Cited in: Ducharme, A., & Watford, L., Explanation of assessment areas (handout).

10. Ducharme & Watford.

11. Lapp, 1992, p. 49.

12. Krueger, W. C. F. (1929). The effect of overlearning on retention. *Journal of Experimental Psychology, 12,* 71 - 78.

13. Weiten, W., Lloyd, M. A., & Lashley, R. L. (1990). *Psychology applied to modern life: Adjustment in the 90s* (3rd ed.). Pacific Grove, CA: Brooks/Cole.

14. Bromage, B. K., & Mayer, R. E. (1986). Quantitative and qualitative effects of repetition on learning from technical text. *Journal of Educational Psychology, 78*(4), 271–78.

15. Zechmeister, E. B., & Nyberg, S. E. (1982). *Human memory: An introduction to research and theory.* Pacific Grove, CA: Brooks/Cole.

16. Kalat, J. W. (1990). *Introduction to psychology* (2nd ed.). Belmont, CA: Wadsworth, p. 295.

17. Underwood, B. J. (1957). Interference and forgetting. *Psychological Review, 64,* 49 - 60.

18. Fowler, M. J., Sullivan, M. J., & Ekstrand, B. R. (1973). Sleep and memory. *Science, 179,* 302–304.

19. Thorndyke, P. W., & Hayes-Roth, B. (1979). The use of schemata in the acquisition and transfer of knowledge. *Cognitive Psychology, 11,* 83–106.

20. Craik, F. I. M., & Lockhart, R. S. (1972). Levels of processing: A framework for memory research. *Journal of Verbal Learning & Verbal Behavior, 11,* 671–84.

21. Raugh, M. R., & Atkinson, R. C. (1975). A mnemonic method for learning a second-language vocabulary. *Journal of Educational Psychology, 67,* 1–16.

22. Intons-Peterson, M. J., & Fournier, J. (1986). External and internal memory aids: When and how often do we use them? *Journal of Experimental Psychology: General, 116,* 267–80.

23. Bower, G. H. (1970). Organizational factors in memory. *Cognitive Psychology, 1,* 18–46.

24. Bower, G. H., & Clark, M. C. (1969). Narrative stories as mediators of serial learning. *Psychonomic Science, 14,* 181–82.

25. Weiten, W., Lloyd, M. A., & Lashley, R. L. (1990). *Psychology applied to modern life: Adjustment in the 90s* (3rd ed.). Pacific Grove, CA: Brooks/Cole, p. 24. Adapted from Bower & Clark, 1969.

26. Paivio, A. (1986). *Mental representations: A dual coding approach.* New York: Oxford University Press.

27. McDaniel, M. A., & Einstein, G. O. (1986). Bizarre imagery as an effective memory aid: The importance of distinctiveness. *Journal of Experimental Psychology: Learning, Memory & Cognition, 12,* 54–65.

28. Crovitz, H. F. (1971). The capacity of memory loci in artificial memory. *Psychonomic Science, 24,* 187–88.

CLASSROOM ACTIVITIES

1. *How's your memory?* Ask each student to take a few minutes to make up a list of 14 terms (not people) related to some *one* subject with which he or she is familiar. (Examples: cars, health, the college.) For the 15th term, have them add the name of a famous person, such as a movie actor.

   Ask students to swap lists face down with someone else in the class. When everyone has someone else's list, have them turn them over and take 10 seconds (being timed by you) to try to memorize the 15 terms. Then tell them to turn the piece of paper over and write as many terms as they can on the back.

   In class discussion, ask students how many terms they were able to remember in 10 seconds. Did everyone recall the name of the movie star or other person on this list? What does this experiment say about people's ability to remember new terms they will need to memorize in a subject they've never studied before?

2. *What's your favorite learning style?* Have students look at their scores in response to Personal Exploration #5.1, "How Do You Learn Best?" Do they individually tend to favor the auditory, visual, kinesthetic, or mixed-modality learning style?

   Have students read the text for an explanation of what their scores mean. Then divide the class into small groups (three to five students) for discussion of their learning style. Have them consider such questions as: Does your learning style suggest you will learn some subjects more easily than you will others? Will you have difficulty learning from lectures or from reading, probably the two principal means by which knowledge is conveyed in college (and in life)? What should you resolve to do if you've found out that you have a harder time learning by some methods than others?

3. *Finding examples of the seven memorizing strategies.* Divide the class into seven small groups with nearly equal numbers of people in each group. Each group should take *one* of the seven memorizing strategies discussed: relaxation, over-learning, distributed practice, avoiding interference, depth of processing, verbal memory aids, visual memory aids. With others in the group, have each student come up with as many ways as possible to illustrate how they could use the particular learning strategy. Later have them share the best examples with others in the class. Invite discussion or other examples from the class.

JOURNAL ENTRY #5.1: WHAT ARE THE TOUGHEST SUBJECTS TO MEMORIZE? What subjects do you worry you will have the most trouble memorizing? Why is this? What tricks can you use from this chapter to change this?

_____

_____

_____

_____

_____

_____

_____

_____

JOURNAL ENTRY #5.2: WHAT HAVE YOU HAD TO MEMORIZE IN THE PAST? In what kind of areas have you had to do extensive memorizing in the past? Examples might be music, athletic moves or plays, dramatic roles, or skills in conjunction with a job. What motivated you to remember? How did you go about doing the memorization?

_____

_____

_____

_____

_____

_____

_____

_____

JOURNAL ENTRY #5.3: WHAT IS YOUR BEST LEARNING STYLE? Which is your predominant learning style—sight, hearing, or touch? What kind of work can you do to improve your skills with other learning styles?

_____

_____

_____

_____

_____

_____

_____

_____

JOURNAL ENTRY #5.4: WHAT NAMES OR AREAS OUTSIDE OF COLLEGE DO YOU NEED TO DO MEMORIZING? Think of some nonacademic areas in which it might be useful for you to do extensive memorizing. For example, you might want to learn the names of everyone where you work, or features of the product or service associated with your work. Or you might want to memorize some features of the city in which you live, such as various commute routes. How would you go about a program of memorizing?

_____

_____

_____

_____

_____

_____

_____

_____

6 lectures

the importance of note taking

IN THIS CHAPTER: Now we come to some techniques that will truly benefit you for the rest of your life:

■ *Making lectures work:* Whatever you think of lectures, they can be made to work for you.

■ *Memorizing material:* How to use the "5R steps" to memorize information from a lecture.

■ *Optimizing the classroom:* How to fight boredom and fatigue.

Lecturing may be an efficient way for instructors to convey information. Is it a good way for students to receive it?

I do a great deal of teaching through discussion and small-group activities, but I also do a fair amount of lecturing, as do most instructors. Lecturing is certainly an easy way for instructors to transfer knowledge—they talk and students listen. Perhaps this is why the lecture system is one of the mainstays of college teaching. Whether it is efficient for any given student, however, depends a lot on his or her preferred learning style.

Lectures, Learning Styles, & Life

PREVIEW Because you can't control the way information is conveyed to you, either in college or in your career, it's important to become comfortable with the lecture method. This means discovering how to extract material from the lecture and learn it.

Of the four learning styles I described in Chapter 5—auditory, visual, kinesthetic, and mixed modality—lectures would seem to favor auditory learners. *Auditory learners*, you'll recall, use their voices and their ears as the primary means of learning.

But suppose you're not an auditory learner. That is, suppose you're a *visual learner* and favor pictures or words written down. Or you're *kinesthetic* and favor touching and physical involvement. (If you're *the mixed-modality type*, you can function in all three learning styles.)

In the work world, too, you don't always have a choice about the method by which information is conveyed to you. You may often have to attend a meeting, presentation, speech, or company training program. There, as I pointed out earlier, the "examination" will consist of how well you recall and handle the information in order to do your job.

It's important, therefore, that you learn to get comfortable with the lecture method of teaching. Thus, you have two tasks:

- ■ *Be able to extract material:* You need to be able to *extract* the most information out of a lecture—that is, take useful notes, regardless of your learning preference and the instructor's style.

- ■ *Be able to learn material:* You need to be able to *learn* the lecture material so that you can do well on tests.

The rest of this chapter shows you how to accomplish this.

Making Lectures Work: What They Didn't Tell You in High School

PREVIEW Cutting classes has been found to be associated with poor grades. Being in class, even a boring one, helps you learn what the instructor expects. It also reflects your attitude about your college performance—whether you want to get successfully through school or merely slide by. Being an active participant means bringing syllabus and textbooks to class and doing the homework and reviewing previous assignments in order to be ready for each new lecture.

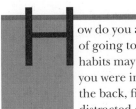

ow do you approach the whole matter of going to class? Many of your classroom habits may have been picked up while you were in high school. Do you sit in the back, find yourself constantly distracted during lectures, have difficulty taking notes? To get an idea of your present performance in the classroom, try Personal Exploration #6.1.

LISTENING QUESTIONNAIRE: HOW'S YOUR CLASSROOM PERFORMANCE?

Read each statement and decide how the habit reflects your listening. Answer as follows:

"Yes"—if you use the habit over half your listening time.
"No"—if you don't use the habit very much at all.
"Sometimes"—if you use the habit periodically.

1. Do you often doodle while listening?

   ❑ Yes
   ❑ No
   ❑ Sometimes

2. Do you show attending behaviors through your eye contact, posture, and facial expressions?

   ❑ Yes
   ❑ No
   ❑ Sometimes

3. Do you try to write down everything you hear?

   ❑ Yes
   ❑ No
   ❑ Sometimes

4. Do you listen largely for central ideas as opposed to facts and details?

   ❑ Yes
   ❑ No
   ❑ Sometimes

5. Do you often daydream or think about personal concerns while listening?

   ❑ Yes
   ❑ No
   ❑ Sometimes

6. Do you ask clarifying questions about what you do not understand in a lecture?

   ❑ Yes
   ❑ No
   ❑ Sometimes

7. Do you frequently feel tired or sleepy when attending a lecture?

   ❑ Yes
   ❑ No
   ❑ Sometimes

8. Do you mentally review information as you listen to make connections among points?

   ❑ Yes
   ❑ No
   ❑ Sometimes

9. Do you often call a lecture boring?

   ❑ Yes
   ❑ No
   ❑ Sometimes

10. Do you recall what you already know about a subject before the lecture begins?

    ❑ Yes
    ❑ No
    ❑ Sometimes

11. Do you generally avoid listening when difficult information is presented?

    ❑ Yes
    ❑ No
    ❑ Sometimes

12. Do you pay attention to the speaker's nonverbal cues?

    ❑ Yes
    ❑ No
    ❑ Sometimes

13. Do you often find yourself thinking up arguments to refute the speaker?

    ❑ Yes
    ❑ No
    ❑ Sometimes

14. Do you generally try to find something of interest in a lecture even if you think it's boring?

    ❑ Yes
    ❑ No
    ❑ Sometimes

(continued on next page)

15. Do you usually criticize the speaker's delivery, appearance, or mannerisms?

❑ Yes

❑ No

❑ Sometimes

16. Do you do what you can to control distractions around you?

❑ Yes

❑ No

❑ Sometimes

17. Do you often fake attention to the speaker?

❑ Yes

❑ No

❑ Sometimes

18. Do you periodically summarize or recapitulate what the speaker has said during the lecture?

❑ Yes

❑ No

❑ Sometimes

19. Do you often go to class late?

❑ Yes

❑ No

❑ Sometimes

20. Do you review the previous class lecture notes before attendin class?

❑ Yes

❑ No

❑ Sometimes

■ SCORING

Count the number of "Yes" answers to *even-numbered* items: _____

Count the number of "Yes" answers to *odd-numbered* items: _____

■ INTERPRETATION: The even-numbered items are considered *effective* listening habits.

The odd-numbered items are considered *ineffective* listening habits.

If you answered an item as "Sometimes," determine how often and under what circumstances you find yourself responding this way. Identify the areas where you have written "Yes" or "Sometimes" to odd-numbered items and write an explanation here:

_____

_____

_____

_____

_____

_____

_____

_____

_____

_____

CLASS ATTENDANCE & GRADES. In high school, I was required to attend every class every school day. What a surprise, then, when I got to college and found that in many classes professors didn't even take attendance and that I was free to cut if I chose. Of course, it was easy to be selective about which classes to go to and which not. In the wintertime, for instance, it wasn't hard to choose between staying in a warm bed and getting up for an 8:00 A.M. class—particularly if I thought that instructor or the subject was boring.

However, in those early days I was not aware of an important fact: *poor class attendance is associated with poor grades.* According to one study, "unsuccessful" students—those defined as having grades of C-minus or below—were found to be more commonly absent from class than "successful" students, those with a B average or above.[1] *(See* ■ *Panel 6.1.)*

"But," students may say, "what if I find the lecture's practically useless? Why should I waste my time?"

There are two answers to this—things they don't usually tell you in high school:

■ *Being in class helps you learn what the instructor expects—and to anticipate exams:* Even if the instructor is so hard to follow that you learn very little from the lectures, it's still important to go to class. "If nothing else," one set of writers points out, "you'll get a feel for how the instructor thinks. This can help you to anticipate the content of exams and to respond in the manner your professor expects."[2]

■ *Going to class goes along with a successful attitude about college in general:* There are probably two kinds of students: passive students, or those who try to slide by in school, and active students, or those who try to triumph in school.

Students who try to *slide by* in school are those who look for all the ways to pass their courses with the least amount of effort: they cut class, borrow other students' notes, cram the night before exams, and so on.

Students who try to *triumph* in school take the attitude that, sure, there are certain shortcuts or efficiencies to making one's way through college (this book is full of such tips). However, they realize that always trying to cut corners is not productive in the long run. Thus, among other things, they try to attend every class.

Which one would an employer want to hire? Here again we have the relevance of college to life outside college: *A can-do attitude in higher education is the kind of quality needed for you to prevail in the world of work.*

BEING AN ACTIVE PARTICIPANT: PREPARING FOR CLASS. Being an active rather than passive student means becoming involved in the course. Besides attending regularly and being on time for class, try to prepare for your upcoming classes, doing the following:

■ *Use the course syllabus as a basic "road map":* The syllabus is a very important document. **The *syllabus* (pronounced "*sill*-uh-buss") is a course outline or guide that tells you what readings are required, what assignments are due when, and when examinations are scheduled.** This basic road map to the course is a page or more that the instructor hands out on the first class day.

PANEL 6.1

Successful and unsuccessful students' class attendance. According to one study, attendance was much better among successful students (B average or above) than unsuccessful students (C– minus or below).

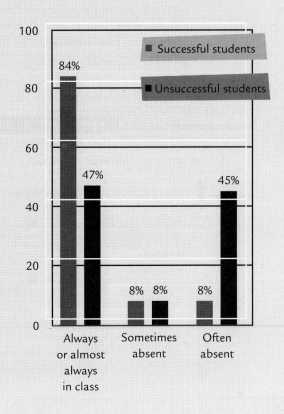

It's a good idea to three-hole-punch the syllabus and include it in the front of your binder or staple it inside the front of your notebook. That way you will automatically bring it to class and can make any changes to it that the instructor announces (such as a new date for a test).

- **Do the homework before the lecture:** A syllabus will often show that certain readings go along with certain lectures. It usually works best if you do the readings *before* rather than after the lectures. Like putting your toe in the water, this will help you know what to expect. If you do the homework first, you'll understand the instructor's remarks better.

- **Anticipate the lecture:** Not only will doing the required readings before class prepare you for the lecture, but so will reading over your lecture notes from the last class. Often the next lecture is a continuation of the last one. In addition, you can look at the syllabus to see what's expected.

  When doing the homework, develop questions on the readings. Bring these to class for clarification.

- **Bring the textbook to class:** Some people come to class carrying only a notebook and pen (and some don't even bring those). Are they the A and B students? If I had to guess, I would say they are not the top grade getters.

  Students who are successful performers in college don't feel they always have to travel light. Besides their notebook they also carry the principal textbook and other books (or supplies) relevant to the course. This is because instructors often make special mention of material in the textbook, or they draw on the text for class discussion. Some instructors even follow the text quite closely in their lectures. Thus, if you have the text in the classroom, you can follow along and make marks in the book, writing down possible exam questions or indicating points of emphasis.

The 5R Steps: Record, Rewrite, Recite, Reflect, Review

PREVIEW Because the greatest amount of forgetting happens in the first 24 hours, you need not just a note-*taking* system but also a note-*reviewing* system. Five steps for committing lecture notes to long-term memory are: Record, Rewrite, Recite, Reflect, and Review.

Many students have the idea that they can simply take notes of a lecture and then review them whenever it's convenient—perhaps the night before a test. And it's easy to think you are doing well when you attend every class and fill page after page of your notebook.

However, simply writing everything down—acting like a human tape recorder—by itself doesn't work. *The name of the game, after all, is to learn the material, not just make a record of it.* Writing things down now but saving all the learning for later is simply not efficient. As I mentioned elsewhere, research shows that the most forgetting takes place within the first 24 hours, then drops off. The trick, then, is to figure out how to reduce the forgetting of that first 24 hours.

Effective learning requires that you be not only a good note *taker* but also a good note *reviewer.* This may mean you need to change the note-taking and note-learning approach you're accustomed to. However, once these new skills are learned, you'll find them invaluable not only in college but also in your career. One method that has been found to be helpful in note taking and note learning consists of five steps known as **the _5R steps_, for Record, Rewrite, Recite, Reflect, Review.** They are:

- **Step 1—Record:** Capture the main ideas.

- **Step 2—Rewrite:** Following the lecture, rewrite your notes, developing key terms, questions, and summaries.

- **Step 3—Recite:** Covering up the key terms, questions, and summaries, practice reciting them to yourself.

- **Step 4—Reflect:** To anchor these ideas, make some personal association with them.

- **Step 5—Review:** Two or three times a week, if possible, review your notes to make them more familiar.

"Too much!" I hear students say. "I've got a lot of things to do. I can't be forever rehashing one lecture!"

Actually, the system may not take as much time as it first looks. Certainly it need not take much more *effort* than if you try to learn it all by cramming—absorbing all the material in one sitting.

In any event, studies show that increased practice or rehearsal not only increases retention. It also improves your *understanding* of material, because as you go over it repeatedly, you are able to concentrate on the most important points.[3]

You probably can appreciate this from your own experience in having developed some athletic, musical, or other skill: the more you did it, the better you got. Like an actor, the more you practice or rehearse the material, the better you will be able to overcome stage fright and deliver your best performance on examination day.

Let's consider what these five steps are:

STEP 1: RECORD. You'll see many of your classmates with pens racing to try to capture every word of the lecture. Don't bother. You're not supposed to be like a court reporter or a secretary-stenographer, recording every word. You should be less concerned with taking down everything than in developing a *system* of note taking. Here is how the system works:

- **Leave blank margins on your note page:** This is a variation on what is known as the *Cornell format* of note taking. *(See Panel 6.2.)* Draw a vertical line, top to

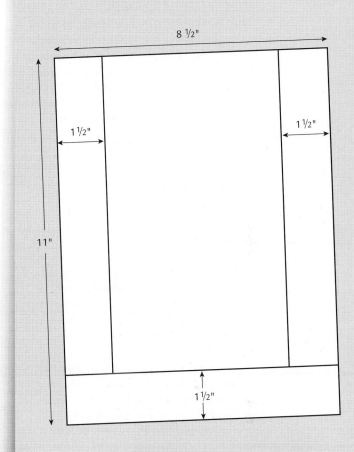

PANEL 6.2

Blank margins. Draw rules on your note paper as shown. (This is a variation on the "Cornell method" of note taking.)

bottom, 1–1/2 inches from the left edge of the paper, a similar line 1–1/2 inches from the right side, and a horizontal line 1–1/2 inches up from the bottom. As I explain below, you will use these blank margins for review purposes.

- **Take notes in rough paragraph form:** At some point you may have been told to take notes in outline form, using the standard "I, A, 1, a," format. If you're good at this, that's fine. However, most professors don't lecture this way, and you should not have to concentrate on trying to force an outline on the lecture material.

Simply take your notes in rough paragraph form. Put extra space (a line or two) between new ideas and divisions of thought. Don't try to save on the cost of notepaper by cramming notes onto every line of the page.

- **Try to capture the main ideas:** Don't try to take down everything the instructor says. Not only will this create a mass of information that you will have to sort through later, it will also interfere with your learning. Instead of forcing you to pay attention and concentrate on what's important, you become simply a tape recorder. An extremely important part of your note-taking system, then, is to try to capture just the key ideas. More on this below.

- **Develop a system of abbreviations:** Some people take highly readable notes, as though preparing to let other people borrow them. You shouldn't concern yourself primarily with this kind of legibility. The main thing is that *you* be able to take ideas down fast and *you* be able to read them later.

Thus, make up your own system of abbreviations. For example, "w.r.t" means "with regard to"; "sike" means "psychology"; "para" is borrowing the Spanish word for "in order to." *(See* ■ *Panel 6.3.)*

By adopting these practices, you'll be well on your way to retaining more information than you have in the past.

STEP 2: REWRITE. *This is extremely important.* The point of this step is to counteract the brain's natural tendency to forget 80% of the information in the first 24 hours.

As soon as possible—on the same day in which you took lecture notes—you should do one of two things:

1. *Either recopy/rewrite your notes, or*

2. *At least go over them to familiarize yourself and to underline key issues and concepts and make notations in the margins.*

Personal shorthand. These are some commonly used abbreviations. If you wish, you can tear out or photocopy this list and tape it inside the cover of your binder or notebook.

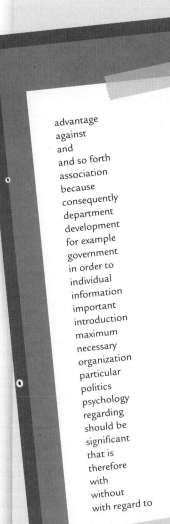

advantage	adv
against	vs
and	+
and so forth	etc
association	assoc
because	bec or cuz
consequently	∴
department	dept
development	devmt
for example	ex or eg
government	govt
in order to	i.o.t.
individual	indiv
information	info
important	impt
introduction	intro
maximum	max
necessary	nec
organization	org
particular	partic
politics	pol
psychology	psych or sike
regarding	re
should be	s/b
significant	signif
that is	i.e.
therefore	∴
with	w/
without	w/o
with regard to	w.r.t.

Of course, it's not *necessary* to recopy your notes. The point I must emphasize, however, is that this very activity will give you the extra familiarization that will help to imprint the information in your mind.

Alternatively, if you don't have time or aren't strongly motivated to rewrite your notes, you should take 5 or 10 minutes to make use of the blank margins you left around your notes. (You should also do this if you rewrite your notes.) Whichever method you use, by rewriting and underlining you reinforce the material, moving it from short-term into long-term memory.

Here's what to do:

- **Read, rewrite, and highlight your notes:** Read your notes over. If you can, rewrite them—copy them over in a separate notebook or type them up on a word processor—with the same margins at the left, right, and bottom as I described above. Now read the notes again, using highlighter pen or underlining to emphasize key ideas.

- **Write key terms in the left margin:** In the left margins, write the key terms and main concepts. *(See ■ Panel 6.4.)* Reviewing these important terms and concepts is a good way of preparing for objective questions on tests, such as true-false or multiple-choice questions.

- **Write one or two questions in the right margin:** On the right side of each page, write two questions about the material on the page. *(See ■ Panel 6.4 again.)* Reviewing these questions later will help you prepare for tests featuring essay questions or subjective questions.

- **Write a summary on the last page:** At the bottom of the last page of that day's notes, summarize in a few words the material in the notes. *(See ■ Panel 6.4 again.)* Some students write these summaries in red or green ink. With this eye-catching color, they can then flip through their notes and quickly take in all the summary information.

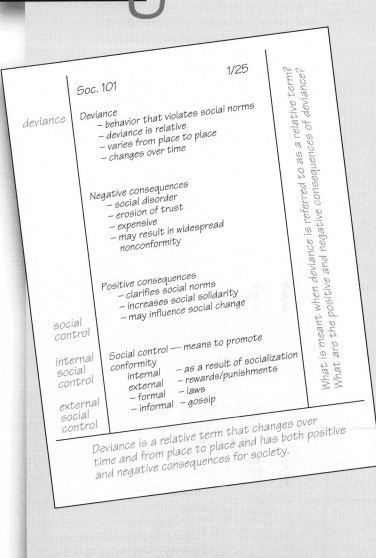

PANEL 6.4 ■ Use of margins.

I cannot stress enough how important it is to take time—*absolutely no later than one day after your class*—to go over your notes, rewriting them if you can but certainly writing key terms, questions, and summaries at the end. *Special note:* If you have a personal computer with a word processing program, the rewriting is not as time consuming as it sounds.

STEP 3: RECITE. Another reinforcement technique is *recitation*. This consists of covering up your detailed notes and using the key terms or concepts in the left margin to say out loud (or under your breath to yourself) what you understand your notes to mean. You can also do this with the questions in the right margin and the summary in the bottom margin.

Recitation is an activity you can do at your desk, on the bus, when you're doing homework, or when you have 5 or 10 minutes between classes. It is a particularly effective reinforcing technique because the activity of verbalizing gives your mind time to grasp the ideas and move them from short-term to long-term memory.

STEP 4: REFLECT. Reflecting is something you can do in the first few minutes you sit in class waiting for the next lecture to begin. You can also do this sitting on the train or bus or in your car.

Look over your notes from the previous class period in the course and try to make some *personal associations* in your mind with the material. Such personal associations will help to anchor the material. For example, if you're learning about European history, imagine how you might link some of these facts to a movie you've seen that was set in that period.

STEP 5: REVIEW. Two or three times a week, review all your notes, using the techniques of recitation and reflection to commit the information to memory. At first you may find that the review takes longer, but as you get more familiar with the material the review will get easier. At the end of the semester or quarter you will then have perhaps 80% of the lecture information stored in your long-term memory. The remaining 20% can be learned in the days before the exam. Unlike the process of cramming, having this much material already memorized will give you much more confidence about your ability to succeed on the test.

Optimizing the Classroom Game

PREVIEW The best way to fight boredom and fatigue in the classroom is to make attending class a game. Three ways to improve your classroom game are to learn (1) to focus your attention, (2) to participate, and (3) to overcome classroom obstacles.

The way to deal with attending class is to treat it as a game. The point of the game is to struggle against two enemies to get the grade you want. The two enemies are *boredom* and *fatigue:*

- **Boredom:** Boredom is a very real factor. Television may have raised our expectations as to how stimulating education ought to be. However, many instructors—indeed, most people in general—can't be that interesting all the time.

- **Fatigue:** Fatigue can also be a real factor. This is particularly so for students who are struggling with other demands, such as those of work and family, or who short themselves on sleep.

As a student, then, you need to turn yourself into an active listener and active participant in the classroom to get past these two hurdles.

Let's consider three ways to improve your classroom game. They are:

- Learning to focus your attention
- Learning to participate
- Learning to overcome classroom obstacles

LEARNING TO FOCUS YOUR ATTENTION. Once you've come to class, what do you do then? You learn to pay attention. Being attentive involves *active listening*, which is different from the kind of passive listening we do when "listening" to television (sucking at the electric bottle, as they say). Active listening is, in one writer's description, "paying attention so that your brain absorbs the meaning of words and sentences."[4]

Being an active listener requires that you do the following:

- ■ *Take listening seriously:*[5] Make up your mind you will listen. Everything begins with your attitude—hence this decision. Students can coast through the college classroom experience yawning, daydreaming, and spacing out, thereby missing a lot, or they can *decide* to listen.

    Making the commitment to learn and taking an active part in obtaining information also improves your ability to remember the material. If you find your mind wandering, pull your thoughts back to the present and review mentally what the speaker has been saying.

- ■ *Sit up front and center:* For a variety of reasons, some students don't want to sit at the front of the class. However, when you go to a musical event or stage performance, you probably *want* to sit down front—because you're interested and you want to see and hear better.

    Sitting in the front and center rows in the classroom will also help you hear and see better, of course. Moreover, the very act of sitting in that place will actually stimulate your interest. This is because you have taken the physical step of *making a commitment*—of putting yourself in a position to participate more. (Also, you'll be less likely to talk to classmates, write letters, or fall asleep if you're where the instructor can see you.)

- ■ *Stay positive and pay attention to content, not delivery:* If you *expect* a lecture to be boring or lacking in content, I guarantee you it will be. By contrast, if you suppress negative thoughts, ignore distractions about the speaker's style of delivery or

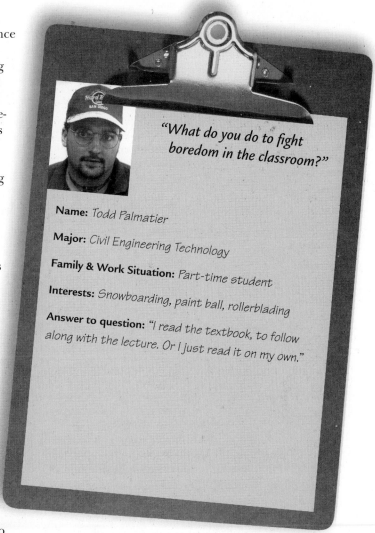

"What do you do to fight boredom in the classroom?"

Name: Todd Palmatier

Major: Civil Engineering Technology

Family & Work Situation: Part-time student

Interests: Snowboarding, paint ball, rollerblading

Answer to question: *"I read the textbook, to follow along with the lecture. Or I just read it on my own."*

body language, and *encourage the instructor with eye contact, interested expression, and attentive posture,* you will find yourself much more involved and interested in the subject matter.

If you find yourself disagreeing with something the speaker says, don't argue mentally, but suspend judgment. (Maybe make a note in the margin and bring the matter up later during class discussion.) Assess the instructor's reasoning, then make up your mind.

- ■ *Listen for "bell" phrases and cues to determine what is important:* All lecturers use phrases and gestures that should "ring a bell" and signal importance.

    A *bell phrase*—also called a *signal word* or *signal phrase*—**is an indicator of an important point. Bell phrases are important because they indicate you** should note what comes after them and remember them. Examples of bell phrases are: "Three major types . . ."; "The most important result is . . ."; "You should remember . . ."; "Because of this . . ."; "First . . . second . . . third . . ."

A *bell cue* is an action or gesture that indicates important points. Examples are (1) diagrams or charts; (2) notes on the board; (3) pointing, as to something on the board or a chart; (4) underlining of, or making a check mark by, keywords; (5) banging a fist; and (6) holding up fingers.

When a class is long or tedious, you can turn it into a game by telling yourself you will try to detect as many bell phrases and cues as possible. Then, every time you pick up one, put a check mark in your notes. You'll find when you do this you'll become more actively involved. Not only does it fight boredom and fatigue but it also increases the quality of your note taking.

Even if you're somewhat shy and hate to get involved in class participation, the preceding suggestions will sharpen your listening skills, comprehension, and memorization, which will help you perform well on tests. If you *really* want to be a peak-performing student, however, you should go to the next step—participation.

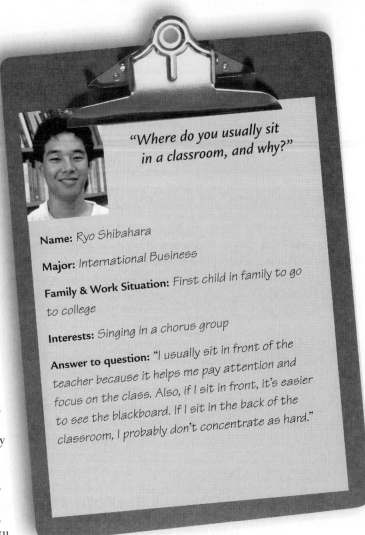

"Where do you usually sit in a classroom, and why?"

Name: Ryo Shibahara

Major: International Business

Family & Work Situation: First child in family to go to college

Interests: Singing in a chorus group

Answer to question: "I usually sit in front of the teacher because it helps me pay attention and focus on the class. Also, if I sit in front, it's easier to see the blackboard. If I sit in the back of the classroom, I probably don't concentrate as hard."

LEARNING TO PARTICIPATE. Are you the type of person who prefers to be invisible in the classroom? No doubt you've noticed many students are. They sit in the back row, never ask questions, and can go an entire semester without talking to the instructor.

In doing this, one can probably scrape by. However, life does not reward the passive. If you ever need a reference from an instructor for a job or for graduate or professional school, how will you know whom to ask if you've never given the instructor an opportunity to know you? When you're starting on your

career, what skills will you be able to draw on to speak up in meetings, give presentations, or persuade authority figures of your point of view? As I've said all along, the skills you practice in the college classroom, regardless of subject, really are practice for life outside of or after college.

For many students, shyness and lack of assertiveness are very real, even incapacitating problems. I deal with these elsewhere in the book (in Chapter 11), and if it's an important issue for you, I urge you to skip ahead and read that material soon. Even those who are not shy or assertive are often reluctant to "make a fool of myself," to risk being laughed at.

> ## *"If you can't let go of the fear of 'being laughed at,' there is a real question as to whether you'll be able to get what you want."*

However, there comes a time in life when, *if you can't push beyond these limitations and let go of the fear of "being laughed at," there is a real question as to whether you'll be able to get what you want in your career and in your relationships.* Learning to participate in a public dialogue is simply part of the growth process.

Class participation, whether in a lecture or a discussion section, further reinforces memorization because it obliges you to become actively engaged with the material and to organize it in your mind. Some suggestions regarding participation are as follows:

- **Do your homework:** There is an understood contract—namely, that you should have kept up with the homework assignments, such as the textbook readings. That way you won't embarrass yourself by asking questions or making remarks about something you are already supposed to have read.

- **Respect the opinions of others:** If the questions or remarks of others seem off-the-wall or biased, don't try to trash them. A spirit of cordiality and absence of intimidation is necessary to keep learning channels open and tempers cool.

- **Follow your curiosity:** We've all had the experience of holding back on asking a question, then hearing someone else raise it and be complimented by the professor with "That's a very good question!" Follow your instincts. You have a right to ask questions, and the more you do so, the more you will perfect this particular art.

LEARNING TO OVERCOME CLASSROOM OBSTACLES. You now know what to do if the instructor or subject matter is boring. What do you do if the instructor speaks too fast or with an accent? If your shorthand or ear is not good enough to keep up, here are some strategies:

- **Do your homework before class:** If you keep up with the reading assignments, doing them before the lecture rather than afterward, you'll often be able to mentally fill in gaps and select key points.

- **Leave holes in your notes:** Whenever you miss something important, leave spaces in your notes, with a big question mark in the margin. Then seek to fill in the missing material through other methods, as explained below.

- **Trade notes with classmates:** If you and others in class take readable notes (even using private shorthand), you can easily make photocopies of your notes and exchange them. Two or three students may find that among them they are able to pick up most of a lecture.

- **Use a tape recorder:** The trick here is not to make a tape recorder a *substitute* for note taking. Then you'll merely be taking the same amount of time to listen to the lecture again—and perhaps still be confused. Use the tape recorder as a backup system, one in which you can use the fast-forward and reverse buttons to go over material you had trouble following in class. (Remember to get permission from the instructor to use a tape recorder in his or her class.)

- **Ask questions—in class or after:** If the instructor has a question period, you can ask questions to clarify what you missed. Or see the instructor after class or during his or her office hours.

  Note: Some students are reluctant to talk to instructors during office hours for fear of "bothering" them. But you're not bothering them; that's what they're there for. Instructors are *paid* to be available for your questions.

Onward

PREVIEW You'll be exposed to lectures all your life.

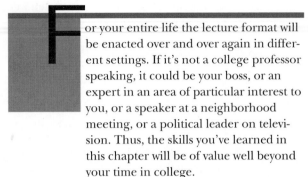

For your entire life the lecture format will be enacted over and over again in different settings. If it's not a college professor speaking, it could be your boss, or an expert in an area of particular interest to you, or a speaker at a neighborhood meeting, or a political leader on television. Thus, the skills you've learned in this chapter will be of value well beyond your time in college.

NOTES

1. Lindgren, H. C. (1969). *The psychology of college success: A dynamic approach.* New York: Wiley.

2. Weiten, W., Lloyd, M. A., & Lashley, R. L. (1990). *Psychology applied to modern life: Adjustment in the 90s* (3rd ed.). Pacific Grove, CA: Brooks/Cole, p. 22.

3. Bromage, B. K., & Mayer, R. E. (1986). Quantitative and qualitative effects of repetition on learning from technical text. *Journal of Educational Psychology, 78*(4), 271–78.

4. Pauk, W. (1989). *How to study in college.* Boston: Houghton-Mifflin, p. 122.

5. Lucas, S. E. (1989). *The art of public speaking.* New York: Random House.

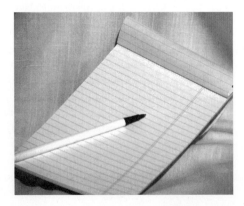

CLASSROOM ACTIVITIES

1. *How well does your learning style suit the lecture method of teaching?* Have the class, in a small- or large-group situation, look back at Personal Exploration #5.1 in Chapter 5. Ask each student to determine which learning style—auditory, visual, kinesthetic, or mixed-modality—he or she seems to favor.

   Then ask students to discuss the following questions: What experiences have you had that make you think you like one learning style better than others (if that's the case)? How well does your learning style relate to the lecture method of presenting information? In a work situation, have you had any difficulty with retaining information from presentations and meetings? Since not everything in life is delivered to you in an easy manner, what kinds of strategies would you recommend for getting the most out of the lecture system?

2. *How's your classroom performance?* Have students look at the results of their Personal Exploration #6.1, "Listening Questionnaire: How's Your Classroom Performance?"

   In a small group situation, ask students to go through this Personal Exploration and discuss some of the items to which they answered "Yes." Discussion questions: What things are you doing right? What things need changing? Since changing one's behavior is not always easy, what kinds of prompts or reinforcement will you give yourself to help you change negative behavior to positive behavior?

3. *What are examples of bell phrases and bell cues?* Ask students to look at their lecture notes from other classes. (Alternatively, have them monitor two of their lectures in other courses this week in preparation for this class discussion.) Questions for discussion: What bell phrases and bell cues do you observe your instructors using? How does putting yourself in a state of alertness to these cues affect your levels of boredom and fatigue?

JOURNAL ENTRY #6.1: SHOULD YOU CHANGE YOUR NOTE-TAKING BEHAVIOR? How should you change your note-taking habits from your accustomed methods?

_____

_____

_____

_____

_____

_____

_____

_____

JOURNAL ENTRY #6.2: WHICH INSTRUCTORS DO YOU HAVE TROUBLE WITH? What kinds of instructors, or what particular instructors, do you have trouble following when they lecture? Why, and what can you do about it?

_____

_____

_____

_____

_____

_____

_____

JOURNAL ENTRY #6.3: ARE YOU TOO SELF-CONSCIOUS ABOUT OTHER STUDENTS? Are you afraid other students will laugh at you for being too obviously engaged in the lecture and learning process? Are you afraid they will consider you some sort of wimp because you're not obviously detached, indifferent, or supposedly cool? Why does this bother you? What does this self-consciousness—this tremendous concern about how people think about you—imply for your future in college or in a career?

_____

_____

_____

_____

_____

_____

_____

JOURNAL ENTRY #6.4: HOW DO YOU RATE YOURSELF AS A STUDENT PERFORMER? For each of the following activities, rate yourself according to the following standard:

A   Excellent
B   Above average
C   Average
D   Below average
F   Poor

1. Active listener in class		A B C D F
2. Consistent attendance		A B C D F
3. Participate and ask questions		A B C D F
4. Involvement in study groups		A B C D F
5. Use of bell cues and bell phrases		A B C D F
6. Do readings prior to class		A B C D F
7. Effectively and consistently use 5 Rs in note-taking		A B C D F

reading

getting everything you need to know from what you read

IN THIS CHAPTER: It's possible you won't have to do much reading after you complete your higher education, except for pleasure or curiosity. More likely, however, because of the explosion of facts caused by information technology, you will have to keep reading to continually update your skills and keep ahead in your career. In this chapter, then, you will learn a valuable skill—namely, *how to read to remember.*

The chapter offers two kinds of reading systems:

■ *Reading System #1:* The SQ3R Method consists of surveying, questioning, reading, reciting, and reviewing.

■ *Reading System #2:* The 3Rs Method consists of reading, recording, and reciting.

Reading is—select one—
(a) fun
(b) boring
(c) difficult

Which describes your feelings? Myself, I always thought reading was fun when I was growing up—provided it was a novel, a magazine, or a newspaper.

Textbooks? Well . . .

As a beginning college student, here's what I would do when I sat down to read a textbook: I would plow through a chapter the way I went through a novel, reading it just one time. I would also deliberately skip over any pictures and tables and charts and chapter summaries, which I thought were "just extra stuff." Thus, I could tell myself "This chapter is really only 24 pages, not 35."

See what I was doing? I was more intent *on simply getting through the assignment as quickly as possible* than on trying to learn it. However, this supposed time-saving method didn't work, for it certainly didn't help me do well on tests.

What are your thoughts about the whole business of reading in higher education? To get an idea, try Personal Exploration #7.1.

Reading for Pleasure Versus Reading for Learning

PREVIEW Reading for pleasure is different from reading for learning. With most pleasure reading you need only remember the information briefly, holding it in your short-term memory. With reading for learning, the information must be stored in your long-term memory, so that you can recall it for tests. This means you must read material more than once. Accordingly, you

need to treat textbooks seriously. You also need to understand what their basic features are—title page, copyright page, table of contents, preface, glossary, appendix, bibliography, and index. Finally, you need to know what "advance organizers" are for purposes of surveying material.

Maybe you already think you read pretty well. After all, you've been doing it for most of your life.

Or maybe you don't feel comfortable about reading. You prefer television to print. Or you think you get information better when someone tells it to you. Or you find English a hard language to follow.

Whatever your skills, *there are techniques to improve your reading abilities so that you can better handle subjects at the level of higher education.* Some of them I'll describe in this chapter. If you don't find what you need here (for example, you feel you need help in reading English as a second language), you can get assistance through your college's learning center or lab.

TWO TYPES OF READING. Reading is principally of two types—for pleasure and for learning:

- **For pleasure:** You can read action-adventure, romances, sports, and similar material just one time, for amusement. This is the kind of material that appears in many novels, magazines, and newspapers. You don't have to read it carefully, unless you want to.

- **For learning:** Most of the other kind of reading you do is for learning of some sort, because you *have* to understand it and perhaps retain it. For instance, you certainly have to pay close attention when you're reading a cookbook or instructions on how to fix a car.

Reading for learning is something you will have to do all your life, whether it's

WHAT DO YOU KNOW ABOUT THE READING PROCESS?

Perhaps you regard the reading of textbooks as a reasonably straightforward activity. Or perhaps you find the whole process dreary or mysterious or scary. Answer "Yes" or "No" depending on whether you agree or disagree with the following statements.

1. Reading makes unusual or unique demands on a reader.

   _____ Yes   _____ No

2. Reading is a form of the thinking process. You read with your brain, not your eyes.

   _____ Yes   _____ No

3. Reading is a one-step process.

   _____ Yes   _____ No

4. Effective readers constantly seek to bring meaning to the text.

   _____ Yes   _____ No

5. Many comprehension problems are not just reading problems.

   _____ Yes   _____ No

6. Good readers are sensitive to how the material they are reading is structured or organized.

   _____ Yes   _____ No

7. Speed and comprehension are independent of each other.

   _____ Yes   _____ No

■ ANSWERS

1. *False.* Reading actually does not make unusual demands on a reader. The same mental processes you use to "read" people's faces or grasp the main idea of a situation you observe are used when you read.

2. *True.* Your eyes simply transmit images to the brain. Improving your reading means improving your thinking, not practicing moving your eyes faster or in a different way.

3. *False.* Reading includes three steps: (a) preparing yourself to read (thinking about what you already know about a subject and setting purposes for reading); (b) processing information; and (c) reacting to what you read.

4. *True.* When they are not comprehending, they take steps to correct the situation.

5. *True.* If you fail to understand something you are reading, it could be because it is poorly written. More likely, however, you lack the background information needed to comprehend—you wouldn't understand it even if someone read it aloud to you. Perhaps you need to read an easier book on the same subject first.

6. *True.* Good readers know the subject matter and main idea of each paragraph and understand how each paragraph is organized (for example, sequence, listing, cause and effect, comparison and contrast, definition).

7. *False.* The more quickly you can understand something, the faster you can read it. However, "speed" without comprehension is meaningless. Reading is more than just allowing your eyes to pass over lines of print.

studying to get a driver's license or finding out how much medicine to give an infant. Indeed, what many managers and administrators are doing all day, when they read reports, letters, and memos, is reading to learn.

But here's the difference between those kinds of reading for learning and reading textbooks: *In higher education, you'll often have to read the same material more than once.* The reason, of course, is that in higher education you have to *understand and memorize* so much of what you read.

READING TO FEED YOUR LONG-TERM MEMORY. "Oh, boy," you may think. "You mean there's no way I can just read stuff once and get it the first time?"

Perhaps you can if you're the sort who can memorize the code to a bicycle or locker combination lock with just one glance. Most people, however, need more practice than that.

This has to do with the notion of short-term memory versus long-term memory. As I described in Chapter 5, the retention of information drops rapidly in the first 24 hours after you've been exposed to it (the "forgetting curve"). Short-term memory is roughly anything you can't hold in mind for more than 24 hours. Long-term memory refers to information you retain for a good deal longer than 24 hours.

Some students might try to make these facts an argument for cramming—holding off until the last day before a test and then reading everything at once. However, there is no way such postponement can really be effective. Many instructors, for instance, have *cumulative* final exams. They test you not just on the new material you're supposed to have learned since the last exam. Rather, they test you on *all* the material back to the beginning of the course. If you opt for cramming, this puts you in the position of having to cram for the *whole course*. In sum: you need to do the kind of reading that will feed your long-term memory.

TREAT TEXTBOOKS SERIOUSLY. Some students regard their textbooks as troublesome or uninteresting but unfortunately necessary (and expensive) parts of their instruction. Or they think of the books as being perhaps useful but not vital (and so they try to avoid buying them).

There's a likelihood, however, that *half or more of your study time will be devoted to such books.* Thus, when you think about what your college education *is*, half of it is in your books. You need, then, to treat them as the tools of your trade (your trade being a student)—just as you would an instruction manual if your job required you, say, to tear down and fix

motorcycles or to lead a tour group around your state.

With that in mind, here are a few tips for extracting some benefits from your textbooks:

- *Look the text over before you take the course:* If you have any doubts about a course you're contemplating taking, take a look in the bookstore at the textbook(s) and any other reading materials that will be required for it. This way you can see what the course will cover and whether it is too advanced or too low-level in the light of your previous experience.

- *Buy your books early:* In my first couple of semesters as a first-year student I would dawdle as long as a week or 10 days before buying some of my books. Not a good idea. The school term flies by awfully fast, and I lost the advantage of a head start. (Also, sometimes when I waited too long the books were sold out.)

- *Look the text over before the first class:* The reason, of course, is that in higher education you have to understand and memorize so much of what you read. If you are familiar with the principal text before you walk into your first class, you will know what the course is going to cover and know how to use the book to help you. Taking a couple of minutes to go from front to back—from title page to index—will tell you what resources the book offers to help you study better.

BECOME FAMILIAR WITH THE BASIC FEATURES. To get a sense of what a book is like, you need to look for eight particular features in the front and back of the book. *(See* ■ *Panel 7.1.)*

- *Title page:* At the front of the book, **the *title page* tells you the title, edition number (if later than the first edition), author, and publisher.** Often the title can give you a sense of the level of difficulty of the book—for example, *Introduction to Business* (introductory level) versus *Intermediate Accounting* (higher level).

- *Copyright page:* **The *copyright page* (on the back of the title page) tells you the date the book was published.** With some

Looking over a textbook.
Principal features to look for in a textbook.

▼ Title page

POPULATION
An Introduction to Concepts and Issues
Fifth Edition

John R. Weeks
San Diego State University

Wadsworth Publishing Company
Belmont, California
A Division of Wadsworth, Inc.

▼ Table of Contents

DETAILED TABLE OF CONTENTS

▼ Copyright page

To Deanna

Editor: Serina Beauparlant
Editorial Assistant: Marla Nowick
Production: Greg Hubit Bookworks
Print Buyer: Randy Hurst
Permissions Editor: Peggy Meehan
Copy Editor: Kathleen McCann
Manuscript Editor: Deanna Weeks
Cover: Henry Breuer
Compositor: Bi-Comp, Incorporated
Printer: Arcata Graphics Fairfield

The cover illustration shows countries in proportion to population. Adapted by the author from United Nations data.

This book is printed on acid-free paper that meets Environmental Protection Agency standards for recycled paper.

© 1992 by Wadsworth, Inc. All rights reserved. No part of this book may be reproduced, stored in a retrieval system, or transcribed, in any form or by any means, without the prior written permission of the publisher, Wadsworth Publishing Company, Belmont, California 94002.

1 2 3 4 5 6 7 8 9 10—96 95 94 93 92

Library of Congress Cataloging in Publication Data
Weeks, John Robert, 1944–
    Population : an introduction to concepts and issues / John R.
Weeks. — 5th ed.
      p. cm.
    Includes bibliographical references and index.
    ISBN 0-534-17346-2
    1. Population. I. Title.
HB871.W43 1992
304.6—dc20
                          92-6251
                          CIP

▼ Preface

PREFACE

Population growth in the 1950s and 1960s could have been likened to a runaway train without an engineer, veering perilously close to a collision course with shortages of food and resources. That specter was altered somewhat by the events of the 1970s, especially by a few hopeful signs of a downturn in the birth rates of several large developing nations. In the 1980s and the 1990s the imagery has changed from the collision course to something equally terrifying. We are faced with a situation analogous to an immense locomotive hurtling down the track at a speed faster than the roadbed can tolerate. The engineer is groping for the brakes, but if and when those brakes are fully applied, the train will still cover a huge distance before it comes to a halt. How much havoc will the charging locomotive of population wreak before it stops, and what condition will we be in at that point? These are two of the most important questions that face the world.

Over the years I have found that most people are either blissfully unaware of the enormous impact that population growth and change have on their lives, or else they have heard so many horror stories about impending doom that they are nearly overwhelmed whenever they think of population growth. My purpose in this book is to shake you out of your lethargy (if you are one of those types), without necessarily scaring you in the process. I will introduce you to the basic concepts of population studies and help you develop your own demographic perspective, enabling you to understand some of the most important issues confronting the world. My intention is to sharpen your perception of population growth and change, to increase your awareness of what is happening and why, and to help prepare you to cope with (and help shape) a future that will be shared with billions more people than there are today.

(continued next page)

▼ Bibliography

BIBLIOGRAPHY

14 Abelson, P.
    1975a "The world's disparate food supplies."
           Science 187: editorial.
14 1975b "Food and nutrition." Science 188
           (4188):501.
11 Adamchak, D., A. Wilson, A. Nyanguru, and J.
    Hampson
    1991 "Elderly support and intergenerational
          transfer in Zimbabwe: an analysis by
          gender, marital status, and place of
          residence." The Gerontologist 31:505–
          13.
4   Adelman, C.
    1982 "Saving babies with a signature." Wall
          Street Journal, 28 July.
5   Adlakha, A., and D. Kirk
    1974 "Vital rates in India 1961–71 estimated
          from 1971 census data." Population
          Studies 28(3):381–400.
7   Agassi, J., and I. C. Jarvie
    1959 Hong Kong. London: Oxford Press.
8   Ahlburg, D., and M. Schapiro
    1984 "Socioeconomic ramifications of chang-
          ing cohort size: an analysis of U.S. post-
          war suicide rates by age and sex." De-
          mography 21(1):97–105.
6   Ahonsi, B.
    1991 "Report on the seminar on anthropologi-
          cal studies relevant to the sexual trans-
          mission of HIV, Sonderborg, Denmark,
          1990." IUSSP Newsletter 41:79–103.
4   Akin, J., R. Bilsbarrow, D. Guilkey, B. Popkin, D.
    Benoit, P. Cantrelle, M. Garenne, and P. Levi
    1981 "The determinants of breast-feeding in
          Sri Lanka." Demography 18(3):287–
          308.

4   Akpom, C., K. Akpom, and M. Davis
    1976 "Prior sexual behavior of teenagers at-
          tending rap sessions for the first time."
          Family Planning Perspectives 8:203–6.
12 Alba, R., and J. Logan
    1991 "Variations on two themes: racial and
          ethnic patterns in the attainment of sub-
          urban residence." Demography 28:431–
          53.
16 Allan, C.
    1981 "Measuring mature markets." American
          Demographics 3(3):13–17.
1,12 Alonso, W., and P. Starr
    1982 "The political economy of national sta-
          tistics." Social Science Research Council
          Items 36(3):29–35.
16 Alsop, R.
    1984 "Firms still struggle to devise best ap-
          proach to black buyers." Wall Street
          Journal, 25 October.
    American Demographics
    1982 "The demographic future." The
          Monthly Report of International Demo-
          graphics (brochure).
16 1983 "Here comes 1984." American Demo-
          graphics 5(6):11.
6   Anderson, B., and B. Silver
    1989 "Patterns of cohort mortality in the So-
          viet population." Population and Devel-
          opment Review 15:471–502.
    Ankrah, E. M.
    1991 "AIDS and the social side of health." So-
          cial Science and Medicine 32:967–80.
8   Aries, P.
    1962 Centuries of Childhood. New York: Vin-
          tage Books.

530

▼ Appendix

APPENDIX
The Life Table,
Net Reproduction Rate,
and Standardization

THE LIFE TABLE
  Probability of Dying
  Deaths in the Life Table
  Number of Years Lived
  Expectation of Life
  Other Applications of the Life Table

NET REPRODUCTION RATE AND MEAN LENGTH OF GENERATION

STANDARDIZATION

509

▼ Glossary

GLOSSARY

This glossary contains words or terms that appeared in boldface type in the text. I have tried to include terms that are central to an understanding of the study of population. The chapter notation in parentheses refers to the chapter in which the term is first discussed in detail.

abortion the expulsion of a fetus prematurely; a miscarriage—may be either induced or spontaneous (Chapter 4).

abridged life table a life table (see definition) in which ages are grouped into categories (usually five-year age groupings) (Appendix).

accidental death loss of life unrelated to disease of any kind but attributable to the physical, social, or economic environment (Chapter 6).

achieved characteristics those sociodemographic characteristics such as education, occupation, income, marital status, and labor force participation, over which we do have some degree of control (Chapter 9).

age/sex pyramid graph of the number of people in a population by age and sex (Chapter 8).

age/sex–specific death rate the number of people of a given age and sex who died in a given year divided by the total number of people of that age and sex (Chapter 6).

age-specific fertility rate the number of children born to women of a given age divided by the total number of women that age (Chapter 4).

age stratification the assignment of social roles and social status on the basis of age (Chapter 11).

age structure the distribution of people in a population by age (Chapter 8).

Agricultural Revolution change that took place roughly 10,000 years ago when humans first began to domesticate plants and animals, thereby making it easier to settle in permanent establishments (Chapters 2 and 14).

alien a person born in, or belonging to, another country who has not acquired citizenship by naturalization—distinguished from citizen (Chapter 7).

Alzheimer's disease a disease involving a change in the brain's neurons, producing behavioral shifts; a major cause of senility (Chapter 11).

ambivalence state of being caught between competing pressures and thus being uncertain about how to behave properly (Chapter 5).

amenorrhea temporary absence or suppression of the menstrual discharge (Chapter 4).

amino acids building blocks from which proteins are formed (Chapter 14).

anovulatory pertaining to a menstrual cycle in which no egg is released (Chapter 4).

antinatalist based on an ideological position that discourages childbearing (Chapter 3).

arable describes land that is suitable for farming (Chapter 14).

ascribed characteristics sociodemographic characteristics such as gender and race and ethnicity, with which we are born and over which we have essentially no control (Chapter 9).

average age of a population one measure of the age distribution of a population—may be calculated as either the mean or the median (Chapter 8).

521

▼ Index

INDEX

of the more rapidly changing fields, such as computer science, you hope for as recent a book as possible.

- *Table of contents:* **The *table of contents* lists the principal headings in the book.** Sometimes a "brief contents" will list just parts and chapters, and a "detailed contents" will list other major headings as well.

- *Preface:* **The *preface* tells you the intended audience for the book, the author's purpose and approach, why the book is different, and perhaps an overview of the organization.** (The preface—which may also be called "Introduction" or "To the Student"—may go in front of the table of contents.)

- *Bibliography:* Appearing at the back of the book or at the end of each chapter, **the *bibliography,* or "Notes" section, lists sources or references used in writing the text.** This section can be a good resource if you're writing a term paper for the course. Scanning the textbook's bibliography may suggest some valuable places to start.

- *Glossary:* In the back of the book, **the *glossary* is an alphabetical list of key terms and their definitions, as found in the text.** Quite often the same terms appear within the main body of the text in **boldface** (dark type) or *italics* (slanted type).

- *Appendix:* Also in the back of the book, **the *appendix* contains supplementary material, material of optional or specialized interest.** Examples are tables, charts, and more detailed discussion than is contained in the text. Often there is more than one appendix. Engineering or business students, for instance, will often find time-saving tables contained in appendixes.

- *Index:* **The *index* is an alphabetically arranged list of names and subjects that appear in the text, giving the page numbers on which they appear.** Sometimes there are two indexes—a name index and a subject index. The index is an *extremely* useful tool. If you're not sure a topic is discussed in the book, try looking it up in the index.

UNDERSTAND WHAT "ADVANCE ORGANIZERS" ARE. As I discuss shortly, one concept underlying many reading strategies is that of surveying. **A *survey* is an overview.** That is, you take a couple of minutes to look through a chapter to get an overview of it before you start reading it.

Surveying a chapter has three purposes:

1. *It gets you going:* Getting started reading on a densely packed 35-page chapter can be difficult. Surveying the material gets you going, like a slow warm-up lap around the track.

2. *It gives you some familiarity with the material:* Have you ever noticed that when you're reading on a subject with which you're familiar you read more rapidly? For example, you might read slowly about an event reported in the morning paper but read more rapidly a story about that same event in the evening paper or a different newspaper. When you survey a chapter in a textbook, you begin to make it familiar to you. Notice, then, that the survey is not a waste of time. *It enables you to read faster later.*

3. *It gives you "advance organizers" to help you organize information in your mind:* As you do your overview you pick up what are called "advance organizers." ***Advance organizers* are mental landmarks under which facts and ideas may be grouped and organized in your mind.** Thus, when you go to read the chapter itself, you already have some advance information about it.

Textbooks provide some or all of the following *advance organizers.* It's a good idea to pay attention to these when doing a survey of a chapter.

- *Chapter table of contents:* You can find a breakdown of the headings within the chapter at the front of the book (in the table of contents). Some textbooks repeat this outline of the contents at the beginning of each chapter.

- *Learning objectives:* Not all books have this, but many texts have learning objectives. ***Learning objectives* are topics you are expected to learn, which are listed at the beginning of each chapter.** This usually starts out with a sentence something like: "After you have read this chapter, you should be able to . . ." The list of objectives then follows.

For example, learning objectives in an introductory computer book might be: "Explain what desktop publishing is" or "Discuss the principal features of word processing software."

- **Chapter summary:** Many textbooks have a summary at the end of the chapter, describing key concepts of the chapter. *Be sure to read the chapter summary FIRST,* even though you probably won't understand everything in it. It will help you get an overview of the material so it will seem somewhat familiar to you later.

In this book, instead of having a summary at the end of each chapter, I have put a summary (called "PREVIEW") following every main section heading. This section-head summary describes the material you are about to read in the section.

- **Review or discussion questions:** These, too, may appear at the end of the chapter. Sometimes review or discussion questions can be quite important because *they ask some of the questions that will be asked on the test.* Be sure to skim through them.

- **List of key terms:** Key terms may appear in **boldface** type (dark type) or *italics* (slanted type) within the text of the chapter. Sometimes key terms also appear in a list at the end of the chapter.

- **Headings, subheadings, and first sentences:** Read anything that appears as a heading; then read the first sentence following the heading.

Of course, a lot of the advance organizers that you read during the survey step are not going to make complete sense. But some of them will. And most of the material will have a familiar, hence somewhat comfortable, feeling to it when you come back to it on subsequent steps.

In the rest of this chapter I describe two reading systems devised to help students get the most out of textbooks.

Reading System #1: The SQ3R Method

PREVIEW The five-step SQ3R method stands for: *Survey, Question, Read, Recite, Review.* Its advantage is that it breaks down reading into manageable segments that require you to understand them before proceeding.

There's a war on! We must teach them to read faster!"

Maybe that's what psychologist Francis P. Robinson was told in 1941. In any event, Robinson then set about to devise an intensified reading system for World War II military people enrolled in special courses at Ohio State University. Since then, many thousands of students have successfully used his system or some variation. The reason the system is effective is that it *breaks a reading assignment down into manageable portions that require you to understand them before you move on.*

Robinson's reading system is called the SQ3R method. **The *SQ3R reading method* stands for five steps: Survey, Question, Read, Recite, Review.**[1] Let's see how you would apply these to the chapter of a textbook you are assigned to read.

STEP 1: S—SURVEY. As I said, a *survey* is an overview. You do a quick 1- or 2-minute overview of the entire chapter before you plunge into it. Look at the advance organizers—the chapter outline or learning objectives, if any; the chapter headings; and the summary, if any, at the end of the chapter. The point of surveying is twofold:

- **You establish relationships between the major segments:** Surveying enables you to see how the chapter segments or sections go together. Understanding how the parts fit in with the whole helps you see how the chapter makes sense.

- **You see where you're going:** If you know where you're going, you can better organize the information as you read. This is just like reading over directions to someone's house before you leave rather than bit by bit while traveling.

Next you apply Steps 2 through 4—Question, Read, Recite—*but only to one section at a time, or to an even smaller segment.* That is, you apply the next three steps section by section, or even paragraph by paragraph, if the material is difficult. You apply the last step, Step 5, Review, after you have finished the chapter.

STEP 2: Q—QUESTION. Take a look at the heading of the first section and turn it into a question in your mind. For example, if the heading (in a book about computers) is "Basic Software Tools for Work and Study," ask "What does 'Basic Software Tools' mean?" If the heading is to a subsection, do the same. For example, if the heading is "Word Processing," ask, "How does word processing work?"

Questioning has two important effects:

- **You become personally involved:** By questioning, you get actively involved in your reading. And personal involvement is one of the most fundamental ways to commit information to memory.

- **You identify the main ideas:** Giving the heading this kind of attention pinpoints the principal ideas you are now going to read about. And it is the main ideas that are important, after all, not the supporting details.

If you are proceeding on a paragraph-by-paragraph basis because the material is difficult (as in technical courses, such as physics), there may not be any heading that you can convert to a question. In that case, you'll need to put Step 3, Read, before Step 2: you read the paragraph, then create a question about that paragraph.

Incidentally, it's perfectly all right (indeed, even desirable) at this stage to move your lips and ask the question under your breath.

STEP 3: R—READ. *Now* you actually do the reading—but only up to the next section heading (or paragraph). Note, however, that you do not read as though you were reading a popular novel. Rather, *you read with purpose—actively searching to answer the question you posed.* If you don't seem to understand it, reread the section until you can answer the question.

What is the difference between passive and active reading? If you were reading a murder mystery *passively,* you would just run your eyes over the lines and wait, perhaps mildly curious, to see how things came out. If you were reading that mystery novel *actively,* you would constantly be trying to guess the outcome. You would be asking yourself such questions as: Who was the killer? What was that strange phone call about? What motive would she have for the murder? What was that funny business in his background? And you would be searching for the answers.

You don't need to do that with recreational reading. Reading a textbook, however, should *always* be an active process of asking questions and searching for answers. That's why you have to take study breaks from time to time (perhaps 5 minutes every half hour), because this type of reading is not effortless.

In addition, especially if the segment is somewhat long, you should read (perhaps on a second reading) for another purpose:

- **You should determine whether the section asks any other questions:** The question you formulated based on the section heading may not cover all the material in the segment. Thus, as you read, you may see other questions that should be asked about the material.

- **Ask those questions and answer them:** You probably get the idea: the Question and Read steps are not completely separate steps. Rather, you are continually alternating questions and answers as you read through the segment.

Some examples of questions you might frame in your mind as you read a textbook are:

> *What is the main idea of this paragraph?*
>
> *What is an example that illustrates this principle?*
>
> *What are the supporting facts?*
>
> *Who is this person and why is he or she considered important?*
>
> *What could the instructor ask me about this on the exam?*
>
> *What is there about this that I don't understand?*

If necessary, as you stop and think about key points, you may want to write brief notes to trigger your memory when you get to Step 5, Review.

STEP 4: R—RECITE. When you reach the end of the section, stop and look away from the page. *Recite* the answer you have just discovered for the question you formulated. You should practice this in two ways:

- **Recite the answer aloud:** When I say "aloud," I don't mean so loud that you have other students in the library looking at you. But there's nothing embarrassing about talking subvocally to yourself—that is, moving your tongue within your mouth while your lips move imperceptibly. When you move the muscles in your lips and mouth and throat, this vocalizing or subvocalizing helps lay down a memory trace in your mind.

I can't stress enough the importance of reciting aloud or nearly aloud. As Walter Pauk writes, "Reciting promotes concentration, forms a sound basis for understanding the next paragraph or the next chapter, provides time for the memory trace to consolidate, ensures that facts and ideas are remembered

accurately, and provides immediate feedback on how you're doing. . . ."[2] Pauk also mentions experiments that show that students who read and recite learn much better than students who just read.

- **Say the answer in your own words:** When you formulate the answer in your own words (perhaps using an example), rather than just repeating a phrase off the page, you are required to *understand* it rather than just memorize it. And when you understand it, you *do* memorize it better.

If you did not take any notes for review earlier, you may wish to at this point. The notes should not be extensive, just brief cues to jog your memory when you move to Step 5, Review.

Don't move on to the next segment until you're sure you understand this one. After all, if you don't get it now, when will you? Once you think you understand the section, move on to the next section (or paragraph) and repeat steps 2, 3, and 4.

STEP 5: R—REVIEW. When you have read all the way through the chapter (or as far as you intend to go in one study session), section by section in Question-Read-Recite fashion, you are ready to test how well you have mastered your key ideas. Here's how to do it:

- **Go back over the book's headings or your notes and ask the questions again:** Repeat the questions and try to answer them without looking at the book or your notes. If you have difficulty, check your answers.

- **Review other memory aids:** Read the chapter summary and the review questions. Then skim the chapter again, as well as your notes, refreshing your memory.

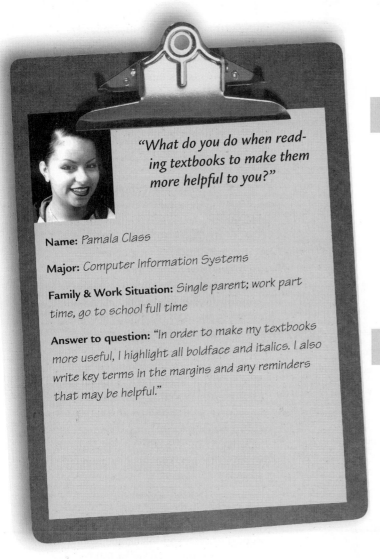

"What do you do when reading textbooks to make them more helpful to you?"

Name: Pamala Class

Major: Computer Information Systems

Family & Work Situation: Single parent; work part time, go to school full time

Answer to question: "In order to make my textbooks more useful, I highlight all boldface and italics. I also write key terms in the margins and any reminders that may be helpful."

Reading System #2: The 3Rs Method

PREVIEW The three-step 3Rs method stands for: *Read, Record, Recite.* The method has no survey step, but it helps you retain material through reading, rereading, underlining, making questions, and self-testing.

The *3Rs reading system* has three steps for mastering textbooks: *Read, Record, Recite.* This system was described by Walter Pauk, who says it "is perfect for students who like to move quickly into a textbook chapter, or for those who face exams with little time for intensive study."[3] In other words, if (against all advice) you have to resort to cramming, use this method.

STEP 1: READ. There is no surveying or questioning of material first, as in the SQ3R method. Rather, you just start reading and read a section or several paragraphs. Then do as follows:

■ *Ask what you need to know:* Return to the first paragraph and ask yourself, "What do I need to know in this paragraph?"

■ *Read and reread for answers and say aloud:* Read and reread the paragraph until you can say aloud what you need to know about it.

STEP 2: RECORD. The SQ3R method, previously discussed, says nothing about making marks or writing in the book, although you can do so if it helps. However, in Step 2 of the 3Rs method you are *required* to mark up the book. Here's how:

■ *Underline key information:* Once you can say aloud what you need to know, you should underline the key information in the book. It's important that you *underline just the key information—terms, phrases, and sentences*—not line after line of material. This is so that when you come back to review, you will see only the essential material.

■ *Write a brief question in the margin:* After underlining, write a *brief question* in the

Underlining & questions. In Step 2, you underline key information and write questions in the margin.

How Television Works

[Handwritten margin notes:]

What are 8 depts of TV station?

① Sales — What duties? What are 2 types of Advertising?

② Programming — What Duties?

O & O — Define
Affiliates — Define
How Differ?

Independents — Define

What are Syndicators?

[Text of the sample page:]

a TYPICAL television station has eight departments: ① sales, ② programming (which includes news as well as entertainment), ③ production, ④ engineering, ⑤ traffic, ⑥ promotion, ⑦ public affairs, and ⑧ administration.

People in the *sales* department sell the commercial slots for the programs. Advertising is divided into *national* and *local* sales. Advertising agencies, usually based on the East Coast, buy national ads for the products they handle. Ford Motor Company, for instance, may buy time for a TV ad that will run simultaneously all over the country. But the local Ford dealers who want you to shop at their showrooms buy their ads directly from the local station. These ads are called local (or spot) ads. For these sales, salespeople at each station negotiate packages of ads, based on their station's rates. These rates are a direct reflection of that station's position in the ratings.

The *programming* department selects the shows that you will see and develops the station's schedule. Network-owned stations, located in big cities (KNBC in Los Angeles, for example), are called O & O's, which stands for owned-and-operated. Stations that carry network programming but are not owned by the networks are called affiliates.

O & O's automatically carry network programming, but affiliates are paid by the network to carry its programming, for which the network sells most of the ads and keeps the money. The affiliate is allowed to insert into the network programming a specific number of local ads, for which the affiliate keeps the money.

Because affiliates can make money on network programming and don't have to pay for it, many stations choose to affiliate themselves with a network. When they aren't running what the network provides, affiliates run their own programs and keep all the advertising money they collect from them.

More than one-third of the nation's commercial TV stations operate as independents. Independent stations must buy and program all their own shows, but independents also can keep all the money they make on advertising. They run some individually produced programs and old movies, but most of their programming consists of reruns of shows that once ran on the networks. Independents buy these reruns from program services called syndicators. Syndicators also sell independently produced programs such as *Donahue*, *The Oprah Winfrey Show*, and *Wheel of Fortune*. These programs are created and

180
CHAPTER FIVE

---

margin that asks for the information you've underlined. (*See* ■ *Panel 7.2.*) Forming questions is extremely important to the 3Rs System, so you must be sure to do this.

After you finish this step for these paragraphs, proceed to the next segment or paragraphs and again Read and Record.

Incidentally, a word about underlining: I've sat in libraries and watched students reading a chapter for the first time, underlining the text as they go. At the end, if they are using a green pen, say, the entire chapter looks like a mess of green paint. Obviously, this kind of underlining doesn't work. The point is to use your pen or highlighter to mark only *important things*, not *everything*. This is why it's best to read the chapter (or section) first without underlining, then reread it, doing your underlining on the second reading. (Note: Be sure to use pen or highlighter. If you use felt tip markers or Magic Markers, the ink will go through the paper—indeed, perhaps through five or more pages.)

STEP 3: RECITE. After you've finished doing Steps 1 and 2 for the chapter, go back to the beginning. Now you will do the Recite step for the entire chapter, as follows:

■ *Cover the page and ask yourself each question:* Use a folded piece of paper or your hand to cover the printed page of the text except for the questions you've written in the margins. Ask yourself the questions.

■ *Recite aloud and check your answers:* Recite *aloud* the answer to each question. ("Aloud" can mean talking to yourself under your breath.) Then lift the paper and check your answer. If you're not clear on the answer, ask and answer again. Put a check mark in the margin if you need to come back and review again.

Continue the Recite step until you get to the end of the chapter. Then go back and look at the places where you've left a check mark.

is to devote enough time and practice to the subject. The third step is to avail yourself of such tools as flash cards or index cards; diagrams, charts, and maps; and cassette tapes.

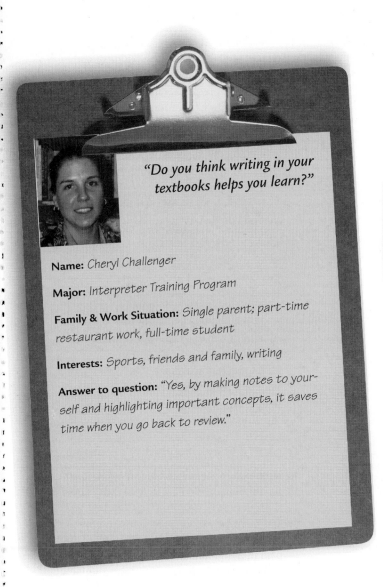

"Do you think writing in your textbooks helps you learn?"

Name: *Cheryl Challenger*

Major: *Interpreter Training Program*

Family & Work Situation: *Single parent; part-time restaurant work, full-time student*

Interests: *Sports, friends and family, writing*

Answer to question: *"Yes, by making notes to yourself and highlighting important concepts, it saves time when you go back to review."*

Some students, even though they may be smart in many ways, go into a panic when confronted with a particular subject—technical subjects such as math or chemistry or detail-oriented subjects such as foreign languages, history, or literature. The specific advice for coping here is:

- *Take steps to reduce your anxiety.*

- *Devote more time and practice to your assignments, and don't fall behind.*

- *Use special tools for information organizing and study.*

Let's consider these matters.

REDUCING YOUR ANXIETY. "Math anxiety" is very real for a number of people, as is anxiety about the other subjects mentioned. Students may believe that math requires a logical ability or special knack that they don't think they have. With science they may think there is only one way to solve problems. With history, literature, or foreign languages, they may think they don't have a good enough memory for details.

Here's what to do:

- *Learn your inner voice:* The first step is to learn what your inner voice is saying, to pinpoint those inhibiting pronouncements from within. This inner voice, the *Voice Of Judgment (VOJ)*, is the internal broadcast that goes on in all of us.

  As one book describes it, the Voice Of Judgment "condemns, criticizes, attaches blame, makes fun of, puts down, assigns guilt, passes sentence on, punishes, and buries anything that's the least bit unlike a mythical norm."[4]

- *Pinpoint your negative thoughts:* Once you've identified the negative thoughts ("I'm not smart enough to grasp this

Dealing with Special Subjects: Math, Science, Languages, & Others

PREVIEW Mathematics, science, social science, history, foreign languages, and literature may be areas of study that require more study effort than you're accustomed to. The first step is to reduce your anxiety, using positive self-talk. The second step

stuff"), speak them aloud or write them down. Usually, such thoughts come down to two matters:

(1) *"I don't understand it now, so I never will."* If you think about this, however, you'll realize that there have been many times in the past when you haven't understood something but eventually did. After all, there *was* a time when you couldn't read, ride a bicycle, drive a car, or whatever.

(2) *"Everybody else is better at this subject than I am."* If you do a reality check—by asking your classmates—you'll find that this just isn't so. Probably a number of people will, if they're honest, say they aren't confident about this subject.

■ *Replace your negative thoughts with positive self-talk:* Now try to replace the VOJ and use your inner voice as a force for success. You do this by using *positive self-talk*, which can help you control your moods, turn back fear messages, and give you confidence.[5,6] **Positive self-talk consists of giving yourself positive messages.**

The messages of positive self-talk are not mindless self-delusions. Rather they are messages such as "You can do it. You've done it well before" that correct errors and distortions in your thinking and help you develop a more accurate internal dialogue.[7]

Stop and try Personal Exploration #7.2 to identify your negative thoughts, then figure out how to make them positive, using positive self-talk.

■ *Deal with the stresses:* The sense of unpleasantness that the anxiety-provoking subject evokes may be felt in a physical way—as clammy hands, constricted breathing, headache, or other kinds of panicky reactions. In Chapters 8 and 10 I describe ways to deal with stress, such as techniques of relaxation and visualization.

For now, however, just try this: Every time you have to deal with a troublesome subject, take a slow, deep breath and slowly exhale; then repeat. Then tell yourself, "Now I'm ready to deal with this subject calmly and methodically, taking however long it takes." If the anxiety begins to resurface, repeat the slow, deep breathing twice.

DEVOTE ENOUGH TIME. Once you've dealt with the emotional barriers, then be prepared to spend more time on the subject. It doesn't matter that it takes you longer to learn math, physics, French, or whatever than it will some other students; you're doing this for yourself. (The chances are, however, that a difficult subject for you is also a difficult subject for many others.)

Spending more time on the subject involves the following:

■ *Keep up with the assignments:* Don't fall behind. Subjects such as math and foreign languages are *cumulative* or *sequential* kinds of knowledge: it's difficult to understand the later material if you don't understand the earlier material.

Thus, if you feel yourself slipping, *get help right away.* Seek assistance from a classmate, the instructor, teaching assistant, or a tutor. If you're worried about confiding your anxieties to someone involved with the subject, see your faculty advisor. Or go to the campus counseling center and seek the advice of a counselor.

■ *Review the previous assignment before starting the present one:* Precisely because later skills depend on having mastered earlier skills, it's a good idea to review the previous assignment. Being confident you understand yesterday's material will give you the confidence to move on to today's assignment.

● ● ● ● ● ● ● ● ● ● ● ● ● ● ● ●

"If you feel yourself slipping, get help right away."

● ● ● ● ● ● ● ● ● ● ● ● ● ● ● ●

■ *Apply the SQ3R or 3Rs reading method:* Difficult subjects are precisely the kinds of subjects in which you need to go over things several times, constantly asking questions and marking up the text. The two reading methods described earlier in this chapter will help here.

NEGATIVE THOUGHTS & POSITIVE THOUGHTS

Think of certain subjects you are anxious about and listen to what your inner voice (your Voice Of Judgment) says about you. (*Examples:* "My mind is always in confusion when I'm confronted with math problems." "I'm the kind of person who can barely change a light bulb, let alone operate a microscope." "I'm not as good as other people at figuring how a foreign language works." "If I ask the question I want to ask, people will think I'm dumb.")

1. _____
_____
_____
_____
_____
_____
_____

2. _____
_____
_____
_____
_____
_____

3. _____
_____
_____
_____
_____
_____

4. _____
_____
_____
_____

Now try to replace these negative thoughts with positive self-talk. (*Examples:* "I can solve math problems when I approach them calmly and deliberately and give myself time." "Just as I've learned [basketball, weaving, or some other skill] in the past, so I can learn a foreign language without having to compare myself to others." "Smart people ask questions rather than withhold questions.")

1. _____
_____
_____
_____
_____

2. _____
_____
_____
_____
_____

3. _____
_____
_____
_____
_____

4. _____
_____
_____
_____

■ **Work practice problems:** Math and foreign languages require that you learn specific skills as well as information. Accordingly, you should work all practice problems that are assigned, whether math problems or language exercises. For example, you should work practice problems at the end of every section within the book and also those at the end of every chapter.

■ **Take frequent breaks—and remind yourself of why you're doing this:** Needless to say, studying difficult material is a frustrating business. Go easy on yourself. If you feel you're beating your head against the wall, take frequent breaks. Study some other material for awhile.

When you come back to your original work, remind yourself why you're studying it—for example, "I need to study chemistry because it's important to my nursing career."

■ *Do lab assignments:* Some subjects require use of a laboratory. For biology or chemistry, for example, there is often a lecture portion, in which you take notes about concepts from a lecturer, and a lab portion, in which you do experiments or other hands-on tasks. *The two kinds of classes are not independent of each other:* what's learned in the lab reinforces what's learned in the lecture.

Foreign language classes also have laboratories, usually places to practice listening to audiocassette tapes. Since repetition is essential for learning languages, language labs can be very effective.

USE SPECIAL TOOLS FOR STUDYING. A whole bag of tools is available for helping to organize information and make special study guides to help you learn difficult subjects. Some of these tools, such as diagrams and charts, may be especially helpful if your learning style tends to be more visual than verbal.

The tools are as follows:

■ **Flash cards or index cards: A _flash card_ is a card bearing words, numbers, or pictures that is briefly displayed as a learning aid.** A flash card may be a 3×5 index card that you make up yourself. Or it may be part of a set of cards that you buy in the bookstore to use to study biological terms, foreign language vocabulary, or whatever.

If you're making up a flash card yourself, write the key term, concept, or problem that you are trying to grasp on the front and the explanation or answer on the back. Don't forget that you can put several terms on one side and their answers on the reverse. For example, for a history course you might list the name of a treaty followed by such questions as "Year?" "Signers?" "Purpose?" "Consequences?" You would list the answers on the back of the card.

Flash cards can be used for all kinds of subjects. For literature classes, you can write the name of a short story or poem on one side and its meaning on the other. For history, you can write the name

of an important person or document on the front and the chief characteristics on the back. For math, you can write a term or formula on one side and its definition, meaning, or calculations on the other. In science, you can state the theory or scientist on the front and the important principles or hypothesis associated with it or him/her on the back.

When you use flash cards, you can sort them into three piles according to how well you've memorized them: (1) cards you know well; (2) cards you know but respond slowly to or are vague about; (3) cards you don't know. You'll find it's pleasing to watch the "I know" pile grow.

Carry a few flash cards with you wherever you go. Then, while at a bus stop or stuck in traffic or while on your work break, you can take them out and practice answering the questions on them.

■ *Diagrams, charts, and maps:* Drawing diagrams of concepts helps reinforce learning in two ways: (1) It helps your *visual sense*, because you can see the ideas. (2) It helps your *kinesthetic sense*, or sense of touch, because you are actually creating something with your hand.

There are all kinds of ways to sketch out concepts and information. What follows are only a few ideas.

(a) _Study diagrams_ **are literal representations of things from real life, which you have rendered in your own hand.** This type of artwork is especially useful in the biological sciences: You can draw and label the parts of a cell, the bones in the head, the arteries and veins of the circulatory system. *(See* ■ *Panel 7.3a.)*

(b) _Process diagrams_ **are useful for representing the steps in a process and thus are useful in such subjects as biology, geology, or environmental science.** For example, you might sketch the process of photosynthesis, the process of global warming, or the geological formation of an ancient lake. *(See Panel* ■ *7.3b.)*

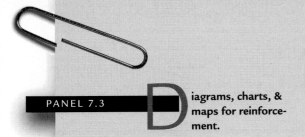

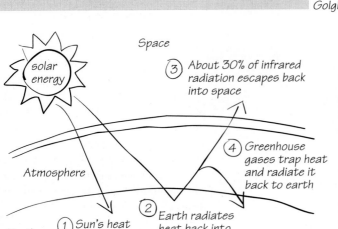

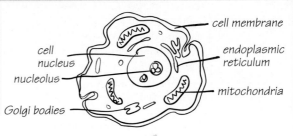

D iagrams, charts, & maps for reinforcement.

■ a. Study diagram—example of drawing and labeling a cell.

Gases: CFCs from air conditioning; CO_2 from industry, deforestation, & burning of fossil fuels; methane & nitrous oxide from cattle

■ b. Process diagram—example of representing steps in global warming.

■ c. Concept map—example of visual diagram of concepts in Maslow's hierarchy of needs.

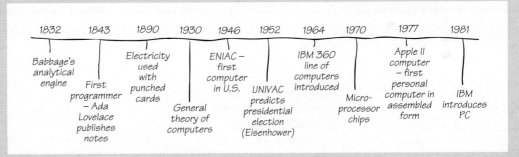

■ d. Time line—example of historical development of the computer.

	Hinduism	Judaism	Christianity	Islam
Principal geographic locations	India	Israel, Europe, Americas	Especially Europe & Americas; adherents worldwide	Asia, North Africa, Central Africa
Type (number of gods)	Polytheistic	Monotheistic	Monotheistic	Monotheistic
Holy book(s)	Mahabharata, Ramayana	Torah	Bible	Koran

■ e. Comparison chart—example of concepts of various world religions.

(c) **_Concept maps_ are visual diagrams of concepts.** For example, you can make a drawing of psychologist Abraham Maslow's famous hierarchy of needs, the parts of a symphony, or the five departments of a typical business organization. *(See Panel ■ 7.3c.)*

(d) **_Time lines_ are sketches representing a particular historical development.** They are useful in memorizing historical processes, such as the buildup to the Civil War or the growth of computer technology. A time line consists of simply a vertical line with "tick marks" and labels, each indicating the year and its important event. *(See Panel ■ 7.3d.)*

(e) **_Comparison charts_ are useful for studying several concepts and the relationships among them.** Headings are listed across the top of the page and down the left side of the page; the concepts are then briefly described in a grid in the middle of the page. For example, you might compare various religions by listing their names across the top (such as *Christianity, Buddhism, Hinduism*), the principal categories of comparison down the side (*Deity, Holy book, Principal countries*), and then the specifics within the grid. *(See Panel ■ 7.3e.)*

■ **_Cassette tapes:_** Elsewhere I mentioned that taping lectures can provide a kind of reinforcement, particularly if the lecturer is hard to follow (though taping is no substitute for note taking). Listening to cassette tapes is also valuable for certain specific subjects such as language study. The heart of learning a foreign language is repetition and practice. Thus, if you have a Walkman-type portable audiotape player or a tape deck in your car, during spare moments in your day you can use it to listen to tapes on which you have recorded new vocabulary terms, verb forms, and idioms.

Onward

PREVIEW Reading is half your education.

Reading, as I said, may well constitute half your education during the next few terms or years—reading textbooks, that is. There is also reading of another sort that you will do—namely, reading your lecture notes. Thus, some of the reading skills you have learned in this chapter will apply to the previous chapter on lectures.

In the next chapter, we will put together what you've learned from the lecture and the reading chapters and show you how to apply the knowledge to tests.

NOTES

1. Robinson, F. P. (1970). *Effective study* (4th ed.). New York: Harper & Row.

2. Pauk, W. (1989). *How to study in college* (4th ed.). Boston: Houghton Mifflin, p. 181.

3. Pauk, 1989, 171.

4. Ray, M., & Myers, R. (1986). *Creativity in business.* Garden City, NY: Doubleday, p. 42.

5. Donahue, P. A. (1989). Helping adolescents with shyness: Applying the Japanese Morita therapy in shyness counseling. *International Journal for the Advancement of Counseling, 12,* 323–32.

6. Zastrow, C. (1988). What really causes psychotherapy change? *Journal of Independent Social Work, 2,* 5–16.

7. Braiker, H. B. (1989, December). The power of self-talk. *Psychology Today,* 24.

1. *What facts about reading are a surprise to you?* Have students look at the answers they checked for Personal Exploration #7.1, "What Do You Know About the Reading Process?" In a group-discussion situation, ask them to consider which statements they were surprised to find the opposite of what they thought. Why did they think this? Does anything they've learned change their previous attitudes toward reading?

2. *What do you think of textbooks?* If half a student's education is in the textbooks, it's important to determine what his or her attitude is toward them. Ask students to list on a piece of paper three negative things that come to mind about textbooks, then list three positive things.

   In class discussion, ask students to describe some of their feelings about textbooks, then consider some of the following questions. If you didn't have textbooks, what would you use instead to get the same information? Would it be more efficient? How much money in a quarter or semester do you spend on recreation and how does that compare to the money spent on books? When you're learning something for work or personal interest, what kinds of sources of information do you use?

3. *Practicing the SQ3R method.* This activity may be performed all in class, or partly out of class and partly in class. Divide the class into small groups of four. Then have each group divide into two teams (Team A and Team B) of two people each.

   Select two earlier chapters from this book on which the teams are to practice the SQ3R. One team practices the method on one chapter, the other team on the other chapter.

   Next, instruct the members of Team A, without looking at the text, to respond to a quiz on the chapter by Team B. Then reverse the roles. Afterward, have the class discuss how well the method worked for them. Ask them what they would do differently.

4. **Negative thoughts and positive thoughts.** Have students look over their responses to Personal Exploration #7.2, "Negative Thoughts & Positive Thoughts." Ask everyone to copy out a couple of examples (anonymously) on a piece of paper and then hand them into you.

   Read aloud (or copy on the black-board) examples for class discussion. Ask students to respond to the following questions: Are there some negative thoughts that seem to be fairly common? How are they hindrances to doing well in school and in life? What do students think of the idea of replacing "negative inner voices" with "positive inner voices"?

JOURNAL ENTRY #7.1: ARE THERE SOME "SPEED READING" TRICKS YOU DON'T KNOW ABOUT? Be honest: After reading this chapter, do you still think there is some shortcut for absorbing all the volumes of material you'll need to read? Is there some "speed reading" trick that hasn't been mentioned? How do you think this might work? Why don't you do some research to find out what this might be?

_____

_____

_____

_____

_____

_____

_____

JOURNAL ENTRY #7.2: WHAT HAVE YOU LEARNED FROM READING IN THE PAST? No doubt at some point in the past you had to learn a lot of material from reading. (Examples: Material necessary to do your job, religious studies, government paperwork.) What was it? How did you go about absorbing it?

_____

_____

_____

_____

_____

_____

JOURNAL ENTRY #7.3: HOW COULD YOUR PRESENT READING SYSTEM BE IMPROVED? What is your present system for marking up and reviewing textbooks? What mistakes have you made (for example, doing too much underlining or reading only once)? What specific techniques could you use to correct these mistakes?

_____

_____

_____

_____

_____

_____

_____

_____

_____

JOURNAL ENTRY #7.4: HOW DO YOU STUDY ESPECIALLY CHALLENGING MATERIAL? Do you do anything different in studying more challenging material—such as mathematics, foreign language, or history—than you do in studying "regular" subject matter? How is your approach different? What does your Voice Of Judgment tell you about your inadequacies in handling certain types of material (math, for example)?

_____

_____

_____

_____

_____

_____

8 tests

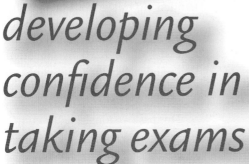

developing confidence in taking exams

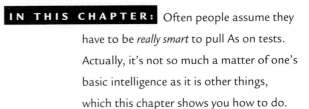

*You are not a victim.
You are here by choice.
You hope college will help
you be your best and
lead to your ultimate
happiness.*

Perhaps this is the outlook to have the next time you're facing exams. Remember why you're in college in the first place. You are not a prisoner or a conscript. You're here because you expect college to enhance your life. Exams may not be fun, but they are simply part of the experience of higher education—an experience you have *chosen* to undertake.

Thus, the attitude to take is "Since I'm here in school voluntarily and want it to enhance my life, I might as well become good at one of the important things school requires—taking tests."

Taking Charge of Taking Tests

PREVIEW Becoming expert at tests means psyching out the instructor, learning how to prepare for specific tests, knowing what to bring to the test, and getting off to the right start in the testing room.

Taking charge of taking tests has four components:

- Psyching out the instructor
- Learning how to prepare for specific tests
- Knowing what to bring to the test
- Getting started right in the testing room

PSYCHING OUT THE INSTRUCTOR. Instructors not only have different ways of teaching, they also have different ways of testing. Some will test mainly on the textbook, some mainly on the lecture material, some on both. It's up to you to be a *detective*—to figure out the instructor's method of operating and to plan accordingly. Actually, this is usually not hard to do. The aim of an instructor, after all, is not to trick you with questions on the test but to find out what you know.

Following are some ways to get a jump on the test by finding out what the instructor will do:

- *Look at the course syllabus:* The syllabus handed out by the instructor on the first class day is often a good guide for test preparation. As I mentioned elsewhere, the syllabus is a course outline or guide that tells you what readings are required, when assignments are due, and when examinations are scheduled.

  This basic roadmap to the course may tell you a lot about testing. It may tell you what kind of weight testing has in the overall course grade. It may indicate if low grades may be made up. It may describe what happens if the test is missed. It may indicate if the lowest grade on a series of tests is dropped when the instructor is determining your average grade for all tests.

- *Look at instructor handouts:* Frequently instructors hand out potential essay questions in advance, or they prepare study guides. Handouts show what the instructor thinks is important. Like an actor learning your lines, you can use such material to practice taking the test. This can not only help prepare you by giving you sample material, it may also help reduce that kind of stage fright–like condition known as test anxiety.

- *Ask about the specific test:* Particularly before the first test in a class, when you don't know what's coming, make a point to ask the instructor (in class or during office hours) the following:

(1) How long will the test last?

(2) How much will the test results count toward the course grade?

(3) What types of questions will appear on the test? Will they be true-false? multiple-choice? fill-in? essay? all of these? Different questions require different test-taking strategies, as I'll show in a few pages.

It's also fair to ask the instructor what is most important for you to know. Some instructors may emphasize certain subject areas over others, or they may emphasize the lecture material over the textbook.

■ *Ask to see copies of old tests:* Some instructors may be willing to provide you with copies of old tests or with the kinds of questions they are inclined to ask. Don't feel it's somehow impolite or incorrect to ask to see old tests. (Sometimes old tests are on file in the library.)

■ *Consult students who have taken the course:* If you know others who have already taken the course, ask them about their test experiences. See if you can get them to share old exams so you can look at what kinds of questions the instructor likes to ask. Indeed, an item from an old test may even reappear on the one you will take, since there are only so many ways to ask a question. (But don't count on it.)

■ *In lectures watch for "bell phrases" and "bell cues":* As I mentioned in Chapter 6, all lecturers use phrases and gestures that should "ring a bell" and signal importance.

A *bell phrase* **is a verbal indicator of an important point.** Examples of bell phrases are: "Three major types . . . ," "The most important result is . . . ," and "You should remember. . . ."

A *bell cue* **is an action or gesture that indicates important points.** Examples are pointing, as to something on the board or a chart; underlining keywords or making a check mark by them; and holding up fingers.

LEARNING HOW TO PREPARE FOR A SPECIFIC TEST. In addition to the foregoing suggestions, there are strategies to employ when preparing for a specific test.

■ *Rehearse study-guide or other practice questions:* Some textbook publishers produce a separate study guide, which you can buy at the campus bookstore. **A** *study guide* **is a booklet that contains practice questions, along with their answers, covering material in the textbook.** Available for a fairly modest price, the study guide represents an excellent investment because *it gives you a trial run at various types of questions similar to those that are apt to be asked on the test.*

A variation on the paper-and-print study guide now being seen more frequently is the electronic study guide. **An** *electronic study guide* **is a floppy disk that students can use on their personal computer (IBM-style or Apple Macintosh) to rehearse practice questions and check their answers.**

Some textbooks also have practice questions at the end of the chapters, with answers to some or all of them in the back of the book.

■ *Form study groups with other students to generate practice questions:* Forming study groups with some of your classmates is an excellent way to generate possible test questions—especially essay questions—and quiz one another on answers. Moreover, study groups offer reinforcement and inject a bit of social life into your studying.

■ *Develop self-study practice sessions:* Besides study guides and study groups, a useful preparation strategy is simply to have your own periodic practice sessions. Every week set aside time to go through your notes and textbooks and compose practice tests. Specifically:

(1) Practice reviewing material that is emphasized. This includes anything your instructor has pointed out as being significant. Practice defining key terms, the terms presented in *italics* or **boldface** in the text. This is an area, incidentally, where you can make excellent use of flash cards. **A** *flash card* **is a card bearing words, numbers, or pictures that is briefly displayed as a learning aid.**

(2) Practice reviewing material that is enumerated, presented in numbered

lists (such as the 13 vitamins or warning signs for heart disease). Enumerations often provide the basis for essay and multiple-choice questions.

(3) Practice answering questions on material on which there are a good many pages of coverage, either in the text or in the lecture notes. Answer questions you've written in the text margins and in your lecture notes. Formulate essay questions and outline answers.

■ *Study throughout the course:* The best way to prepare for exams is *not* to play catch-up. Elsewhere (Chapter 5) I mentioned the idea of overlearning. **_Overlearning_ is continuing to repeatedly review material even after you appear to have absorbed it.** Of course, to overlearn, you must first have learned. This means keeping up with lecture notes and textbooks, rereading them so that you really get to know the material. Space your studying rather than cramming, since it is *repetition* that will move information into your long-term memory bank.

■ *Review the evening and morning before the test:* The night before a test, spend the evening reviewing your notes. Then go to bed without interfering with the material you have absorbed (as by watching television). Get plenty of rest—there will be no need to stay up cramming if you've followed the suggestions of this book. The next morning, get up early and review your notes again.

KNOWING WHAT TO BRING TO THE TEST.

Asking to borrow a pencil or pen from the instructor on exam day because you forgot to bring one will not get you off to a good start. It makes you feel and look as though you're not exactly in charge. Thus, be sure to bring some sharpened pencils (#2 if the tests are machine-scored) or pens (preferably blue or black ink; no red, a color instructors often use for grading).

Besides pencils or pens, other items you should bring are:

■ *A watch:* If the examination room has no clock, you'll need a watch to be able to budget your time during the test.

■ *Blue book or paper and paper clips:* Some instructors will hand out "blue books" for examinations or require that you bring some along. (They're usually for sale in the campus bookstore.) Otherwise, bring some paper to write on and some paper clips (or small stapler) to attach pages together.

■ *Calculator, dictionary, formulas, or other aids:* Some instructors allow you to bring items to assist test-taking. Be sure to give yourself the extra edge by availing yourself of these learning aids if they're permitted!

In math, business, and science courses, you may be allowed to have a calculator.

In foreign language or literature courses, you may be permitted access to a dictionary.

In some math, statistics, business, engineering, and science courses, instructors may allow you to jot down formulas on index cards and bring them to the test.

GETTING STARTED RIGHT IN THE TESTING ROOM.

It's important to extend the feeling of "taking charge" to the environment of the testing room. Here's how:

■ *Arrive on time:* Have you ever been sitting in an exam room and watched some fellow students arrive late, perhaps having overslept? You have to feel sorry for them. They're clearly starting at a great disadvantage, and their faces show it.

Arrive early. Or if arriving early makes you nervous, because it means listening to other students talk about the test, then arrive on time.

■ *Find a good test-taking spot:* Find a spot where you won't be distracted. Sitting near the front of the room is good, where you won't see a lot of other people. Or sitting in your normal spot may make you feel comfortable. Some people like the back of the room because other people can't see them—or see how nervous they are.

How to Cope with Test Anxiety in the Classroom

PREVIEW Five short-term strategies exist for coping with test anxiety in the classroom. (1) Press fists against your closed eyes and squint. (2) Drop your head forward and slowly roll it left and right. (3) Alternately tense your muscles, then let go. (4) Concentrate on breathing slowly in and out. (5) Try positive self-talk.

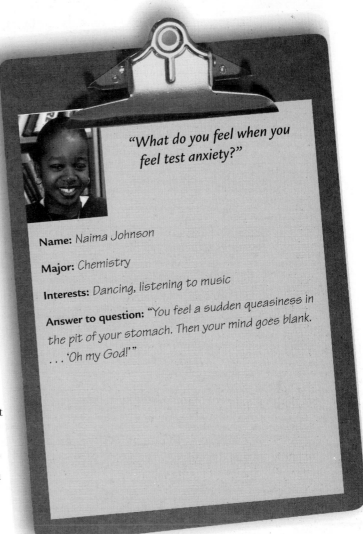

"What do you feel when you feel test anxiety?"

Name: Naima Johnson

Major: Chemistry

Interests: Dancing, listening to music

Answer to question: "You feel a sudden queasiness in the pit of your stomach. Then your mind goes blank. . . . 'Oh my God!'"

Dry mouth. Rapid breathing. Quickened pulse. Taut muscles. Sweating. Nausea. Headache. These are just some of the *physical* symptoms—which I well recall myself—associated with test anxiety. Then there are the *mental* aspects: panic, mental blocks, foreboding, dread. "You're going to freeze up," the inner Voice Of Judgment says. "You *know* you're going to flunk!"

Test anxiety consists of thoughts and worries (the mental component) and feelings and sensations (the physical component) of stress linked to test taking. Test anxiety has much in common with other kinds of *performance anxiety*—the stresses associated with first dates, public speaking, job interviews, pregame nervousness, stage fright, and the like.

Anxiety is an indicator of the importance we attach to an event and of our concern that we will not succeed. Thus, anxiety is *normal* under these circumstances. In fact, a certain amount of anxiety can actually be *helpful.* As you've probably noticed in other kinds of challenges (games, for example), some anxiety makes you focus your attention and gets yourself "up" to perform. The problem lies in the kind of test anxiety that hinders your performance. What can be done about it?

The best recipe for alleviating feelings of panic is to be prepared. If you've reviewed the material often enough, you can have butterflies in your stomach and still feel confident that you'll pull through. Beyond that, there are various techniques for coping with stress (such as relaxation training and visualization, which I describe in Chapter 10).

Five techniques for handling test anxiety in the classroom are the following.

1. PRESS FISTS AGAINST YOUR CLOSED EYES & SQUINT. This exercise will give you a moment to blank out tensions and distractions. Here's how it works (best not to try this if you wear contact lenses):

Press your fists against your closed eyes.

Squint or tightly close your eyes at the same time.

After a few seconds, take your hands away and open your eyes.

2. DROP YOUR HEAD FORWARD & SLOWLY ROLL IT LEFT & RIGHT. Do the following exercise five times:

Drop your head forward on your chest.

Roll it slowly over to your left shoulder, then slowly over to your right shoulder.

3. ALTERNATELY TENSE YOUR MUSCLES & THEN LET GO. If a particular part of your body, such as your shoulders, is tense, try this tense-and-relax activity. The effect is to make you aware of the relaxed feeling after you have released the tension.

Take a deep breath and hold it.

Make the muscles in the tense place even more tense. Hold tightly for a few seconds.

Then let out your breath and release the tension.

You can do this for other parts of your body (chest, neck, and so on) or for all parts simultaneously.

4. CONCENTRATE ON BREATHING SLOWLY IN & OUT. This activity will calm some of the physical sensations in your body. Do this for 2–5 minutes.

Focus your mind on your breathing.

Breathe slowly through your nose.

Deeply and slowly inhale, filling your lungs.

Then slowly exhale through your mouth.

Avoid taking short breaths.

Once your breathing is calm and regular, you can concentrate on the test.

5. TRY POSITIVE SELF-TALK. When the Voice Of Judgment within you says "You're going to flunk!" make an effort to replace this and other negative thoughts with positive ones. Say to yourself: "Nonsense! I studied enough, so I know I'll be okay."

See Personal Exploration #8.1, opposite page.

The Six-Step Examination Approach

PREVIEW The six-step examination approach consists of the following: (1) Unload. (2) Review subjective questions. (3) Do objective questions. (4) Do subjective questions. (5) Do questions left undone. (6) Proofread.

Once you have settled your nerves with some of the exercises described in the previous section, you need to apply a strategy for taking the test itself. The six-step system discussed here has three purposes. First, it is a very efficient method for tackling a test. Second, it helps you stave off panic because it gives you a plan to follow. Third, it helps you build confidence.

The six steps are:

1. Unload on the back of the test.

2. Review, but don't answer, the subjective questions.

3. Answer the objective questions.

4. Answer the subjective questions.

5. Answer questions left undone.

6. Proofread the examination.

MORE ON NEGATIVE THOUGHTS & POSITIVE THOUGHTS

What kinds of negative thoughts do you have during tests? Pretend you are sitting in an examination room. Listen to what your inner voice (the Voice Of Judgment) is saying, and write down the thoughts below. *Examples:*

"My mind is a blank; I can't remember anything!"

"I'm going to flunk, and my life will be ruined!"

"Everyone else is leaving early; they're smarter than I am!"

1. _____

_____

_____

2. _____

_____

_____

3. _____

_____

_____

4. _____

_____

_____

Now try to replace these negative thoughts with positive thoughts, using positive self-talk. Write your responses below. *Examples:*

"Breathe easy, and you'll start to remember some things. If not, come back to the question later."

"Even if you flunk, you'll survive. But don't get distracted. Just concentrate on each step of the test."

"Leaving early doesn't mean they're smarter, maybe the reverse. Just focus on the test, not other students."

1. _____

_____

_____

2. _____

_____

_____

_____

3. _____

_____

_____

_____

4. _____

_____

_____

STEP 1: UNLOAD ON THE BACK OF THE TEST.

The first thing you should do after getting the test from your instructor is to *put your name on it.* (You'd be surprised how many students simply forget to sign their examination sheet, baffling the instructor and delaying posting of the final grade.)

After signing it, *without looking at any of the questions,* flip the examination sheet over and simply *unload.* **Unloading means taking 2–3 minutes to jot down on the** **back of the exam sheet any keywords, concepts, and ideas that are in your mind.** These are things that you think might be on the test. They may also be things that you feel a bit shaky about— that is, things you've only recently studied and need to get down on paper while you still have them in mind.

Unloading is important for two reasons:

- **It relieves anxiety:** Just "blowing out" all the information pent up in you at the outset of the test can be extremely useful in helping overcome test anxiety.

- **It helps prevent forgetting:** One term or one idea can be like a string attached to a whole train of ideas that make up an entire essay. Unloading may well produce a key term or idea that leads to a string that you can pull on later in the test.

There is nothing illegal or unethical about unloading. It is not cheating so long as the things you unload are the product of your own brain and not cribbed from somewhere.

STEP 2: REVIEW, BUT DON'T ANSWER, THE SUBJECTIVE QUESTIONS. After unloading, flip the test over. Skip over any objective questions (true-false, multiple-choice) and go to the subjective questions. **_Subjective questions_ are those that generally require long answers, such as essay-type questions or those requiring lists as answers.** Examples of such questions are:

Describe the principal causes of the Civil War.

List the four operations of a computer system.

Compare and contrast the main schools of psychology.

You should also take 2–3 minutes to do a form of unloading: Write *keywords* in the margins next to each question. These keywords will help to serve as a rough outline when you start answering. Don't, however, immediately begin writing answers to the subjective questions (unless these are the only kinds of questions on the exam). Rather, proceed next to the objective questions on the test.

STEP 3: ANSWER THE OBJECTIVE QUESTIONS. _Objective questions_ **are those that are true-false, multiple-choice, matching, and fill-in.** There's a good reason for answering these objective questions before answering any subjective questions: *the very process of answering may help supply you with extra details for helping you answer your subjective*

questions. It may also help you answer a subjective question that you didn't know when you reviewed it in Step 2.

This method of operating shows how you can use the test as a tool. That is, your recognition of the answer to an objective question may help you to recall other material that may help you later in the test.

Answer the objective questions as quickly as you can. Don't spend any time on questions you're not sure of. Rather, circle or star them and return to them later.

STEP 4: ANSWER THE SUBJECTIVE QUESTIONS. When grading the test, instructors often assign more importance to some subjective questions than to others. That is, they will judge the answer to one question to be worth, say, 30% of the test grade and another to be worth 10%. Quite often the point values may be mentioned on the examination sheet. If they are not, raise your hand and ask the instructor or test giver. It's your right as a student to know.

To make efficient use of your time, do the following:

- **Read the directions!** This is obvious advice, and it applies to all types of test questions. However, since subjective questions usually have more point values than objective questions do, you want to be sure you don't misunderstand them.

- **Either answer the easiest first . . . :** Answer the *easiest* subjective questions first.

- **. . . Or answer the highest-value questions first:** Alternatively, answer the subjective questions with *the greatest point values* first.

STEP 5: ANSWER QUESTIONS LEFT UNDONE. By this point you will have answered the easiest questions or the ones that you have most knowledge about. As you get toward the end of the test period, now is your chance to go back and try answering the questions you left undone—those you circled or starred.

A word about guessing: *Unless the directions say otherwise,* often an *unanswered* question will count off just as much as an *incorrectly answered* question, especially on objective questions. Thus, *unless the instructor or test says there's a penalty for guessing,* you might as well take a guess.

STEP 6: PROOFREAD THE EXAMINATION.

If you get through all your questions before the end of the examination period, it's tempting to hand in your test and walk out early. For one thing, you'll be dying to find relief from the pressure cooker. Secondly, you may think it somehow looks as if you're smarter if you're one of the first to leave. (However, it's not so. Often it's the ones who don't know, and who have given up, who leave early.)

The best strategy, however, is: If you have any time left, use it. By staying you give yourself the extra edge that the early leavers don't. During this remaining time, look over the test and *proofread* it. Correct any misspellings. Reread any questions to make sure you have fully understood them and responded to them correctly; make any changes necessary to your answers.

Mastering Objective Questions

PREVIEW Different strategies may be employed for the different types of objective questions— for true-false, multiple-choice, matching, or fill-in-the-blank questions.

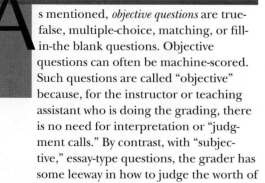

A s mentioned, *objective questions* are true-false, multiple-choice, matching, or fill-in-the blank questions. Objective questions can often be machine-scored. Such questions are called "objective" because, for the instructor or teaching assistant who is doing the grading, there is no need for interpretation or "judgment calls." By contrast, with "subjective," essay-type questions, the grader has some leeway in how to judge the worth of the answer.

Here are three general strategies to apply to objective questions:[1]

■ *Guess, unless there's a penalty:* With objective questions, *never leave an answer blank,* unless the instructor or test indicates there's a penalty for guessing. Note: Some instructors have grading systems for objective tests that penalize guessing. (For example, a correct answer may count +1, a nonresponse −1, and a wrong answer −2.) Thus, be sure you know the ground rules before you guess.

■ *If penalty exists, guess after eliminating half of the choices:* If the instructor does take points off for guessing, take a guess anyway when you can eliminate half or more of the options—for example, two out of four choices on a multiple-choice test.

■ *Allow second thoughts, if you've prepared:* Answer objective questions reasonably quickly, and make a check mark for any answer that you're unsure about. You may decide to change the answer when you do a final survey, based on information suggested to you by later items on the test.

"Contrary to the popular advice about never changing answers, *it can be to your advantage to change answers,*" say educators Tim Walter and Al Siebert (the emphasis is theirs). "The research evidence shows that when students have prepared well for an examination, the number of students who gain by changing answers is significantly greater than the number of students who lose by changing answers."[2]

The key here is "prepared well." If you've studied well for the test, your second thought may be more apt to be correct.

HANDLING TRUE-FALSE QUESTIONS. *True-false questions* **are statements that you must indicate are either "true" or "false."**

With such items, you have a 50% chance of getting each one right just by guessing. Thus, instructors may try to put in statements that seem true but on close reading actually are not.

Here are some strategies for handling true-false questions:

■ *Don't waste a lot of time:* Go through the true-false items as quickly as you can. Don't spend time agonizing over those you don't know; they usually aren't worth a lot of points compared to other parts of the test. Moreover, later questions may jog your memory in a way that suggests the correct answers.

■ *Be aware that more answers are apt to be true than false:* True-false tests generally contain more true answers than false ones. Thus, mark a statement true unless you know for sure it is false.

■ *Be aware longer statements tend to be true:* Statements that are longer and provide a lot of information *tend* to be true, though not always so. Read the statement carefully, however, to be sure no part of it is false.

■ *Read carefully to see that every part is true:* For the answer to be true, every part of the statement must be true. That is, a statement is false if *any part of* it is false. (Example: "The original Thirteen Colonies included Massachusetts, Virginia, and Illinois" is a false statement because the last state was not a member, though the first two were.)

■ *Look for qualifier words:* Qualifier words include the following: *all, none, always, never, everyone, no one, invariably, rarely, often, usually, generally, sometimes, most.*

Two suggestions to follow are these:

(1) Statements that use *absolute* qualifier words, such as "always" or "never," are usually false. (Example: "It's always dry in Nevada" is false because it does rain there some times.)

(2) Statements that use *moderating* qualifier words, such as "usually" or "often," tend to be true more often than not. (Example: "It's generally dry in Nevada" is true.)

HANDLING MULTIPLE-CHOICE QUESTIONS. *Multiple-choice questions* **allow you to pick an answer from several options offered,** generally between three and five choices. The question itself is called the *stem.* The choices of answers are called the *options.* Incorrect options are known as *distractors* because their purpose is to distract you from choosing the correct option. Usually only one option is correct, but check the test directions (or ask the instructor) to see if more than one answer is allowed.

There are two kinds of strategies to apply to multiple-choice questions—*thinking strategies* and *guessing strategies.*

Here are some *thinking strategies:*

■ *Answer the question in your head first:* Read the question and try to frame an answer in your mind before looking at the answer options. This will help you avoid being confused by "distractor" options.

■ *Eliminate incorrect answers first:* Read *all* the options, since sometimes two may be similar, with only one being correct.

(Beware of trick answers that are only partly correct.) Eliminate those options you know are incorrect. Then choose the correct answer from those remaining.

■ *Return to questions that are difficult:* Mark those questions that are difficult and return to them later if time permits. Spending time mulling over multiple-choice questions may not pay off in the points the instructor allows per question. Moreover, later questions in the test may trigger a line of thought that may help you with answers when you come back.

■ *Try out each option independently with the question:* If you're having trouble sorting out the options, try reading the question and just the first option together. Then try the question and the second option together. And so on. By taking each one at a time, you may be able to make a better determination.

■ *Be careful about "All of the above" or "None of the above":* The options "All of the above" or "None of the above" are often the correct choices. However, you have to examine the alternatives carefully. Make sure that *all* of the other options apply before checking "All of the above." Make sure *no one* other option is correct before marking "None of the above."

■ *Look for opposite choices:* If two choices are opposite in meaning, one is probably correct. Try to eliminate other choices, then concentrate on which of these two opposite options is correct.

Here are some *guessing strategies* for multiple-choice questions:

■ *Guess, if there's no penalty:* Unless the instructor has indicated he or she will take points off for incorrect answers, you might as well guess, if you don't know the answer.

■ *Choose between similar-sounding options:* If two options have similar words or similar-sounding words, choose one of them.

■ *If options are numbers, pick in the middle:* If the alternative options indicated consist of numbers, high and low numbers tend to be distractors. Thus, you might try guessing at one of the middle numbers.

■ *Consider that the first option is often not correct:* Many instructors think you should have to read through at least one incorrect answer before you come to the correct answer. Thus, when you're having to guess, consider that there's a high probability that the first option will be incorrect.

■ *Pick a familiar term over an unfamiliar one:* An answer that contains an unfamiliar term is apt to be a distractor, although many students tend to assume otherwise. If you're having to make a guess, try picking an option with a familiar term.

As I said with the true-false questions, when you go back and review your answers, don't be afraid to change your mind, if you realize that you could have made a better choice. The idea that you should always stick with your first choice is simply a myth.

HANDLING MATCHING QUESTIONS. *Matching questions* **require you to associate items from one list with items from a second list.** For example, on a history test you might be asked to associate eight famous political figures listed in Column A with the time period in which each one lived, as listed in Column B.

Strategies for handling matching questions are as follows:

■ *Ask if items can be used more than once:* With most matching-questions tests, each item in one column has its unique match in the other column. However, it's *possible* that items can be used for more than one match. That is, an item in Column B may fit several items in Column A. If you're not sure, ask the instructor.

■ *Read all choices before answering, then do the easy matchings first:* Before making your choices, read all options in both columns. Then work the easy items first. Matching the easier items first may help you match the tougher ones later by a process of elimination.

If you may use an item only once, cross off each item as you use it. (If items can be used more than once, put a check mark next to the ones you have used, rather than crossing them out.)

Put a question mark next to the matchings you're not sure about. If time permits, you can go back later and take another look at them.

HANDLING FILL-IN-THE-BLANK QUESTIONS. Also known as *sentence-completion questions*, __fill-in-the-blank questions__ **require you to fill in an answer from memory or to choose from options offered in a list.** Often the answers are names, definitions, locations, amounts, or short descriptions. Frequently there are clues contained within the incomplete sentence that will help you with your answer.

Strategies for working fill-in-the-blank tests are as follows:

- *Read the question to determine what kind of answer is needed:* Reading the question carefully will tell you what kind of fact is needed: a key term? a date? a name? a definition? By focusing on the question, you may be able to trigger an association from your memory bank.

- *Make sure the answer fits grammatically and logically:* Be sure that subject and verb, plurals, numbers, and so on, are used grammatically and logically. For example, if the statement says "a ____," don't put in "hour" and if it says "an ____," don't put in "minute." "*A* hour" and "*An* minute" are not grammatical.

As I've suggested with the other types of objective questions, you should put a star or question mark beside those items you're not sure about. Later material on the test may prompt your memory when you come back to review them.

Mastering Written Examinations: Short & Long Essays

PREVIEW Two types of written examinations are short-answer essay and long-answer essay. The strategy for the short-answer essay is to determine the amount of detail needed, depending on time available, point value, and your knowledge. The strategy for the long-answer essay is to meet the standards for relevance, completeness, accuracy, organization, logic, and clarity. This means reading the directions, looking for guiding words; determining choice of essay question; brainstorming ideas and making an outline of your position, supporting details, and summary; writing the three parts of the essay; making sure the essay is clear; and watching your time.

n __written examinations__ **you are generally required to write essays, either short or long.** Both types of essays may be on the same exam. In either case, the point values for answers usually count more than those for answers to objective questions.

- *Short-answer essay:* **A** __short-answer essay__ **may be a brief one-word or one-sentence answer to a short-answer question, a one- or two-paragraph essay, or a list or diagram.** Usually you are asked to write a response to just one question.

- *Long-answer essay:* **A** __long-answer essay__ **generally requires three or more paragraphs to answer.** You may be required to answer one question or several questions, all in the same essay.

Let's consider strategies for both of these.

HANDLING THE SHORT-ANSWER ESSAY.

Frequently tests contain questions that require only a short answer—anywhere from a single word to two or three paragraphs. Examples:

State the name of a particular theory. (This might be a one- or two-word answer.)

Define a certain term. (Could be done in a sentence.)

List the basic steps in a process. (Could be several words or sentences or a list.)

Describe a particular scientific study. (Might require a paragraph.)

Identify and describe three causes of a particular event. (Might be done in two or three paragraphs.)

Your strategy here is to provide the instructor with enough information (but not an excessive amount) to show that you understand the answer—whether it's a list, some brief sentences, or a few paragraphs.

How much detail should you provide? This is sometimes difficult to determine. After all, the question "Identify and describe three causes of the Civil War" could run to several pages. To decide how much detail is appropriate, you need to make a judgment based on three factors:

- *Time available:* How much time do you have for other questions on the exam? You may need to allow for an upcoming long essay question, for example.

- *Point value:* What is the relative weight (number of points) that the instructor assigns to short-answer questions compared with other questions?

- *Your knowledge:* How much do you know about the topic? The instructor might take points off if you volunteer information that is erroneous.

In general, it's best to write down just the minimum you think necessary. If you're in doubt, write out a response to one short-answer question, then take it up to the instructor and ask if it's long enough.

HANDLING THE LONG-ANSWER ESSAY.

The long-answer essay (and to some extent the short-answer essay) is sometimes considered a *subjective* test. This notion would seem to imply there are no "objective" facts and that it's up to the grader to determine how good your answer is. Actually, there usually *are* objective facts, and the instructor looks for them in your answer.

What strategy should you follow on a long-answer question? According to one clinical psychologist and instructor of first-year seminar courses, research shows that instructors award the greatest number of points when an essay answer meets the following six standards:[3]

1. *Relevance:* The answer sticks to the question. That is, the facts and points set down are relevant to the question.

2. *Completeness:* The question is answered completely.

3. *Accuracy:* The information given is factually correct.

4. *Organization:* The answer is organized well.

5. *Logic:* The answer shows that the writer can think and reason effectively.

6. *Clarity:* Thoughts are expressed clearly.

Basically, then, two things are important in answering essay questions: First, *you need to know your facts.* Second, *you need to present them well.*

. . . .

"Two things are important in answering essay questions: you need to know your facts and you need to present them well."

. . . .

Let us now proceed to outline a strategy for answering long-answer essay questions.

- **Read the directions!** This instruction is important for *all* test questions, of course. However, it is especially important here because of the amount of time you're required to invest in responding to long-answer essay questions and the high point values attached to them.

  In failing to read the directions carefully, students may answer only one question when three have been asked. Or they may answer three when only one has been asked (thereby depriving themselves of time to respond adequately to later test questions). Or they may go off on a tangent with an answer that earns no credit. I don't know how many times I've written in the margin of a test, "Nice response, but it misses the point. Did you read the directions?"

  Reading the directions will help you stay on the topic, thereby helping you to meet Standard #1 above—making the answer *relevant*.

- **Look for guiding words in the directions:** When you read the directions, look for guiding words—key task words such as *discuss*, *define*, or *compare*—which may guide your answer. **Guiding words are common words that instruct you in the task you are to accomplish in your essay-question answer.**

  Common guiding words are *analyze, compare, contrast, criticize, define, describe, discuss, enumerate, explain, evaluate, illustrate, interpret, outline, prove, relate, state, summarize,* and *trace*. A list of guiding words and their definitions appears in the box on the opposite page. *(See ■ Panel 8.1.)*

  As you read the directions, *circle or underline the guiding words* so that you know exactly what is required of you. This will help you achieve Standards #2 and #3—making your answer *complete* and *accurate*.

  Often, for instance, I will ask students to "compare and contrast" two ideas. However, some students will show only the similarities ("compare") and not the differences ("contrast"), thus answering only half the question and getting only

half the points. Circling guiding words will help you avoid such oversights.

- ***If you have a choice of essay questions, read them all:*** Some tests will allow you to choose which of, say, two or three essay questions you want to answer. In order to take your best shot, read all such questions, circling the guiding words. Then pick the essay question you think you can answer best.

- ***Brainstorm ideas:*** Now it's time to go to work—by doing some brainstorming and then making an outline. It's best to make your notes on a separate sheet of scratch paper. (If you use a part of the exam-questions sheet or blue book, be sure to cross them out afterward. You don't want to confuse the grader and have your notes figured into your point values—unless you're attaching the outline because you've run out of writing time.)

  Here's how to proceed:

(1) Do a little brainstorming. **Brainstorming means jotting down all the ideas that come to mind in response to the directions in the question.** Just blow out as many ideas as you can that seem to be pertinent. Do this for a minute or two. This will help ensure that you haven't left anything out—helping you to achieve Standard #2, *completeness*.

(2) Next read through your notes and *underline the important ideas.* These will become the basis for your outline and your essay.

- ***Make an outline of your prospective answer:*** At this point you may feel yourself under extreme pressure to simply begin writing. However, by taking another minute to make an outline you will help achieve Standard #4—your answer will be *organized*.

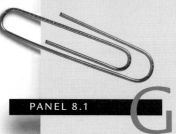

Guiding words. These key words appear in essay-question directions as part of the examination vocabulary. As you read the instructions, circle or underline such words so that you will be sure to focus your answer.

When an examination states . . .	*You should . . .*
Analyze	Explain the major parts or process of something.
Apply	Show function in a specific context.
Compare	Show similarities.
Contrast	Show differences.
Criticize (Critique) (Evaluate) (Examine)	Present your view (positive or negative) of something, giving supporting evidence for your position.
Define	Give the meaning of a word or expression. (Giving an example often helps.)
Demonstrate	Show function.
Describe	Present major characteristics.
Differentiate	Distinguish between two (or more) things.
Discuss (Review)	Give a general presentation of the question. (Give examples or details to support the main points.)
Enumerate	Present all the items in a series, as on a numbered list or outline.
Experiment	Try different solutions to find the right one.
Explain	Show how and why; clarify something.
Formulate	Devise a rule workable in other situations; put together new parts in several ways.
Identify	Label or explain.
Illustrate	Present examples of something.
Interpret	Explain the meaning of one thing in the context of another.
Justify	Give reasons why; argue in support of a position.
Organize	Put together ideas in an orderly pattern.
Outline	Present main points and essential details.
Perform (Solve) (Calculate)	Work through the steps of a problem.
Propose	Suggest new idea of your own for consideration.
Restate	Express the original meaning of something in new words.
Revise	Put together items in new order.
Sketch (Diagram)	Outline; draw picture or graph.
Summarize	Present core ideas.
Trace	Present a sequence; start at one point and go backward or forward in order of events.
Translate	Convert from one system to another.

Some examples:

Identify the parts of the cell.	[On a drawing of a cell, label the nucleus, cytoplasm, cell membrane, etc.]
Define seasonal affective disorder.	[Give the meaning of the term—for example, "Condition in which people become seriously depressed in winter and normal or slightly manic in summer."]

PANEL 8.2 outline of the parts of a long-answer essay. The answer consists of three parts: Your Position, Supporting Details, and Summary.

The essay question:
CRITICIZE OR DEFEND THE PROPOSITION THAT CAPITAL PUNISHMENT BENEFITS SOCIETY.

Possible outline for answer:

**Part 1,
Your Position:**
State your position in response to essay question.

1. Doesn't benefit.

**Part 2,
Supporting Details:**
List keywords representing 3 or so facts supporting your position.

2. Why not:
   a. Doesn't deter murders (FBI stats—compare states)
   b. Innocent executed (names)
   c. C.P. applied more to poor than rich (names)

**Part 3,
Summary:**
Restate your position; include supporting "mini-fact."

3. C.P. not mark of civilized society. Canada, England, Japan lower murder rate, no C.P.

My students have found that a certain formula for an outline seems to help them organize their thoughts and touch on the main points of the answer. The outline formula consists of three parts— Your Position, Supporting Details, and Summary. *(See* ■ *Panel 8.2.)*

Part 1, *Your Position,* states your position or viewpoint in response to the question being asked. It says what you are going to write about.

Part 2, *Supporting Details,* lists the supporting evidence for your position. These might be three or more facts. In your outline, jot down keywords that represent these facts.

Part 3, *Summary,* restates your position. It may include an additional supporting "mini-fact."

One reason for making an outline is that *if you run out of time and can't finish, you can attach the outline to your test answer and get partial credit.*

■ *Do Part 1, Your Position, by rewriting the test question, stating your position, and listing the evidence:* Now begin writing Part 1 of the essay, Your Position. If you follow the formula for the first paragraph that I describe, you will show your instructor that you are achieving Standard #5— your answer is *logical.*

(1) In the first sentence, include part of the examination question in your answer (without using the exact same words the instructor used). This will help you overcome inertia or anxiety and get going.

(2) Next state the position or point of view you will take.

(3) Then list, in sentence form, the facts you will discuss as evidence to support your position, starting with the strongest points in order to make a good impression.

Your first paragraph might read as shown in the example to the right. (See ■ *Panel 8.3.*)

PANEL 8.3

Example of a first paragraph for a long-answer essay. The first sentence restates the examination question or direction. The second sentence states the position you will take. The third, fourth, and fifth list the facts you will discuss as evidence to support your position.

The essay question or direction:

CRITICIZE OR DEFEND THE PROPOSITION THAT CAPITAL PUNISHMENT BENEFITS SOCIETY.

The first paragraph of your long-answer essay:

Whether capital punishment actually benefits society has long been a controversial issue in the United States.

[This first sentence somewhat restates the test question.]

I will argue that in the long run it does not.

[This second sentence states your position.]

As evidence, I offer the following supporting facts: First, capital punishment has not been found to deter future murders. Second, some innocent prisoners have been executed by mistake. Third, capital punishment is applied disproportionately to poor people.

[These last three sentences list the supporting facts for your position, which you will develop in subsequent paragraphs.]

Let us consider these three facts . . .

[This is a transition sentence. You will now develop each of the three facts into a full paragraph.]

Let us consider these three facts.
One of the strongest arguments for capital punishment is that the example of execution of murderers deters others from committing murders themselves. Thus, we would expect homicide rates to be lower in states with capital punishment laws than in states without them. However, this is not always the case. According to FBI crime statistics,

[Notice the supporting detail.]

Homicide rates in Southern states, most of which feature capital punishment, are higher than they are in many states in the Midwest, in which the strongest penalty for a homicide conviction is a life sentence. For instance, Georgia, which has capital punishment, has a higher murder rate than Minnesota, which does not.

[Notice additional supporting detail.]

Proponents of capital punishment also assume that the criminal justice system doesn't make mistakes . . .

[Notice the transition sentence to the next paragraph of supporting evidence.]

- *Do Part 2, Supporting Details, by expanding each fact into a paragraph:* Now you take the supporting facts you stated in sentence form in the first paragraph and address them separately. Take each fact and expand it into a full paragraph with supporting details. *(See ▪ Panel 8.4 at left.)* Use transitional sentences to connect the supporting details so that the reader can follow the progress of your discussion.

- *Do Part 3, Summary, by writing a paragraph summarizing your position and adding a supporting mini-fact:* The conclusion is basically a summary paragraph in which you simply restate your position. If you have an additional supporting mini-fact (or a supporting detail you've forgotten until now), this can "punch up" your ending a bit and bring your essay to a dramatic close. *(See ▪ Panel 8.5 at right.)*

- *As you write your essay, make sure it's clear:* Here are some tips to help you achieve Standard #6—*clarity.*

(1) *Write legibly,* using a pen rather than a pencil (which is difficult to read) and writing neatly rather than using a frantic scrawl. Because, as I said, grading of essay questions is somewhat subjective, you don't want to irritate the instructor by making your answer hard to read and risking lowering your points.

(2) *Write on one side of the paper only.* Writing on both sides will make the ink show through. Writing on one side also leaves you the opposite side of the page as a place to write an insert later in case you've forgotten something.

(3) *Leave generous space between paragraphs and in the margin.* Leaving space gives you an opportunity to add material later in such a way that you don't have to cram it in and make it hard to read.

(4) *Proofread.* If you have time, go back over your answer and check for grammar, spelling, and legibility so as to boost the clarity of your effort.

- **Watch your time:** Throughout the test you should keep track of your time, periodically checking to see how much time you have left. Answer the easy questions first, to build confidence, but after that give more time to questions that are worth more points.

As a student I used to think test-taking was often a matter of luck or having some sort of inherited smarts. However, you can see from the foregoing that it's pretty much a *learned* skill. And there's no question you're capable of learning it.

The Important Matter of Academic Honesty

PREVIEW Academic honesty is very important. Types of dishonesty include the following: (1) Cheating, or using unauthorized help. (2) Plagiarism, or presenting someone else's ideas as one's own. (3) Fakery, or inventing material. (4) Lying, by omission or commission.

People will commit such dishonest behaviors for several reasons: (1) They think what they're doing is a "white lie that won't hurt anyone." (2) They are in a crisis and are desperate. (3) They think "everyone does it." You can determine whether behavior is ethical by looking at yourself in the mirror, asking what your parents or friends would say, or asking if you could defend the behavior in court. Penalties for dishonesty in higher education could be a failing grade, suspension, or expulsion. Alternatives to cheating are (1) being prepared or (2) negotiating with the instructor.

PANEL 8.5　Example of summary paragraph.

In conclusion, I believe capital punishment is not the mark of a civilized society but rather its opposite.

[This first sentence restates your position.]

Other nations of the developed world, with far lower homicide rates than ours—Canada, England, Japan—have long since abolished this extreme form of punishment.

[This second sentence adds a last supporting mini-fact.]

It's time that we join them.

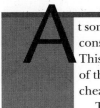

At some point in this book we need to consider the matter of academic honesty. This is as good a place as any, since one of the areas where problems arise is cheating on tests.

There are all kinds of ways to be less than honest in higher education: use crib sheets for tests, exchange signals with other test takers, give instructors false reasons for being late ("I was ill"; "I had car problems"), plagiarize term papers (pass off others' material as your own), buy "canned" term papers already prepared by commercial firms—the devices are endless.

A good place to examine one's values is in the area of academic honesty. To get a sense of some of the areas you may well encounter, take a look at Personal Exploration #8.2, at right.

TYPES OF ACADEMIC DISHONESTY. Academic dishonesty is of several principal types—cheating, plagiarism, fakery, and lying:

- *Cheating: Cheating* **is using unauthorized help to complete a test, practice exercise, or project.** This can mean writing crib notes of critical dates and names for a history test on one's shirt cuff or under the bill of a baseball cap. It can mean arranging a signal with other test takers to exchange answers. It can mean stealing a look at someone else's exam booklet or of a copy of the test before it is given out. It can mean copying someone else's laboratory notes, or field project notes, or computer project.

- *Plagiarism: Plagiarism* **means presenting another person's ideas as one's own.** For example, some students, having no opinions of their own about, say, a novel they've been assigned to write a report about, may try to pass off the comments of a literary critic as their own ideas. (If you can't come up with any ideas of your own but you simply agree with the critic's ideas, that's okay. Only be sure to *cite* the critic.)

- *Fakery: Fakery* **is when a person makes up or fabricates something.** Inventing data for a science experiment, for example, would be fakery.

- *Lying: Lying* **is simply misrepresentation of the facts.** Lying may be by omission or commission.

    In lying by *omission,* crucial facts are simply left out. For example, a student might explain a late paper with "I had computer problems," when what she really means is that the person whose computer she often borrows had to use it.

    In lying by *commission,* facts are simply changed. For example, a student might say his paper was late "because I was sick," when in fact he was just partying.

    The most outrageous, and risky, form of lying is passing off work as your own on which you have expended very little or no effort—for example, a term paper bought from a commercial firm.

WHY DO PEOPLE LIE OR CHEAT? According to Sissela Bok, professor of ethics at Brandeis University and author of the book *Lying,* people lie or cheat for one of three principal reasons:[4]

- *Just a little white lie:* People say to themselves they're just telling a little white lie. "It doesn't hurt anybody," they say, "so who cares?" Often, however, the lie *does* hurt somebody. In a course in which students are graded on a curve, for example, the honest term-paper writers who gave up their weekends to meet a course deadline may be hurt by the person who stayed up partying, then lied about being sick when handing in the paper late.

- *Desperation:* People may feel obliged to cheat because of a crisis. To save face with themselves they may say, "I don't usually do this, but here I really have to do it." This is the rationalization of students handing in a phony research paper bought from a term-paper factory because they didn't allow themselves enough time to research and write the paper themselves.

HOW WOULD YOU RESPOND TO CHALLENGES TO HONESTY?

College can throw you into situations that pose basic ethical conflicts. To see how you might fare, answer the following "Yes" or "No":

1. If I were in a classroom taking a final exam and saw two *friends* exchanging secret signals about the answers, I would do the following:

    a. Tell them afterward that I was ticked off because I'd studied hard and they hadn't, and their cheating might affect my grade.

      ❏ Yes ❏ No

    b. Probably say nothing to them.

      ❏ Yes ❏ No

    c. Report them in an unsigned (anonymous) note to the instructor.

      ❏ Yes ❏ No

    d. Complain personally to the instructor.

      ❏ Yes ❏ No

2. If I saw two students who were *unknown* to me exchanging secret signals in a test situation, I would do the following:

    a. Do nothing about it, although I might be contemptuous of them or even upset.

      ❏ Yes ❏ No

    b. Report them in an unsigned (anonymous) note to the instructor, identifying their location in the classroom and what I saw.

      ❏ Yes ❏ No

    c. Complain personally to the instructor.

      ❏ Yes ❏ No

3. I wouldn't cheat on a test myself, but I would not turn in a friend who cheated.

    ❏ Yes ❏ No

4. Lying about why I am late with a paper or missed a class is just a "white lie" that harms no one.

    ❏ Yes ❏ No

5. Higher education (and the world) is so competitive that sometimes you have to bend the rules just to survive.

    ❏ Yes ❏ No

6. So many people cheat. Cheating is wrong only if you get caught.

    ❏ Yes ❏ No

7. If you don't cheat, you're just an honest loser in a world where other people are getting ahead by taking shortcuts.

    ❏ Yes ❏ No

8. I try to be honest most of the time, but sometimes I get in a jam for time and am forced to cheat.

    ❏ Yes ❏ No

9. There's nothing wrong with buying a term paper written by someone else and passing it off as my own.

    ❏ Yes ❏ No

10. If instructors look the other way or don't seem to be concerned about cheating, then I'd be a fool not to take advantage of the system and cheat.

    ❏ Yes ❏ No

■ MEANING OF THE RESULTS

See the discussion in the text.

■ *"Everyone does it":* This is a very common excuse. As one graduate student at the Massachusetts Institute of Technology said, commenting on a 1991 cheating scandal attributed to extreme academic pressures, students see cheating take place, and "they feel they have to. People get used to it, even though they know it's not right."[5]

People who cheat in higher education, suggests University of Southern California psychology professor Chaytor Mason, are those "who don't think they're smart enough to make it by themselves. One of the greatest threats people feel is being considered unacceptable or stupid."[6]

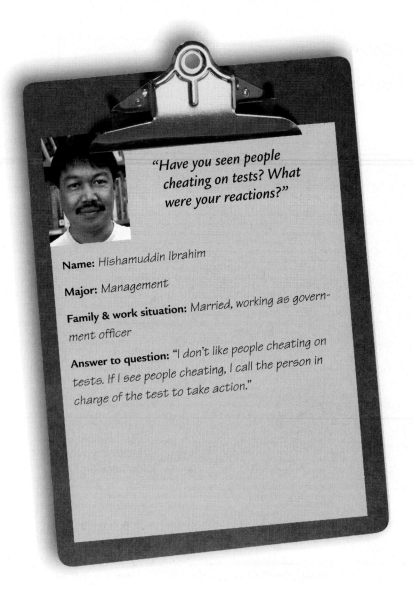

"Have you seen people cheating on tests? What were your reactions?"

Name: Hishamuddin Ibrahim

Major: Management

Family & work situation: Married, working as government officer

Answer to question: "I don't like people cheating on tests. If I see people cheating, I call the person in charge of the test to take action."

polls show that students in higher education are deeply concerned with "the moral and ethical standards in our country."[8] Thus, the place for ethics and morality starts with you.

If you have any doubt about the ethical question of something you're doing, you might put yourself through a few paces recommended by a crisis-management expert for business people who are worried about whether they are committing fraud:[9]

- *The Smell Test:* Can you look yourself in the eye and tell yourself that the position you have taken or the act you are about to undertake is okay? Or does the situation have a bad smell to it? If it does, start over.

- *The What-Would-Your-Parents-Say Test:* This is far more demanding. Could you explain to your parents (or family) the basis for the action you are considering? If they are apt to give you a raised eyebrow, abandon the idea. (You might actually have to deal with your parents or family, of course, if you were found to be cheating and were expelled from school.)

- *The Deposition Test:* A deposition is testimony taken under oath by lawyers. Could you swear in court that the activity you are doing is right? Or if a future employer or graduate or professional school asked if your grades were satisfactory, could you show them a transcript of your courses containing no Fs—the automatic failing grade given students caught cheating?

Many people who are bent on cheating, then, are probably less concerned with looking like a crook than with looking like a schnook. And that certainly shows *their* values. Clearly, this dilemma can be avoided by developing adequate study skills and scheduling enough time for studying.

IMAGINING YOU'RE FOUND OUT. If cheating seems to have been widespread in some places, ethics appear to be making a comeback. According to Michael Josephson, head of the Los Angeles–based Joseph and Edna Josephson Institute for the Advancement of Ethics, studies show that "90% of adults say they want to be considered ethical."[7] According to an executive for The Roper Organization,

THE PENALTIES FOR CHEATING. No matter how much you might be able to rationalize cheating to yourself or to anyone else, ignorance of the consequences is not an excuse. Most colleges spell out the rules somewhere against cheating or plagiarizing. These may be embodied in student conduct codes handed out to new students at the beginning of the year. Where I teach, instructors frequently give students a handout, as I do, at the first class that states that "If reasonable evidence exists that indicates you have cheated, you will receive a failing grade."

In general, the penalties for cheating are as follows:

- *Failing grade:* You might get a failing grade on the test, the course, or both. This is the slap-on-the-wrist punishment. Actually, it's usually automatic with a cheating or plagiarism offense and is given out *in addition to* other penalties.

  Of course, if you think you might fail the course anyway, you might be inclined to think, "Why not take the chance and cheat?" The reason not to do it is the additional penalties, which could vitally affect your future—as well as your feelings about yourself.

- *Suspension:* **Suspension means you are told you cannot return to school for a given amount of time, usually a semester or quarter or a year.**

- *Expulsion:* **Expulsion means you are kicked out of school permanently; you are not allowed to return.** This penalty is especially bad because it could make it very difficult to transfer to another school.

ALTERNATIVES TO CHEATING: PREPARATION & NEGOTIATION. Some students cheat routinely, but most do so only once, probably because they are desperate.[10] Let us make some suggestions on how one can avoid cheating:

- *Be prepared:* Some pretty obvious advice is simply: Be prepared. This usually comes down to a matter of developing your time-management and study skills. Overcoming bad habits such as procrastination or spending too much time on nonacademic things will probably eliminate even the thought of cheating. Getting the assistance of a tutor may also help.

- *Negotiate with the instructor for more time:* So your instructor is an intimidating figure? You assume he or she won't listen to an explanation of your situation? As an instructor myself, I understand how it's possible to fall behind, and I'm always open to a reasonable explanation from my students.

  Note that there may be other times in your life when you'll have to nervously explain to some authority figure why something you were responsible for didn't work out. Explaining to an instructor why you need more time to

study for a test or to write a paper is simply practice for those other occasions. It's possible you could push back the deadline a couple of days, which may be all you need. Or you might need to take an "Incomplete" in the course, which would allow you to make it up the following term. (Some schools, however, allow "Incompletes" only for medical reasons.)

Of course it's possible the instructor may deny your request, but at least you made the effort. If that's the case, grit your teeth, pull an all-nighter, do the best you can in the short time you have, and make a resolution never to put yourself in this bind again. Learning from experience is the first step toward change.

But don't cheat. That could really mess up your future. And it certainly reflects poorly on the values you would like to think you hold.

Onward

PREVIEW If you still have high levels of anxiety about testing, you can try other stress-busting techniques.

If, after reading this chapter, you get into a testing situation and find that your anxiety is still much too high, don't give up hope. One way to deal with such tensions is with relaxation training, as I discuss in Chapter 10, using creative visualization and similar methods. Another way, which has been found to be effective in alleviating anxiety-producing situations, is with systematic desensitization. This consists of replacing one's anxiety with relaxation. A visit to the counseling department of your school may show you how to avail yourself of such techniques.

This was an important chapter because it showed you valuable techniques for being successful on tests. It also asked you to take a hard look at matters of academic honesty and how they relate to your core values. Both apply in the world outside of higher education.

NOTES

1. Walter, T., & Siebert, A. (1990). *Student success* (5th ed.). Fort Worth, TX: Holt, Rinehart and Winston, pp. 96–97.

2. Walter & Siebert, 1990.

3. Starke, M. C. (1993). *Strategies for college success* (2nd ed.). Englewood Cliffs, NJ: Prentice Hall, p. 82.

4. Bok, S. Cited in: Venant, E. (1992, January 7). A nation of cheaters. *San Francisco Chronicle*, p. D3; reprinted from *Los Angeles Times*.

5. Dobrzeniecki, A. Quoted in: Butler, D. (1991, March 2). 73 MIT students guilty of cheating. *Boston Globe*, p. 25.

6. Mason, C. Quoted in: Venant, 1992, p. D4.

7. Josephson, M. Quoted in: Venant, 1992, p. D3.

8. Himmelfarb, S. (1992, June 1). Graduates feel anxious, not just about jobs [letter]. *New York Times*, p. A14.

9. Woodell, M. L. (1991, November 24). Fraud? Imagine you're in the spotlight. *New York Times*, sec. 3, p. 11.

10. Tetzeli, R. (1991, July 1). Business students cheat most. *Fortune*, pp. 14–15.

CLASSROOM ACTIVITIES

1. ***Walking in your instructor's shoes: preparing for an exam.*** This activity requires that each student have a copy of this text plus his or her lecture notes from this course. Divide the class into small groups of three to five people each.

   Ask each group to come up with four possible long-answer essay questions (those requiring three or more paragraphs, asking for comparison/contrast and the like) that might be asked on the next test. Suggest students use the kinds of tips described in this chapter to "walk in the instructor's shoes" and psych out what kinds of questions are apt to be asked.

   Ask students to share with the larger class the questions that were developed. Have them explain the reasoning behind their choices.

2. ***What kind of negative thoughts do you have during tests?*** Have students look at their responses to Personal Exploration #8.1, "More on Negative Thoughts & Positive Thoughts." Or have them, along with others in a small group, write down a list of negative thoughts that they sometimes have during test situations. Ask students to also describe the circumstances that generate such negative thoughts.

   Next ask students to generate a list of positive thoughts to replace the negative thoughts. Have them share their responses and conclusions with the class.

3. ***Applying exam strategies.*** Ask students to take a few minutes to look through Chapter 7 (on Reading) and write out five examination-style questions. There should be *one example each* of true-false, multiple-choice, matching, fill-in, and subjective (essay) questions.

   Now have each student join with four other people in a team and exchange all their questions (25 in all) with a second team. Each team should work through all the 25 questions it received, applying the techniques learned in the present chapter to trying to solve them.

   Later students may share their strategies with the rest of the class.

4. ***Have you ever cheated? What do you think of cheaters?*** This is a class-wide discussion activity. The instructor hands out pieces of scratch paper (it's important that all pieces of paper look pretty much alike). Each student is to describe on a piece of paper in 25 words or less one of the following: (a) An incident in which you cheated in school. (b) An incident of cheating you observed in school. (c) An incident of cheating you observed in some other situation.

   Tell students *not* to put their names on the paper. Have them carefully fold up their answers, which are then collected. Have students then take turns coming up to the front of the class, drawing one of the folded comments from a hat or box, then reading it aloud. Ask everyone to discuss the comments. Are there any circumstances under which cheating is excusable? What are the rules of your school's academic integrity standards?

JOURNAL ENTRY #8.1: HOW HAVE YOU PREPARED FOR TESTS IN THE PAST? Consider how you have prepared for tests in the past. How successful has your routine been? Which techniques would you take from this chapter that you would use in the future?

_____

_____

_____

_____

_____

_____

_____

JOURNAL ENTRY #8.2: HOW AFFECTED ARE YOU BY TEST ANXIETY? How big a roadblock is test anxiety for you? Which techniques will you try to employ to reduce it next time?

_____

_____

_____

_____

_____

_____

_____

JOURNAL ENTRY #8.3: WHAT TYPES OF TESTS ARE DIFFICULT FOR YOU? What kinds of tests do you do the worst on—true-false, multiple-choice, matching, fill-in-the-blank, short-answer essay, or long-answer essay? How will you change your approach in the future?

_____

_____

_____

_____

_____

_____

_____

_____

JOURNAL ENTRY #8.4: WHAT ABOUT CRAMMING FOR TESTS? Are you used to cramming for tests? How do you feel about this method? How will you break this habit in the future?

_____

_____

_____

_____

_____

_____

_____

communication

writing great papers

IN THIS CHAPTER: Does the idea of having to write a paper make you ill? Maybe that's because you don't have a formula for doing it. You'll probably have to write a number of papers in school—and in your career (when they're called "reports"). Now's your chance, then, to develop a strategy for doing them.

This chapter considers the following:

■ *How to target your audience:* What instructors look for in a written presentation, such as a research paper.

■ *Making a written presentation:* The five phases of conceptualizing, researching, and writing a paper.

Writing papers is mainly just academic busywork and not required much outside of college—right?

That's what I used to think. I thought these were just temporary skills I had to learn so instructors would have some basis for grading me.

After I graduated, however, I found out otherwise. The training I had developed in doing researching and writing, I discovered, was *very* important in building a career. If you need to research a business report, make a presentation to clients, or contribute to a newsletter, for instance, you'll be glad you learned how.

For now, though, it's a great benefit to learn how to use the library, pull information together, and present your research well. These are vital skills for success in higher education.

What Do Instructors Look for in a Term Paper?

PREVIEW Instructors grade term papers according to three criteria: (1) Demonstration of originality and effort. (2) Demonstration that learning took place. (3) Neatness, correctness, and appearance of the presentation.

Writing may be something you do for yourself. For instance, you can keep a journal or diary about your feelings, observations, and happenings; this is *personal writing*. Or you can write songs or poetry or musings; this is *expressive writing*. Or you can keep private notes about something you're working on, to help you sort out what you think. Here, however, let us consider a kind of writing you do for other people—specifically term papers for instructors.

Think about the meaning of the word "term" in *term paper*. Doing the paper is supposed to take the greater part of a school *term*—that is, a semester or quarter. Thus, it is supposed to be a paper based on extensive research of a specific subject. When finished it should probably run 10 or more double-spaced pages done on a typewriter or word processor. (This is equivalent to about 20 handwritten pages.) Sometimes you may have to give an oral presentation instead of writing a paper, but much of the work is the same. Because so much effort is required, no wonder instructors often consider the term paper to be worth *50% of the course grade.* This suggests why it's worth giving it your best shot, not just knocking it out over a weekend. (This is the equivalent of cramming for a test.)

Perhaps the best way to get oriented is to ask, *How do instructors grade term papers?* There are probably three principal standards:[1]

- Demonstration of originality and effort

- Demonstration that learning took place

- Neatness, correctness, and appearance of the presentation

1. DEMONSTRATION OF ORIGINALITY & EFFORT. *Are the ideas in your paper original and does the paper show some effort?* Instructors are constantly on the lookout for papers that do not represent students' own thoughts and efforts. These papers can take three forms, ranging from most serious (and dangerous to the student) to least serious:

- ***"Canned" or lifted papers:*** Papers known as "canned" papers may be *bought from commercial term-paper-writing services.* Or they may be *rewritten or lifted from old papers,* as from those of other students.

  Beware of submitting a paper that is not your own. The instructor might recognize it as the work of a student who was there before you or suspect the style is not yours. If you're found out, you'll not only flunk the course but probably will be put on some form of academic probation. This means you might be suspended or expelled from school.

- **_Plagiarized papers:_** The ideas and/or expression in a paper may be **_plagiarized;_** **that is, another person's ideas are passed off as one's own.** For instance, a student may copy passages from another source without giving credit to the source.

  Most instructors have developed a sensitivity to plagiarism. They can tell when the level of thought or expression does not seem appropriate for student writing. Moreover, lifting others' ideas goes against the very nature of why you're supposed to be in higher education to begin with. That is, you're supposed to be here to help yourself learn ways to meet challenges and expand your competence. In any case, plagiarism can also result in an F in the course and possible suspension from school.

- **_Unoriginal, no-effort papers:_** Quite often students submit papers that _show no thought and effort._ They consist of simply quoting and citing—that is, rehashing—the conflicting ideas of various experts and scholars. There is no evidence that the student has weighed the various views and demonstrated some critical thinking. A 10-page paper that shows original thinking is always better than a 20-page paper with lots of footnotes but no insights of your own.

  This leads us to point 2, about learning.

2. DEMONSTRATION THAT LEARNING TOOK PLACE. Instructors want to see you demonstrate the very reason why you're supposed to be in an institution of higher learning in the first place: _Does the paper show that you've learned something?_

How do you show that you're learning? My suggestion is this: _Ask a question for which the term paper provides the answer._ Examples of questions are as follows.

"Do men and women view 'date rape' differently?"

"Are alcohol and cigarettes really 'gateway' drugs to illegal drug use?"

"How did the Vietnam War affect the U.S. approach to the war in Bosnia?"

"What's the best way to dispose of radioactive waste?"

Always try, if you can, to make the question one that's important or interesting to you. That way you'll be genuinely motivated to learn something from the answer. At the end of your paper, you'll be able to demonstrate that learning took place. For example, you might conclude "When I first looked into the question of date rape, I wondered whether men and women view the matter differently. As the research in this paper has shown, I have found that. . . ."

3. NEATNESS, CORRECTNESS, & APPEARANCE OF PRESENTATION. Like most readers, instructors prefer neatness over messiness, readability over unreadability. Studies show that instructors give papers a higher grade if they are neat and use correct spelling and grammar. The third standard, then, involves form. _Is your paper typed and proofread and does it follow the correct form for footnotes and references?_

Let's consider these points:

- **_Typed versus handwritten:_** All instructors _prefer_—and many _require_—that you hand in a paper that has been produced on a typewriter or word processor rather than handwritten. Even if you're only a hunt-and-peck typist, it's best to try to render the final version of your term paper on a typewriter or word processor. (A word processor is easier for people who make lots of typing mistakes.) Or hire someone else to type it, if you can afford it.

- **Correct spelling and grammar:** As you write, look up words in the dictionary to check their spelling. Proofread the final version to correct any mistakes and bad grammar. (And if you're using a word processor, run the final draft through a spelling-checker program, in addition to proofreading it yourself.)

  You may be sick and tired of your paper when you finally get done with it. Nevertheless, you would hate to blow it at the end by allowing the instructor to mark it down because you overlooked the small stuff.

- **Follow correct academic form:** Different academic disciplines (English and psychology, for example) have their preferred footnote and bibliography styles. Be sure to follow any directions your instructor gives for these and any other requirements for the form of the paper.

  Now you know what you're aiming for. Let's see how to achieve it.

Writing a Term Paper: Five Phases

PREVIEW The five phases of producing a term paper are as follows. (1) Pick a topic. (2) Do initial research and develop an outline. (3) Do further research. (4) Sort notes, revise the outline, and write a first draft. (5) Revise, type, and proofread the paper.

The audience for a term paper, I said, is an instructor. Writing for instructors is different from other writing. It's not the same, for example, as an essay accompanying an application for admission to university, college, or vocational-technical school. Nor is it the same as an article for the school paper or a letter of complaint to a landlord or government official. Nor is term-paper writing the same as writing an article for an academic journal; it is usually less formal and rigorous than that.

In this section, I'll explain how to prepare a term paper for an instructor. There are five principal phases:

- **Phase 1:** Picking a topic

- **Phase 2:** Doing initial research and developing a preliminary outline

- **Phase 3:** Doing your research—using the library

- **Phase 4:** Sorting your notes, revising the outline, and writing a first draft of the paper

- **Phase 5:** Revising, typing, and proofreading your paper

Be mindful of the fact that the grade on the term paper will count heavily toward the grade in the course. Thus, you should try to spread these phases over the semester or quarter—not do them all in one week or a few days.

Phase 1: Picking a Topic

PREVIEW The first phase, *picking a topic,* has five parts. (1) Set a deadline for picking a topic. (2) Pick a topic important to the instructor and interesting to you. (3) Refine proposed topics into three questions. (4) Check topics with the instructor.

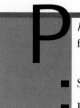*hase 1 consists of picking a topic.* This has five parts:

- Set a deadline for picking the topic

- Pick a topic important to the instructor and interesting to you

- Refine your proposed topics into three questions

- Check with your instructor

SET A DEADLINE FOR PICKING YOUR TOPIC. Students often procrastinate on this first step. However, the most important advice I can give you about writing papers is: START EARLY. By beginning early, you'll be able to find a topic that interests you. Moreover, you'll avoid pitfalls such as picking a subject that is too narrow or too large.

Thus, *as soon as you get your instructor's guidelines for the term paper, set a deadline for picking the topic.* In your lecture notes, on a page by itself, write a big note to yourself:

*** DEADLINE: PICK TERM PAPER TOPIC BY TUESDAY NOON! ***

In addition, put this on your To Do list and on your weekly planner.

PICKING A TOPIC: TWO CRITERIA. There are two criteria for picking a topic. Pick something that is (1) important to your instructor and (2) interesting to you.

■ *Topics important to the instructor:* You need to determine what is important to your instructor because he or she is the sole audience for your paper.

How do you find out what the instructor believes is significant? First, if he or she has provided any written guidelines, read them carefully. If the assignment is given verbally, take precise notes. You'll also get a better idea of what's important when you meet with the instructor to discuss your proposed topics, as I describe.

■ *Topics interesting to you:* Motivation is everything. Thus, whenever possible, try to choose a topic that interests you. It also helps if you already know something about it. To determine what might be suitable, look through your lecture notes to see what things pop out at you.

Don't be afraid of mistakes. The fear of making a mistake, of failing, is quite common. It occurs because most of us have been rewarded while growing up for producing "right" answers. However, sometimes you *want* to permit yourself

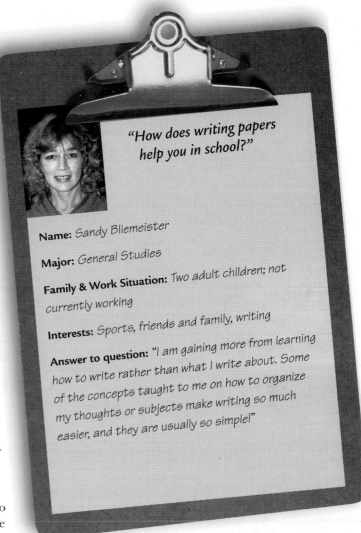

"How does writing papers help you in school?"

Name: Sandy Bliemeister

Major: General Studies

Family & Work Situation: Two adult children; not currently working

Interests: Sports, friends and family, writing

Answer to question: "I am gaining more from learning how to write rather than what I write about. Some of the concepts taught to me on how to organize my thoughts or subjects make writing so much easier, and they are usually so simple!"

mistakes because that allows you to come up with fresh ideas.

By saying that no ideas are too risky or embarrassing, you allow yourself to consider information you'd normally ignore. Judgment and criticism are necessary later in the problem-solving process. However, if they occur too early, you may reject many ideas, some of which are fragile and imperfect but may be made mature later.

Try brainstorming. The word *brainstorming* was coined by advertising man Alex Osborn for a type of group problem solving in which several people work simultaneously on a specific problem. However, you can use this method by yourself. Four rules govern the procedure, according to Osborn:

(1) No evaluations or judgments are permitted, which might cause people to defend rather than generate ideas.

(2) Think of the wildest ideas possible, in order to decrease individual judgment among individual members.

(3) The more ideas the better—quantity is more important than quality and, in fact, quantity leads to quality.

(4) Build on and modify the ideas of others whenever possible, which will lead to ideas superior to the original ones.[2]

EXPRESSING PROPOSED TOPICS AS THREE QUESTIONS. By the time your self-imposed deadline arrives for choosing your topic, you should have three alternative ideas. Because your purpose is to demonstrate that you're learning, these should be expressed as questions.

For example, for an introductory health course, you may decide on the following possible topics.

"What diets are most effective for weight loss?"

"Does meditation prolong life in cancer patients?"

"Does wearing helmets reduce motorcycle injuries?"

Are some of these questions too broad (diets) or too narrow (helmets)? In the next step, you'll find out.

CHECKING TOPIC IDEAS WITH YOUR INSTRUCTOR. It's now a good idea to take your topic questions and show them to your instructor (after class or during office hours). Questions to ask are the following:

■ *Is it important enough?* Ask "Do you think any of these topics are important enough to be worth exploring in a term paper?" The answer will indicate whether you are meeting the first criterion in selecting a topic—does the instructor think it's significant?

■ *Is the scope about right?* Ask "Do you think the topic is too broad or too narrow in scope?" The instructor may suggest ways to limit or vary the topic so you won't waste time on unnecessary research. He or she can also prevent

you from tackling a topic that's too advanced. Equally important, the instructor may be able to suggest some books or other resources that will help you in your research.

What if you're in a large class and have difficulty getting access to your instructor (or teaching assistant)? In that case, go to the library and ask a reference librarian for an opinion on the topic's importance and scope. In addition, of course, he or she will be able to steer you toward some good sources of information for your research.

Phase 2: Doing Initial Research & Developing an Outline

PREVIEW The beginning of Phase 2, *doing initial research,* consists of using the library's card catalog and guide to periodicals to determine the scope of research material. The second part of Phase 2, *developing an outline,* means doing a tentative outline suggesting the paper's beginning (introduction), middle (body), and end (conclusion). The beginning and middle pose questions you hope your research will answer.

Phase 2 consists of doing initial research and developing an outline. If it took you one week to decide on a topic, it should take you another week to do Phase 2. Here, too, you should write a big note to yourself (and also put it on your weekly calendar and To Do list):

*** DEADLINE: CHECK OUT RESEARCH FOR TERM PAPER BY WEDNESDAY 5 P.M.! ***

The idea here is to satisfy yourself about two things:

- **Research material:** Is enough material available to you so that you can adequately research your paper?

- **Rough outline:** Do you have a rough idea of the direction your paper will take?

INVESTIGATING RESEARCH MATERIAL. This step need not take long—perhaps a half hour in the library. The idea is to look in a handful of places to get a sense of the research material accessible to you. Two places to look in particular are:

- **Card or online catalog:** Look under the subject listing in the library's card catalog or online catalog to see what books exist on your topic. Don't assume, however, that just because the books are listed they are easily available. (They may be checked out, on reserve, or in another campus library. An online catalog may tell you if they're checked out.) Look up some call letters for relevant titles, then visit the shelves and see what books you can find.

- **Guide to periodicals:** Magazines and journals are apt to be more up to date than books. Check the *Reader's Guide to Periodical Literature* or computerized catalog to see what articles are available in your topic area. Jot down the names of the periodicals, then check with the reference librarian to see if they are available to you.

Further information about the library, including use of the card catalog and guide to periodicals, is given in Phase 3, Research. This preliminary investigation, however, gives you an overview of the subject.

DEVELOPING AN OUTLINE. While you're in the library doing your first research you should also do a preliminary outline.

Many people resist doing an outline because they think "I don't know where I'm going until I've been there." That is, they think they won't know their direction until they've done all the research

and thought about the material. Or they think an outline is somehow going to lock them in to an approach that might not work out.

The purpose of doing a preliminary outline now is twofold. First, it will save you time later. Second, it will provide you with a general road map. You can always change the outline later. But if you set out without one, you may waste time wandering around before you get a sense of direction.

Take a sheet of paper and write *OUTLINE #1* across the top. Then fill in the following three parts—*I. Beginning, II. Middle,* and *III. End.*[3]

I.   *BEGINNING—the introduction*

The beginning or introduction describes the *one or two main questions your paper will try to answer.* In the final paper, the beginning will be one or two paragraphs.

Example: "How smart are college athletes?" "Are college athletics dominated by 'dumb jocks'?"

II. *MIDDLE—the body*

The middle or body of the outline describes *some specific questions your paper will try to answer.* These are detailed questions that will help you answer the main questions.

Examples: "What's the grade-point average (GPA) of college football, baseball, and basketball players?" "What's the GPA of competitive swimmers, gymnasts, and tennis players?" "What percentage of athletes graduate compared to most students?" "What percentage drop out?" "What proportion of athletes in pro sports are college graduates?" "Are top athletes usually top scholars, such as Phi Beta Kappa, magna cum laude, Rhodes Scholars?" And so on.

III. *END—the conclusion*

You won't know the end or conclusion, of course, until you've done the research and answered your questions. For now, *just state that you will write a conclusion based on your answers.*

Here are some techniques for developing your outline:

■ *Write questions on index cards:* Get a stack of 3 × 5 index cards or cut sheets of notepaper into quarters. On each card or quarter-page, write a question you want to answer about your topic. *Write as many questions as you can think of, both general and detailed.*

■ *Organize index cards into categories:* Now sort your 3 × 5 cards into stacks. The stacks represent whatever categories come to mind. One stack might contain a few general questions that will make up your introduction. The others will make up specific categories for the body of the outline.

What kinds of categories might you have? Some might be stacks of similar kinds of questions. Some might be advantages and disadvantages, or cause and effect, or compare and contrast. Do whatever kind of grouping seems sensible to you.

■ *Write out your outline:* Copy out the categories and questions into the outline form shown above. You now have a road map to follow to begin your research.

Note: If you are used to a computer, you may find an *outlining program* useful rather than 3 × 5 cards. This kind of software allows you to brainstorm and sort out ideas onscreen.

After developing it, show your outline to your instructor.

He or she will be able to determine at a glance whether you seem to be headed in the right direction.

Phase 3: Doing Your Research—Using the Library

PREVIEW Phase 3, *doing research,* usually means using the library. This requires learning the parts of the library; discovering how to use librarians and the catalog; knowing how to locate books, periodicals and journals, and reference materials; and finding out how to use other libraries. Low-tech ways of collecting information involve use of 3 × 5 cards. High-tech ways involve the use of photocopiers and computers.

hase 3 consists of doing your research, which usually means making use of the library. In this section, let us consider these aspects:

■ Parts of the library

■ Using librarians and the catalog

■ Locating books

■ Finding periodicals and journals

■ Finding reference materials

■ Using other libraries

■ Low-tech ways to collect information: 3 × 5 cards

■ High-tech ways to collect information: photocopiers and personal computers

FINDING YOUR WAY AROUND THE LIBRARY.
Particularly at a large university, you may find that the library is a lot larger than those you're accustomed to. Indeed, there may be several libraries on campus, plus access to libraries elsewhere. The most important one for first-year students is the *central library,* the principal library on campus.

The central library has several parts:

■ *Main section:* The main section includes six parts:

(1) The desk where you check books out

(2) The catalog (card or computerized) listing books

(3) A reference section, with dictionaries, encyclopedias, and directories

(4) A periodicals section displaying current newspapers, magazines, and journals

(5) A section (perhaps called the "stacks") housing books

(6) A section housing back issues of periodicals

■ *Other sections:* In addition, the central library usually has some special sections:

(1) A media center, or section containing audiotapes and videotapes

(2) A section for reserve books, which have been set aside by instructors for certain courses

(3) A vertical file containing pamphlets on special topics

(4) A government documents section

■ *Other services—study areas and machines:* Most campus libraries also provide study areas. Indeed, because the whole purpose of the library is to enable students to do serious work, there are relatively few distractions there.

Finally, there may be several kinds of machines available for your use. Examples are machines for reading microfilm and microfiche (materials on film),

terminals for accessing databases and indexes, and machines for making photocopies. Some libraries provide typewriters or word processors. Some also have machines providing access to audiotapes, CDs, videotapes, slides, films, filmstrips, videodisks, computer floppy disks, and/or CD-ROM disks.

If you have not had a formal orientation to the library, whether videotaped presentation or actual tour, now is the time. If possible, do it before you're under a tight deadline for a research paper, so you won't have to do your research under panic conditions. Some institutions offer a credit course in how to use the library—something I would recommend to anyone.

The principal resource, the trained navigators, as it were, are the *reference librarians.* Don't hesitate to ask for their help. That's what they're there for. They can tell you if the library has what you need and show you how to get started. Reference librarians are also the people to hunt up when you have exhausted other resources. They may refer you to special sources within the library or to different libraries on or off campus.

HOW TO FIND WHAT YOU WANT IN BOOKS.
Books may be found on open shelves in the main section of the library. In some places, they may also be back in the "stacks," requiring a library page or runner to go get them. Or they may be in special libraries located elsewhere on campus, such as those attached to the business school or the law school. Or they may be available by means of **inter-library loan, a service that enables you to borrow books from other libraries.** Allow extra time—several days or even a couple of weeks—and perhaps a small fee, when you're obtaining a book through interlibrary loan.

To find a book, you may use a *card catalog, CD-ROM computerized catalog,* or *online computerized catalog:*

- **The card catalog: A library _card catalog_ contains information about each book typed on a 3-by-5-inch card, stored in wooden file drawers.** This is the system that has been used by libraries for decades.

  Libraries have three kinds of card catalog listings for books: _title, author,_ and _subject_. Thus, you can find _The Right and the Power: The Prosecution of Watergate_ by Leon Jaworski in three ways. The first is by title—under "R." (Words such as "The," "A," and "An" are omitted if they are the first word in a title.) The second is by author's last name—under "J." The third is by subject—under "United States, petitioner"; "Nixon, Richard Milhous"; or "Watergate Affair." _(See ■ Panel 9.1, opposite page.)_

  When doing research papers, you'll probably often use the subject catalog. Standardized subject headings are listed in the reference work _Library of Congress Subject Headings,_ which the reference librarian can help you find.

- **CD-ROM computerized catalog: _CD-ROM catalogs_ look like music compact disks (CDs), except that they are used to store text and images. CD-ROM stands for Compact Disk—Read Only Memory.** To use a CD-ROM, you put the disk into the microcomputer's CD-ROM drive, then follow directions (perhaps on Help screens) for searching by title, author, or subject.

  An advantage of CD-ROMs is that you can use keywords to search for material. **_Keywords_ are any words you use to find specific information.** For example, you could use the keywords "National Socialism" to look for books about Hitler and the Nazi Party.

  A drawback of CD-ROMs, however, is that a disk cannot be updated. Instead a new disk must be produced, which your library may do every month or so. Thus, any CD-ROM catalog you consult may lag slightly behind the library's acquisitions.

- **Online computerized catalog: _Online computerized catalogs_ require that you use a computer terminal or microcomputer that has a wired connection to a database.** Online catalogs have all the advantages of CD-ROMs, including the ability to do keyword searches. However, they are more quickly updated. Moreover, they may contain additional information, such as whether or not a book has been checked out. The instructions for using online catalogs appear on the computer keyboard and/or on the display screen (in Help screens). _(See ■ Panel 9.2, below.)_

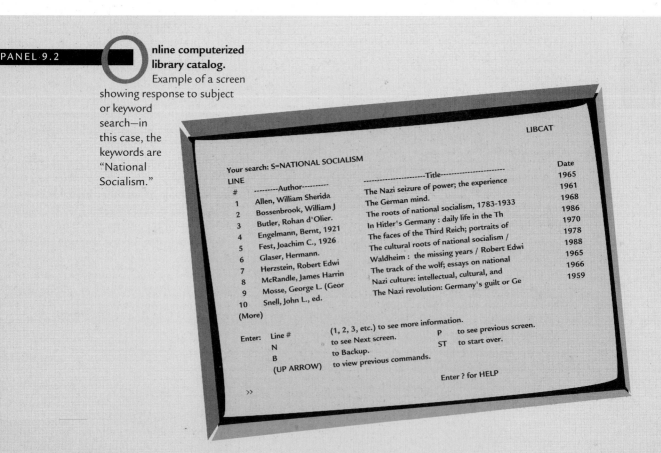

PANEL · 9.2

Online computerized library catalog. Example of a screen showing response to subject or keyword search—in this case, the keywords are "National Socialism."

Your search: S=NATIONAL SOCIALISM

LIBCAT

LINE #	Author	Title	Date
1	Allen, William Sherida	The Nazi seizure of power; the experience	1965
2	Bossenbrook, William J	The German mind.	1961
3	Butler, Rohan d'Olier.	The roots of national socialism, 1783-1933	1968
4	Engelmann, Bernt, 1921	In Hitler's Germany : daily life in the Th	1986
5	Fest, Joachim C., 1926	The faces of the Third Reich; portraits of	1970
6	Glaser, Hermann.	The cultural roots of national socialism /	1978
7	Herzstein, Robert Edwi	Waldheim : the missing years / Robert Edwi	1988
8	McRandle, James Harrin	The track of the wolf; essays on national	1965
9	Mosse, George L. (Geor	Nazi culture: intellectual, cultural, and	1966
10	Snell, John L., ed.	The Nazi revolution: Germany's guilt or Ge	1959

(More)

Enter: Line #   (1, 2, 3, etc.) to see more information.   P   to see previous screen.
        N   to see Next screen.   ST   to start over.
        B   to Backup.
        (UP ARROW)   to view previous commands.

Enter ? for HELP

>>

Three kinds of card catalog listings: title, author, subject. The same book may be found on cards in the three separate catalogs. Note the subject headings at the bottom of the card. These offer more categories that could produce other books pertinent to your area of research.

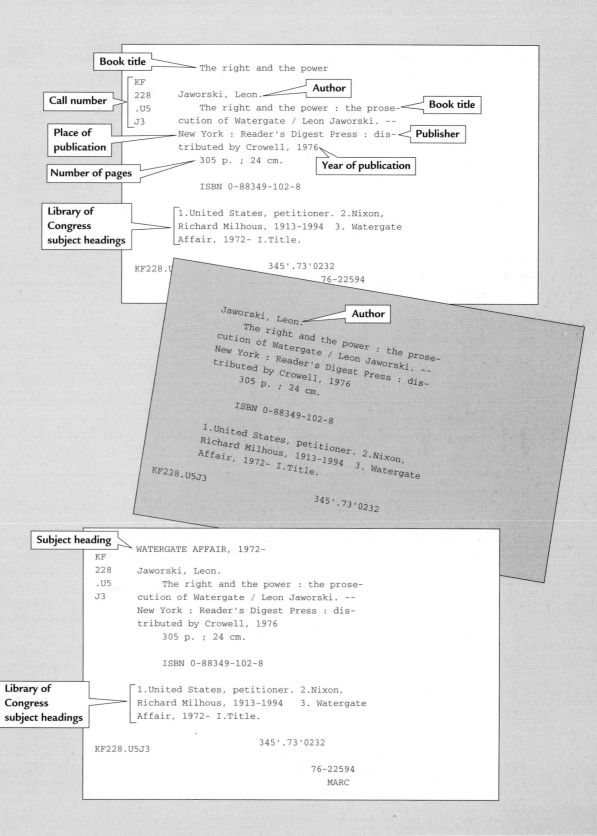

Note: *Books in Print* is an annual reference work—organized by title, author, and subject—that lists most books currently in print in the United States. By using the subject category you can also find books in your area of research, although they won't necessarily be in your school's library.

Most schools' libraries use the Library of Congress system of call numbers and letters. Get the call numbers from the card or computerized listing, then use a map of the library to find the appropriate shelves. Once you've found your book, look at other books in the general vicinity to see if they could be useful.

If you can't find a book on the shelves and decide you really need it, ask a librarian for help. It may be in the reference section or on reserve for a class. If it has been checked out, ask the library to put a hold on it for you when it's returned. Or ask for help getting another copy through interlibrary loan.

HOW TO FIND WHAT YOU WANT IN NEWSPA-PERS, MAGAZINES, & JOURNALS. You can see what general newspapers, magazines, and journals are available by simply looking at the open shelves in the periodicals reading room. A list of the library's holdings in periodicals should also be available at the main desk.

Here are some avenues for finding articles in the research area you're interested in. *(See ■ Panel 9.3, opposite page.)*

- *Newspaper indexes:* In the United States, the newspapers available nationally and in many campus libraries are *The New York Times, The Wall Street Journal,* and *USA Today.* Some schools may also subscribe to other respected newspapers such as *The Washington Post* or *The Los Angeles Times.* Some newspapers print indexes that list information about the articles appearing in their pages. Examples are *The New York Times Index* and *The Wall Street Journal Index.* Look also for *Newspaper Abstracts* and *Editorials on File.*

  In addition, your library may subscribe to computerized databases providing bibliographical information about articles appearing in hundreds of magazines and newspapers. Ask the librarian how

you can use *Data Times, DIALOG,* or the reference services of *CompuServe, America Online, Prodigy,* or *Nexis.*

- *Magazine indexes:* The index for the 100 or so most general magazines, many probably available in your library, is the *Readers' Guide to Periodical Literature.* This lists articles appearing in such well-known magazines as *Time, Newsweek, Reader's Digest, Psychology Today,* and *Business Week.*

  Other indexes, available in printed, microfilm, or CD-ROM form, are *Magazine Index, Newsbank, InfoTrac, Business Index,* and *Medline.*

- *Journal indexes and abstracts:* Journals are specialized magazines, and their articles are listed in specialized indexes and databases. Examples range from *Applied Science and Technology Index* to *Social Science Index.*

  In addition, there are indexes called **_abstracts_, which present paragraphs summarizing articles along with bibliographical information about them.** Examples range from *Biological Abstracts* to *Sociological Abstracts.*

  Some journal indexes are accessed by going online through a computer. For example, *PsycLit* is a bibliographic database to *Psychological Abstracts.*

HOW TO FIND OTHER REFERENCE MATERIALS. All kinds of wonderful other reference materials are also available to you. Here's a short list:

- *Dictionaries, thesauruses, style books:* Need to look up specialized terms for your paper? The reference section of the library has not only standard dictionaries but also specialized dictionaries for technical subjects. Examples range from *Dictionary of Biological Sciences* to *Webster's New World Dictionary of Computer Terms.*

  In addition, you may find a thesaurus helpful in your writing. **A _thesaurus_ lists synonyms, or words with similar meanings.** This is a great resource when you can't think of the exact word you want when writing.

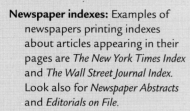

Newspaper indexes: Examples of newspapers printing indexes about articles appearing in their pages are *The New York Times Index* and *The Wall Street Journal Index.* Look also for *Newspaper Abstracts* and *Editorials on File.*

Examples of computerized databases providing information about newspaper articles are *Data Times, Dialog, CompuServe, America Online, Prodigy,* and *Nexis.*

Magazine indexes: The *Readers' Guide to Periodical Literature* lists articles appearing in well-known American magazines.

Other indexes, available in printed, microfilm, or CD-ROM form, are *Magazine Index, Newsbank, InfoTrac, Business Index,* and *Medline.*

Journal indexes and abstracts:

Examples of indexes and databases for specialized journals are *Accountants' Index, Applied Science and Technology Index, Art Index, Business Periodicals Index, Computer Data Bases, Education Index, Engineering Index Monthly, General Science Index, Humanities Index, Medline,* and *Social Science Index.*

Examples of indexes called abstracts are *Biological Abstracts, Chemical Abstracts, Historical Abstracts, Psychological Abstracts,* and *Sociological Abstracts.*

Some computerized online indexes to journals are available, such as *PsycLit,* a bibliographic database to *Psychological Abstracts.*

Specialized dictionaries: Examples of specialized dictionaries for technical subjects are *Dictionary of Biological Sciences, Dictionary of Film Terms, Dictionary of Quotations, Dorland's Illustrated Medical Dictionary, Grove's Dictionary of Music and Musicians, Mathematical Dictionary,* and *Webster's New World Dictionary of Computer Terms.*

Encyclopedias, almanacs, and handbooks: Examples of encyclopedias on specialized subjects are *Cyclopedia of World Authors, Encyclopedia of Associations, Encyclopedia of Banking and Finance, Encyclopedia of Bioethics, Encyclopedia of Religion and Ethics, Encyclopedia of Sports, Encyclopedia of World Art, Thomas Register of American Manufacturers,* and *The Wellness Encyclopedia.*

Examples of specialized almanacs, handbooks, and other reference sources are *The Business Writer's Handbook, Comparisons, The Computer Glossary, Facts on File, The Guinness Book of World Records, Keesing's Record of World Events, Literary Market Place, The Pacific Rim Almanac,* and *The Secret Guide to Computers.*

Government literature: Publications published by the U.S. Government are listed in *The Monthly Catalog* and *PAIS (Public Affairs Information Service).*

Computer networks: Examples of guides to computerized information networks are *Directory of Online Databases, Encyclopedia of Information Systems and Services,* and *Guide to the Use of Libraries and Information Services.*

Finally, there are various style books for helping you do footnotes and bibliographies, such as *The Chicago Manual of Style*.

- **Encyclopedias, almanacs, handbooks:** No doubt the library has various kinds of standard encyclopedias, in printed and CD-ROM form. As with dictionaries, there are also encyclopedias on specialized subjects. Examples range from *Cyclopedia of World Authors* to *The Wellness Encyclopedia*.

  There are also all kinds of specialized almanacs, handbooks, and other reference sources. Examples range from *The Business Writer's Handbook* to *The Secret Guide to Computers*.

- **Government literature:** A section of the library is probably reserved for information from both the federal government and state and local governments. The most prolific publisher in the world is the United States government. To find out publications pertinent to your subject, look in *The Monthly Catalog* and *PAIS (Public Affairs Information Service)*.

- **Computer networks:** This is a vast subject in itself. Now many libraries subscribe to computerized information networks, such as DIALOG, ERIC, ORBIT, and BSR. Directories and guides exist to help you learn to use these services. Examples are *Directory of Online Databases, Encyclopedia of Information Systems and Services*, or *Guide to the Use of Libraries and Information Services*.

  In addition, there are many online information services: America Online, CompuServe, Prodigy, and Microsoft Network. Many schools also provide access to the Internet, the so-called network of networks, which unifies over 36,000 individual computer networks.

HOW TO USE OTHER LIBRARIES. In big universities, various departments and schools often have their own libraries. Thus, the libraries of, say, the business school or medical school will have material that the main library does not. In addition, you may find a visit to local city or county libraries worthwhile or the libraries of other colleges nearby. Although you probably won't be allowed to check out materials, you can certainly use the materials available to the general public.

LOW-TECH WAYS TO COLLECT INFORMATION: 3 × 5 CARDS. Some materials (principally books) you'll be able to check out and have access to at your usual writing desk. However, most libraries won't let you take out magazines, encyclopedias, and general reference materials. Thus, you'll need to be able to take notes in the library.

Traditional 3 × 5 index cards are useful because you can write one idea on each card, then later sort the cards as you please. Index cards should be used in three ways—as *source cards, information cards*, and *idea cards*. (See ■ Panel 9.4.)

- **Source cards:** Use *source cards* to keep track of bibliographical information. At the time you're looking up your sources, you can jot down the call letters on these cards. Specifically:

  (1) For each *journal article*: Write down the author's last and first name (for example, "Anderson, Dave"), title of article, title of journal, month and year, volume and issue number, and page numbers.

  (2) For each *book*: Write down the author's (or editor's) name, book title, edition, city and state of publication, name of publisher, year of publication (listed on the copyright page), and pages you referred to, if necessary.

  Later, when you type your references, you'll be able to arrange these source cards in alphabetical order by authors' last names.

- **Information cards:** Use *information cards* to copy down information and quotations. This is the actual research material you will use. The card will have three areas:

  (1) *Source abbreviation:* At the top of each card, put an abbreviated version of the source, including the page number. (Example: "Anderson 1995, p. 35." If you have two 1995 Anderson references, label them *a* and *b*.) If you use more

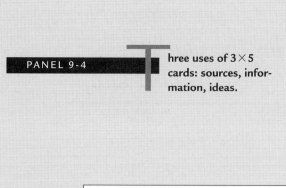

Three uses of 3 × 5 cards: sources, information, ideas.

than one card for a single source, number the cards.

(2) *Information:* In the lower part of the card, write the information. If it's a direct quote, enclose it in quotation marks.

(3) *Keyword zone:* Reserve the top right corner of the card as a "keyword zone." In this area put one or two keywords that will tie the card to a place on your outline. (Example: "Graduation Rates.") The keyword can also tie the card to a new subject, if it is not on the outline.

■ *Idea cards:* Use *idea cards* to jot down ideas that occur to you. To make sure you don't mix them up with information cards, write "IDEA #1," "IDEA #2," and so on, at the top.

To keep the cards organized, keep them in three separate stacks each wrapped in a rubber band.

a. *Source card:* Use source cards to keep track of bibliographical information.

Anderson, Dave. "Real College Champions Are the Ones Who Graduate."
New York Times July 6, 1995, p. B5.

b. *Information card:* Use information cards to write down information to be used in the paper; put quoted material in quotation marks.

Anderson 1995 p. B5   Graduation Rates
NCAA issued graduation rates at its 302 Division I
schools for all 1st-year students compared with student-
athletes (men & women) who entered college in 1988-89
school year. No breakdown of sports documented.

"Based on its graduation numbers, Penn State (77%
student-athletes, 79% all students) deserved to be the
top-ranked football team last season..."

"Of basketball's Final Four teams, North Carolina had the
best rates (76% student-athletes, 85% all students)."

c. *Idea card:* Use idea cards to jot down ideas that occur to you.

IDEA #1

Find out: Do many college athletes not graduate
because they don't have time-management
skills to handle both studies and sports?

HIGH-TECH WAYS TO COLLECT INFORMATION: PHOTOCOPIERS & PORTABLE COMPUTERS. Using 3×5 cards is a traditional though low-tech way of collecting information. They can also be somewhat time-consuming, since you're required to write out everything by hand.

Two high-tech ways to collect information in the library are the use of photocopiers and portable computers.

- *Photocopiers:* When you find an article from which you'd like to quote extensively, it may make sense to simply use the library's photocopying machines. Sometimes this means feeding the machine a lot of dimes, but the time saving may still be worth it. Some libraries allow students to open charge accounts for use of these machines.

    For organizing purposes, you can then take scissors and cut up the photocopied material. Then write the source abbreviation and page number in one margin and the "keywords" in the other.

- *Portable computers:* Having a portable computer with a word processing program can be a godsend in collecting library information. (If your library has desktop word processors installed on the premises, you might also be able to use them.) Some researchers also use hypertext programs. An example is the HyperCard software on the Apple Macintosh, which electronically simulates 3×5 "cards" and "stacks" that can be manipulated.

    Even if you're not very fast on the keyboard, it may still be faster than writing out your information by hand. Follow the same format as you would for 3×5 cards.

    Personal Exploration #9.1 lets you try your hand at researching a topic or author.

Phase 4: Sorting Your Notes, Revising the Outline, & Writing the First Draft

PREVIEW In Phase 4, you first determine your writing place, then sort your notes, revise your outline, and write a thesis statement and working title. You next write your first draft—middle first, then beginning, then end. In writing, you should make your point and give support, quoting experts, avoiding irrelevancies, and giving sources.

P*hase 4 consists of sorting your notes, revising your outline, and writing a first draft of the paper.* The research phase may have taken a lot of work, but now it's time to put it all together.

ESTABLISHING YOUR WRITING PLACE. What kind of writing environment suits you best is up to you. The main thing is that it *help you avoid distractions.* You may also need room to spread out, even be able to put 3×5 cards and sources on the floor. If you write in longhand, a table in the library may do. If you write on a typewriter or word processor, you may need to use a desk or table at home.

Some other tips:

- *Allow time:* Give yourself plenty of time. A first draft of a major paper should take more than one day.

- *Reread instructions:* Just before you start to write, reread the instructor's directions regarding the paper. You would hate to find out afterward that you took the wrong approach because you overlooked something.

Ready? Begin.

RESEARCH: LOOKING UP A TOPIC IN THE LIBRARY

Think of a topic that you are required to research for another class or just for your own interest. Then use three methods to locate three different sources of information about it.

■ A. YOUR TOPIC

The topic for which I am doing research is _____
_____
_____

■ B. FINDING SUBJECT HEADINGS

Check the *Library of Congress Subject Headings* for two subject headings that will lead to information about your topic. Write them down here:

1. _____
_____
_____

2. _____
_____
_____

■ C. FINDING BOOKS

Look in the subject section of the library's card catalog or electronic catalog. Write down information for three books on your subject. Information should include authors' names, book titles, city and name of publisher, year of publication (look on copyright page), call number.

1. Book #1:
_____
_____
_____

2. Book #2:
_____
_____
_____
_____

3. Book #3:
_____
_____
_____
_____

■ D. FINDING MAGAZINE, JOURNAL, AND NEWSPAPER ARTICLES

Use three sources to find three different articles. One should be from a magazine, one from a journal, and one from a newspaper.

1. **Article from a Magazine:** Use the *Reader's Guide to Periodical Literature* to find an article on your topic. Write down the author's names, article title, name and date of magazine, volume number, article page numbers, and call number. Find the article and write down the first and last sentence in it.

_____
_____
_____
_____
_____
_____

2. **Article from a Journal:** Use another periodical index to find another article on your subject, this time from an academic journal. (An example is *Applied Science and Technology Index;* see other examples in Panel 9.3.) Write down the periodical index used,

the authors' names, article title, name and date of journal, volume and issue number, article page numbers, and call number. Find the article and write down the first and last sentence in it.

_____
_____
_____
_____
_____

3. **Article from a Newspaper:** Use a newspaper index to find an article on your topic. (Examples are the *New York Times Index* and the *Wall Street Journal Index.*) Write down the newspaper index used, the author's names, article title, name and date of newspaper, section and page numbers, and call number. Find the article and write down the first and last sentence in it.

_____
_____
_____
_____
_____

■ E. FINDING OTHER SOURCES

Use other sources to find more information—for example, government literature, encyclopedias, or computer networks.

1. _____
_____

2. _____
_____

SORTING YOUR NOTES & REVISING YOUR OUTLINE. In gathering your information, you may have been following the questions that appeared on your preliminary outline. However, the very process of doing research may turn up some new questions and areas that you hadn't thought of. Thus, your 3 × 5 cards or source materials may contain information that suggests some changes to the outline.

Here's what to do:

- **Sort your information cards:** Keeping your eye on the keywords in the upper right corner of your 3 × 5 cards (or other source material), sort the information material into piles. *Each pile should gather together information relating to a similar question or topic.*

    Now move the piles into the order or sequence in which you will discuss the material, according to your preliminary outline.

- **Revise your outline:** The piles may suggest some changes in the order of your outline. Thus, you should now take a fresh sheet of paper, write *OUTLINE #2* at the top, and redo the questions or categories.

    By now you will be able to write answers to some or all of your questions. *As you rework the outline, write answers to the questions you have listed.* Refer to the sources of your information as you write. For example, suppose you have the question "What percentage of basketball players graduate compared to most students?" You might write:

    "NCAA 1995 study: No breakdown by sports. However, at basketball Final Four schools, graduation rates were as follows: North Carolina 76% student-athletes, 48% all students; UCLA 56% and 77%; Arkansas 39% and 41%; Oklahoma State 38% and 40% (Anderson 1995, p. B5)."

    Resequence the topics so that they logically seem to follow, with one building on another.

- **Write a thesis statement and working title:** When you get done with reworking and answering questions in *II. Middle* of your outline, go back up to *I. Beginning.*

Revise the main question or questions into a thesis statement. **A _thesis statement_ is a concise sentence that defines the purpose of your paper.** For example, your original main questions were "How smart are college athletes?" and "Are college athletics dominated by 'dumb jocks'?" These might now become your thesis statement:

"Though graduation rates of college athletes are lower than those for other students, some individual athletes are among the best students."

The thesis statement will in turn suggest a working title. **A _working title_ is a tentative title for your paper.** Thus, you might put down on your outline: *Working title: "How Smart Are College Athletes?"*

WRITING YOUR FIRST DRAFT. The first draft has one major purpose: *to get your ideas down on paper.* This is not the stage to worry about doing a clever introduction or choosing the right words or making transitions between ideas. Nor should you concern yourself about correct grammar, punctuation, and spelling. Simply write as though you were telling your findings to a friend. *It's important not to be too judgmental about your writing at this point.* Your main task is to get from a blank page to a page with *something* on it that you can refine later.

Proceed as follows:

- **Write the middle:** Skip the beginning, letting your thesis statement be the introduction for now. Instead, follow Outline #2 for *II. Middle* to write the body of your paper, using your information cards to flesh it out. Set down your answers/ideas one after the other, without worrying too much about logical transitions between them. Use your own voice, not some imagined "scholarly" tone.

    Follow some of the writing suggestions mentioned in the next section, "Some Writing Tips."

- **Write the beginning:** When you have finished setting down the answers to all the questions in the middle, go back and do *I. Beginning.* By starting with the middle, you'll avoid the hang-up of

fellowships, and graduate and professional schools. Today the 'strong-back, weak-brain' athlete of yesteryear is largely a myth."

SOME WRITING TIPS. In writing the first draft of the middle, or body, of the paper, you should try to get something down that you can revise and polish later. Thus, don't worry too much if this initial version seems choppy; that's why a first draft is called a "rough" draft.

As you write, follow these guidelines:

■ *Make your point and give support:* The "point" you want to make is the answer to each question. (For example, your question might be "Does football require more intelligence than other major sports?") In your writing, this answer will become a statement. Example:

"It's possible that football requires greater intelligence than other major sports do."

Then support the statement with evidence, data, statistics, examples, and quotations. Example:

"Memorizing and executing scores or hundreds of different plays, for instance, takes a lot of intelligence. When scouts for pro football teams look over college players, one question they ask is, 'How is he at learning the playbook?'" (Then footnote the source.)

■ *Quote experts:* It makes your statements or arguments much more convincing when you can buttress them with brief quotes from experts. Quoting authorities also can make your paper much more interesting and readable to the instructor. One caution, however: don't overdo it with the quotations. Keep them brief.

■ *Avoid irrelevancies:* Don't think you have to use all your research. That is, don't feel you have to try to impress your instructor by showing how much work you've done in your investigation. Just say what you need to say. Avoid piling on lots of irrelevant information, which will only distract and irritate your reader.

■ *Give the source of your data and examples:* Your instructor will want to know where you got your supporting information. Thus, be sure to provide sources. These can be expressed with precision on the

trying to get your paper off the ground or of writing an elegant lead. Also, having done the middle, you'll have a solid idea, of course, of what your paper is about. You'll know, for instance, which questions and answers are the most important. These may be different from the questions you asked before you did your research.

Now, then, you'll be able to write the introduction with some confidence. An example might be:

"A common image many people have of college athletes is that they are 'dumb jocks.' That is, they may be good on the playing field but not in the classroom. Is this true? The facts vary for different sports, colleges, class levels, and other factors. This paper examines these differences."

■ *Write the end:* Finally, you write *III. End.* The end is the conclusion. It does not include any new facts or examples. It provides just the general answer or answers to the main question or questions raised in the beginning. This is the answer you've arrived at by exploring the questions in the middle section. It's possible, of course, that your conclusion will be tentative. It's all right to state that further research is needed.

An example of the end of a paper might be as follows:

"As we have seen, although the dropout rate is higher for players in some sports and in some schools, it is not in others. Moreover, college athletes often graduate with honors, and some go on not only to professional sports but also to Rhodes scholarships, Fullbright and Wilson

final draft, following the particular foot-note and bibliography ("works cited") style you've decided on. For now put some sort of shorthand for your sources in the first draft.

For instance, at the end of the sentence above about the football play-book, you could provide the author, year, and page for the source in parentheses. Example: " '. . . learning the playbook?' (Wahlstrom 1997, p. 23)."

- *Jot down ideas:* As you proceed through the first draft, jot down any ideas that come to you that don't immediately seem to fit anywhere. You may find a place for them later.

- *Take breaks:* Professional writers find that physical activity gives the mind a rest and triggers new ideas. The brain needs to disengage. Take short breaks to relax. Go get a soda, take a walk outside, or other-wise move your body a bit. Take pen and paper and jot down thoughts.

LETTING THE DRAFT SIT. Many students write papers right up against their deadlines. It's far, far better, however, if you can get the first draft done early and let it sit in a drawer for a day or so. This will allow you to come back and revise it with a fresh perspective.

Phase 5:
Revising, Finalizing, & Proofreading Your Paper

PREVIEW Ideally the fifth phase should take as much time as the first four. This final phase consists of seven parts. (1) Read the paper aloud or have someone else read it. (2) Delete irrelevant material. (3) Write transi-tions and do reorganizing. (4) Do fine tuning and polishing. (5) Type the paper. (6) Proofread the paper. (7) Make a copy.

The last phase, Phase 5, consists of revising, finalizing, and proofreading your paper. How much time should revising take? One suggestion is this: Phases 1–4 should take half your time, and Phase 5 should take the other half of your time. This rule shows the importance that is attached to revision.

The steps to take in revision are as follows:

- Read the paper aloud or get someone else to read it

- Delete irrelevant material

- Write transitions and do any reorganizing

- Do fine tuning and polishing

- Type the paper

- Proofread the paper

- Make a copy

READ ALOUD OR HAVE SOMEONE ELSE READ DRAFTS OF YOUR PAPER. It's hard for us to spot our own mistakes, particu-larly during a silent reading. To better catch these, try the following:

- *Read your draft aloud to yourself:* If you read aloud what you've written, whether first draft or revised draft, you'll be able to spot missing words, awkward usage, and missing details.

- *Get feedback from another person:* By having a friend, family member, or the instructor read any of your drafts, you can get the help of an "editor." (You can offer to read friends' papers in exchange.) Any additional feedback can be valuable.

  SPECIAL NOTE: *Don't take the criticism personally.* If your readers say your paper is "illogical" or "vague," they are not implying you're stupid. When people criticize your draft, they are not criticiz-ing you as a human being. Moreover, remember you don't have to do what they say. You're looking for suggestions, not commandments.

DELETE IRRELEVANT MATERIAL. The best way to start the revision is to take a pencil and start crossing out words. Like a film maker cutting scenes so a movie won't run too long (and bore the audience), you should cut your paper to its essentials.

This is what editors call "blue penciling." Strive for conciseness and brevity. As a mental guideline, imagine someone writing "Repetitious!" or "Wordy!" in the margin. Be ruthless. First cut unnecessary sections, pages, and paragraphs. Then cut unnecessary sentences, phrases, and words. Cut even your best ideas and phrases—those gems you're proud of—if they don't move the essay along and advance your case.

WRITE TRANSITIONS & DO ANY REORGANIZING. You may have written the first draft fairly rapidly and not given much thought to making transitions—logical connections—between thoughts. You may also have deleted such connections when you blue-penciled material above. Now's the time to make sure the reader is able to move logically from one of your ideas to another.

You may well discover while doing this that your paper needs to be reorganized, that your outline isn't working right. There are two ways to handle this:

- *Low-tech reorganizing—scissors and glue:* You can use scissors to cut up your paper, then move the cut-up sections around. Use glue (paste) or transparent tape to attach the sections to blank pieces of paper. This activity is known as "cutting and pasting."

- *High-tech reorganizing—word processing:* The same kind of resequencing can be done electronically with a word processing program by using the "block move" function. You use the "block" command to mark the beginning and end of a section. Then you go to another location in the document and use the "move" command to transfer that marked-off section to it.

DO FINE TUNING & POLISHING. Now you need to take a pencil and do a final editing to make sure everything reads well.

Some suggestions:

- *Have a thesis statement:* Make sure the introduction to the paper has a thesis statement that says what the main point of your paper is.

- *Guide the reader:* Tell the reader what you're going to do. Introduce each change in topic. Connect topics by writing transitions.

- *Present supporting data:* Make sure you have enough examples, quotations, and data to support your assertions.

- *Don't be wordy:* Don't be infatuated with the exuberance and prolixity of your own verbosity. Don't use big words when short ones will do. Delete unnecessary words.

- *Check grammar and spelling:* Check your paper for grammatical mistakes. Also check for spelling. Look up words you're not sure about.

- *Follow correct style for documentation:* Follow the instructor's directions, if any, for documenting your sources. The humanities, for example, follow the style developed by the Modern Language Association. The social sciences follow the style developed by the American Psychological Association. Guidebooks are available in the campus bookstore.

In general, the preferred style nowadays is to identify the author's last name and the page reference within parentheses. For example:

"One sportswriter points out that extenuating factors were ignored in the NCAA survey (Anderson B5)."

You then present a complete description of each source in an alphabetical listing at the end of the paper entitled "Works Cited." *(See ■ Panel 9.5.)*

THE PRESENTATION: TYPE YOUR PAPER.

Presentation is important. Some instructors accept handwritten papers, but they'd rather not, since they're harder to read. In a job interview situation, you have to sell yourself not only with your experience but also by the way you dress and present yourself. Similarly, you have to sell your paper not only by its ideas but by its presentation.

Thus, its best to type your paper or have it typed. You need not be expert; using two fingers instead of ten just means typing will take a little longer. If you have access to a personal computer, you'll find typing is even less of a chore, because it's easier to fix mistakes. You can type (keyboard) on the machine, print out a draft, and make corrections on the draft with a pencil. Then you can type in the corrections and print out a clean draft.

PROOFREADING.

In the past have you had papers come back from the instructor with red ink circling spelling and grammatical mistakes? Those red circles probably negatively affected your final grade, marking you down from, say, an A– to a B+.

With your paper in beautiful final-typed form (and the hand-in deadline perhaps only hours away), it may be tempting not to proofread it. You may not only be supremely tired of the whole thing but not want to "mess it up" by making handwritten corrections. Do it anyway. The instructor won't have any excuse then to give you red circles for small mistakes. (If you're using a word processor, providing a completely clean final draft is very easy.)

PANEL 9.5

Documentation. The preferred style of documentation is to identify the author's last name with the page reference within parentheses in the text. The complete source is then presented at the end of the paper in a "Works Cited" section.

Example of citation in text:

One New York Times sportswriter points out that extenuating factors were ignored in the NCAA's survey comparing student athlete and nonathlete graduation rates. "No breakdown of courses was presented, either pre-med or pre-unemployed," he says. "No breakdown of sports was documented, either football or field hockey" (Anderson B5).

Example of "Works Cited" section:

WORKS CITED

Anderson, Dave. "Real College Champions Are the Ones Who Graduate." New York Times 6 July 1995, B5.

Hyatt, Carole and Linda Gottlieb. When Smart People Fail. New York: Simon and Schuster, 1987.

Rice, Phillip L. Stress and Health. 2nd ed. Pacific Grove, CA: Brooks/Cole, 1992.

MAKE A COPY. Papers do get lost or stolen after they've been handed in (or on a student's way to handing it in). If you typed your paper on a word processor, make sure you save a copy on a floppy disk. If you typed it on a typewriter or hand-wrote it, use a photocopying machine at the library or an instant-printing shop to make a copy.

Important note: Another good reason for retaining a copy of your paper is that you may be able to expand on the subject in subsequent papers later. I've known students who gradually explored a particular topic to the point where in graduate school it finally became the subject of their doctoral dissertation.

Onward

PREVIEW Education is more than memorizing subjects.

Learning to conceive, research, and write papers is learning how to think. American education has been criticized because students are required to memorize subjects rather than to understand and analyze them. However, as Wisconsin student James Robinson points out, future survival lies in knowing how to solve problems. "If we do not know how to analyze a problem," he says, "how are we ever going to compete in the real world? The problems we are going to face are not all going to be written down in a textbook with the answers in the back. . . . As students, we must realize that we need to come up with our own solutions."[4]

Robinson is right. And the final payoff is this: It has been found that students who learn how to think do better not only in school but in life.[5]

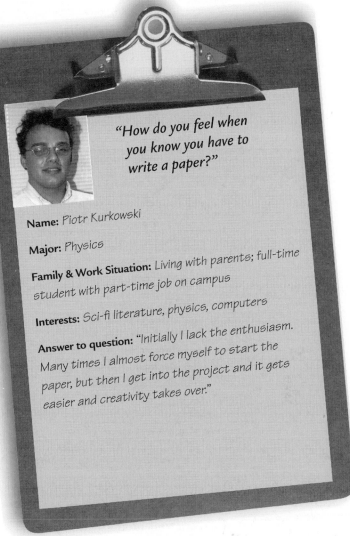

"How do you feel when you know you have to write a paper?"

Name: Piotr Kurkowski

Major: Physics

Family & Work Situation: Living with parents; full-time student with part-time job on campus

Interests: Sci-fi literature, physics, computers

Answer to question: "Initially I lack the enthusiasm. Many times I almost force myself to start the paper, but then I get into the project and it gets easier and creativity takes over."

NOTES

1. Walter, T., & Siebert, A. (1990). *Student success: How to succeed in college and still have time for your friends.* Fort Worth, TX: Holt, Rinehart and Winston, pp. 108–109.

2. Osborn, A. (1953). *Applied imagination.* New York: Scribner's.

3. Walter & Siebert, 1990, p. 103.

4. Robinson, J. R. (1991, November 6). [Letter to editor.] U.S. students memorize, but don't understand. *New York Times,* p. A14.

5. Elder, J. (1991, January 6). A learned response. *New York Times,* sec. 4A, p. 23.

1. ***Getting going on a research paper.*** Have students form into small groups (four to six students each). Then ask them to select one of the following topics: *horse racing, magnetic resonance imaging, information literacy, population control, urban crime, long-distance running, retirement planning, Mayan ruins.* (Or ask students to consult with you about another topic.)

   Each group is to develop a number of questions on the topic. They are then to use the questions to produce an outline. Group members should write their names at the top of the outline and turn it into the instructor.

2. ***Looking up a topic in the library.*** This activity involves out-of-class time because it requires a visit to the library. Students are to follow the instructions of Personal Exploration #9.1, "Research: Looking Up a Topic in the Library." They may develop the topic agreed upon in Classroom Activity #1 above or may develop a topic required for a paper in another class. They should research the sources requested in the Personal Exploration, either by themselves or in a team with three to five other students.

   Later have students discuss the following questions in class. What types of information were the easiest to locate and why? Which the most difficult? Is your approach to locating sources low-tech or high-tech and how? How could searching for information be enhanced? What did you learn about the library?

3. ***How do you handle footnotes and references?*** Finding the correct form for footnotes and/or references may seem somewhat daunting to many students. With a little bit of out-of-class time for research and a bit of in-class time for discussion, however, they may learn to feel more comfortable with this important part of writing papers.

   Instruct students to find correct references for three kinds of source material: (1) books, (2) articles from periodicals, and (3) other sources (such as encyclopedias and government publications). Point out that different academic disci-plines have their own preferred reference and footnoting styles.

   In the library, students are to find and copy out footnote and reference styles for books, articles, and other sources that will appear in (a) papers they will submit in most of their courses, and (b) papers they will submit in courses in their major or prospective major.

   Later selected examples can be posted on the board. Ask the class to discuss the differences among the various forms.

JOURNAL ENTRY #9.1: WRITING ABOUT SOMETHING IMPORTANT TO YOU
Write a few words about something that is very important to you, such as a particular person or event that profoundly affected you. (Use a separate sheet of paper, if you wish.) Describe how writing helps you understand it.

_____

_____

_____

_____

_____

_____

_____

_____

JOURNAL ENTRY #9.2: WHAT MORE DO YOU NEED TO FIND OUT ABOUT THE LIBRARY? How comfortable are you with using the college library? For each of the following library resources, rate yourself on your confidence in using that resource for research. Use the following system:

A = Very comfortable
B = Comfortable
C = Somewhat uncertain
D = Very uncertain
F = Totally unfamiliar

1. Online card catalog   A   B   C   D   F

2. Microfiche   A   B   C   D   F

3. Interlibrary loan   A   B   C   D   F

4. Newspaper, magazine, and journal indexes   A   B   C   D   F

5. Specialized dictionaries   A   B   C   D   F

6. Internet and/or other computerized networks   A   B   C   D   F

Look at those you rated C, D, or F. What specific steps could you take to become more comfortable with them?

_____

_____

_____

_____

_____

_____

_____

_____

_____

_____

_____

JOURNAL ENTRY #9.3: WHAT DO YOU NEED TO FIND OUT ABOUT FOOTNOTES AND BIBLIOGRAPHIES? One subject that might have been discussed in more detail in this chapter was the proper form for footnotes and bibliographies. Is this an area in which you need further help? Who can give you the assistance you need?

_____

_____

_____

_____

_____

_____

_____

_____

JOURNAL ENTRY #9.4: WHAT IF YOU WERE TO BE A PROFESSIONAL WRITER?

If you were to be a professional writer, what kinds of things would you like to write about? For what kinds of publications?

_____

_____

_____

_____

_____

_____

_____

_____

_____

special section: survival skills for commuters

"For those of you who do not know the commute pain, imagine sitting in bumper-to-bumper traffic, sucking up exhaust from cars and double-trailer trucks, watching out for lane jumpers and going only 10 miles in 30 minutes. Then imagine your commute is only one-third complete."

So writes a California man whose job changed from off hours to regular hours and as a result turned his 30-mile drive to work from 30 minutes to 90 minutes—one-way.[1] "I never had to go from 70 mph to a dead stop on the freeway every work day," he continues. "And then inch along and stop and inch along and stop and inch along and stop."

Of course, not all students who drive to campus have to do so during that wretched time period known as "rush" hour. (Was there ever a worse word choice?) Nor, in fact, do all commuter students drive. But nearly all have to make constant adjustments between their different worlds.

Adjusting to the Transition Between the Parts of Your Life

How well do you make the transition between the different sectors of your life? All of us have to deal not only with the *physical* separation between home, school, and (often) work but also with the way we *think and act* in each realm. Some people (called "segmenters"), according to Christena Nippert-Eng, draw wide boundaries between the compartments of their lives. For example, at home they avoid all thoughts of work; at work they completely shut out their personal life. Others ("integrators") blend their different worlds. For example, some may go back and forth several times during the day between work (or school) and home, or they may invite co-workers (or fellow students) to their homes.[2]

The problem for some commuter students is that being on campus or at work may be manageable, because these realms are fairly orderly. Home, however, may be full of noisy housemates or children, yet you have to do your studying there anyway. How do you make the mental transitions across these boundaries?

What's required is to figure out your personal style. It may be best, for example, to stay on campus after class and do your studying there, where it's quiet. Or, if this is impossible, you keep a To Do list—a "road map of the day"—to provide the organizing boundaries you need to make transitions.[3] You religiously follow the study schedule you drew up according to the description in Chapter 4.

Dealing with Commuting

Not only do you have to adjust to the constant change among the the different compartments of your life. You also have to adjust to the travel that connects them.

Although, particularly for students, public transportation may be advantageous because you may be able to study while on board a bus or train, these days most people rely on cars to get places. The use of public transit, particularly of bus service, is declining throughout the United States. In Chicago, for instance, the number of bus and train rides dropped 38% from 1980 to 1995.[4] Nationwide, car poolers dropped 19% between 1980 and 1990.[5] Moreover, with the rise in two-income families (there are nearly 31 million two-earner couples in the U.S.), more people are combining commuting to work with personal business matters—which includes shopping, visits to day care, and taking college classes—which often rules out ride-sharing and public transit.[6]

Still, is a car an absolute must?

Do You Need a Car?

Often people think they *need* a car, but they really don't. For many people, particularly young people, it may really come down "to the difference between want and need," says one psychologist. "You would very much like to have a car: for independence, for status, and for the sense of power you feel when you drive," she says. "But you don't need one."[7]

Adds another writer, our dependence on a car "often has more to do with our lack of imagination and willingness to be flexible than it does on any real necessity." Indeed, he says, a simple shift in attitude—learning to view a car as a luxury rather than as a necessity—can save you a great deal of money.[8]

WHAT DOES A CAR REALLY COST?

If you get a used car for $3000, say, that's equivalent to approximately 600 hours of labor at minimum wage. That's about like taking a semester off and working full time. Most new cars, of course, cost much more—$10,000 and up. And they'll cost you a lot more than that if you make monthly payments on an auto loan or lease rather than buying one for cash saved in advance.[9] In general, the less you pay for a car, the less it will cost in sales taxes and motor-vehicle fees and the less you will pay to insure it.

But buying a car is just the beginning. The average cost of owning and operating a car—including gas, tires, battery, repairs, and so on—works out to 45 cents a mile, according to the American Automobile Manufacturers Association.[10] Thus, if you drive an average of 12,000 miles a year, you are spending $5400 annually on the car. And this *does not* include parking fees or bridge or turnpike tolls.

ALTERNATIVES TO CAR OWNERSHIP

Besides public transit and ride-sharing, what is the alternative to driving your own car? An obvious one is: Live close to campus or job, which can allow you to walk or ride a bicycle. Many people, says Eric Tyson, author of *Personal Finance for Dummies*, never consider this option. "Most assume that it would be too expensive," he says. "But a decrease in transportation costs by living close to work [and school] might more than make up for an increase in housing costs."[11] If you can't move closer to campus or work, you might also consider moving closer to a public-transportation route. As mentioned, from a student's point of view, public transit may provide a bonus in that you may be able to get some studying done while you're traveling.

If moving is out of the question and the travel time and crowds on public transit are too inconvenient, you might also consider a motorcycle or motor scooter. Motorcycles have become enormously popular—so much so, in fact, that they are more apt to be stolen than cars. This means you should chain your bike to an immovable object such as a lamp post, since thieves often use Freon to freeze the handlebar lock, then smash it with a hammer.[12] Motor scooters are less expensive and are easier to drive. However, motorcycle and scooter insurance isn't as competitive as car insurance.[13] Moreover, if you're involved in an accident, the outcome may be a lot more serious than if it happened to you in a car.

The Expert Driver: How to Steer Clear of Your Next Accident

If you drive a car, motorcycle, or bicycle, you have two concerns: to avoid injuring yourself and to avoid injuring others. Often, of course, both concerns overlap.

DRIVING TO AVOID HURTING YOURSELF

Young drivers, ages 15–24, have the highest death rates, owing to lack of experience and judgment. The second highest death rate is among drivers over the age of 75 (tied with those in the 25–44 age group), owing to slowing of reaction times and deterioration of the senses. Regardless of the current age group in which you find yourself, you can reduce the chances of injuring or killing yourself by doing the following:

- **Don't cause—or respond to—provocation:** "I have a nasty, dangerous habit, one that could kill me and anyone near me," says journalist William J. Cook. "And I am not finding it easy to break."[14] The habit? When in his car he expresses his feelings all too vividly—making obscene gestures—when someone in another vehicle gives him provocation, such as honking at him for not moving fast enough when the light turns green.

  Nowadays there are so many nuts (including young, poorly educated males with criminal records) on the highways that this kind of behavior could lead to disaster. The number of violent driving incidents involving deaths or injuries—caused by guns, knives, clubs, tire irons, and cars themselves—increased 51% between 1990 and 1995. "What used to be just two people screaming at each other is now one person losing it and pulling the trigger," says Lou Mizell, a security expert who conducted a study on aggressive driving for the AAA Foundation for Traffic Safety.[15]

  What should you do? First follow this rule above all others: *Don't respond to provocation!* If someone tailgates you or crowds in front of you, remember you're not in a contest of driving to win. You're just trying to get somewhere. If you holler an insult or lean on the horn, you may find someone following too closely or otherwise on the way toward an unpleasant encounter. (If that happens, don't drive home, advises one highway patrolman. "Drive instead to a public place, such as a police or fire station, service station, or shopping center."[16] Telephone the police.)

  Second, *don't provoke others yourself!* Avoid glaring at other drivers. In fact, avoid making eye contact at all. (This is what professional limousine drivers are trained to do.) And don't do the kind of aggressive things that you would object to yourself, such as tailgating or hogging the passing lane.

- **Use seat belts:** The percentage of people admitting to "seat-belt nonuse" varies tremendously, but an average of 30% of the population still does not use seat belts.[17] However, there is no reason *not* to use seat belts.

  Whereas some health behaviors are somewhat complex, such as exercising or losing weight, there is nothing complicated about putting on a seat belt. Yet the 2 seconds it takes to buckle up can reduce the chances of accidental death by 50%—an incredible amount of protection in return for the tiny effort invested.[18]

  Some people think there's no need to buckle up when on short trips or when not driving fast. However, three-quarters of all crashes are within 25 miles of home and 80% of deaths and injuries occur under 40 mph.[19] Some people also think that in a crash they would be better off being "thrown clear," although actually they would be 25 times more likely to be killed. Finally, although you may be a good driver yourself, you may not be able to prevent someone else—a drunk driver, say—from hitting you.

  To repeat: *The single most effective thing you can do in a car to protect your life is to use a seat belt.*

Crash avoidance and survival techniques

- **Always try to avoid a head-on crash:** Your chances of surviving almost any other crash are better than of surviving a head-on collision.

- **Go off-road, if necessary:** Get rid of the idea that your car *always* belongs on the pavement. If you are close to having an on-road collision, and pedestrians, bicyclists, or motorcyclists are not in your way, *drive off the road.* Driving onto a sidewalk or lawn or into a field may save your life.

- **Steer your way clear and brake gently off-road:** As you drive off the pavement, try to steer to avoid skidding. Also, don't brake too hard when you're off road, which may trip up the vehicle and cause it to roll over.

- **Hit a car going your way:** If you are about to crash into a car stopped in front of you or approaching you, and have to hit another vehicle, *hit one going in the same direction you are.* Hitting one traveling beside you in the next lane will have less impact than hitting one in front.

- **Hit objects that will yield somewhat, and hit with a glancing blow:** If you have to have a collision, don't hit a massive immovable object, such as a concrete abutment or a brick building. Try to pick something that has some "give," such as small trees, parked cars, or wood-frame buildings. Whatever object you run in to, try to give it a glancing blow, which will lessen the impact.

- *Know crash-avoidance driving techniques:* Many people don't know how to handle themselves when driving in bad weather. They drive as fast on rain-slicked pavements as they do when it's dry, and wonder why they go into a skid when they hit the brakes. In fog they pull close to the car or truck in front and follow its lights, eliminating room to stop.[20] When someone veers into their lane, they choose a head-on accident rather than risk a less lethal crash to the side or off the road. There are, however, some crash survival techniques that don't square with most people's driving habits which are well worth learning. (*See* ■ *Panel SS.1, above.*)

- *Learn patience to avoid stress:* It has been found that the longer people commute, the higher their blood pressure afterward, the worse the stress they feel, and the more they carry over that stress into their destination afterward.[21] How does one deal with this? You can can practice patience, or what psychotherapist Todd Berger, co-author of *Zen Driving,* calls "moving meditation"—driving with full awareness and relaxed concentration.

  "In Zen driving," he says, "you let go. You drop what you were thinking about before, and you drop your destination. All that matters is what you are doing *right now.* Anything that gets in the way, like anger, fear, or tension, is calmly acknowledged. Then you let the emotion go, and return your attention to the pure experience, and awareness of the present moment. A guy in a pickup truck cuts you off. It makes you mad. You acknowledge the anger, and let it go. Then you go back to total awareness and feeling the car around you."[22]

- *Drive or ride in a safe car:* Big cars are usually safer than small cars in crashes. However, a large car is not necessarily a safer car.[23–25] The critical factor is design, which can compensate for small size and light weight. Cars of whatever size built with tough roofs and sides, a frame designed to absorb collision, interior padding, antilock brakes, and air bags are more apt to protect drivers and passengers than cars not so designed.

DRIVING TO AVOID HURTING OTHERS

The young driver looked down to change a music tape in her dashboard tape deck. When she looked up again, she had drifted slightly off the road and was too late to avoid hitting four bicyclists riding single file, all of whom were killed. This young college student was not only convicted of manslaughter but will have to bear the pain of her experience for the rest of her life.

About 95% of the automobile deaths and injuries are due to careless or reckless driving such as this. (The rest are caused by mechanical failure of the vehicle.)[26] To avoid having a similar tragic episode in your life, here are some driving strategies that experts follow:

- *Surround yourself with a "bubble" of space:* Don't tailgate cars in front, avoid traveling next to cars in other lanes, and try not to let cars behind you crowd you (let them go around). This "bubble" or "defensive space" keeps you away from other cars and gives you some room to maneuver. When you enter situations such as interchanges or heavy traffic, slow down to allow for a smaller bubble.[27]

- *Slow down:* Speed puts a lot of wear and tear on your car and raises the fuel consumption. It is also a leading cause of accidents (19.5% of total accidents). The chance of death roughly doubles for every 10 miles per hour of additional speed over 50.[28] The reasons are simple: the faster you go, the less reaction time you have to stop, the longer your stopping distance, and the heavier the force of impact when you hit something. (*See* ■ *Panel SS.2.*)

Speeding on rain-slicked or icy roads means you have no control over the vehicle. Speed-limit signs indicate the *maximum* speed allowed under *ideal* conditions. This means if you're driving at night or during bad weather, you should drive more slowly.

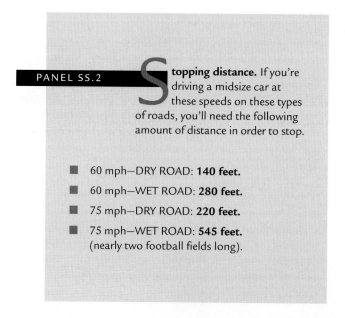

PANEL SS.2

Stopping distance. If you're driving a midsize car at these speeds on these types of roads, you'll need the following amount of distance in order to stop.

- 60 mph—DRY ROAD: **140 feet.**
- 60 mph—WET ROAD: **280 feet.**
- 75 mph—DRY ROAD: **220 feet.**
- 75 mph—WET ROAD: **545 feet.** (nearly two football fields long).

We realize that so many people speed that it can almost make you feel uncomfortable to drive under the speed limit because people may crowd you from behind. But that's *their* problem. *Your* problem is to not let yourself feel harrassed just because you're holding up someone who wants to go faster.

■ *Don't be a red-light bandit:* Not surprisingly, the rules-don't-apply-to-me drivers who try to beat the yellow light at an intersection and find themselves going through on the red are extremely dangerous. In San Francisco, for instance, up to 29% of the injury accidents are caused by drivers who run red lights.[29]

■ *Don't drink and drive:* Alcohol is responsible for about 41% of all automobile accidents and is the leading cause of automobile fatalities.[30] No stronger message can be sent about the reasons for the steady drumbeat of advertising you see begging you not to drink and drive.

■ *Don't become fatigued:* After alcohol, the second cause of serious accidents is fatigue (which is worst from 3 P.M. to 2 A.M.). Drowsiness can be caused not only by lack of sleep but also by certain medications, such as tranquilizers, muscle relaxants, antidepressants, antihistamines, and some cold and flu remedies.[31,32]

■ *Don't smoke and drive:* People who smoke while driving are 50% more likely to be involved in a mishap than those who don't smoke.[33] Fumbling with cigarettes, eye irritation, filmy windshields, and the interference of carbon monoxide with night vision are all reasons.

■ *Don't try to do two things at once:* A nonscientific study of 500 traffic-school students in South Florida found that three-quarters of them said they drink a beverage, eat, or do both while driving. About half admitted applying makeup or writing notes. More than 40% said they sometimes kiss and drive at the same time.[34] You can't do these things and keep your mind on your driving.

Incidentally, many people are convinced they can hold a cellular phone to one ear while maneuvering 1½ tons of metal through traffic. However, one study found that people with a cell phone in the car run a 34% higher risk of having an accident.[35]

MOTORCYCLE SAFETY

Mile for mile, motorcycles are more dangerous than cars, the chief reasons being that they are hard to see and other motorists often forget that motorcycles are there. Some motorcyclists add to their chances of injury by "lane splitting," riding between traffic lanes when cars are slowing or stopped. Despite the argument (not true) that a helmet decreases vision, helmet laws have been shown to reduce head injuries.[36–38]

BICYCLE SAFETY

Bicyclists also benefit from having helmets.[39] Of the 1300 bicyclists killed each year, most die from head injuries, and the odds of injury are six times greater for the unhelmeted compared to the helmeted.[40] In addition, bicyclists need to be sure they are visible to motorists, using bright-colored clothing, reflectors, and headlights and taillights at night. Ride as though your life depended on it, because it does: stop at stop signs, signal for turns, use bike lanes when available, and when riding with others proceed single-file rather than side by side. (*See* ■ *Panel SS.3.*)

Bicycle safety
Bicycling is . . .

■ **. . . Like driving a car in some respects:** Many of the same traffic laws apply, including those of stop signs and traffic signals. Signal (using hand signals) your intention to change directions. Go in a straight line and don't weave. Slow down on rainy days.

■ **. . . But you're much less visible than a car:** Drivers don't see bicycles as readily as they do other cars. Thus, at night you should have a rear red reflector, a light emitting a bright beam forward and to the sides, and reflectors on the frame or wheels, or reflecting tape on your clothes. In the daytime, wear bright clothes.

■ **. . . And much more vulnerable than a motorist:** You need to be especially alert to the hazards of the road. Check for cars before you make a turn. Watch for sewer grates, pot holes, gravel, and low-hanging branches. Keep at least one hand on the handlebars. Avoid clothing that might get caught in the chain or spokes (long scarves and coats or baggy trousers or dresses). Wear a helmet.

NOTES

1. Wright, S. E. (1996, October 13). Is there any hope for Silicon Valley's worst commute? *San Jose Mercury News,* pp. 1P, 3P.

2. Nippert-Eng, C. (1996). *Home and work.* Chicago: University of Chicago Press.

3. Shellenbarger, S. (1996, July 17). Making the trip home from work takes more than just a car ride. *Wall Street Journal,* p. B1.

4. Castaneda, C. J. (1996, August 16). Public transit: Competing against cars, and losing. *USA Today,* p. 8A.

5. Castaneda, C. J., & Sharn, L. (1996, August 16). Car pools: Too much time and trouble for a lot of riders. *USA Today,* p. 8A.

6. Tyson, R. (1996, August 16). Commutes get longer as jobs shift to suburbs. *USA Today,* p. 1A.

7. Hamilton, E. (1996, August 8). When should a teen get a car? *Point Reyes Light,* p. 6.

8. Tyson, E. (1996, August 18). Kicking the car habit. *San Francisco Examiner,* pp. D–1, D–2.

9. Tyson, E. (1996, September 1). If you must drive, consider all costs when buying a car. *San Francisco Examiner,* pp. C–1, C–6.

10. American Automobile Manufacturers Association, cited in: Tyson, E., August 18, 1996.

11. Tyson, E., August 18, 1996.

12. Eldridge, E. (1996, July 19). Thieves hog wild over motorcycles. *USA Today,* p. 1B.

13. Castaneda, L. (1996, July 4). Scooters—easy and economical. *San Francisco Chronicle,* pp. E1, E2.

14. Cook, W. J. (1996, November 11). Mad driver's disease. *U.S. News & World Report,* pp. 74–76.

15. Mizell, L. Quoted in: Castaneda, C. J. (1996, November 7). Violence by malicious drivers up 51% since '90. *USA Today,* p. 1A.

16. Obregon, R. Quoted in: Cook, 1996.

17. Wald, M. L. (1996, October 10). Safety group reports rise in fatalities on highways. *New York Times,* p. A17.

18. Cory, D. (1989, November 12). Seat belt study assesses savings in medical costs and injuries. *New York Times.*

19. Traffic Safety Now. (1987). *Buckle up.* Detroit: Traffic Safety Now, Inc.

20. Cushman, J. H. Jr. (1991, April 27). Officials say little is done to cut crashes in fog. *New York Times,* p. 8.

21. Public Policy Research Institute, University of California, Irvine. (1987). *Orange County annual survey: 1987 final report.* Irvine, CA: University of California.

22. Berger, T. Cited in: Greenwald, J. (1992, April). Driving yourself sane. *Health,* pp. 86 – 89.

23. Meier, B. (1991, November 2). Auto safety vs. fuel economy: Questions of size and design. *New York Times,* p. 12.

24. Hamilton, J. (1991, November/December). Safe by design. *Sierra,* pp. 36 – 39.

25. Cushman, J. H. Jr. (1992, January 14). Auto roll-overs are new target of a U.S. push. *New York Times,* p. A16.

26. National Safety Council. (1988). *Accident facts.* Chicago: National Safety Council.

27. Blyskal, J. (1993, January/February). Crash course: How to steer clear of your next auto accident. *American Health,* pp. 74 – 79.

28. Wald, 1996.

29. Zane, M. (1992, January 28). More drivers running the signals. *San Francisco Chronicle,* p. A1.

30. Johnson, K. V., & Dowling, C. (1996, July 2). After decade of decline, a deadly statistic rises. *USA Today,* p. 2A.

31. Brody, J. E. (1990, July 5). Why drivers fall asleep, and how to avoid becoming a statistic. *New York Times,* p. B8.

32. Lamberg, L. (1996, June). Who me? Fall asleep at the wheel? *American Health,* pp. 84 – 87.

33. Deutsch, G. (1990, October). Cruise control. *Men's Health,* pp. 47, 82.

34. Associated Press. (1992, July 23). Drivers keep themselves busy. *San Francisco Chronicle,* p. D3.

35. Violanti, J., in March 1996 *Accident Analysis & Prevention;* reported in: Associated Press (1996, March 19). Study shows car-phone users in more crashes. *San Francisco Chronicle,* pp. A1, A11.

36. Sosin, D. M., Sacks, J. J., & Holmgreen, P. (1990). Head injury-associated deaths from motorcycle crashes: Relationship to helmet-use laws. *Journal of the American Medical Association,* 264, 2395–99.

37. Braddock, M., Schwartz, R., Lapidus, G. et al. (1992). A population-based study of motorcycle injury and costs. *Annals of Emergency Medicine,* 21, 273 – 78.

38. Muelleman, R. L., Mlinek, E. J., & Collicott, P. E. (1992). Motorcycle crash injuries and costs: Effect of a reenacted comprehensive helmet use law. *Annals of Emergency Medicine,* 21, 266 – 72.

39. Williams, M. (1991). The protective performance of bicyclists' helmets in accidents. *Accident Analysis & Prevention,* 23, 119 – 31.

40. Thompson, R., Rivara, F., & Thompson, D. (1989, May 25). A case-control study of the effectiveness of bicycle safety helmets. *New England Journal of Medicine,* 320, 1361 – 67.

no
stress

taking care of yourself mentally

IN THIS CHAPTER: Health is not just avoiding illness. It is also about managing stress. This chapter considers the following topics:

■ *Causes and manifestations of stress:* How to identify the stresses of college.

■ *Managing stress:* Five strategies for handling stress.

> *A great deal of the college experience, unfortunately, consists of stress.*

This can be particularly true of the *commuter* college experience, which adds the tensions of travel to those of studying and exams.

However, as you probably suspect, stress won't end with graduation, so it's important to learn how to cope with it. Indeed, there's even a *good* kind of stress, one that propels you to accomplish the things you want to do.

Stress: Causes & Manifestations

PREVIEW Three principal worries of college students are: (1) anxiety over wasting time, (2) anxiety over meeting high standards, and (3) feelings of being lonely. To these are added other worries of life: the commuter rat-race, work, family, age, minority status, and ability. *Stress* is the body's reaction, *stressors* are the source of stress. Stressors may be small irritating hassles, short-duration crises, or long-duration strong stressors. A source of stress may be negative and cause "distress" or positive and cause "eustress." Stress may produce certain physical reactions: skin problems, headaches, gastrointestinal problems, and high blood pressure. Stress may also produce emotional reactions such as nervousness and anxiety, and burnout.

Stress or burnout is one of the greatest causes of students leaving school without graduating.[1] I say that not to alarm you but simply so you'll know that any feelings of anxiety or tension you have are *commonplace* for college students.

THE WORRIES OF STUDENTS. College students, says one psychologist, are most hassled by three things:[2]

■ *Anxiety over wasting time:* To be in college is to always feel like you should be studying—particularly if you haven't yet set up a time-management system. Students who don't draw up a schedule of their study times and stick to it are particularly apt to suffer constant anxiety over wasting time.

■ *Meeting high standards:* Another worry for students is whether or not they can meet the high standards of college. They may worry that they won't do well enough to get top grades. Or they may worry that they won't do well enough even to get passing grades and will flunk out.

■ *Being lonely:* Many college students feel lonely from time to time. They may be lonely because they presently have no friends with common interests, no one with whom to share their worries, or no current love relationship.

THE WORRIES OF LIFE. To the stresses of being a college student you can also add the other stresses in your life. These might include the following:

■ *The commuter rat-race:* Is commuting stressful? You should know. "Driving is emotional," says one writer. "Vile epithets spew in cars the way they do in torture chambers."[3] Says another: "What is it about cars that turn rational human beings into seething monsters? Behavior that we would not tolerate nor dare use outside our car is commonplace within it."[4]

Of course, commuting by bus, train, or subway can be stressful, too. Jolting over potholes in an overdue, packed bus, after having waited for it in the rain, is no fun, and in some major cities a great many people spend more than an hour a day commuting. But bus service has declined 12% from 1980 to 1995, as suburbs have replaced cities as the main workplace destinations.[5]

As a result, more and more people commute by car, mostly as lone drivers, since car pooling is often not an option. Interestingly, suburban residents have a higher chance of experiencing injury or death from either traffic accidents or crime (19.2 out of 1000) than city residents do (16 out of 1000). That is, automobiles and auto accidents lead to more deaths and injuries in the suburbs than guns and drugs do in urban settings.[6]

- **Work:** Work can be extremely stressful, the result of tyrannical supervisors, unpleasant customers or coworkers, physical strains, boredom, constant deadlines, and many other difficulties. One poll found that 25% of employed adults said job stress or pressure interfered with their off-the-job relationships, and 20% said such stress had affected their physical health.[7]

- **Family:** Housework and parenting can be quite stressful. Domestic chores—shopping, cooking, child care, and so on—not only require a great deal of effort, they are one of the greatest sources of deep tension in a marriage, according to one eight- year study.[8] Housework produces stress not only because of the extra hours of work it entails but also because of its effects on family relationships.

- **Age:** Life may be more stressful at certain ages than others.[9] Those under age 25, for example, must deal with the stresses of new relationships, marriage, pregnancy, and career choice. People between 40 and 44 must cope with mortgage and other heavy expenses, changes in work responsibilities, deaths and illnesses of relatives, children moving out, and menopause. People over age 60 may have to deal with financial changes caused by retirement, major illnesses and health changes, and death of a spouse.

- **Minority status:** Research indicates that blacks of all classes and ages continually experience more stress than whites do.[10, 11] If some of this stress may be associated with having low incomes, it has been shown that racism produces stress regardless of income. For instance, one nationwide study of 200 upper-income African-Americans found they still face discrimination despite their economic advantages.[12] Blacks in the study reported numerous instances of hearing racial epithets and even of being suspected of being criminals.

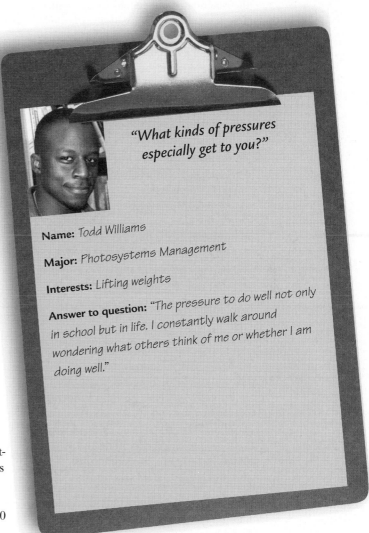

"What kinds of pressures especially get to you?"

Name: Todd Williams

Major: Photosystems Management

Interests: Lifting weights

Answer to question: "The pressure to do well not only in school but in life. I constantly walk around wondering what others think of me or whether I am doing well."

- *Ability:* People with disabilities suffer stresses others might have no inkling of, according to several studies.[13, 14] For instance, one wheelchair-bound woman said her greatest difficulty is simply in getting around. Just because buses are equipped to pick up people in wheelchairs, she observed, doesn't mean that they do. "You get passed up by the drivers," she reported. "The equipment breaks down."[15]

TYPES OF STRESSORS: THE CAUSES OF STRESS. To understand how to fight stress, you need to understand the difference between *stress* and *stressors*. **Stress is the reaction of our bodies to an event. The source of stress is called a *stressor*.** Stressors may be specific and may range from small to large. That is, they may cover everything from a question you don't understand on a test all the way up to a death in your family.

Some characteristics of stressors are as follows:

- *Three types:* There are three types of stressors—*hassles*, *crises*, and *strong stressors*. **A *hassle* is simply a frustrating irritant,** such as a term-paper deadline.

   A *crisis* is an especially strong source of stress, such as a horrible auto accident. Though it may be sudden and not last long, it may produce long-lasting psychological (and perhaps physical) effects.

   A *strong stressor* is a powerful, ongoing source of extreme mental or physical discomfort, such as a back injury that keeps a person in constant pain. It can dramatically strain a person's ability to adapt.

   From these terms, it would appear the stressors of college aren't so bad compared to other things that can happen. That is, your main experience is one of *hassles* rather than crises or strong stressors.

- *Distressors or eustressors:* One famous expert on stress, Canadian researcher Hans Selye, points out that stressors can be either negative or positive.[16]

   When the source of stress is a negative event, it is called a *distressor* and its effect is called *distress*. An example of a distressor is flunking an exam or being rejected in love. Although distress can be helpful when one is facing a physical threat, too much of it may result in depression and illness.

   When the source of stress is a positive event, it is called a *eustressor* and its effect is called *eustress* (pronounced "you-stress"). An example of a eustressor is getting an A on an exam or falling in love. Eustress can stimulate a person to greater coping and adaptation.

   We can't always prevent distressors. However, we can learn to recognize them, understand our reactions to them, and develop ways of managing both the stressors and the stress. Eustressors, on the other hand, are what impel us to do our best. Examples are the pressure to win games, to make the dean's list, to try out a new activity, to ask out someone new for a date.

- *The number, kind, and magnitude of stressors in your life can affect your health:* When stressors become cumulative they can lead to depression and illness. Several years ago, physicians Thomas Holmes and Richard Rahe devised a "future illness" scale.[17] The scale, known as the Holmes-Rahe Life Events Scale, identifies certain stressors (life events), both positive and negative. These are stressors that the physicians found could be used to predict future physical and emotional problems.

   You may wish to try Personal Exploration #10.1, which contains a version of this scale, the Student Stress Scale. This was designed for people of the traditional student age, 18–24 (although anyone can take it). Note that the scale includes both negative and positive sources of stress.

TYPES OF STRESS: YOUR PHYSICAL & PSYCHOLOGICAL REACTIONS TO THE STRESSORS. Stress—your internal reactions to the stressor—has both physical and emotional sides. Physically, according to researcher Selye, stress is "The nonspecific response of the body to any demand made upon it."[18] Emotionally, stress is the feeling of being overwhelmed. According to one authority, it is "the perception that events or circumstances have challenged or exceeded a person's ability to cope."[19]

Specifically, the stress reactions, for you and for most other students, could take the following forms:

- **Physical reactions:** All diseases are to some extent disorders of adaptation.[20] Often, however, an adaptation to stress appears in a particular part of the body—what doctors call a person's

---

PERSONAL EXPLORATION #10.1

THE STUDENT STRESS SCALE

In the Student Stress Scale, each event, such as beginning or ending school, is given a score that represents the amount of adjustment a person has to make in life as a result of the change. In some studies, people with serious illnesses have been found to have high scores on similar scales.

■ DIRECTIONS

Check off the events you have experienced in the past 12 months.

POINTS

1. Death of a close family member	❑	100
2. Death of a close friend	❑	73
3. Divorce of parents	❑	65
4. Jail term	❑	63
5. Major personal injury or illness	❑	63
6. Marriage	❑	58
7. Firing from a job	❑	50
8. Failure of an important course	❑	47
9. Change in health of a family member	❑	45
10. Pregnancy	❑	45
11. Sex problems	❑	44
12. Serious argument with close friend	❑	40
13. Change in financial status	❑	39
14. Change of scholastic major	❑	39

15. Trouble with parents	❑	37
16. New girl- or boyfriend	❑	37
17. Increase in workload at school	❑	36
18. Outstanding personal achievement	❑	36
19. First quarter/semester in school	❑	31
20. Change in living conditions	❑	30
21. Serious argument with an instructor	❑	30
22. Lower grades than expected	❑	29
23. Change in sleeping habits	❑	29
24. Change in social activities	❑	29
25. Change in eating habits	❑	28
26. Chronic car trouble	❑	26
27. Change in the number of family get-togethers	❑	26
28. Too many missed classes	❑	25
29. Change of college	❑	24
30. Dropping of more than one class	❑	23
31. Minor traffic violations	❑	20

Total points: _____

■ SCORING

To determine your stress score, add up the number of points corresponding to the events you checked

■ INTERPRETATION

If your score is 300 or higher, you are at high risk for developing a health problem.

If your score is between 150 and 300, you have a 50-50 chance of experiencing a serious health change within two years.

If your score is below 150, you have a 1-in-3 chance of a serious health change.

The following can help you reduce your risk:

- Watch for early signs of stress, such as stomachaches or compulsive overeating.
- Avoid negative thinking.
- Arm your body against stress by eating nutritiously and exercising regularly.
- Practice a relaxation technique regularly.
- Turn to friends and relatives for support when you need it.

"stress site." My own stress site, for instance, is the neck or back, when tension is felt as a knot in the muscles there. Some people I know grind their teeth. Others develop nervous tics or perspire excessively.

Do you have a "stress site"? Some physical reactions to stress are *skin problems, headaches, gastrointestinal problems, susceptibility to colds and flus,* and *high blood pressure.* [21-24]

■ ***Psychological reactions:*** Individual emotional reactions to stress cover a wide range. Among them are *nervousness and anxiety,* expressed as irritability, difficulty concentrating, and sleep disturbances. Nervousness and anxiety also are expressed in feelings of dread, overuse of alcohol and other drugs, and mistakes and accidents. Another emotional reaction is *burnout,* a state of physical, emotional, and mental exhaustion. [25, 26]

Managing Stress

PREVIEW You can adapt to or cope with stress. *Adaptation* is not changing the stressor or stress. Some ways of adapting are use of drugs and other escapes such as television watching, junk-food eating, or sleeping. *Coping* is changing the stressor or your reaction to it. There are five strategies for coping: (1) Reduce the stressors. (2) Manage your emotional response. (3) Develop a support system. (4) Take care of your body. (5) Develop relaxation techniques.

egardless of your age, you have already found ways to deal with stress in your life. The question is: Are these ways really the best? For instance, on some campuses, students drink a lot of alcohol—and I mean *a lot.* Why? "Stress!" seems to be the answer. Actually, however, heavy alcohol use only leads to *more stress.*[27]

DO YOU CONTROL STRESS OR DOES STRESS CONTROL YOU? Unfortunately, we can't always control the stressors in our lives, and so we will experience stress no matter what we do. Thus, which is more important—what happens to you, or how you handle it? Clearly, learning how to *manage* stress—minimize it or recover from it—is more important.

There are two principal methods of dealing with stress—adaptation and coping.

■ ***Adaptation:*** **With** <u>adaptation</u>**, you do not change the stressor or the stress.** An example is getting drunk. Adaptation is the *bad* way of handling stress.

■ ***Coping:*** **With** <u>coping</u>**, you do change the stressor or change your reaction to it.** For example, if you're feeling stressed about handing in a paper late, you go talk to the instructor about it. This is the *good* way of handling stress.

ADAPTATION: THE NONPRODUCTIVE WAYS OF HANDLING STRESS. Some of the less effective ways in which people adapt to stress are as follows:

■ ***Drugs, legal and illegal:*** Coffee, cigarettes, and alcohol are all legal drugs. However, too much coffee can make you tense, "wired." Cigarettes also speed up the heart rate and may make it difficult to get going in the morning. Moreover, they put you under the stress of always having to reach for another cigarette.

Alcohol is perceived as being a way of easing the strain of life temporarily, which is why it is so popular with so many people. The down side, however, is what heavy drinking makes you feel like the next morning—jittery, exhausted, depressed, all conditions that *increase* stress.

Other legal drugs, such as tranquilizers, and illegal drugs, such as marijuana, cocaine, and heroin, may seem to provide relaxation in the short run. However, ultimately they complicate your ability to make realistic decisions about the pressures in your life.

- **Food:** Overeating and junk-food snacking are favorite diversions of many people. The act of putting food in our mouths reminds us of what eased one of the most fundamental tensions of infancy: hunger.

- **Sleep and social withdrawal:** Sleep, too, is often a form of escape from exhaustion and depression, and some individuals will spend more than the usual 7–9 hours required in bed. Withdrawal from the company of others is also usually an unhealthy form of adaptation.

How do you adapt to stress now? Consider the kinds of responses you habitually make to the tensions in your life.

COPING: THE PRODUCTIVE WAYS OF HANDLING STRESS—FIVE STRATEGIES.
Now let me turn from negative adaptations to stress to positive coping mechanisms. There are five strategies for coping with stress, as follows:

1. Reduce the stressors.

2. Manage your emotional response.

3. Develop a support system.

4. Take care of your body.

5. Develop relaxation techniques.

STRATEGY NO. 1: REDUCE THE STRESSORS.
Reducing the source of stress is better than avoidance or procrastination.

"Reducing the stressors" seems like obvious advice. However, it's surprising how long we can let something go on being a source of stress—usually because dealing with it is so uncomfortable.

Examples: Falling behind in your work and having to explain your problem to your instructor. Having misunderstandings with your family, your lover, or people sharing your living space. Running up debts on a credit card.

It may not be easy, but all these problems are matters you can do something about. Getting the advice of a counselor may help. Avoidance and procrastination only make things worse.

STRATEGY NO. 2: MANAGE YOUR EMOTIONAL RESPONSE.
You can't always manage the stressor, but you can manage your reactions. Techniques include understanding and expressing your feelings, acting positively, and keeping your sense of humor and having hope.

Learning how to manage your emotional response is crucial. Quite often you can't do anything about a stressor (being stuck having to read a dull assignment, for example). However, you can do something about your *reaction* to it. (You can tell yourself that resentment gets you nowhere, or choose to see a particular stressor as a challenge rather than a threat.)

Some techniques for managing your emotional response follow:

- **Understand and express your feelings:** Understanding pent-up feelings is imperative. This advice is supported by a study of students at Southern Methodist University. It was found that those who kept a journal recounting traumatic events and their emotional responses had fewer colds and reported fewer medical visits.[28]

Are you one who believes it's not appropriate to cry? Actually, crying helps. In one study, 85% of women and 73% of men reported that crying made them feel better.[29]

■ *Act positively:* To keep their spirits up, some people put up signs of positive affirmation on their bathroom mirrors or over their desks. For example:

DON'T SWEAT THE SMALL STUFF.

ONE DAY AT A TIME.

"NEVER GIVE UP" —Winston Churchill

Can you actually *will* yourself to feel and act positively and affirmatively? There is some evidence this is so. Some studies have found that putting a smile on your face will produce the feelings that the expression represents—facial action leads to changes in mood.[30–32]

You can also make your "inner voice" a force for success. Positive "self-talk" can help you control your moods, turn back fear messages, and give you confidence.[33, 34] Positive self-talk is not the same as mindless positive thinking or self-delusion.[35] Rather, it consists of telling yourself positive messages—such as "You can do it. You've done it well before"—that correct errors and distortions in your thinking and help you develop a more accurate internal dialogue.

■ *Keep your sense of humor and have hope:* There has been a growing body of literature that seems to show that humor, optimism, and hope can help people conquer disease or promote their bodies' natural healing processes.[36–39] There is some disagreement as to how much effect laughter and hope have on healing. Still, so many accounts have been written of the positive results of these two qualities that they cannot be ignored.

• • • • • • • • • • • • • • • • • • • •

"Can you actually will *yourself* to feel and act positively and affirmatively? There is some evidence this is so."

• • • • • • • • • • • • • • • • • • • •

STRATEGY NO. 3: DEVELOP A SUPPORT SYSTEM. *Finding social support is vital for resisting stress. Sources of support are friends—in the true sense—counselors, self-help, and other support groups.*

It can be tough to do things by yourself, so it's important to grasp a lesson that many people never learn: *You are not alone. No matter what troubles you, emotional support is available—but you have to reach out for it.*

Some forms of support are as follows:

■ *Talk to and do things with friends:* True friends are not just people you know. They are people you can trust, talk to honestly, and draw emotional sustenance from. (Some people you know quite well may actually not be very good friends in this sense. That is, the way they interact with you makes you feel competitive, anxious, or inferior.) Friends are simply those people you feel comfortable with, regardless of age or social grouping.

It's vital to fight the temptation to isolate yourself. Studies show that the more students participate in activities with other students, the less they suffer from depression and the more they have feelings of health.[40]

■ *Talk to counselors:* You can get emotional support from counselors. Paid counselors may be psychotherapists, ranging from social workers to psychiatrists. Unpaid counselors may be clergy or perhaps members of the college student services.

Sources of free counseling that everyone should be aware of are telephone "hot lines." Here, for the price of a phone call, callers can find a sympathetic ear and various kinds of help. (Hot lines are listed under the heading of CRISIS INTERVENTION SERVICE in the telephone-book Yellow Pages. Other forms of stress counseling are listed under the heading STRESS MANAGEMENT AND PREVENTION.)

■ *Join a support group:* This week an estimated 15 million Americans will attend one of about 500,000 meetings offered by some form of support group.[41] Self-help organizations cover all kinds of areas of concern. There are many on various types of drug addiction and offering help to adult children of alcoholics. Others range from single parenting to spouse abuse to compulsive shopping to "women who love too much" to various forms of bereavement. Some of these groups may exist on or near your campus.

In the true self-help group, membership is limited to peers. There is no professional moderator, only some temporarily designated leader who makes announcements and calls on people to share their experiences. This is in contrast with group-therapy groups, in which a psychologist or other therapist is in charge.

STRATEGY NO. 4: TAKE CARE OF YOUR BODY.
Taking care of the body helps alleviate stress in the mind. Techniques include eating, exercising, and sleeping right and avoiding drugs.

The interaction between mind and body becomes particularly evident when you're stressed. If you're not eating and exercising well, or are short on sleep, or are using drugs, these mistreatments of the body will only make the mind feel worse.

STRATEGY NO. 5: DEVELOP RELAXATION TECHNIQUES.
There are three relaxation techniques for de-stressing yourself. One is progressive muscular relaxation, which consists of tightening and relaxing muscle groups. A second is mental imagery, which consists of visualizing a change. A third is meditation, which consists of focusing on removing mental distractions.

There is an entire body of extremely effective stress reducers that most people in North America have never tried at all.[42] They include the following:

- **_Progressive muscular relaxation:_ The technique of _progressive muscular relaxation_ consists of reducing stress by tightening and relaxing major muscle groups throughout your body.** If you like, take 10 minutes to try the following.

(1) *Get comfortable and quiet.* Sit down or lie in a comfortable setting where you won't be disturbed. Close your eyes.

(2) *Be aware of your breathing.* Breathe slowly in through your nose. Exhale slowly through your nose.

(3) *Clench and release your muscles.* Tense and relax each part of your body two or more times. Clench while inhaling. Release while exhaling.

(4) *Proceed through muscles or muscle groups.* Tense and relax various muscles, from fist to face to stomach to toes. (A good progression is: Right fist, right biceps. Left fist, left biceps. Right shoulder, left shoulder. Neck, jaw, eyes, forehead, scalp. Chest, stomach, buttocks, genitals, down through each leg to the toes.)

Mental imagery: <u>*Mental imagery*</u> is also known as <u>*guided imagery*</u> and <u>*visualization.*</u> **It is a procedure in which you essentially daydream an image or desired change, anticipating that your body will respond as if the image were real.** The accompanying box shows how to do mental imagery. *(See* ■ *Panel 10.1, below.)*

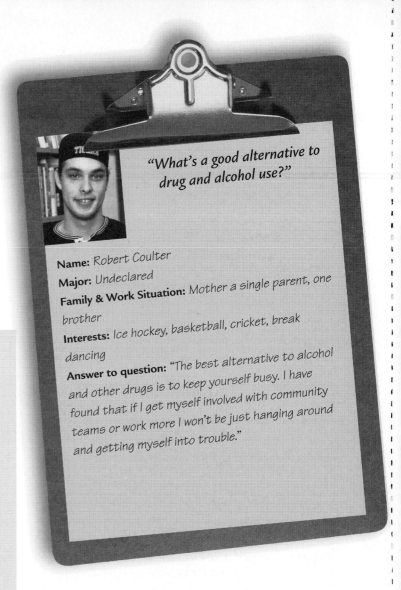

"What's a good alternative to drug and alcohol use?"

Name: Robert Coulter

Major: Undeclared

Family & Work Situation: Mother a single parent, one brother

Interests: Ice hockey, basketball, cricket, break dancing

Answer to question: "The best alternative to alcohol and other drugs is to keep yourself busy. I have found that if I get myself involved with community teams or work more I won't be just hanging around and getting myself into trouble."

PANEL 10.1 **M**ental imagery. It's recommended that you devote 10 minutes or so to this procedure.

Get comfortable and quiet: Remove your shoes, loosen your clothes, and sit down or lie in a comfortable setting, with the lights dimmed. Close your eyes.

Breathe deeply and concentrate on a phrase: Breathe deeply, filling your chest, and slowly let the air out. With each breath, concentrate on a simple word or phrase (such as "One," or "Good," or a prayer). Focus your mind on this phrase to get rid of distracting thoughts. Repeat.

Clench and release your muscles: Tense and relax each part of your body, proceeding from fist to face to stomach to toes.

Visualize a vivid image: Create a tranquil, pleasant image in your mind—lying beside a mountain stream, floating on a raft in a pool, stretched out on a beach. Try to involve all five senses, from sight to taste.

Visualize a desired change: If you're trying to improve some aspect of your performance, such as improving a tennis serve, visualize the act in detail: the fuzz and seam on the ball, the exact motion of the serve, the path of the ball, all in slow detail.

■ *Meditation:* <u>*Meditation*</u> **is concerned with directing a person's attention to a single, unchanging or repetitive stimulus. It is a way of quelling the "mind chatter"**—the chorus of voices that goes on in the heads of all of us. An age-old technique, the purpose of meditation is simply to eliminate mental distractions and relax the body. The box opposite shows one method.[43] *(See* ■ *Panel 10.2.)*

PANEL 10.2

Meditation. Meditation includes the repetition of a word, sound, phrase, or prayer. Whenever everyday thoughts occur, they should be disregarded, and you should return to the repetition. The exercise should be continued for 10 minutes or so.

Herbert Benson, M.D., author of *The Relaxation Response* and *Your Maximum Mind,* offers the following simple instructions for meditation:

- Pick a focus word or short phrase that is firmly rooted in your personal belief system. For example, a Christian person might choose the opening words of Psalm 23, "The Lord is my shepherd"; a Jewish person, "Shalom"; a nonreligious individual, a neutral word like "One" or "Peace."

- Sit quietly in a comfortable position.

- Close your eyes.

- Relax your muscles.

- Breathe slowly and naturally, and as you do, repeat your focus word or phrase as you exhale.

- Assume a passive attitude. Don't worry about how well you're doing. When other thoughts come to mind, simply say to yourself, "Oh, well," and gently return to the repetition.

Onward

PREVIEW Your body is not expendable.

any people treat their bodies as if they were expendable, but in the end they find they are not. Probably the more you let stress cause you to abuse your health, the less energy you'll have as well as less self-esteem. Sooner or later, we all learn we have to take care of Number One.

1. Anonymous. (1987, October). The perils of burnout. *Newsweek on Campus.*

2. Lazarus, R. S. (1981, July). Little hassles can be hazardous to health. *Psychology Today,* p. 61.

3. Hamilton, W. (1996, June/July). Automotivational counseling. *Buzz,* p. 128.

4. Lowery, S. (1991, December 26). Honk if you're a rude driver. *San Francisco Chronicle,* p. B5. Reprinted from *Los Angeles Daily News.*

5. Castaneda, C. J. (1996, August 16). Public transit: Competing against cars, and losing. *USA Today,* p. 8A.

6. Anonymous (1996, April 15). Study says cars pose greatest risk in suburbs. *San Francisco Chronicle,* p. A2. Reprinted from *Los Angeles Times.*

7. Gallup Organization, Associated Press. (1990, January 12). Working at the wrong job. *San Francisco Chronicle,* p. C1. [October 1989 survey for National Occupational Information Coordinating Committee.]

8. Hochschild, A., & Machung, A. (1989). *The second shift: Working parents and the revolution at home.* New York: Viking Penguin.

9. Timmrick, T. C., & Braza, G. (1980). Stress and aging. *Geriatrics, 25,* 113.

10. Jung, J., & Khalsa, H. K. (1989). The relationship of daily hassles, social support, and coping to depression in Black and White students. *Journal of General Psychology, 116,* 407–417.

11. Ulbrich, P. M., Warheit, G. J., & Zimmerman, R. S. (1989). Race, socioeconomic status, and psychological distress: An examination of differential vulnerability. *Journal of Health and Social Behavior, 30,* 131–146.

12. Feagin, J., Associated Press. (1990, September 22). Even upper-income blacks suffer race bias, study shows. *San Francisco Chronicle,* p. A8.

13. Turner, R. J., & McLean, P. D. (1989). Physical disability and psychological distress. *Rehabilitation Psychology, 34,* 225–242.

14. Reich, J. W., Zautra, A. J., & Guarnaccia, C. A. (1989). Effects of disability and bereavement on the mental health and recovery of older adults. *Psychology and Aging, 4,* 57–65.

15. Anonymous. Despite rights law, the disabled say there's a long way to go. (1990, September 1). *San Francisco Chronicle,* p. A16. Reprinted from *Los Angeles Times.*

16. Selye, H. (1974). *Stress without distress.* New York: Lippincott, pp. 28–29.

17. Holmes, T. H., & Rahe, R. H. (1967). The social readjustment rating scale. *Journal of Psychosomatic Research, 11,* 213–18.

18. Selye, 1974, p. 27.

19. Lazarus, R. S., & Forlman, S. (1982). Coping and adaptation. In W. D. Gentry (Ed.). *Handbook of behavioral medicine.* New York: Guilford Press.

20. Hinkle, L. E., Jr. (1987). Stress and disease: The concept after 50 years. *Social Science & Medicine, 25,* 561 - 66.

21. Kiecolt-Glazer, J., & Glaser, R. (1988). Major life changes, chronic stress, and immunity. *Advances in Biochemical Psychopharmacology, 44,* 217–24.

22. Kiecolt-Glazer, J. et al. (1987) Stress, health, and immunity: Tracking the mind/body connection. Presentation at American Psychological Association meeting, New York, August 1987.

23. Kannel, W. B. (1990). CHD risk factors: A Framingham study update. *Hospital Practice, 25,* 119.

24. Eliot, R., & Breo, D. (1984). *Is it worth dying for?* New York: Bantam Books.

25. McCulloch, A., & O'Brien, L. (1986). The organizational determinants of worker burnout. *Children & Youth Services Review, 8,* 175–90.

26. Girdano, D. A., & Everly, G. S., Jr. (1986). *Controlling stress and tension.* Englewood Cliffs, NJ: Prentice-Hall.

27. Matthews, A. (1993, March 7). The campus crime wave. *New York Times Magazine,* pp. 38–42, 47.

28. Anonymous. (1987, August). Dear diary. *American Health.*

29. Mee, C. L., Jr. (Ed.). (1987). *Managing stress from morning to night.* Alexandria, VA: Time-Life Books.

30. Zajonc, R. B. (1985). Emotion and facial efference: A theory reclaimed. *Science, 228,* 15–21.

31. Adelmann, P. K., & Zajonc, R. B. (1989). Facial efference and the experience of emotion. *Annual Review of Psychology, 40,* 249–80.

32. Zajonc, R. Cited in: Goleman, D. (1989, June 29). Put on a happy face—it really works. *San Francisco Chronicle,* p. C10. Reprinted from *New York Times.*

33. Donahue, P. A. (1989). Helping adolescents with shyness: Applying the Japanese Morita therapy in shyness counselling. *International Journal for the Advancement of Counselling, 12,* 323–32.

34. Zastrow, C. (1988). What really causes psychotherapy change? *Journal of Independent Social Work, 2,* 5–16.

35. Braiker, H. B. (1989, December). The power of self-talk. *Psychology Today,* p. 24.

36. Cousins, N. (1979). *Anatomy of an illness.* New York: Norton.

37. Dillon, K. M., Minchoff, B., & Baker, K. H. (1985–86). Positive emotional states and enhancement of the immune system. *International Journal of Psychiatry in Medicine, 15,* 13–18.

38. Long, P. (1987, October). Laugh and be well? *Psychology Today,* pp. 28–29.

39. Siegel, B. (1986). *Love, medicine, and miracles.* New York: Harper & Row.

40. Reifman, A., & Dunkel-Schetter, C. (1990). Stress, structural social support, and well-being in university students. *Journal of American College Health, 38,* 271–77.

41. Leerhsen, C., et al. (1990, February 5). Unite and conquer. *Newsweek,* pp. 50–55.

42. Snyder, M. (1988). Relaxation. In J. J. Fitzpatrick, R. L. Taunton, & J. Q. Benoliel (Eds.). *Annual review of nursing research, 8,* 111–28. New York: Springer.

43. Benson, H. (1989). Editorial: Hypnosis and the relaxation response. *Gastroenterology, 96,* 1610.

1. *How much stress do you have in your life?*
Ask students to complete Personal Exploration #10.1, "The Student Stress Scale." Each student should list on a sheet of paper his or her Top Ten Stressors, drawing on this Personal Exploration, if necessary.

Students should then meet in a small group (three to five students), designate a secretary or recorder, and develop a master list from their separate lists. After identifying the top five stressors for the group, students should discuss how the stressors affect their behaviors and feelings and how they have ineffectively coped with such stressors in the past. They should then discuss how they would hope to deal with them in the future.

If time permits, students may share their experiences with the class as a whole.

2. *Practicing a relaxation technique.* The instructor should select *one* of the three relaxation techniques described in this chapter—*progressive muscular relaxation, mental imagery,* or *meditation*—for 10 minutes of practice by the class as a whole. Read aloud from this book the steps for the particular method. *Important: Tell students that whenever everyday thoughts occur they are to disregard them and return to the relaxation procedure.*

After the 10 minutes are up, ask students to discuss their experience. Questions for discussion: Do you actually feel more relaxed? Did you almost fall asleep? Was it difficult to disregard the intrusion of everyday thoughts? Were you too aware of others in the room? Do you think the technique might work in private?

3. *What role does drinking and drugging play?*
Ask students in the class to discuss *someone they know* (don't allow them to use names) who seems to have a drinking or drug problem. Does the person say that stress plays a role? Does he or she admit to having a problem? Why or why not, in the student's opinion?

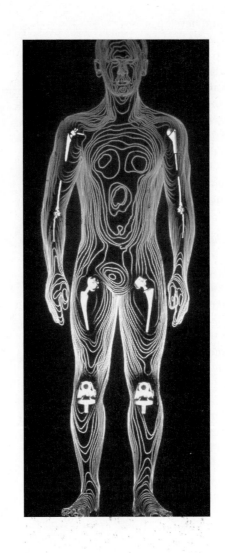

JOURNAL ENTRY #10.1: HOW DO YOU REACT TO STRESS? What kind of psychological reactions do you have to stress (for example, irritability, impatience, depression)? What kind of physiological reactions do you have to stress (for example, insomnia, upset stomach, tiredness)? List your reactions and compare them to the reactions of other people you know.

_____

_____

_____

_____

_____

_____

_____

_____

_____

JOURNAL ENTRY #10.2: HOW DO YOU DEAL WITH STRESS? What kinds of things do you do to reduce the feelings of stress? What kinds of things *could* you do?

_____

_____

_____

_____

_____

_____

_____

_____

JOURNAL ENTRY #10.3: IS THERE A RELATIONSHIP BETWEEN STRESS AND "PARTYING"? Give some thought to the whole matter of "partying," or heavy drinking and/or drugging. How much of it do you see around you? Have you been affected by it? Is stress a contributor?

_____

_____

_____

_____

_____

_____

_____

_____

JOURNAL ENTRY #10.4: WHAT ARE YOUR DRINKING/DRUGGING HABITS? Do you routinely get intoxicated or high? Has it affected your academic work or relations with others? What do you think you should do about it?

_____

_____

_____

_____

_____

_____

_____

_____

relationships

managing conflict, assertiveness, & sexual risks

IN THIS CHAPTER: Some students think as much—or more—about their relationships as they do about their academic work. How you deal with other people—particularly love relationships—can have a lot of bearing on your happiness. In this chapter, we consider the following:

■ *Relationships and communication:* The nature of intimate relationships and how to handle conflict.

■ *Assertiveness:* Assertiveness versus aggressiveness and nonassertiveness.

■ *HIV and AIDS:* What you should know about these feared sexual diseases.

■ *Safer sex:* Rules for safer sex.

What are the two most important personal issues in life?

Love and work, said psychologist Sigmund Freud. Or *"romance and finance,"* as I've heard other people put it.

What about you? Are relationships and career issues important matters in *your* life? I know they certainly are for me. Ending war, poverty, and disease are certainly of greater significance for humankind in general, of course. However, for most people the two most important *personal* issues are love and work.

We consider money and career issues in Chapters 12 and 13. Here let's look at relationships.

Conflict & Communication: Learning How to Disagree

PREVIEW Communication consists of ways of learning to disagree. In bad communication, you become argumentative and defensive and deny your own feelings. In good communication, you acknowledge the other person's feelings and express your own openly. Expert listening consists of tuning in to your partner's channel. It means giving listening signals, not interrupting, asking questions skillfully, and using diplomacy and tact. Most important, it means looking for some truth in what the other person says. To express yourself, use "I feel" language, give praise, and keep criticism specific.

Why can't people get along better? Must there always be conflict in close relationships, as between lovers, family members, roommates, or housemates? To see what your usual approach to conflict is, try the following Personal Exploration.

PERSONAL EXPLORATION #11.1

WHAT ARE YOUR FEELINGS ABOUT CONFLICT?

Check which *one* of the following statements best describes your feelings when you approach a conflict with someone close to you.

1. ❑ I hate conflict. If I can find a way to avoid it, I will.

2. ❑ Conflict is such a hassle. I'd just as soon let the other person have his or her way so as to keep the peace.

3. ❑ You can't just let people walk over you. You've got to fight to establish your point of view.

4. ❑ I'm willing to negotiate to see if the other person and I can meet halfway.

5. ❑ I'm willing to explore the similarities and differences with the other person to see if we can solve the problem to both our satisfaction.

■ INTERPRETATION

Whichever one you checked corresponds to a particular style of dealing with conflict. They are: (1) avoidance, (2) accommodation, (3) domination, (4) compromise, (5) integration. For an explanation, read on.

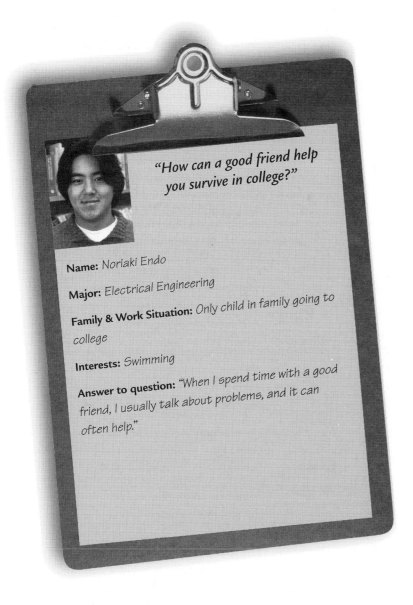

"How can a good friend help you survive in college?"

Name: Noriaki Endo

Major: Electrical Engineering

Family & Work Situation: Only child in family going to college

Interests: Swimming

Answer to question: "When I spend time with a good friend, I usually talk about problems, and it can often help."

Researchers have identified five styles of dealing with conflict, one of which is probably closest to yours.

1. *Avoidance: "Maybe It Will Go Away."*
   People who adopt this style find dealing with conflict unpleasant and uncomfortable. They hope that by ignoring the conflict or by avoiding confrontation the circumstances will change and the problem will magically disappear. Unfortunately, avoiding or delaying facing the conflict usually means it will have to be dealt with later rather than sooner. By then the situation may have worsened.

2. *Accommodation: "Oh, Have It Your Way!"*
   Accommodation does not mean compromise; it means simply giving in, although it does not really resolve the matter under dispute. People who adopt a style of easily surrendering are, like avoiders, uncomfortable with conflict and hate disagreements. They are also inclined to be "people pleasers," worried about the approval of others. However, giving in does not really solve the conflict. If anything it may aggravate the situation over the long term. Accommodators may be deeply resentful that the other person did not listen to their point of view. Indeed, the resentment may even develop into a role of martyrdom, which will only irritate the person's partner.

3. *Domination: "Only Winning Matters."* The person holding the winning-is-everything, domination style should not be surprised if he or she some day finds an "I'm gone!" note from the partner. The dominator will go to any lengths to emerge triumphant in a disagreement, even if it means being aggressive and manipulative. However, winning isn't what intimate human relationships are supposed to be about; that approach to conflict produces only hostility and resentment.

4. *Compromise: "I'll Meet You Halfway."* Compromise seems like a civilized way of dealing with conflict, and it is definitely an improvement over the preceding styles. People striving for compromise recognize that both partners have different needs and try to negotiate an agreement. Even so, they may still employ some gamesmanship, such as manipulation and misrepresentation, in an attempt to further their own ends. Thus, compromise is not as effective in resolving conflict as integration.

5. *Integration: "Let's Honestly Try to Satisfy Both of Us."* Compromise views solution to the conflict as a matter of each party meeting the other halfway. The integration style, on the other hand, attempts to find a solution that will achieve satisfaction for both partners.

Integration has several parts to it:

- **Openness for mutual problem solving:** The conflict is seen not as a game to be won or negotiated but as a problem to be solved to each other's mutual benefit. Consequently, manipulation and misrepresentation have no place; honesty and openness are a necessary part of reaching the solution. This also has the benefit of building trust that will carry over to the resolution of other conflicts.

- **Disagreement with the ideas, not the person:** There is an important part of integration, which I expand on below. This concept is that partners must be able to criticize each other's ideas or specific acts rather than each other generally as persons. It is one thing, for instance, to say "You drink too much!" It is another to say "I feel you drank too much last night." The first way is a generality that insults the other's character. The second way states that you are unhappy about a particular incident.

- **Emphasis on similarities, not differences:** Integration requires more work than other styles of dealing with conflict (although the payoffs are better). The reason is that partners must put a good deal of effort into stating and clarifying their positions. To maintain the spirit of trust, the two should also emphasize the similarities in their positions rather than the differences.

AREAS OF CONFLICT. The number of subjects over which two people can disagree is awesome. One area about which couples must make adjustments are unrealistic expectations, such as who should do which household chores. Other matters have to do with work and career, finances, in-laws, sex, and commitment/jealousy.[1] Most of the foregoing problems can be overcome with effective communication. Indeed, good communication—to handle conflict and wants—is critical to the success of any relationship.

COMMUNICATION: THERE ARE WAYS TO LEARN HOW TO DISAGREE. The fact that conflict is practically always present in an ongoing relationship does not mean that it should be suppressed. When handled constructively, conflict may bring problems out into the open, where they can be solved. Handling conflict may also put an end to chronic sources of discontent in a relationship. Finally, airing disagreements may lead to new insights through the clashing of divergent views.[2] The key to success in relationships is the ability to handle conflict successfully, which means the ability to communicate well.

BAD COMMUNICATION. Most of us *think* communication is easy, points out psychiatrist David Burns, because we've been talking since we were children.[3] And communication *is* easy when we're happy and feeling close to someone. It's when we have a conflict that we find out how well we really communicate—whether it's good or bad.

Bad communication, says Burns, author of *The Feeling Good Handbook,* has two characteristics:

- **You become argumentative and defensive:** The natural tendency of most of us when we are upset is to argue with and contradict others. The habit of contradicting others, however, is self-defeating, for it creates distance between you and them and prevents intimacy. Moreover, when you are in this stance you show you are not interested in listening to the other person or understanding his or her feelings.

- **You deny your own feelings and act them out indirectly:** You may become sarcastic, or pout, or storm out of the room slamming doors. This kind of reaction is known as *passive aggression.* However, it can sometimes be as destructive as *active aggression,* in which you make threats or tell the other person off.

There are a number of other characteristics of bad communication. One is *martyrdom,* in which you insist you're an innocent victim. A second is *hopelessness,* in which you give up and insist there's no

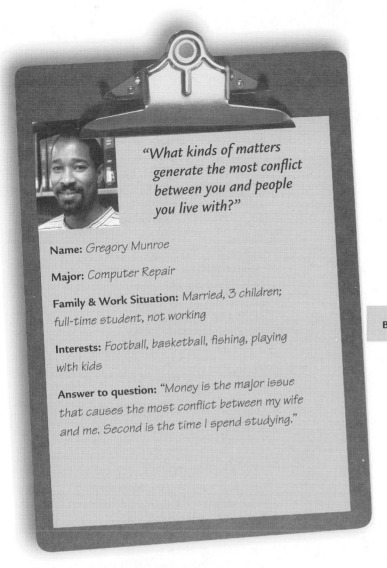

"What kinds of matters generate the most conflict between you and people you live with?"

Name: Gregory Munroe

Major: Computer Repair

Family & Work Situation: Married, 3 children; full-time student, not working

Interests: Football, basketball, fishing, playing with kids

Answer to question: "Money is the major issue that causes the most conflict between my wife and me. Second is the time I spend studying."

point in trying to resolve your difficulties. A third is *self-blame,* in which you act as if you're a terrible, awful person (instead of dealing with the problem). A fourth is *"helping,"* in which instead of listening you attempt to take over and "solve" the other person's problem. A fifth is *diversion,* in which you list grievances about past "injustices" instead of dealing with how you both feel right now.

GOOD COMMUNICATION. "Most people want to be understood and accepted more than anything else in the world," says Burns.[4] Knowing that is taking a giant first step toward good communication.

Good communication, according to Burns, has two attributes:

- **You listen to and acknowledge the other person's feelings:** You may be tempted just to broadcast your feelings and insist that the other agree with you. It's better, however, if you encourage the other to express his or her emotions. Try to listen to and understand what the other person is thinking and feeling. (I expand on listening skills below.)

- **You express your own feelings openly and directly:** If you only listen to the other person's feelings and don't express your own, you will end up feeling short-changed, angry, and resentful. When you deny your feelings, you end up acting them out indirectly. *The trick, then, is to express your feelings in a way that will not alienate the other person.*

BECOMING EXPERT AT LISTENING. If communication is listening, how is that done? Some ideas are offered by Aaron Beck, director of the Center for Cognitive Therapy at the University of Pennsylvania. In his book *Love Is Never Enough,* he suggests the following listening guidelines:[5]

- **Tune in to your partner's channel:** Imagining how the other person might be feeling—putting yourself in the other's shoes—is known as *empathy,* trying to experience the other's thoughts and feelings. The means for learning what the other's thoughts and feelings are can be determined through the other steps.

- **Give listening signals:** Use facial expressions, subtle gestures, and sounds such as "uh-huh" and "yeah" to show your partner you are really listening. Beck particularly urges this advice on men, since studies find that women are more inclined to send responsive signals. Talking to someone without getting feedback is like talking to a wall.

- **Don't interrupt:** Although interruptions may seem natural to you, they can make the other person feel cut off. Men, says Beck, tend to interrupt more than women do (although they interrupt other men as often as they do women). They would do better to not express their ideas until after the partner has finished talking.

- **Ask questions skillfully:** Asking questions can help you determine what the other person is thinking and keep the discussion going—provided the question is not a *conversation stopper*. "Why" questions can be conversation stoppers ("Why were you home late?"). So can questions that can have only a yes-or-no answer.

Questions that ask the other's opinion can be *conversation starters*. (Example: "What do you think about always having dinner at the same time?") Questions that reflect the other's statements help convey your empathy. (Example: "Can you tell me more about why you feel that way?") The important thing is to ask questions *gently*, never accusingly. You want to explore what the other person is thinking and feeling and to show that you are listening.

■ *Use diplomacy and tact:* All of us have sensitive areas—about our appearance or how we speak, for example. This is true of people in intimate relationships as much as people in other relationships. *Problems in relationships invariably involve feelings.* Using diplomacy and tact in your listening responses will help build trust to talk about difficulties.

An especially wise piece of advice about listening comes from David Burns: *Find SOME truth in what the other person is saying and agree with it.* Do this even if you feel that what he or she is saying is totally wrong, unreasonable, irrational, or unfair. This technique, known as *disarming*, works especially well if you're feeling criticized and attacked.

If, instead of arguing, you agree with the other person, it takes the wind out of his or her sails. Indeed, it can have a calming effect. The other person will then be more open to your point of view. Adds Burns: "When you use the disarming technique, you must be genuine in what you say or it will backfire. You can always find some valid way to agree, no matter how illogical the person's accusations might seem to you. If you agree with them in a sincere way, they will generally soften and will be far more willing to listen to you."[6]

BECOMING EXPERT AT EXPRESSING YOURSELF. It is often tempting to use the tools of war—attacking and defending,

withdrawing and sulking, going for the jugular. However, these will never take you as far in resolving conflicts in intimate relationships as will kinder and gentler techniques.

In expressing yourself, there are two principal points to keep in mind:

■ *Use "I feel" language:* It's always tempting to use accusatory language during the heat of conflict. (Examples: "You make me so mad!" or "You never listen to what I say!") However, this is sure to send the other person stomping out of the room.

A better method is simply to say "I feel" followed by the word expressing your feelings—"frustrated"; "ignored"; "attacked"; "nervous"; "unloved." This way you don't sound blaming and critical. (Compare this to saying "You make me . . ." or "You never . . .") By expressing how you feel, rather than defending the "truth" of your position, you can communicate your feelings without attacking the other person.

■ *Express praise and keep criticism specific:* Most of us respond better to compliments than to criticism, and most of us seek appreciation and fear rejection. In any conflict, we may disagree with a person's *specific act or behavior*. However, we need not reject the other as a person.

For example, you might want to say, "When we go to parties, you always leave me alone and go talk to other people." It's better, however, to combine criticism with praise. For example: "I'm proud to be with you when we go to parties, and I hope you are of me. However, I think we could have even more fun if we stay in touch with each other when we're at a party. Does this seem like a reasonable request?"[7]

Assertiveness: Better than Aggressiveness or Nonassertiveness

PREVIEW Aggressiveness is expressing yourself in a way that hurts others. Nonassertiveness is not expressing yourself, giving in to others and hurting yourself. Assertiveness is expressing yourself without hurting either others or yourself. Both men and women have assertiveness problems, women sometimes being too passive, men too aggressive, although the reverse is also true. Developing assertiveness means observing your own behavior in conflict situations, visualizing a model for assertiveness, and practicing assertive behavior.

t's important to learn to express your disappointments, resentments, and wishes without denying yourself. Yet you also don't want to put other people down or make them angry. This means learning to be *assertive*.

Assertiveness doesn't mean being pushy or selfish but rather being forthright enough to communicate your needs while respecting the needs of others. Being assertive is important in intimate relationships, of course. However, it's also important in many other social interactions in which speaking out, standing up for yourself, or talking back is necessary.

AGGRESSIVE, NONASSERTIVE, & ASSERTIVE BEHAVIOR. Let us consider three types of behavior: aggressiveness, non-assertiveness, and assertiveness. (Distinctions among these behaviors have been put forth in two interesting books by psychologists Robert Alberti and Michael Emmons. They are *Your Perfect Right* and *Stand Up, Speak Out, Talk Back!* [8,9]) The definitions are as follows:

- **Aggressiveness—*expressing yourself and hurting others:* Aggressive behavior means you vehemently expound your opinions, accuse or blame others, and hurt others before hurting yourself.**

- **Nonassertiveness—*giving in to others and hurting yourself:* Nonassertive behavior — also called *submissive* or *passive behavior* —means consistently giving in to others on points of difference. It means agreeing with others regardless of your own feelings, not expressing your opinions, hurting yourself to avoid hurting others. Nonassertive people have difficulty making requests for themselves or expressing their differences with others. In a word, they are *timid*.**

- **Assertiveness—*expressing yourself without hurting others or yourself:* Assertiveness is defined as acting in your own best interests by expressing your thoughts and feelings directly and honestly. It means standing up for yourself and openly expressing your personal feelings and opinions, yet not hurting either yourself or others. Assertiveness is important in enabling you to express or defend your rights.**

It's important to learn to *ask for what you want in a civilized way, without hurting the feelings of the other person.* This is what assertive behavior is all about. Consider what happens if you try aggressive or nonassertive behavior. Aggressive behavior probably won't help you get what you want because your pushiness or anger creates disharmony and alienates other people. It may also make you feel guilty about how you treated others. Nonassertive behavior also may not help you get what you want. Though it may be an attempt to please others by not offending them, it may actually make them contemptuous of you.[24] In addition, nonassertive behavior leads you to suppress your feelings, leading to self-denial and poor self-esteem.

You need to know, however, that assertive behavior will not always get you what you want. Probably no one form of behavior will. Still, if performed correctly, it may improve your chances. The reason is that assertive behavior is not offensive to other people. This makes them more willing to listen to your point of view.

ASSERTIVENESS & GENDER STEREOTYPES.

It has been suggested that behaving assertively may be more difficult for women than men. This is because many females have supposedly been socialized to be more passive and submissive than men.[11] For example, some women worry that acting boldly in pursuing success will make them appear unfeminine.[12] Indeed, by the college years, women may view an act of assertive behavior as more aggressive when done by females than by males.[13]

However, many men have assertiveness problems, too. Some males have been raised to be nonassertive, others to be aggressive rather than assertive. Some researchers suggest that actually more males than females need to be trained in assertiveness to modify their typically more aggressive behavior.[14]

To get an idea of your assertiveness, try Personal Exploration #11.2 at right.

DEVELOPING ASSERTIVENESS.
There are different programs for developing assertiveness, but most consist of four steps:[15]

- *Learn what assertive behavior is:* First you need to learn what assertive behavior is, so that you know what it is supposed to be like. You need to learn how to consider both yours and others' rights.

- *Observe your own behavior in conflict situations:* You then need to monitor your own assertive (or nonassertive) behavior. You need to see what circumstances, people, situations, or topics make you behave aggressively or nonassertively. You may find you are able to take care of yourself (behave assertively) in some situations, but not in others.

- *Visualize a model for assertiveness:* If possible, you should try to find a model for assertiveness in the specific situations that trouble you and observe that person's behavior. Role models are important in other parts of life, and this area is no exception. If possible, note how rewarding such behavior is, which will reinforce the assertive tendencies.

- *Practice assertive behavior:* Of course the only way to consistently behave assertively is to practice the behavior. You can do this as a rehearsal, carrying on an imaginary dialogue in private with yourself. Or you can actually role-play the behavior, practicing the assertive behavior with a good friend, counselor, or therapist.

HIV & AIDS

PREVIEW HIV (Human Immunodeficiency Virus) may progress over about 10 years into AIDS (Acquired Immune Deficiency Syndrome). HIV is diagnosed through an antibody test, but the test cannot predict if the virus will become AIDS. HIV may infect both sexes and is principally transmitted by unprotected sex and by shared drug needles.

Formerly called venereal diseases, *sexually transmitted diseases (STDs)* **are infectious diseases that are transmitted as a result (usually) of sexual contact.** There are many STDs. They include hepatitis B, herpes, human papilloma virus (HPV), chlamydia, gonorrhea, syphilis, parasite infections, and HIV and AIDS. These are growing rapidly, bringing considerable suffering and even death.

HIV & AIDS: THE MODERN SCOURGE.
We will focus on HIV and AIDS because they are recent threats and because they have produced all kinds of misunderstandings. HIV and AIDS are two different things:

HOW ASSERTIVE ARE YOU?

Answer "Yes" or "No" to each of the following statements.

1. When a person is blatantly unfair, do you usually fail to say something about it to him or her?

   ❏ Yes ❏ No

2. Are you always very careful to avoid all trouble with other people?

   ❏ Yes ❏ No

3. Do you often avoid social contacts for fear of doing or saying the wrong thing?

   ❏ Yes ❏ No

4. If a friend betrays your confidence, do you tell him or her how you really feel?

   ❏ Yes ❏ No

5. Would you insist that a roommate do his or her fair share of cleaning?

   ❏ Yes ❏ No

6. When a clerk in a store waits on someone who has come in after you, do you call his or her attention to the matter?

   ❏ Yes ❏ No

7. Do you find that there are very few people with whom you can be relaxed and have a good time?

   ❏ Yes ❏ No

8. Would you be hesitant about asking a good friend to lend you a few dollars?

   ❏ Yes ❏ No

9. If someone who has borrowed $5 from you seems to have forgotten about it, would you remind this person?

   ❏ Yes ❏ No

10. If a person keeps on teasing you, do you have difficulty expressing your annoyance or displeasure?

    ❏ Yes ❏ No

11. Would you remain standing at the rear of a crowded auditorium rather than look for a seat up front?

    ❏ Yes ❏ No

12. If someone kept kicking the back of your chair in a movie, would you ask him or her to stop?

    ❏ Yes ❏ No

13. If a friend keeps calling you very late each evening, would you ask him or her not to call after a certain time?

    ❏ Yes ❏ No

14. If someone starts talking to someone else right in the middle of your conversation, do you express your irritation?

    ❏ Yes ❏ No

15. In a plush restaurant, if you order a medium steak and find it too rare, would you ask the waiter to have it recooked?

    ❏ Yes ❏ No

16. If a landlord of your apartment fails to make certain necessary repairs after promising to do so, would you insist on it?

    ❏ Yes ❏ No

17. Would you return a faulty garment you purchased a few days ago?

    ❏ Yes ❏ No

18. If someone you respect expresses opinions you strongly disagree with, would you venture to state your own point of view?

    ❏ Yes ❏ No

19. Are you usually able to say no when people make unreasonable requests?

    ❏ Yes ❏ No

20. Do you think that people should stand up for their rights?

    ❏ Yes ❏ No

■ INTERPRETATION

There is no scoring system. You can figure out what the answers *should* be.

Now it becomes a matter of rehearsing the response so you'll be able to act assertively the next time it's required. What will you do the next time the landlord fails to make repairs? Or the people in your household don't do their fair share of cleaning? Or you need to ask the waiter to have your steak cooked some more?

- **HIV:** *HIV*, or *human immunodeficiency virus*, the virus causing AIDS, brings about a variety of ills. The most important is the breakdown of the immune system, which leads to the development of certain infections and cancers.

    Two variants of the virus are HIV-1 and HIV-2. *HIV-1* causes most of the AIDS cases in the United States. *HIV-2* is the dominant strain in Africa; cases are now showing up in the United States.

- **AIDS:** *AIDS* stands for *acquired immune deficiency syndrome*, a sexually transmitted disease that is caused by HIV. It is characterized by irreversible damage to the body's immune system. As a result, the body is unable to fight infections, making it vulnerable to many diseases, such as pneumonia. So far, AIDS has proven to be always fatal.

    Because HIV and AIDS are life-and-death matters, it's important that you have *accurate knowledge* about them. Doing Personal Exploration #11.3 will help you determine what you know.

PERSONAL EXPLORATION #11.3

WHAT DO YOU KNOW ABOUT HIV & AIDS?

Answer "Yes" or "No" to each of the following statements:

1. There is no known cure for AIDS.
   - ❏ Yes   ❏ No

2. AIDS is caused by inheriting faulty genes.
   - ❏ Yes   ❏ No

3. AIDS is caused by bacteria.
   - ❏ Yes   ❏ No

4. A person can "carry" and transmit the organism that causes AIDS without showing symptoms of the disease or appearing ill.
   - ❏ Yes   ❏ No

5. The organism that causes AIDS can be transmitted through semen.
   - ❏ Yes   ❏ No

6. Urinating after sexual intercourse makes infection with AIDS less likely.
   - ❏ Yes   ❏ No

7. Washing your genitals after sex makes infection with AIDS less likely.
   - ❏ Yes   ❏ No

8. Sharing drug needles increases the chance of transmitting the organism that causes AIDS.
   - ❏ Yes   ❏ No

9. The organism that causes AIDS can be transmitted through blood or blood products.
   - ❏ Yes   ❏ No

10. Donating blood makes it more likely you will be exposed to HIV.
    - ❏ Yes   ❏ No

11. You can catch AIDS like you catch a cold because whatever causes AIDS can be carried in the air.
    - ❏ Yes   ❏ No

12. You can get AIDS by being in the same classroom as someone who has AIDS.
    - ❏ Yes   ❏ No

13. You can get AIDS by shaking hands with someone who has AIDS.
    - ❏ Yes   ❏ No

14. A pregnant woman who has HIV can give AIDS to her baby.
    - ❏ Yes   ❏ No

15. Having a steady relationship with just one sex partner decreases the risk of getting AIDS.
    - ❏ Yes   ❏ No

16. Using condoms reduces the risk of getting AIDS.
    - ❏ Yes   ❏ No

17. A test to determine whether a person has been infected with HIV is available.
    - ❏ Yes   ❏ No

18. A vaccine that protects people from getting AIDS is now available to the public.
    - ❏ Yes   ❏ No

■ **CORRECT ANSWERS**

1. Yes	7. No	13. No
2. No	8. Yes	14. Yes
3. No	9. Yes	15. Yes
4. Yes	10. No	16. Yes
5. Yes	11. No	17. Yes
6. No	12. No	18. No

In the United States and Canada, HIV now affects 1.3 million people. For 449,000 people the HIV infections have developed into AIDS. In the 15-year history of the disease, 358,000 people in North America have already died of AIDS.[16] In the United States, presently as many as one in 300 adults has HIV (it's higher among men than among women).[17] Half of those infected are under age 25. *AIDS is the leading cause of death for men and women in the United States between the ages of 25 and 44.*[18]

Who gets HIV? Half of HIV infections in the United States were in gay and bisexual men, a quarter were in intravenous drug users, and about 15% were acquired heterosexually.[19] The greatest increases have been among women.

The really scary thing is that people with HIV *often show no outward symptoms of illness*—FOR PERHAPS AS LONG AS 9 YEARS! Thus, a person can be a carrier and infect others without anyone knowing it.[20] The estimated average time from HIV infection to first symptom is 5 years and to AIDS 8–10 years.[21] (See ■ Panel 11.1.)

Maybe you've heard these numbers thrown around before. What's interesting, however, is how little attention people pay to numbers. So, one out of every 20 Americans will be infected by HIV by the year 2000? "So what?" you may think. "It's not going to be me. Anyway, I don't want to be preached to." Despite all the warnings, AIDS continues to spread among young gay men.[22] And despite all the widespread messages about the value of condoms, the use of condoms actually declines as teenagers get older—perhaps because older students switch to birth-control pills or other methods that protect against pregnancy, not realizing they are of no use against HIV.[23]

Many people can't put a face on AIDS. If you live in the city, however, you are probably more apt to know, or at least to have met, people with AIDS. You know, then, that it's not the kind of glamorous disease portrayed on MTV's "The Real World," which edits out night sweats and diarrhea, making the symptoms not real at all.[24]

PANEL 11.1 **F**our important facts about HIV and AIDS.

1. AIDS itself comes only at the end of a long, slow collapse—averaging 8–10 years in adults—of the body's immune system.

2. Often there are *no symptoms of illness* during the development of the disease, which means for perhaps 7–9 years.

3. So far *no one has ever recovered from AIDS.*

4. Yet *not everyone who has been exposed to HIV has gotten AIDS—so far*—just as not everyone exposed to the polio virus develops paralysis.

TESTING FOR HIV. How does a person find out whether he or she has HIV? The answer is by taking a standard blood test called the *HIV antibody test.* The test does not detect the virus itself. Rather it detects the antibodies that the body forms in response to the appearance of the virus. (Antibodies are molecules that are secreted into the bloodstream, where they bind to the invading virus, incapacitating it.)

Negative test results *can* mean positive news: the HIV may not be present. *Positive* test results *can* mean negative news: the HIV may be present. Still, anyone taking these tests needs to be aware of certain cautions:

- **Antibodies to the virus may not develop immediately:** If the test results are negative, it may mean the body has not been exposed to HIV. But it may also mean that antibody formation has not yet taken place. The time it takes for most people to develop antibodies is about 1–3 months, though it varies. Some people do not develop antibodies until 6–12 months have elapsed since exposure to the organism. (Meanwhile the person may be infected and continue to infect others.)

- **Be aware that testing labs can make errors:** If performed correctly, the tests themselves can be highly accurate, detecting antibodies in 99.6% of HIV-infected people. The problem is that some medical labs have problems with high error rates in their testing.[25]

- **Tests cannot predict AIDS:** Currently, tests can show that a person has HIV. They cannot predict whether that HIV will develop into AIDS.

WHO GETS HIV/AIDS & HOW. The most recent figures, from 1992, show that the predominant number of reported U.S. HIV cases were transmitted by male homosexual sex (about half). This was followed by those transmitted by intravenous drug users (25%). The fastest-growing group, 15%, were transmitted by heterosexual sex. (The remaining percentage resulted from blood transfusions, treatments for blood-clotting disorders, transmission from mothers to infants, and accidental contacts.)[26]

However, the number of women infected with HIV through heterosexual sex is on the rise, with three times as many women being infected in 1992 as eight years earlier (compared with about a doubling of infections among men).

In fact, there is some evidence that *men are more efficient at infecting women than women are at infecting men.*[27] Studies seem to show that increasingly women are becoming HIV-infected through unprotected sex with bisexual men or male intravenous drug users.[28] Indeed, women are the fastest-growing category of people affected by the epidemic, particularly women of color.[29]

Some Rules for Safer Sex

PREVIEW One way to reduce the risk of exposure to STDs is to ask the right questions of prospective sexual partners. The answers, however, provide no guarantees. The safest form of sex for preventing transmission of STDs is abstinence and other behavior in which body fluids are not exchanged. The next least risky is protected sex, such as that using condoms. High-risk behavior involves sexual exchange of body fluids or use of intravenous needles. Long-term mutually monogamous relationships are an especially important consideration.

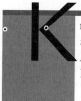

"Know your sexual partner," medical authorities advise. Concerned about AIDS and other STDs, many students have taken the advice to heart.

Unfortunately, they may go about it the wrong way, says psychologist Jeffrey D. Fisher.[30] Students try to gauge their risks by asking other students about their home town, family, and major. Or they try to judge their sexual chances on the basis of the other person's perceived "social class," educational level, or attractiveness.[31]

Do such external clues work? No, says Fisher. These are useless and irrelevant facts, not guides to safe sex.

How can you be sure that sex is really safe? The answer is: you can't. However, there are things that you can do to *reduce* your risks.

ASKING PROSPECTIVE PARTNERS ABOUT THEIR SEXUAL HISTORY.

However embarrassing the conversation, it can be helpful for people to explore their prospective partners' sexual histories before getting involved. Here are some questions to ask:[32]

- **STD tests:** "Have you ever been tested for HIV or for other STDs? Would you be willing to have an HIV test?"

- **Previous partners:** "How many sexual partners have you had?" (The more partners, the higher the STD risk.)

- **Prostitution:** "Have you ever had sex with a prostitute?" Or, "Have you ever exchanged sex for money or drugs?" (If so, was protection used?)

- **Bisexuality:** For a woman to ask a man: "Have you ever had a male sexual partner?" For a man to ask a woman: "Have you ever had a sexual partner who was bisexual?"

- **IV drug use:** "Have you—*or your sexual partners*—ever injected drugs?" (Previous sexual partners can transmit HIV or hepatitis they got by sharing needles.)

Even if you ask all the right questions, however, you still can't be sure of the answers. Someone may state with absolute honesty and sincerity that he or she has never had a genital infection or HIV. But that person may have an infection and not know it.

Even people who have had an HIV test can't prove they are HIV negative. The test measures the presence of antibodies (which fight HIV) that can take 6 months or more to develop. So a person can become infected and infect others during the 6 months required for the antibodies to show. He or she can also, of course, become infected after taking the test.

Truth is the first casualty in war, it is said. Some think it is also the first casualty in sexual behavior.[33] Clearly, the bottom line is that simply asking a prospective sexual partner about HIV does not by itself guarantee safer sex.[34]

THREE LEVELS OF RISK: HIGH-RISK SEX, SAFER SEX, SAVED SEX.

In general, there are three levels of risk in sexual behavior:

- **Very risky—unprotected sex and other behavior:** Behavior that is high-risk for the transmission of STDs includes all forms of sex in which body fluids may be exchanged. By body fluids, I mean semen, vaginal secretions, saliva, or blood (including menstrual blood). These are transmitted through unprotected vaginal, oral, or anal sex.

  High risks also include behavior having to do with the intravenous injection of drugs, a prime means of transmitting STDs. Certainly you shouldn't share IV needles yourself. Moreover, you should avoid sexual contact with someone who is an IV drug user or whose previous partner was. Avoid having sexual contact with people who sell or buy sex, who are often IV drug users.

- **Somewhat risky—"safer" sex:** The next best step to ensuring safe sex—actually, only saf*er* sex—is to use *latex condoms.* "Safer" sex is still somewhat risky, but at least it minimizes the exchange of body fluids. One example of safer-sex behavior is deep (French) kissing. Another is vaginal intercourse using latex condoms with **nonoxynol-9, a spermicide that kills STD organisms.** (Condoms are described in detail on the next page.)

- **Lowest risk—"saved sex":** The safest kind of sex avoids the exchange of semen, vaginal secretions, saliva, or blood. The principal kind of "saved sex" is abstinence. **Abstinence is the voluntary avoidance of sexual intercourse and contact with a partner's body fluids.**

  Saved sex includes massage, hugging, rubbing of bodies, dry kissing (not exchanging saliva), masturbation, and mutual manual stimulation of the genitals. In all cases, contact with body fluids is avoided. *The trick in practicing safe-sex activity is not to get swept away and end up practicing unsafe sex.*

SOME SEX, SOME RISK. If you've decided that abstinence is not for you, what should you do? The principal kinds of advice are as follows:

- **Use precautions universally:** If you choose to have sex, then CONSISTENTLY use safer-sex measures, such as a condom and spermicide, with ALL partners. This means all sexual partners, not just those you don't know well or those you think may be higher risk. Doing this means you'll have to learn to overcome any embarrassment you may feel about talking with your partner about using condoms.

- **Keep your head clear:** Be careful about using alcohol and other drugs with a prospective sexual partner. Drugs cloud your judgment, placing you in a position of increased vulnerability.

- **Practice mutual monogamy:** Having multiple sexual partners is one of the leading risk factors for the transmission of STDs. Clearly, mutual monogamy is one way to avoid infection.

    Be aware, however, that even apparent monogamy may have its risks. If one partner has a secret sexual adventure outside the supposedly monogamous relationship, it does not just breach a trust. It endangers the other's life—especially if the unfaithful partner is not using condoms.

    In addition, you may be in a monogamous relationship but have no idea if your partner was infected previously. To be on the safe side, it's suggested the two of you wait several weeks while remaining faithful to each other. Then both of you should take a test to see if HIV antibodies are present. This gives some indication (though not absolutely) that the partner is currently free of infection.

ALL ABOUT CONDOMS. A _condom_ is a thin sheath made of latex rubber or lamb intestine. (See ■ Panel 11.3.) (Though called "natural skin," lamb intestine is not as safe as latex.) A condom comes packaged in rolled-up form. It should then be unrolled over a male's erect penis, leaving a little room at the top to catch the

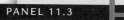

PANEL 11.3 **H**ow to buy and use condoms.

- **How to Buy**

    Materials: Buy latex, not natural membrane or lambskin. Latex is less apt to leak and better able to protect against HIV transmission. Inexpensive foreign brands are suspect.

    Sizes: The FDA says condoms must be between 6 and 8 inches in length when unrolled. (The average erect penis is 6 1/2 inches.) Condoms labeled _Regular_ are 7 1/2 inches. Instead of "Small" for condoms under 7 1/2 inches, manufacturers use labels such as _Snug Fit._ Instead of "Large" for condoms over 7 1/2 inches, manufacturers use labels such as _Max_ or _Magnum._

    Shapes: Most condoms are _straight-walled._ Some are labeled _contoured,_ which means they are anatomically shaped to fit the penis and thus are more comfortable.

    Tips: Some condoms have a _reservoir_ at the end to catch semen upon ejaculation. Others do not have a reservoir, in which case they should be twisted at the tip after being put on.

    Plain or Lubricated: Condoms can be purchased _plain_ (unlubricated) or _lubricated,_ which means they feel more slippery to the touch. There are four options:
    1. Buy a plain condom and don't use a lubricant.
    2. Buy a plain condom and use your own lubricant, preferably water-based (such as K-Y Jelly or Astroglide).
    3. Buy a lubricated condom pregreased with silicone-, jelly-, or water-based lubricants.
    4. Buy a _spermicidally lubricated_ condom, which contains _nonoxynol-9,_ a chemical that kills sperm and HIV. This is probably the best option.

Strength: A standard condom will do for vaginal and oral sex. Some people believe an *"extra-strength"* condom is less apt to break during anal sex, although this is debatable.

Gimmicks: Condoms come with all kinds of other features:

1. *Colors:* Red, blue, green, and yellow are safe. Avoid black and "glow in the dark," since dyes may rub off.
2. *Smell and taste:* Latex smells and tastes rubbery, but some fragranced condoms mask this odor.
3. *Adhesive:* Condoms are available with adhesive to hold them in place so they won't slip off during withdrawal.
4. *Marketing gimmicks:* Condoms are sold with ribs, nubs, bumps, and so on, but unless the additions are at the tip and can reach the clitoris they do no good whatsoever.

■ *How to Use*

Storage: Condoms should be stored in a cool, dry place. Keeping them in a hot glove compartment or wallet in the back pocket for weeks can cause the latex to fail.

Opening package: Look to see that the foil or plastic packaging is not broken; if it is, don't use the condom. Open the package carefully. Fingernails can easily damage a condom.

Inspection: Make sure a condom is soft and pliable. Don't use it if it's brittle, sticky, or discolored. Don't try to test it for leaks by unrolling, stretching, or blowing it up, which will only weaken it.

Putting on: Put the condom on before any genital contact to prevent exposure to fluids. Hold the tip of the condom and unroll it directly onto the erect penis. (If the man is not circumcised, pull back the foreskin before rolling on the condom.) Gently pinch the tip to remove air bubbles, which can cause the condom to break. Condoms without a reservoir tip need a half-inch free at the tip.

Lubricants: *Important!* If you're using a lubricant of your own, *don't use an oil-based lubricant.* Oil-based lubricants—examples are hand lotion, baby oil, mineral oil, and Vaseline—can reduce a latex condom's strength by 90% in as little as 60 seconds. Saliva is not recommended either.

Use a water-based or silicone-based product designed for such use, such as K-Y Jelly or spermicidal compounds containing nonoxynol-9.

Add lubricant to the outside of the condom before entry. If not enough lubricant is used, the condom can tear or pull off.

Slippage and breakage: If the condom begins to slip, hold your fingers around the base to make it stay on. If a condom breaks, it should be replaced immediately.

If ejaculation occurs after a condom breaks, apply a foam spermicide to the vagina at once.

After ejaculation: After sex, hold the base of the condom to prevent it from slipping off and to avoid spillage during withdrawal. Withdraw while the penis is still erect. Throw the used condom away. (Never reuse condoms.) Wash the genitals.

semen. Some condoms are marketed with a "reservoir" at the end for this purpose.

A condom provides protection for both partners during vaginal, oral, or anal intercourse. It keeps semen from being transmitted to a man's sexual partner and shields against contact with any infection on his penis. It also protects the male's penis and urethra from contact with his partner's secretions, blood, and saliva.

These thin, tight-fitting sheaths of latex rubber or animal skin are available in all kinds of colors, shapes, and textures. They also come with or without a reservoir tip and are available dry or lubricated. Spermicide-coated condoms, including those with nonoxynol-9, have been shown to be effective in killing sperm.[35] When buying condoms, always check the expiration date. Also, don't store them in places where they might be exposed to heat (wallets, glove compartments), which causes latex to deteriorate.

Unfortunately, *condoms are not perfect protection.* They only *reduce* the risk of acquiring HIV infection and other STDs. Note that *reducing the risk is not the same as eliminating the risk.* If the condom is flawed or it slips off or breaks, there is suddenly 100% exposure. (And possibly to a disease that is 100% fatal.)

Condoms break most frequently when couples use oil-based lubricants or engage in prolonged sex. A condom may also be weakened if couples attempt their own "quality testing" (such as blowing up condoms to test for leaks).

Onward

PREVIEW Ignorance about love and sex is not bliss.

Love and sexual passion are among the most powerful human forces. So powerful are they, in fact, that they lead people sometimes to take chances or make decisions they might not otherwise make. For instance, students who did not use a condom during sex often report they got carried away, "out of control." Or they say they did not plan ahead when they became sexually involved.[36]

We are surrounded by words and images about love and sex. However, a great many people, including many college-educated people, are surprisingly uninformed about these subjects. Unfortunately, we live in a time when ignorance in relationship and sexual matters can no longer be considered bliss.

NOTES

1. Weiten, W., Lloyd, M. A., & Lashley, R. L. (1991). *Psychology applied to modern life: Adjustment in the 90s* (3rd ed.). Pacific Grove: CA: Brooks/Cole.

2. Weiten, Lloyd, & Lashley, 1991, p. 179.

3. Burns, D. D. (1989). *The feeling good handbook.* New York: Plume.

4. Burns, 1989, p. 371.

5. Beck, A. (1989). *Love is never enough.* New York: HarperPerennial.

6. Burns, 1989, p. 379.

7. Crooks, R., & Baur, K. (1990). *Our sexuality* (4th ed.). Redwood City, CA: Benjamin/Cummings, p. 268.

8. Alberti, R. E., & Emmons, M. L. (1970). *Your perfect right: A guide to assertive behavior.* San Luis Obispo, CA: Impact.

9. Alberti, R. E., & Emmons, M. L. (1975). *Stand up, speak out, talk back!* New York: Pocket.

10. Jakubowski-Spector, P. (1973). Facilitating the growth of women through assertive training. *Counseling Psychologist, 4,* 75–86.

11. Weiten, Lloyd, & Lashley, 1989.

12. Horner, M. J. Toward an understanding of achievement related conflicts in women. *Journal of Social Issues, 28,* 157–76.

13. Freundl, P. C. (1981, August). Influence of sex and status variables on perceptions of assertiveness. Paper presented at meeting of the American Psychlogical Association, Los Angeles.

14. Smye, M. D., & Wine, J. D. (1980). A comparison of female and male adolescents' social behaviors and cognitions: A challenge to the assertiveness literature. *Sex Roles, 6,* 213–30.

15. Weiten, Lloyd, & Lashley, 1991.

16. Global AIDS Policy Coalition, United Nations AIDS Program, reported in: Perlman, D. (1996, July 5). A bit less gloom in AIDS battle. *San Francisco Chronicle,* pp. A1, A17.

17. Centers for Disease Control and Prevention, cited in: Krieger, L. (1996, July 7). 1 in 300 U.S. adults infected, says report. *San Francisco Examiner,* p. A-8.

18. Merson, M. H. 1996, August 5). How to fight AIDS. *Newsweek,* p. 18.

19. Centers for Disease Control and Prevention, cited in: Painter, K. (1996, July 8). AIDS estimate for USA lowered. *USA Today,* p. 1D.

20. Blattner, W. A. (1991). HIV epidemiology: past, present, and future. *Faseb Journal, 5,* 2340–48.

21. Giesecke, J., Scalia-Tomba, G., Hakansson, C. et al. (1990). Incubation time of AIDS: Progression of disease in a cohort of HIV-infected homo- and bisexual men with known dates of infection. *Scandinavian Journal of Infectious Diseases, 22,* 407–411.

22. Painter, K. (1996, July 9). AIDS spreads among young gays despite warnings. *USA Today,* 1D.

23. Painter, K. (1996, July 10). Push to abstain doesn't lower teen sex rates. *USA Today,* 1D.

24. Phillips, L. (1996, July 20). How teens handle the HIV virus. *San Francisco Chronicle,* p. A23.

25. Snell, J. J., Supran, E. M., Esparza, J. et al. (1990). World Health Organization quality assessment programme on HIV testing. *Aids, 4,* 803–806.

26. Centers for Disease Control and Prevention, reported in: Burghart, T. (1996, July 7). New HIV cases level off, CDC study says. *Monterey Herald,* pp. 1A, 14A.

27. Padian, N. S., Shiboski, S. C., & Jewell, N. P. (1991). Female-to-male transmission of human immunodeficiency virus. *Journal of the American Medical Association, 266,* 1664–67.

28. Staver, S. (1990, June 1). Women found contracting HIV via unprotected sex. *American Medical News,* pp. 4–5.

29. Kerr, D. L. (1991). Women with AIDS and HIV infection. *Journal of School Health, 61,* 139–40.

30. Fisher, J. D. Cited in: Adler, J., Wright, L., McCormick, J. et al. (1991, December 9). Safer sex. *Newsweek,* pp. 52–56.

31. Montefiore, S. S. (1992, October). Love, lies and fear in the plague years . . . *Psychology Today,* pp. 30–35.

32. Adler et al., 1991.

33. Cochran, S. D., & Mays, V. M. (1993). Sex, lies, and HIV [letter]. *New England Journal of Medicine, 322,* 774–75.

34. Cochran, S. Quoted in: Roberts, M. (1988, December). Dating, dishonesty and AIDS. *Psychology Today,* p. 60.

35. Hatcher, R., Guest, F., Stewart, F. et al. (1990). *Contraceptive technology: 1990–1992.* (15th ed.). New York: Irvington.

36. Workman, B. (1991, May 2). Sex at Stanford not always safe, poll finds. *San Francisco Chronicle,* p. A20.

1. ***What kinds of supporting relationships do you have?*** Have students form into small groups and take turns describing people they know who will give them emotional and other support, if needed, to help sustain them through college. Questions for discussion: What kind of qualities do such people have? Are they good listeners? Do they express their feelings well? If you or others feel short on such support, where can it be found? How can one widen the circle of supportive friends?

2. ***What are your feelings about conflict?*** Ask students to refer to Personal Exploration #11.1, "What Are Your Feelings About Conflict?" Ask them to discuss (in a small or large group) which style of conflict they seem to gravitate to. Questions for discussion: How well does this seem to work for you? As a regular way of operating, what kinds of frustrations does it produce for you? for the people with whom you're in conflict? What alternative style of conflict can you see yourself doing?

3. ***Practicing constructive conflict.*** Have students form into small groups of four people. Each person should select a partner and think up a situation—or act out one from his or her own life—of two people in conflict. For example, student and partner might pretend to be a husband and wife arguing over one not phoning about being late for dinner.

    The couple should pretend to have an argument the way they are accustomed to. Others in the group should then comment on the exchange. The partners should then try to have the same discussion (not argument) using the techniques of good communication described in this chapter; the observers may comment again.

    Then the other couple should act out a disagreement about some other matter, with the first couple offering comments.

4. ***Practicing assertiveness.*** Have students form into groups of three people each. Students should then take turns describing situations in which they were *nonassertive* (passive). They should describe who was involved in the interaction, how they felt about that person or persons, and their feelings about themselves as a result of their nonassertiveness.

    Next students should give the same attention to situations in which they behaved *aggressively*. Finally, they should apply the same considerations to situations in which they were *assertive* in their communication style.

    Ask students to choose one of the incidents in which they behaved nonassertively or aggressively and, with a second group member role-playing the other person, practice behaving assertively in the same situation. The third person in the group should act as observer, monitoring eye contact, voice tone, body posture, and other signs of assertiveness.

    In the group or with the class as a whole, students should discuss what kinds of situations give them the most trouble in being assertive. Ask them to state whether they involve authority figures, strangers, or people close to them. Have them identify role models who might help them become assertive and state what they notice about their behavior.

5. ***What do you know about HIV and AIDS?*** Ask students to refer to Personal Exploration #11.3, "What Do You Know About HIV & AIDS?" In a group situation, large or small, ask them to discuss their feelings about the HIV/AIDS crisis.

    Questions for discussion: What did you not know that this Personal Exploration has taught you? Does HIV/AIDS seem like a real danger to people you know (perhaps including yourself)? What should people be doing to reduce their risk? Do you think heavy use of alcohol or other drugs could play a role in increasing one's risk? What do you think of the kind of sex-soaked culture portrayed in movies and other mass media in relation to the AIDS epidemic?

JOURNAL ENTRY #11.1: HOW DO YOU HANDLE CONFLICT? Write some details about an important relationship (such as parents, boyfriend/girlfriend, spouse, children, professor, boss). Are you satisfied with this relationship? What have you learned in this chapter that might help you to improve it?

_____

_____

_____

_____

_____

_____

_____

_____

JOURNAL ENTRY #11.2: ARE YOU PASSIVE OR AGGRESSIVE? Do you feel you're inclined to be aggressive or to be passive in conflict situations? Imagine yourself having a disagreement with someone (such as an instructor about a grade on a paper or a roommate about living arrangements). Write out a little script about some things you might say to express your point of view without hurting the other person or hurting yourself.

_____

_____

_____

_____

_____

_____

_____

JOURNAL ENTRY #11.3: WHO CAN YOU TALK TO? Do you often feel lonely, unloved, unwanted? Why do you think that is? Who might you talk to about this? (An example is someone at the college counseling service.)

_____

_____

_____

_____

_____

_____

_____

_____

_____

JOURNAL ENTRY #11.4: HOW DO YOU FEEL ABOUT ABSTAINING FROM SEX? Because we live in the Age of AIDS, more and more students are abstaining from sexual relationships. Do you know anyone who has announced this? How do you feel about his or her decision?

_____

_____

_____

_____

_____

_____

_____

_____

_____

JOURNAL ENTRY #11.5: HOW DO YOU FEEL ABOUT BUYING CONDOMS? How difficult emotionally is it for you to buy condoms or to discuss their use with a prospective sexual partner? What are the impediments?

_____

_____

_____

_____

_____

_____

_____

_____

_____

_____

_____

_____

_____

_____

_____

_____

_____

_____

_____

_____

_____

_____

_____

_____

_____

_____

12 money

getting it & using it

IN THIS CHAPTER: Money is a problem for a great many students. Even if they have a steady source of income or spending money, they may still have trouble controlling their spending. This chapter considers the following topics.

- *Managing costs:* Getting and spending

- *Important record keeping:* Money plans and expense records

- *Money handling:* A crash course in strategies

- *Financial aid:* How to get financial help for college

College is a financial struggle for many people. Is it worth it?

Many students are doing whatever it takes financially to get a college education. More first-year students than ever before are now basing their choice of college not on educational reasons but on financial reasons. For example, they may choose an institution because it charges low tuition, offers financial aid, or enables them to live at home.[1] Many students are also having to borrow in order to meet their college expenses. Half the students graduating from college have debts, such as student loans, that have to be repaid.[2] Indeed, the number of students in debt has doubled over the past 10 years.[3]

In addition, more and more students are taking longer than four years to graduate from college, in part because many need to work and go to school part time. At the University of Texas at Austin, for instance, less than half the students who start there as freshmen end up graduating in four years. At San Francisco State University in California, less than a quarter of students graduate within *five* years.[4]

These facts demonstrate that a lot of students are willing to go to great lengths to get a college education. Are the sacrifices worth it? As I showed in Chapter 1, the evidence is that it is. Most college graduates make incomes sufficient to justify their investment in college. As a group, college graduates have nearly always done better than high-school graduates, but in recent years they have widened the gap significantly. During the 1980s, college grads earned about 30% more than high-school graduates. Now they earn *60% more.*[5]

Thus, even if you leave school with a debt of $10,000—the debt of the average student finishing today—you'll probably be able to handle it. Indeed, a year after graduation, college graduates will be making an average (median) annual income of $18,600.[6,7]

Add to this the fact that college graduates usually have happier, more fulfilled lives than people who are not college graduates, and the costs of higher education seem worth it.

Managing Costs: Getting & Spending

PREVIEW Students get their money from their families, jobs, grants and loans, and other sources. They spend it not only on college and living expenses but also in some unpredictable ways. Handling your money is a matter of constantly balancing your income and your expenses.

Probably the best advice that can be given about money is that *you have to pay attention.* "Our inattentiveness toward money is enough of a misperception of reality that it can lead us into trouble," says an economist and former banker. In this way it is dangerous in the same sense that "any misperception of reality can lead to trouble."[8]

Thus, he says, the most important rule is that "you have to keep track of your money. You have to know approximately how much you have, how much you are spending, how much is coming in, what the general direction of your dollar flow is."[9]

If you can do addition and subtraction, that's all that's required to keep track of your money while in college. After all, there are only three parts to basic money management:

- *Getting*—determining your **_income,_** or **where the money comes from**

- *Spending*—determining your **_outgo,_** or **what your expenditures are**

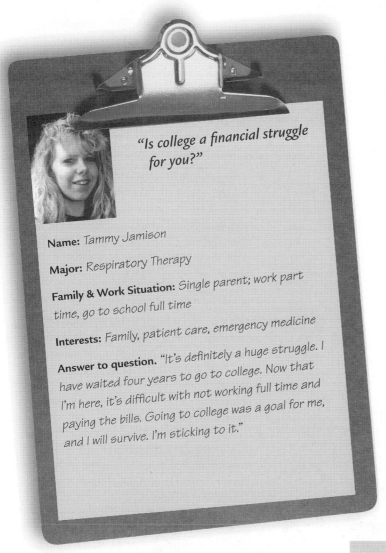

"Is college a financial struggle for you?"

Name: Tammy Jamison

Major: Respiratory Therapy

Family & Work Situation: Single parent; work part time, go to school full time

Interests: Family, patient care, emergency medicine

Answer to question. "It's definitely a huge struggle. I have waited four years to go to college. Now that I'm here, it's difficult with not working full time and paying the bills. Going to college was a goal for me, and I will survive. I'm sticking to it."

Employment: More than half of all students work during summers. Nearly a third work part-time during the school year.

Grants or scholarships: A good portion of college costs are supported by college, federal, or state grants or scholarships, and nearly half of students have access to this resource.

Loans: Many college costs are supported from the Guaranteed (Stafford) Student Loan.

Other sources: Savings not derived from summer or part-time work earnings and other sources make up the rest of the income sources. More than a quarter of all students draw on non-work-related savings as a resource.

Do you have more control over your sources of income than your expenses? That's up to you to decide. Some students get a regular allowance from their parents. Others may have to earn or borrow every cent they get—more evidence of how the world is unfair. On the other hand, those who must go out and scrape up their income themselves have one advantage. They often develop a better sense of the value of money than those who simply have it given to them.

THE SPENDING: YOUR OUTGO. An important moral is: *It's important to distinguish between your needs and your wants.* Sure, you might want to go out and party, to dress right, to treat your friends, but do you need to? You might like to move away from home and have your own apartment, but do you have to?

> **"In spending it's important to distinguish between your needs and your wants."**

■ **Balancing**—determining that you have the income *when you need it* to balance the spending

Let's take a look at these.

THE GETTING: YOUR INCOME. Most people would not consider gambling and robbery efficient sources of income. (Neither are predictable nor look good on a career résumé.) However, there are a variety of other sources. Most students have a mix, as follows:[10]

■ **Family assistance:** Nearly three-quarters of students have this resource.

With the constant drumming of advertising on us from television and other mass media (18,000 messages a day, supposedly), we are always being made to *want* all kinds of things. But, when you think about it, we *need* very little. This can be a healthy point of view to take when you consider your expenses.

Expenses are of the following types:

■ *One-time educational expenses:* These are one-shot expenses for items that you need to buy only once and that might serve you for most of your college years. Examples are bicycle (for getting to or around campus), computer or typewriter, and dictionary and other reference books. Some of these you or your family may already have at home.

■ *Recurring educational expenses:* These are educational expenses that are repeated every quarter or semester. Examples are tuition, registration fees, books and educational supplies, and laboratory fees. Many of these figures you can get from your college catalog.

■ *Housing, food, and clothing expenses:* These are the expenses that it takes just to live: housing, utilities, food. Don't forget to add insurance, such as fire and theft insurance, if you can afford it. You also need to determine your clothing expenses—even if you wear only T-shirts and jeans half the time.

NOTE: Don't underestimate the cost of food. Besides your meals at home, you'll need to allow for meals out and snacks.

■ *Transportation:* If you have a car, this can be a big expense, because you'll need to allow for car insurance, maintenance, and repairs, as well as gas and oil. Parking fees can also be a big item. Many students don't have cars, of course, but need to allow for bus or other commuting fees.

■ *Personal and health expenses:* These include expenses for your laundry, toothpaste and other personal-care products, medicines, and health insurance or college health-center fees.

■ *Telephone expense:* This expense can get tricky, depending on your living arrangements, but it should be budgeted for.

■ *Entertainment:* If you didn't already budget for expenses for snacks and eating out, put them here. Dating, going to musical or athletic events, movies or theater, whatever seems to be fun—add these expenses. Also add as many other entertainment expenses as you can think of. These include CDs, tapes, athletic gear, musical instruments, and so on.

■ *Emergencies and other expenses:* Bad stuff happens, and you need to allow for it. I'm talking about car breakdowns, toothaches, and other emergencies. You may also want to plan for some good stuff—a summer trip, for example, if you can afford it.

THE BALANCING ACT. What if you get most of your money at the beginning of the fall term, but your expenses will go on for the next ten months? One problem that people who don't have a regular allowance or paycheck have to face is *uneven cash flow.* That is, many bills (rent, phone, credit cards) tend to come due at regular intervals. However, the income does not flow in on the same timely basis. Thus, some short-range saving is necessary.

Of course, saving money may not be as much fun as spending it. However, short-range saving sure beats the desperate feeling of not having the funds there when the rent is due. Managing your money, in short, is a constant balancing act between income and outgo.

For many of us, money has a way of just dribbling through our fingers, and we're not really sure where it goes. That's why credit counselors, who help people in debt, have clients keep detailed records of all expenses, even for candy bars and newspapers. Even if you don't have money troubles, before you can *plan* how to manage your money, you need to *observe* your present money patterns. To do this, I suggest doing the Personal Exploration #12.1 for a week, longer if you can. From this information, you can draw up some spending categories and projections, as I will show.

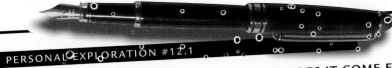

THE MONEY DIAGNOSTIC REPORT: WHERE DOES IT COME FROM, WHERE DOES IT GO?

Tear out or photocopy this page and carry it around with you in an accessible place for a week.

Every time you receive a check or cash (*Money in*), write down its source and the amount. (Example: "Loan from Susie, $10.") Every time you

spend money—whether cash, check, or credit card (*Money out*)—write down the expenditure and the amount. (Example: "Movie, food: $12.")

■ **MONEY IN:** Examples of sources of funds: job, parents, grant, savings, loan, friend, tax refund.

MONEY IN FROM	SUNDAY	MONDAY	TUESDAY	WEDNESDAY	THURSDAY	FRIDAY	SATURDAY

Total received for week: _____

■ **MONEY OUT:** Examples of expenditures: books, meals, bus fare, snacks, phone, rent, entertainment, clothes, laundry.

MONEY OUT FOR	SUNDAY	MONDAY	TUESDAY	WEDNESDAY	THURSDAY	FRIDAY	SATURDAY

Total spent for week: _____

Money Plans &
Expense Record

PREVIEW A money plan, or budget, is of two types. The *yearly money plan* helps you look at the big picture of your income and outgo. The *monthly money plan* helps project ordinary monthly expenses. The money *expense record* tells you what your expenses actually were.

To effectively balance your getting and spending, you need to know where you're going. This requires formulating a *money plan,* the name I prefer rather than *budget,* although they are the same. **A *money plan,* or *budget,* is simply a plan or schedule of how to balance your income and expenses. It helps you see where your money is going to come from and where it is going to go.**

Most students find it useful to have two kinds of money plans:

■ *Yearly:* A yearly money plan helps you visualize the big picture for the school year.

■ *Monthly:* A monthly money plan, which includes "Money in" and "Money out" columns, helps you keep track of your ongoing financial situation.

Let's take a look at these.

THE YEARLY MONEY PLAN. The yearly money plan is your big-picture estimate of your income and expenses for the academic year (for example, September to June). You may be able to obtain much of your financial information from the college catalog. Examples of sources of "Money in" are loans or grants. Examples of kinds of "Money out" are tuition and fees.

Other information you may have to estimate. If you have already established a record of expenses, as in Personal Exploration #12.1, you can use that. You can also collect a month or two of old bills and receipts, cancelled checks, and credit-card statements. Then you can estimate what these expenses would amount to over the course of the school year. If you have not already made out a Yearly Money Plan, I strongly suggest that you spend some time on Personal Exploration #12.2.

THE MONTHLY MONEY PLAN. The monthly money plan is a smaller version of the yearly one. It is particularly useful if you live off campus with your family or housemates or by yourself. Then you are more apt to have several monthly bills, such as rent, phone, water, electricity, gas, and garbage. (Even students living on campus, however, may have monthly credit-card and telephone bills for which they need to plan.)

Developing a monthly money plan requires three steps:

■ *Subtract large one-time expenses from yearly income:* First you need to take your *yearly* income and subtract all your *large one-time* expenses: college tuition, registration fees, meal ticket, textbooks and supplies (total for all terms), and insurance premiums.

Example: Using round figures, suppose you have $18,000 coming in from all sources. This includes loans, grants, part-time and summer work, and help from your family. Suppose your tuition and registration fees are $10,000. Add your rent ($3000), meal ($1500), insurance ($300), and textbooks and supplies ($300 for two semesters). Add your round-trip bus fare from home ($400). The total comes to $15,500. You then subtract $15,500 from $18,000, which leaves $2500.

■ *Divide the remaining sum by the number of months to determine how much you have to spend on everything else:* After subtracting one-time large expenses from your yearly income, you can see how much you have left for other requirements.

THE YEARLY MONEY PLAN: HOW MUCH MONEY COMES IN & GOES OUT DURING A SCHOOL YEAR?

■ **INCOME (FOR 10 MONTHS)**

Examples of money sources: job, grants/scholarships, loans, family, refunds, sale of unneeded belongings, other.

INCOME	SEP	OCT	NOV	DEC	JAN	FEB	MAR	APR	MAY	JUN

Total income: _____

■ **OUTGO (FOR 10 MONTHS)**

Examples of expenses: rent/mortgage, food, tuition, college fees, books/supplies, transportation (including parking), clothes, phone, insurance, medical, child care, personal items, entertainment, other.

OUTGO	SEP	OCT	NOV	DEC	JAN	FEB	MAR	APR	MAY	JUN

Total outgo: _____

Example: Suppose you figure you had $2500 left over after subtracting one-time expenses from yearly income. You would divide that by the number of months in the academic year—that is, nine months (September and June are partial school months). This would give you about $278 a month to spend. This may seem like a lot if you just need to cover snacks and an occasional movie or meal out. However, if you have to support a car or child care or a lot of entertainment, it may not be enough.

■ *Determine other categories of expenses and decide how much to spend each month:* Only you can determine the expenses remaining after your one-time "big ticket" expenses are taken out. The cost of your monthly transportation expenses will differ depending on whether you drive a car, take the bus, or ride a bicycle to class. Expenses for clothing, phone calls, CDs, video rentals, and snacks can vary tremendously, depending mainly on your personal restraint.

One category many students are glad they've created: savings. This category will help you keep a fund for emergencies or special expenses. It may also help you restrain your spending.

Example: Your monthly categories for spending $278 might be as follows, ranging from large to small expenses. *Car* (gas and oil, repairs, parking—insurance is included above): $80. *Entertainment* (including dates): $45. *Personal* (personal-care products): $33. *Meals out:* $30. *Clothes:* $30. *Snacks:* $25. *Phone:* $25. *Savings:* $10.

To set up your Monthly Money Plan, spend a few minutes with the "A. To Plan" portion of Personal Exploration #12.3.

THE EXPENSE RECORD. How do you know if you're overspending in some expense categories? In accordance with the advice at the beginning of the chapter ("Pay attention to your money"), you keep an expense record. The expense record has two parts, daily and monthly:

■ *The daily expense record:* This can be very simple and can be carried around as a shirt-pocket spiral-bound notebook or even as a 3 × 5 card in your wallet or purse. The point is to make this easy so you won't mind doing it.

You need write down only three things: *date, item, cost.* (If you wish, you can also indicate if you paid with cash, check, or credit card—$$, CK, CC.) Examples are:

3/15	*Snack*	*1.50*
3/15	*Gas*	*8.33*
3/16	*Toothpaste*	*2.00*
3/16	*Movie & popcorn*	*6.50*

■ *The monthly expense record:* At the end of the month, you can sort the daily expenses into the different categories of your Monthly Money Plan under the "Actual" column. The categories might be: *Housing & utilities, Meals & snacks, Transportation, Entertainment, Personal supplies, Books & supplies, Savings,* and *Other.* When you add up the different columns, you can then see if you are staying within your budget.

To record your expenses in the coming month, follow the "B. To Record" portion of Personal Exploration #12.3.

Does all this record keeping seem like a lot of boring work? Actually, it's just a series of easy mechanical tasks. The whole reason for doing them is to give you *peace of mind.* After all, disorganization around money and consequent financial problems can affect your emotional well-being in other ways, making it difficult to study. Using these tools can help you avoid those difficulties.

YOUR MONTHLY MONEY PLAN—& YOUR RECORD OF ACTUAL INCOME & OUTGO

Tear out or photocopy the form on page 266. Use this form (1) to plan and (2) to record your income and outgo for the next month.

■ The left side of the form is for *planning and recording Income*—money in.

■ The right side of the form is for *planning and recording Outgo*—money out.

■ **A. TO PLAN**

On the left side of the form ("Income") indicate your predicted sources and amounts of money you expect to receive. *Examples:* "Family," "Job," "Loan," "Grant," "Scholarship," "Tax refund," "Aunt Gladys." Put the amounts in the column headed *Planned*.

On the right side of the form

("Outgo"), first indicate your categories of expenses, from left to right. *Examples:* "Rent," "Phone," "Utilities," "Credit card," "Car payments," "Food," "Transportation," "Clothing," "Entertainment," "Savings," "Miscellaneous." For each category, put in the *predicted* expenses. Put these amounts in the columns headed *Planned*.

■ **B. TO RECORD**

On the left side ("Income"), record the date/source and amount of money coming in. Example: "9/30 job—$200." Record these data in the *Actual* column.

On the right side ("Outgo"), record the date/expenses, amounts, and method of payment ($$ for cash, CK for check, CC for credit card) of

your expenditures within each category. *Example:* Within the category of "Entertainment," you could record "10/15 video rental—$6.00 CK"; "10/18 dinner Amelio's—$12.30 CC"; "10/18 crackers—$1.10 $$."

■ **AT MONTH'S END**

Total up your *predicted* Income and Outgo and compare it with the *actual* Income and Outgo. Use the information to adjust your predicted Money Plan for the next month.

A Crash Course in Money Handling

PREVIEW Controlling spending starts with managing big-ticket purchases, such as housing and transportation, which are often trade-offs. You can also find ways to get inexpensive furniture and computers. Tactics exist for controlling telephone charges and food and clothing purchases. Students need to investigate good banking and ATM sources. They need to know how to manage charge cards and credit cards. They also need to make arrangements to be covered by insurance—health, tenant's, and automobile.

It's almost impossible to grow up in this society and not want to spend more than one's income. The television and print ads just never let us forget life's endless possibilities for parting with our money. Maybe you can't increase your income, but you can almost always find ways to cut spending.

CONTROLLING YOUR SPENDING. Here are some money-saving tips, ranging from big-ticket items to everyday small expenditures:

■ *Housing and transportation:* Many urban students live at home and take bus, streetcar, or subway to campus. Or, particularly in the South and West, they may live at home and drive a car to school.

Housing and transportation sometimes present a trade-off. Living at home

MONTHLY MONEY PLAN & RECORD

INCOME: MONEY IN

Date/Source	Planned Amount	Actual Amount

OUTGO: MONEY OUT

Category Date/Expense/Amount	Category Date/Expense/Amount	Category Date/Expense/Amount	Category Date/Expense/Amount	Category Date/Expense/Amount	Category Date/Expense/Amount

may be cheaper than living in your own apartment, so you can afford to maintain a car. Living in an apartment close to campus may cost more, but you can get around on foot, bicycle, or public transportation.

When comparing prospective rents, be sure to determine if the rent does or doesn't include utilities, such as electricity, water, and garbage collection. Try to take care of your rental unit, by fixing things yourself when possible and making sure to keep up the yard (if there is one). This will help you get back any security deposits when you move out. It will also help you get a favorable reference from the landlord that will assist you in lining up the next rental.

Cars can be expensive. I remember turning a deaf ear to my father's warning that the purchase price of a car was only the beginning. It wasn't until a year later that I knew how expensive my powerful Chevy was in the way of gas, oil, tires, repairs, insurance, and parking. It was then I realized I could have commuted to campus by bus and even taken dates out in a taxi for a whole lot less. On a daily basis, a bus or a bicycle may turn out to be a real bargain.

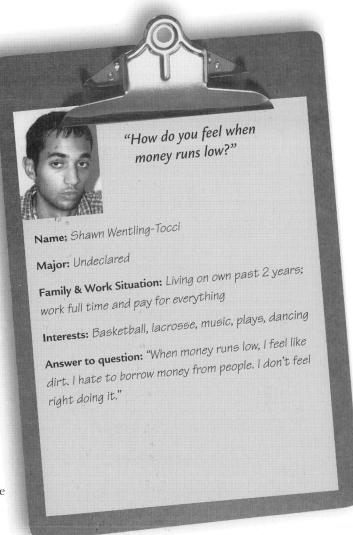

"How do you feel when money runs low?"

Name: Shawn Wentling-Tocci

Major: Undeclared

Family & Work Situation: Living on own past 2 years; work full time and pay for everything

Interests: Basketball, lacrosse, music, plays, dancing

Answer to question: "When money runs low, I feel like dirt. I hate to borrow money from people. I don't feel right doing it."

■ *Computers, furniture, refrigerators:* If you have your own apartment or room, remember that the things that cost the most are also those on which you can cut costs. You don't need to go first class on such big-ticket items as computers and furniture. Do you need a television set, CD player, radio, heater, or fan? Check with your housemates, who may have these. Do you need a bed, a desk lamp, a dresser? All of these may be bought used.

You don't need *both* a typewriter and a computer, but you're well advised to have one or the other. (You might be able to borrow someone else's machine. But what if he or she needs it when you're up against a tight deadline to get a paper done?) Computers may be bought used, especially if all you need them for is typewriter-like purposes, such as writing papers.

Some students like to have a refrigerator in their rooms, either the 2.8 cubic-foot size or the smaller 1.6 cubic-foot size. These may be rented from local organizations (for perhaps $50–$75) or bought outright for $100–$150 from local discount appliance stores.[11] When these costs are shared with housemates, they become manageable.

■ *The telephone:* Probably there's not much hazard in making a lot of local calls—unless you're tying up your family or housemates' phone, too. However, cross-country love affairs and talks with friends at other schools can produce massive long-distance charges.

If you're the one originating the calls, you may find a telephone timer will help you hold calls to 10–15 minutes instead of 2 hours. Also, don't feel you have to answer every incoming call, especially if you're studying. Tell others in your living unit to take a message, then call back later.

■ *Food and clothing:* Food can be a great hidden magnet for cash. Consider what the minimum wage is in this country (around $5 an hour before deductions). Then consider how *little* that will buy in the way of soft drinks, potato chips, and other packaged snacks. Even meals at fast-food places can rapidly drain your money.

Clearly, learning how to cook will save you money, even if it's just spaghetti. So will learning how to shop. Shop from a list, which keeps you disciplined. Don't shop when you're hungry; it tends to make you reach for convenience foods and snacks. Shop for fresh fruits, vegetables, grains, and other foods that are not processed; they are less expensive. Use clip-out coupons from newspapers if they will really save you money. (Don't use them to buy expensive processed foods you would not otherwise buy.)

Some people are hyper-conscious about the way they dress, which is fine, so long as they aren't hooked into following every fashion. There are ways to buy clothes cheaply: at the end of the season, at other sale times, or at used-clothing stores. If you build your wardrobe around one or two colors, you can do a lot of mixing and matching.

You might consider entering into a contest with housemates to find ways of saving money: turning down the thermostat, turning off unnecessary lights, keeping doors and windows closed in winter, buying toilet paper and paper towels in large lots at discount prices

BANKS & ATMS. One student who, with friends, wrote a guide to college survival, suggests keeping two things in mind when choosing a bank.[12] First, find a bank that has automated teller machines (ATMs) that are handy for you. Second, consider all possible hidden costs of the bank in question.

There are many kinds of checking and savings accounts. On standard checking accounts, some banks charge you a monthly fee, some a fee for every check you write, some both. Some checking accounts pay interest if you maintain a high balance, but often the fees will eat up the interest. If you don't write a lot of checks, you might do better with a savings account, which pays interest. Finally, some banks offer a basic banking account, geared to low-income or retired customers. This allows you to write six or so checks per month without additional charge.

ATMs are popular with those who want fast spending money. Indeed, customers who are 18–24 years old conduct a higher share of their transactions at ATMs than any other age group. Most of the youngest ATM users are college students.[13] Clearly, there are some advantages to having an ATM card. For example, you can do transactions during evenings and weekends, when most banks are closed.

CHARGE CARDS, CREDIT CARDS, & DEBIT CARDS. Studies have shown banks and credit-card companies that students are as responsible with credit as most adults. Consequently, campuses have been deluged with ads and applications, trying to entice thousands of students into The Way of Plastic. Indeed, credit-card companies often waive credit histories and income requirements.[14] As a result, 82% of college students have at least one credit card.[15]

Charge cards **are those that require that the bill be paid off every month.** Examples are charge cards given out by American Express and many oil companies.

Credit cards are those that allow the charges to be paid off in installments plus interest, provided you make a minimum payment every month. Examples are those given out by MasterCard, Visa, and Discover.

A third kind of card is the debit card, which can be used at certain stores such as some grocery chains. **The *debit card* enables you to pay for purchases by withdrawing funds electronically directly from your savings or checking account.** That is, the debit card acts in place of a paper check.

The advantage of all three types of cards is convenience: you don't have to carry cash. Credit cards can also give you a loan when you need it.

There are, however, some disadvantages:

- *It's easy to forget you're spending money:* "We'll just put it on plastic," students say. Somehow it's easy to spend $80 on that great coat in the store window when you only have to sign a charge slip. It's a lot more difficult when you have to hand over four Andrew Jacksons. With plastic, you get what you want now without the pain of feeling as if you're paying for it.

- *Debts can pile up:* With debit cards, the money is gone from your checking account as soon as you use it. With American Express and other charge cards, you have to pay the bill every month, just like the phone bill. With Visa, Discover, MasterCard, and other credit cards, however, debts can be carried over to the next month. Credit limits for students typically start at $500. Many students find this line of credit too much of a good thing.

  A survey of students at three Michigan universities found that 10% had outstanding credit-card bills of more than $700. A handful had bills as high as $5000 or $6000.[16] One student was reported to have an $1100 bar tab on his Visa. One first-year law student was $40,000 in debt but unable to stop using her cards.[17]

- *Interest rates can be high:* Credit-card interest rates can be much higher than the rates banks charge for other kinds of loans, such as car loans. (And that's all that a credit card is—a loan.) Many cards charge 18–20% a year. And every month interest is added to the interest.

  NOTE: If you carry a $6297 credit-card balance and make only the minimum $200 payment every month, you'll be paying off that debt for—the next 23 years and 10 months! (And that cost could include over $9570 in interest.)[18]

If you have trouble restraining yourself on your credit cards, there's only one solution: take some scissors and cut them in half.

INSURANCE. A dull subject, you may think, but it's important. Murphy's Law states, "If anything can go wrong, it will."

For a college student, there are two or three important kinds of insurance:

- *Health insurance:* This is absolutely essential. The United States is not a country where it's wise to be without health insurance. If something goes wrong, a hospital somewhere (maybe not a good one) will probably admit you. However, without health insurance you might not get the level of care you need. Moreover, the hospital's business office will bill you anyway.

  Parents' employer health plans can often be extended to cover college-age children up until the age of around 24. In addition, most colleges offer student health plans, and you should check to see what their benefits cover. Are lab tests, surgery, hospital stays, long-term care included? If necessary, pay for supplemental health insurance to cover care not provided on campus.

- *Tenant's insurance:* You should make sure your possessions are covered by insurance against fire and theft. Students who are still dependents of their parents may be covered by their parents' insurance. This is so even if the students live in an off-campus apartment. It assumes, however, that they still live at home during the summer, are registered to vote there, or carry a driver's license with parents' address. Your coverage usually amounts to 10% of your parents' coverage, minus the deductible. Thus, if your parents' plan covers $150,000 and has a $250 deductible, you are covered up to $15,000. If a $2000 computer system is stolen out of your apartment, you'll get that amount back minus $250. Check with your insurance company to make sure you're covered as you should be. If not, you should be able to get a special policy for additional premiums.

If you're self-supporting or emancipated or older than about 23, you'll need to get your own tenant's policy.

■ *Car insurance:* If you have a car and are under age 25 (especially if you're an unmarried male), perhaps you've already found that car insurance is one of the most expensive things you can buy. Indeed, it and all other car expenses should seriously make you think about whether you really need a car at school.

If you have an older car, as so many students do, it may not be worth carrying collision insurance. This is the kind of insurance that covers any repairs (usually with a deductible) should anyone run into you. However, you'll want to carry as much comprehensive insurance as you can in case you run into another car, bicyclist, or pedestrian. You should also be covered for hospitalization for any passengers riding in your car.

With car insurance it's worth getting on the phone with the telephone-book Yellow Pages and doing some comparison shopping. Be sure to ask if you can get a discount on your premiums for maintaining good grades. Some companies offer this.

Financial Aid

PREVIEW Financial aid may consist of gifts, such as grants and scholarships. Or it may consist of self-help assistance, such as loans, part-time work, and college work-study. Most financial aid is considered "need-based," in which you show economic need. However, some aid is "merit-based," such as

academic, music, or sports scholarships. To demonstrate financial need, you or your family must fill out a needs analysis document. Aid is available for parents of students, self-supporting students under 24, and older students.

Student need for financial aid has shot up in recent years. This is partly because colleges have raised their tuition rates but also partly because of changes in the kinds of students going to college. For instance, over the past decade, three-quarters of colleges have reported taking more students over 25 years old. Because most of them are part time, they are not eligible for federal financial aid, so they have turned to the schools themselves to cover their aid requirements.[19]

The purpose of this section is to show you the different sources of financial aid available to you.

GIFTS & SELF-HELP, NEED-BASED & MERIT-BASED. The term *financial aid* **refers to any kind of financial help you get to enable you to pay for college.** There are two ways to distinguish financial aid:

■ *Gifts versus self-help assistance: Gift assistance* **is financial aid you do not have to pay back.** It includes grants and scholarships.

Self-help assistance **is financial aid that requires something in return.** *Loans,* which must be repaid, are one example. *Part-time work* and *college work-study* are others.

■ *Need-based versus merit-based:* Most financial aid is need-based. **With *need-based financial aid,* you or your parents fill out forms stating your resources. The college then determines how much aid needs to be made up from somewhere else.**

Merit-based financial aid **is based on some sort of superior academic, music, sports, or other abilities.**

CAN YOU SHOW YOU NEED IT? *Demonstrated financial need* **means that you have proven you need financial aid according to a certain formula,** such as the Congressional Methodology. To begin to apply for need-based financial aid, you must ask your institution for an application form called a needs analysis document. **The *needs analysis document* is a form for helping people prove their financial need to colleges.** The two federal forms you are most likely to encounter are the *FAF* and the *FAFSA*. Financial aid is available whether you are or are not getting money from your family. It is also available whether you are going it alone as a young person or are going back to school as an older person.

- *Aid for parents of students:* The Congressional Methodology formula considers your family's size, income, net worth, and number of members now in college. It then considers your anticipated costs of attending a particular college. From these two factors, the formula arrives at an estimated family contribution. Colleges then make their own calculations based on this formula. If the results show your family's resources insufficient, you'll get some help.

- *Aid for self-supporting students under 24:* If you're self-supporting, the Congressional Methodology formula counts just your income and assets, not your family's. You must show that you are single, under age 24, and without dependents. You must also show you have not been claimed as a dependent by your parents for two years. Finally, you must show you have had annual resources of at least $4000 during each of these two years.[20]

- *Aid for returning adult students:* Even returning adult students can obtain financial aid based on need. It's a matter of minimizing one's income and assets. (For example, older people can move their savings into retirement plans, which are sheltered from financial aid computations.) Believe it or not, it may also help to apply to an expensive college, according to one piece of advice. The reason is that the more expensive the college is, the more aid one is eligible for.[21]

TYPES OF FINANCIAL AID. We may classify financial aid as grants, scholarships, loans, and work. These are available from several sources: federal, state, college, and private.

- *Grants: Grants* **are gifts of money;** they do not have to be repaid.

  One large need-based grant program from the federal government is the *Pell Grants*, given to undergraduates on the basis of need. Normally Pell Grants are given to families with an annual income of less than $25,000, although there are special exceptions. You should apply in any case. Many colleges will not consider you for other grants unless you've been turned down for a Pell Grant.

  Another need-based federal grant program is the *Supplemental Educational Opportunity Grants (SEOG)*, which are designed to augment other forms of financial aid.

  Some companies also offer their employees grants in the form of educational benefits that allow them to attend school while working. For example, a hospital may pay one of its employees to go to nursing school while he or she continues working.

- *Scholarships: Scholarships* **are usually awarded on the basis of merit,** often academic merit. Sometimes the scholarships are for merit in other areas as well, such as proficiency in a certain sport or musical activity. Examples are various *Reserve Officer Training Corps (ROTC)* scholarships.

  Sometimes scholarships are available for reasons you couldn't possibly predict, and they seem to have nothing to do with merit. For instance, you have a certain last name, have a parent who worked for a certain organization, or are from a certain geographical area. You'll never know what these are unless you start looking. Go to the financial aid office or library and ask for help.

■ *Loans:* **A _loan_ is money you have to pay back, either as money or in some form of work.** There are three well-known federal loan programs.

The *Perkins Loans* allow students to borrow up to $4500 for their first and second years. They can borrow up to $9000 for all undergraduate years. The interest rate is 5%. Repayment begins nine months after graduation (unless you quit or become a student less than half time). The repayment may be spread over 10 years.

The *Stafford Loan Program,* also known as the Guaranteed Student Loans, allows you to borrow money up to $2625 per year for the first and second year. You can borrow up to $4000 for the third year and beyond. Thus, you can accumulate up to $17,250 for your undergraduate years. Loans are made by banks or other private lenders. Repayment doesn't start until six months after you graduate, quit, or drop below half-time student status.

The *Parent Loans for Undergraduate Students (PLUS)* program allows parents to borrow from a private lender for their children's education. They can borrow up to $4000 a year, up to $20,000 for each student and at a rate up to 12%. To be eligible, you have to have applied for a Pell or Stafford first. Parents begin repayment 60 days after receiving the money. Students taking out the loan may wait until 60 days after quitting or graduating from college before beginning repayment.

A more recent kind of loan is a *direct-loan program* by the U.S. Government, designed to cut out bankers' profits, streamline procedures, and help students predict and organize their debts. Depending on their circumstances, graduates can repay their debt over 10 to 30 years. (Most student loans are structured for repayment over 10 years.)[22]

■ *Work:* Many colleges offer part-time work opportunities, usually on campus. Of course, you may also be able to line up part-time work off-campus. In addition, a federally funded need-based program called *College Work-Study* helps colleges set up jobs for students. Typi-cally College Work-Study covers 12–15 hours a week, or up to 40 hours a week during the summer.

Cooperative education programs **allow you to improve your marketability upon graduation by giving you work experience in your major.** The work may go on at the same time as the course work or as part-time school and part-time work. Or the work may alternate with course work—for example, one semester in school and the next semester at work. Pay is often modest, but the experience is what counts. Cooperative education programs are offered at about 1000 schools.

GETTING GOING. Even if you don't think you're eligible for financial aid right now, it might be advisable to go through the application process. At least then you'll know where you stand. And you'll be prepared if something happens to the college funds that you're presently counting on. Help in obtaining financial assistance is offered through a couple of toll-free numbers. Call the Federal Student Aid Information Center at 800-4-FEDAID or the Federal Student Aid Advisory Center at 800-648-3248.

One caution, however: Allow *lots* of time. No one's going to give you any money if you didn't follow their rules and apply within the deadlines posted. Applying for money is just like applying to get into college itself—these things do not happen instantaneously. It will take time for you (or your parents) to fill out the forms and meet a filing deadline (usually far in advance of the first day of the school term). Then it will take college officials time to approve the paperwork before they can send you a check.

Applying for financial aid is just as much a test of adult responsibility as filing an income-tax return. Just as the burden is on you to meet the deadlines and proofs of the tax collector, so it is with financial aid. Thus, be sure to keep copies of all your paperwork in case something gets lost.

Onward

PREVIEW Money concerns are usually lifelong.

Unless they come into a large inheritance or otherwise strike it rich, most people find that money concerns continue after they're out of college. Thus, like other skills in this book, the techniques described here are not just things you need to know for the short run. They are lifelong skills that will benefit you no matter what kind of degree you hold.

NOTES

1. Higher Education Research Institute, University of California at Los Angeles, survey sponsored by American Council on Education. Reported in: Associated Press (1992, January 13). College freshmen feeling pinch. *San Francisco Chronicle*, p. A3.

2. Kelly, D. (1991, February 19). Students leave in deeper debt. *USA Today*, p. 6D.

3. Rigdon, J. E. (1991, January 3). Student loans weigh down graduates. *Wall Street Journal*, p. B1.

4. Seligman, K. (1992, March 29). More and more college students on '7-year plan'. *San Francisco Examiner*, p. A-1.

5. Anonymous. (1995, April 18). The rich get richer faster [editorial]. *New York Times*, p. A16.

6. *Washington Monthly* (1993, March). Cited in: Ouellete, L. (1993, September/October). Class bias on campus. *Utne Reader*, pp. 19–24.

7. Kelly, 1991.

8. Phillips, M. (1974). *The seven laws of money*. Menlo Park, Calif., and New York: Word Wheel and Random House, p. 41.

9. Phillips, 1974, p. 32.

10. Astin, A. W., Dey, E. L., Korn, W. S. et al. (1991). *The American freshman: National norms for fall 1991*. Los Angeles: Higher Education Research Institute, Graduate School of Education, University of California, Los Angeles.

11. Gottesman, G. (1991). *College survival*. New York: Prentice Hall Press, pp. 13–14.

12. Gottesman, 1991, pp. 196 - 97.

13. Melia, M. K. (1992, May). Carry-out cash. *American Demographics*, p. 6.

14. Anonymous (1991, February 9). Credit cards become big part of life. *New York Times*, p. 16.

15. Brookes, A. (1994, November 5). Lesson for teen-agers: Facts of credit-card life. *New York Times*, p. 31.

16. Foren, J. (1991, December 1). College students piling on credit card debt. *San Francisco Examiner*, p. E-9.

17. Kutner, L. (1993, August 19). College students with big credit card bills may be learning an economics lesson the hard way. *New York Times*, p. B4.

18. Dugas, C. (1996, September 27). Paying off cards saves a bundle. *USA Today*, p. 7B.

19. Madden, M. (1996, August 5). Colleges tighten belts. *USA Today*, p. 9B; citing report by American Council on Education, *Campus Trends 1996*.

20. Kiplinger's Changing Times (1988). *Success with your money*. Washington, DC: Kiplinger Changing Times, p. 132.

21. Nemko, M. (1992, June 28). A grown-up's guide to financial aid. *This World, San Francisco Chronicle*, pp. 11–12.

22. Manegold, C. S. (1994, September 19). U.S. has high hopes for a revamped student loan program. *New York Times*, p. A10.

1. *What are common concerns about money?* Have each student write down on a sheet of paper five principal thoughts or worries they have about money. Be sure to tell them *not* to put their names on the paper but to fold it up for collection by the instructor.

   Read aloud some of the responses to the class for discussion purposes. Questions to consider: How common are some of these concerns? What can you do about them? Does it make you feel better knowing that others have the same worries you have?

2. *Where does you money come from and where does it go?* Ask students to bring to class completed versions of Personal Exploration #12.1, "The Money Diagnostic Report." In a small group or with the class at large, have students share any impressions they've gained during the week. Are there any surprises? In what unexpected areas do students find themselves spending too much money?

3. *How can you reduce expenses?* Ask students to bring completed Personal Explorations #12.2 and #12.3 to class. With others in a small group, they should generate a list of largest monthly expenses. Also they should list expenses that they might be able to reduce.

   Ask students to share the lists and money-saving strategies with the rest of the class. Questions for discussion: Which areas are the easiest to reduce spending in and why? Which areas are the most difficult? What have you learned about your needs and your wants? Do you control your emotions or do they control you regarding spending? What can you do to exercise more control over your financial affairs?

4. *The credit-card hassle.* In the class at large, ask students to discuss the problems of credit cards. Questions to consider: What is the psychology behind credit cards that makes them irresistible to use? Suppose instead of using a credit card you had to go apply for a bank loan every time you wanted to buy something.

Would you do it? If you have credit cards, do you know what their interest rates and charges are? How much does that work out to per month on the unpaid balance? Could you cut up your credit cards today and get through the rest of the school year?

5. *There's money out there somewhere.* This activity, which requires some out-of-class time, is to be done in groups of four to six students. Many students are familiar with the basic state and federal programs offering financial aid. The purpose of this exercise is to locate less obvious sources of financial assistance.

   With their group members, students should use the campus library to identify *five* new potential sources of financial aid. (If possible, they should prepare a typed list of potential resources, to be distributed to each person in the class.)

   In class students should report on their findings or distribute their lists. Questions to consider: What were your reactions to the sources of financial assistance available? Do you feel these funds are readily accessible? Have you identified new sources of monetary aid that are directly applicable to your own financial situation?

JOURNAL ENTRY #12.1: WHAT IS UPSETTING ABOUT MONEY? What do you find particularly upsetting to you about money? What does this chapter suggest you might be able to do about it?

_____

_____

_____

_____

_____

_____

_____

_____

_____

_____

_____

JOURNAL ENTRY #12.2: PAYING ATTENTION: HOW MUCH MONEY DO YOU OWE? Some students are only vaguely aware of how much money they owe, including both student loans and credit-card debts. Indeed, they may be off by as much as $5000. Do you know how much you need to repay? How long would it be before you're debt free?

_____

_____

_____

_____

_____

_____

_____

_____

_____

JOURNAL ENTRY #12.3: WHAT DO YOU KNOW ABOUT STUDENT LOANS? Some students talk almost like bankers, computing which loans and repayment schedules are better than others. Have you done comparisons of the various loans available? If not, what kind of action might you take here?

_____

_____

_____

_____

_____

_____

_____

_____

_____

_____

_____

13 work

majors, résumés, & careers

IN THIS CHAPTER: What will you do when you get out of college? What would you *like* to do? Is there necessarily a relationship between your major and your prospective career, and which should you decide on first? These are some of the most important questions you'll ever have to consider. And you're in the unique position of *being able* to consider them now. In this chapter, we consider the following:

■ *Your future:* What do you want to do when you get out of college, and how can you get career advice?

■ *Vocational tests:* What vocational tests can help point you toward a career?

■ *Job hunting:* What are the best ways to find a good job? How can you use a computer to help you in a job search? What are the best ways to write a résumé?

When we go to our jobs, what is it that we are trading for money?

The answer is, simply, our *life energy*.

"Our life energy," explain Joe Dominguez and Vicki Robin, authors of *Your Money or Your Life,* "is our allotment of time here on earth, the hours of precious life available to us." Life energy is all we have. "It is precious because it is limited and irretrievable and because our choices about how we use it express the meaning and purpose of our time here on earth."[1]

Thus, they say, in considering what to do for a living, two questions become important:

- Are you receiving satisfaction and value in proportion to your life energy expended?

- Is the expenditure of life energy in alignment with your values and purpose?

Considering all the ways you might spend your future days, then, what would make you *feel most fulfilled while trading your irretrievable life energy?*

Unfortunately, for a great many people, work does not give them this sense of purpose. According to a Gallup poll, only 41% of the respondents consciously chose the job or career they were in. Of the rest, 18% got started in their present job through chance circumstances, and 12% took the only job available. The remainder were influenced by relatives or friends.[2]

Perhaps the most important finding was this: *Nearly two thirds said that, given a chance to start over, they would try to get more information about career options.*

Maybe, then, you are in a good position to take advantage of others' hindsight: Get as much information as you can about careers and jobs.

What Do You Want to Be After You Graduate?

PREVIEW Some careers have a relationship to one's major, but many others do not. Often the additional training needed can be acquired in graduate school. It's best to decide on a career before a major; advice can be obtained at the college career counseling and job placement center.

In urging you to get career information, I also need to say this: Don't be afraid about making a mistake in a career choice. People make career changes all the time, in all phases of life. Moreover, in the beginning it's natural to go through some trial and error until you find what suits you. Indeed, columnist and business consultant Jack Falvey points out that most people do some casting about: "It is a rare person who knows with certitude what he [or she] wants to be and then follows that dream into the sunset for a lifetime. It is unrealistic to set that [ideal] as a standard."[3]

In fact, in the future the average person is expected to have *four career changes*—and several job changes within each career.[4] Statistically, people change jobs or assignments every 2 1/2 years.[5] The best approach you can take, then, is to be flexible.

IS THERE A RELATIONSHIP BETWEEN MAJORS & CAREERS? Many students assume that to enter most careers you must have the appropriate major. There are three possibilities here:

- *Relationship between career and major:* For some fields, there clearly is a relationship between the major and the career. To be an engineer, nurse, or musician, for example, you should major in engineering, nursing, or music, respectively. This is because the training for the occupation is so specific.

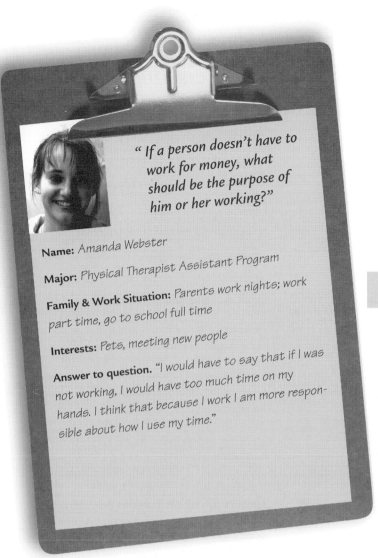

" If a person doesn't have to work for money, what should be the purpose of him or her working?"

Name: Amanda Webster

Major: Physical Therapist Assistant Program

Family & Work Situation: Parents work nights; work part time, go to school full time

Interests: Pets, meeting new people

Answer to question. "I would have to say that if I was not working, I would have too much time on my hands. I think that because I work I am more responsible about how I use my time."

■ *No relationship between career and major:* A great many fields require no specific major at all. You can be a sales representative, a store manager, a police officer, or the like with almost any major.

■ *Relationship between career and graduate training:* For some fields—even seemingly specialized and technical ones—training can be obtained at the graduate level. For example, you could major in history as an undergraduate, then get a master's degree in business, journalism, librarianship, or social work. The master's will enable you to enter one of these fields as a profession. (Some graduate programs may insist that you go back and make up particular undergraduate prerequisite courses that you might have missed.)

Quite apart from considering your career, however, is another important question: What do you want to *study*? For most people, college is a once-in-a-lifetime activity. Regardless of what you're going to do for a living, now's the time to study those things that truly interest you. Philosophy, English literature, ethnic studies, history of science, fine arts, and physical education might not seem directly connected to your career interests. But if you're interested in any of these subjects, the college years are the time to investigate them.

WHAT DO YOU WANT TO DO FOR A CAREER?

How do you find which career might be best for you? You can just leave things to chance, as many people do. Indeed, one out of three students puts off making a career decision until after graduation.[6] Then you can take whatever comes along, hoping everything will just work out for your future happiness.

But consider what it is that makes people want to succeed. University of Rochester psychology professor Edward L. Deci has studied human motivation for many years. According to his research, people do better when they are encouraged to pursue a task for its own sake. They also enjoy it more than those told to do the task for a reward. Or those told they will be punished if they don't perform correctly.[7] Clearly, then, it's worth your while to seek out a career that you really want to do.

CAREER COUNSELING & JOB PLACEMENT CENTER. Career guidance starts with a visit to the career counseling center, which most colleges have. Often this is coupled with the job placement office.

Basically the career counseling and job placement center offers the following services:

■ *Vocational testing:* Tests such as those described in the next section ask you questions about your interests, abilities, and values. They also make suggestions about possible career areas that might interest you.

- **Career counseling:** Career counseling offices usually have lots of information about what occupational fields are expanding. They also can tell you where the jobs tend to be concentrated geographically, the salary levels, and the training required. In addition, they can advise on transferring, as from community college to university.

  You may get one-on-one advice from career advisors. Or you may be steered to job fairs attended by prospective employers or be introduced to alumni working in fields you're considering.

- **Information about graduate school:** Some careers may require an advanced degree. Often the career counseling office provides information on graduate and professional programs and their admissions requirements and costs.

- **Job placement:** Students may think of part-time jobs as simply ways of making money to help get them through college. However, they can also provide valuable work experience that you can leverage later when you're trying to obtain a career-path type of job. The job-placement office can also help you find out about internships or fieldwork jobs associated with your major.

Tests to Help Establish Career Interests

PREVIEW Vocational tests can help people establish their career interests and abilities. One presented here is the "career video" exercise. More formal tools include the Strong/Campbell Interest Inventory and the Edwards Personal Preference Schedule. Visiting the career counseling and job placement office can be a valuable and ultimately time-saving experience.

ow can you identify which occupations might suit your abilities and interests? One way to do this is through vocational testing offered by career counselors. Let's consider some of these tests.

THE "CAREER VIDEO" EXERCISE. John Holland is a psychologist at Johns Hopkins University who has developed a system that divides career areas into six categories based on different interests and skills.[8] Here let us suppose that Holland's six career categories have been produced as a series by a "career introduction video service." (This is sort of a variation on those video dating services you may have seen ads for.) To see which careers appeal to you, try Personal Exploration #13.1.

OTHER TESTS FOR CAREER DECISION-MAKING. A more sophisticated version of the "career video" test is available under the name of the *Vocational Preference Inventory*, developed by John Holland. Holland has also written a *Self-Directed Search Assessment Booklet*. This contains a self-marking test that you can use to examine what occupations you might begin to investigate. A career counselor can give you a further explanation of these valuable tests.

THE "CAREER VIDEO": WHAT INTERESTS & SKILLS ARE YOU ATTRACTED TO?

■ DIRECTIONS

The accompanying description shows a summary of six career videos, labeled 1, 2, 3, 4, 5, 6. Read the description of all six videos. Then answer the questions below.

NUMBER OF VIDEO

a. Which video are you drawn to because it shows the group of people you would *most enjoy* being with? _____

b. Which second video are you drawn to because it shows the people you would *next most enjoy* being with? _____

c. Which video of the third rank are you drawn to because it shows people you would enjoy being with? _____

1. **Objects, things, animals:**

   People in this video are shown working with tools, machines, objects, animals, or plants. They may work outdoors. They have mechanical or athletic skills.

2. **Learning, analyzing, solving:**

   People in this video are shown analyzing and solving problems, learning, observing, discovering. They are curious and have good investigative skills.

3. **Innovating and creating:**

   People in this video are shown being intuitive, creative, imaginative, and artistic. They like to operate in unstructured environments.

4. **Helping and informing:**

   People in this video are shown training, developing, curing, enlightening. They like working with people and often have word skills.

5. **Influencing, performing, leading:**

   People in this video are shown persuading, performing, or managing people. They like working with people in achieving a goal.

6. **Data and details:**

   People in this video are shown executing tasks, following instructions, and working with numbers and facts. They like working with data.

   (continued on next page)

THE "CAREER VIDEO": WHAT INTERESTS & SKILLS ARE YOU ATTRACTED TO?

■ INTERPRETATION

The video numbers represent the following:

1 = *Realistic*
2 = *Investigative*
3 = *Artistic*
4 = *Social*
5 = *Enterprising*
6 = *Conventional*

In general, the closer the types, the less the conflict among the career fields. Here's what the six fields mean.

1. **Realistic:** People in this video consider themselves "doers." They are practical, down-to-earth, mechanically inclined, action-oriented, interested in physical activity.

   Interests may be mechanical or scientific. Examples of occupations: coach, computer graphics technician, electrical contractor, electronics technician, farmer, fitness director, health and safety specialist, industrial arts teacher, jeweler, navy officer, physical education teacher.

2. **Investigative:** If you're this type, you consider yourself a problem solver. You're probably rational and analytical, valuing intellectual achievement. You're thought-oriented rather than action-oriented. You may not be very people-oriented, indeed may be a loner.

   Sample occupations: cattle breeder, college professor, computer programmer, engineer, environmentalist, flight engineer, physician, scientist, urban planner.

3. **Artistic:** As might be expected, artistic people describe themselves as creative. They also consider themselves independent, unconventional, and emotional, valuing self-expression and disliking structure.

   Careers are apt to be in visual or performing arts. Examples of occupations: actor, architect, cartoonist, communications specialist, editor, illustrator, interior decorator, jewelry designer, journalist, librarian, orchestra leader, photographer, public relations person, sculptor.

4. **Social:** Social people value helping others and consider themselves socially concerned and caring and understanding of other people. They are drawn to associating with others in close personal relationships.

   Some careers: career specialist, caterer, convention planner, counselor, home economist, insurance claims specialist, minister, nurse, teacher, travel agent.

5. **Enterprising:** If you consider yourself adventurous, assertive, risk-taking, outgoing, and persuasive, you may be of the enterprising type. Power and prestige are important to you, and you prefer leadership to supporting roles.

   Examples of occupations: banker, city manager, FBI agent, labor negotiator, lawyer, marketing specialist, politician, promoter, real-estate developer, sales representative, television announcer or producer.

6. **Conventional:** Conventional types see themselves as enjoying routine, order, neatness, detail, and structure, as well as prestige and status. They are self-controlled and skilled in planning and organizing.

   Some occupations: accountant, auditor, database manager, hospital administrator, indexer, information consultant, insurance administrator, legal secretary, office manager, personnel specialist, statistician.

Most people are not one distinct type but rather a mixture of types. This is why this Personal Exploration offers second and third choices.

These interpretations may help suggest possible directions for you to pursue for your major and career.

Two other tests used by career counselors are the Strong/Campbell Interest Inventory (SCII) and the Edwards Personal Preference Schedule (EPPS). The Strong/Campbell test enables students to compare their interests to those of people in various occupations. The Edwards tests allows students to discover what their personal needs and preferences are—such as need for order, dominance, helping others, and social orientation.

GOING FOR AN APPOINTMENT AT CAREER COUNSELING. A visit to a career counseling center and the taking of a vocational test might take the better part of an afternoon. But the experience may well save you months or even years of wasted effort. In order to get started on establishing your career path—and the right major—do Personal Exploration #13.2.

WHAT CAN YOU LEARN FROM A VISIT TO THE CAREER COUNSELING & JOB PLACEMENT OFFICE?

The purpose of this assignment is to get you into the Career Counseling and Job Placement Office and have you talk to one of the counselors.

■ DIRECTIONS

Call the Career Counseling Center (or its equivalent on your campus) and make an appointment to come in. Explain to the counselor that you are doing a class assignment for this course. Ask if he or she can spare 15–20 minutes of time for a brief interview. Make an appointment to meet.

My appointment is at (date and time)

_____

_____

with (name of counselor)

_____

_____

at (location)

_____

_____

■ QUESTIONS FOR THE VISIT

Review the interview questions below and add two of your own. Ask the following questions and fill in the blanks.

1. What kind of career counseling services do you offer?

_____
_____
_____
_____
_____
_____
_____
_____
_____
_____
_____

2. What kind of information do you have about occupational fields?

_____
_____
_____
_____
_____
_____
_____
_____
_____

3. What kind of vocational tests do you offer? How long do they take?

_____
_____
_____
_____
_____
_____
_____

4. What kind of information do you have, if any, about graduate and professional schools?

_____
_____
_____
_____
_____
_____
_____
_____
_____
_____

5. If this office has a job placement component, what kind of services does it offer? Does it help students get internships or field-work placements?

_____
_____
_____
_____
_____
_____
_____
_____

The Job of Looking for a Job

PREVIEW Everyone should train in the job of looking for a job. Two ways to investigate jobs are via the informational interview and internships. The computer can also be a job-search tool, as in hunting for online job openings and putting your résumé in an online database. It helps to know techniques for writing résumés, both recruiter-friendly and computer-friendly, chronological and functional. It's also important to know how to write a cover letter to accompany the résumé and how to behave in an interview.

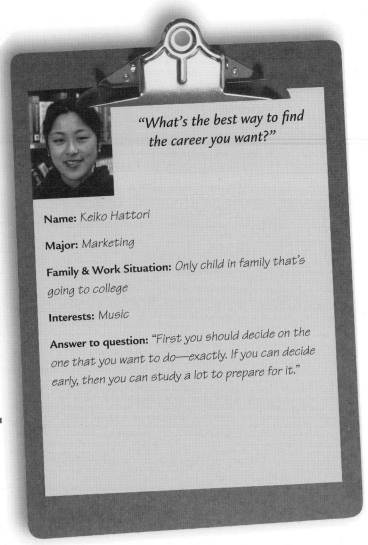

"What's the best way to find the career you want?"

Name: Keiko Hattori

Major: Marketing

Family & Work Situation: Only child in family that's going to college

Interests: Music

Answer to question: "First you should decide on the one that you want to do—exactly. If you can decide early, then you can study a lot to prepare for it."

The average person will go job hunting *eight* times in his or her life," says Richard Bolles. A former clergyman, Bolles is author of *What Color Is Your Parachute?* and other writings about career searching.[9–11] Thus, today one needs to train for the task of *finding and getting* a job as much as for the ability to do the job itself.

Bolles offers several insights on finding that "lucky" job.[12] Luck, he says, favors people who:

■ Are going after their dreams—the thing they really want to do most in the world.

■ Are prepared.

■ Are working hardest at the job hunt.

■ Have told the most people clearly and precisely what they are looking for.

■ Treat others with grace and dignity, courtesy and kindness.

WAYS OF LOOKING FOR JOBS. Listing the various ways of finding jobs would take a book in itself. My suggestion is to go through the Career Counseling Center and find out everything you can about

this subject. I would agree with Jack Falvey, however, when he says that contacts are everything. This means developing relationships with people.

Some unique ways of establishing contacts are as follows:

■ ***The informational interview:*** Students have somewhat of a privileged status just by being students. (This is true for part-time and older students as well as traditional-age full-time students.) That is, everyone knows that they are in a temporary position in life, that of *learning*. Consequently, it is perfectly acceptable for you to write a letter to a high-level executive asking for an *informational interview*. The letter should be written on high-quality paper stock, perhaps even on a letterhead printed with your name and address. (*See* ■ *Panel 13.1.*)

"You may find it hard to believe that some senior management types would clear their calendars for an hour or two just to talk to a student," Falvey observes, "but they do it all the time.[13] After sending the letter, you can make the follow-up phone call. This will probably connect you with a secretary who handles the appointment calendar. Simply remind him or her that you had written to set up a meeting and ask how the executive's calendar looks.

■ *Internships:* Essentially an *internship* gives you the chance to gain inside professional experience within a particular company or organization. What the company gets in return is your labor (sometimes for a modest salary, sometimes for no salary). It also gets the opportunity to bid for your services after college if the people there decide they like you. Internships may be as short as a few days during semester break or as long as a complete summer or school term.

Internships—sometimes called field experiences or cooperative educational experiences—are found everywhere. You can locate these through the Career Counseling Center, of course. You can also simply ask guest speakers or other campus visitors. You might even be able to create your own internship, as by asking an executive during an informational interview.

PANEL 13.1 **E**xample of letter requesting informational interview.

I need your help. I am researching _____ industry (profession). If I could meet with someone of your experience, I am sure I could get enough information in a half hour to give me the direction I need to begin finding out how _____ really works.

As a first-year student studying _____, I find it difficult to understand how everything applies or fits together.

I will call your office in hopes of scheduling an appointment.

WRITING A RECRUITER-FRIENDLY RÉSUMÉ. Writing a résumé is like writing an ad to sell yourself. However, it can't just be dashed off or follow any format of your choosing. It should be carefully designed to impress a human recruiter, who may have some fairly traditional ideas about résumés. (It should also be designed to be put into an employer's computerized database, as I'll describe.)

Some tips for organizing résumés, offered by reporter Kathleen Pender, who interviewed numerous professional résumé writers, are as follows.[14] *(See ■ Panel 13.2.)*

■ *The beginning:* Start with your name, address, and phone number.

Follow with a clear objective stating what it is you want to do. (Example: "Sales representative in computer industry.")

Under the heading "Summary" give three compelling reasons why you are the ideal person for the job. (Example of one line: "Experienced sales representative to corporations and small businesses.")

After the beginning, your résumé can follow either a *chronological* format or a *functional* format.

■ *The chronological résumé:* The chronological résumé works best for people who have stayed in the same line of work and have moved steadily upward in their careers. Start with your most recent job and work backward, and say more about your recent jobs than earlier ones.

The format is to list the dates you worked at each place down one side of the page. Opposite the dates indicate your employer's name and your job title. You can also list a few of your accomplishments, using action words ("managed," "created," "developed"). Omit accomplishments that have nothing to do with the job you're applying for.

■ *The functional résumé:* The functional résumé works best for people who are changing careers or are re-entering the job market. It also is for people who want to emphasize skills from earlier in their careers or their volunteer experience. It is particularly suitable if you have had responsibilities you want to showcase but have never had an important job title.

The format is to emphasize the skills, then follow with a brief chronological work history emphasizing dates, job titles, and employer names.

■ *The conclusion:* Both types of résumés should have a concluding section showing college, degree, and graduation date and professional credentials or licenses. They should also include professional affiliations and awards if they are relevant to the job you're seeking.

■ *The biggest mistakes on résumés:* The biggest mistake you can make on a résumé is to *lie*. Sooner or later a lie will probably catch up with you and may get you fired, maybe even sued.

The second biggest mistake is to have *spelling errors*. Spelling mistakes communicate to prospective employers a basic carelessness.

• • • • • • • • • • • • • • • • •

"The biggest mistake you can make on a résumé is to lie."

• • • • • • • • • • • • • • • • •

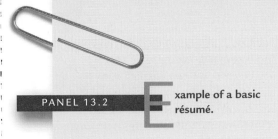

771 Randall Avenue
San Jose, CA 95190

(408) 555-4567

STACEY S. WILLIAMS

OBJECTIVE:

Sales representative in a publishing or communications company in an entry-level position.

SUMMARY OF QUALIFICATIONS:

Experienced with working with general public and in retail selling during summer and Christmas jobs. Superb writing skills developed through college courses and extracurricular activities. Active volunteer in literacy program and discussion forums. Knowledge of Spanish, some French.

BUSINESS EXPERIENCE:

Nov. 22–Dec. 24, 1996   FRY'S ELECTRONICS, San Jose, CA

SALESPERSON, television sets and VCRs.

Nov. 22–Dec. 24, 1995   MACYS, San Jose, CA

SALESPERSON, video games.

SUMMER JOBS:

1991–1995   DEPT. OF PARKS & RECREATION, San Jose, CA

June–Sept. 1995, GATE ATTENDANT, pool area; June–Sept. 1994, GATE ATTENDANT, pool area; June–Sept. 1993, LOCKER ROOM ATTENDANT; June–Sept. 1992, LOCKER ROOM ATTENDANT; June–Sept. 1991, PARK ATTENDANT. Collected tickets, checked residency, painted, cleaned pool area.

EDUCATION:

B. A. in International Relations, minor in Journalism, San Jose State University, San Jose, CA, 1997.

Dean's List, 2 years.

Courses in International Relations: U.S., European, Latin America.

Additional courses in: Principles of Journalism, Feature Writing, Fundamentals of Public Speaking, Principles of Economics, Introduction to Business.

EXTRACURRICULAR ACTIVITIES:

Editor and reporter, college newspaper.

Member, debate team.

Volunteer, Project READ, a literacy program, and of National Issues Forums, network of forums to discuss national issues.

REFERENCES AVAILABLE ON REQUEST

Other résumé dos and don'ts appear in the box at left. *(See ■ Panel 13.3.)*

PANEL 13.3 Résumé dos and don'ts.

There are no hard and fast rules to résumé writing, but these are a few points on which the majority of experts would agree.

■ DO . . .

- Start with a clear objective.
- Have different résumés for different types of jobs.
- List as many relevant skills as you legitimately possess.
- Use jargon or buzzwords that are understood in the industry.
- Use superlatives: biggest, best, most, first.
- Start sentences with action verbs (organized, reduced, increased, negotiated, analyzed).
- List relevant credentials and affiliations.
- Limit your résumé to one or two pages (unless you're applying for an academic position).
- Use standard-size, white or off-white heavy paper.
- Use a standard typeface and a letter-quality or laser-jet printer.
- Spell check and proofread, several times.

■ DON'T . . .

- Lie.
- Sound overly pompous.
- Use pronouns such as I, we.
- Send a photo of yourself.
- List personal information such as height, weight, marital status or age, unless you're applying for a job as an actor or model.
- List hobbies, unless they're directly related to your objective.
- Provide references unless requested. ("References on request" is optional.)
- Include salary information.
- Start a sentence with "responsibilities included:"
- Overuse and mix type styles such as bold, underline, italic, and uppercase.

WRITING A COMPUTER-FRIENDLY RÉSUMÉ. Once upon a time, an employer would simply throw away old résumés or file them and rarely look at them again. Now a company may well use a high-tech résumé-scanning system such as Resumix.[15] This technology uses an optical scanner to input 900 pages of résumés a day, storing the data in a computerized database. The system can search for up to 60 key factors, such as job titles, technical expertise, education, geographic location, and employment history. Resumix can also track race, religion, gender, and other factors to help companies diversify their workforce. These descriptors can then be matched with available openings.

Such résumé scanners can save companies thousands of dollars. They allow organizations to more efficiently search their existing pool of applicants before turning to advertising or other means to recruit employees. For applicants, however, résumé banks and other electronic systems have turned job hunting into a whole new ball game. The latest advice is as follows:

- *Use the right paper and print:* In the past, job seekers have used tricks such as colored paper and fancy typefaces in their résumés to catch a bored personnel officer's eye. However, optical scanners have trouble reading type on colored or gray paper and are confused by unusual typefaces. They even have difficulty reading underlining and poor-quality dot-matrix printing.[16] Thus, you need to be aware of new format rules for résumé writing. *(See ■ Panel 13.4.)*

- *Use keywords for skills or attributes:* Just as important as the format of a résumé today are the words used in it. In the past, résumé writers tried to clearly present their skills. Now it's necessary to use, in addition, as many of the buzzwords or keywords of your profession or industry as you can.

Action words ("managed," "developed") should still be used, but they are less important than nouns. Nouns include job titles, capabilities, languages spoken, type of degree, and the like ("sales representative," "Spanish," "B.A."). The reason, of course, is that a computer will scan for keywords applicable to the job that is to be filled.

Because résumé-screening programs sort and rank keywords, résumés with the most keywords rise to the top of the electronic pile. Consequently, it's suggested you pack your résumé with every conceivable kind of keyword that applies to you. You should especially use those that appear in help-wanted ads.[17]

If you're looking for a job in desktop publishing, for instance, certain keywords in your résumé will help it stand out. Examples might be *Aldus Pagemaker, Compugraphics, DCF, Harvard Graphics, Page Perfect, Quark, PhotoShop.*

USING THE COMPUTER TO LOOK FOR JOBS.

Today there are many computer-related tools you can use to help you in your job search. These range from résumé-writing software to online databases on which you can post your résumé or look for job listings.[18–26] Two types of online job-hunting tools are as follows:

- **Online job openings:** You can search online for lists of jobs that might interest you. This method is called the "armchair job search" by careers columnist Joyce Lain Kennedy, co-author of *Electronic Job Search Revolution.*[27] With a computer you can prowl through online information services, online job ad services, or newspaper online information services. (Examples of online information services are America Online, CompuServe, Prodigy, and Microsoft Network.)

- **Résumé database services:** You can put your specially tailored résumé in an online database, giving employers the opportunity to contact you. Among the kinds of resources for employers are databases for college students and databases for people with experience.

PANEL 13.4

Tips for preparing a computer-scannable résumé. Resumix Inc., maker of computerized résumé-scanning systems, suggests observing the following rules of format for résumé writing:

- Exotic typefaces, underlining, and decorative graphics don't scan well.

- It's best to send originals, not copies, and not to use a dot-matrix printer.

- Too-small print may confuse the scanner; don't go below 12-point type.

- Use standard $8\frac{1}{2} \times 11$-inch paper and do not fold. Words in a crease can't be read easily.

- Use white or light-beige paper. Blues and grays minimize the contrast between the letters and the background.

- Avoid double columns. The scanner reads from left to right.

You may wish to try Personal Exploration #13.3 to draft a résumé using some of the principles just described.

WRITING A GOOD COVER LETTER. Write a targeted cover letter to accompany your résumé. This advice especially should be followed if you're responding to an ad.

Most people don't bother to write a cover letter focusing on the particular job being advertised. Moreover, if they do, say San Francisco employment experts Howard Bennett and Chuck McFadden, "they tend to talk about what *they* are looking for in a job. This is a major turn-off for employers."[28] Employers don't care very much about your dreams and aspirations, only about finding the best candidate for the job.

Bennett and McFadden suggest the following strategy for a cover letter:

- *Emphasize how you will meet the employer's needs:* Employers advertise because they have needs to be met. "You will get much more attention," say Bennett and McFadden, "if you demonstrate your ability to fill those needs."

  How do you find out what those needs are? *You read the ad.* By reading the ad closely you can find out how the company talks about itself. You can also find out what attributes it is looking for in employees and what the needs are for the particular position.

- *Use the language of the ad:* In your cover letter, use as much of the ad's language as you can. "Use the same words as much as possible," advise Bennett and McFadden. "Feed the company's language back to them." This will produce "an almost subliminal realization in the company that you are the person they've been looking for."

- *Take care with the format of the letter:* Keep the letter to one page and use dashes or asterisks to emphasize the areas where you meet the needs described in the ad. Make sure the sentences read well and—very important—that no word or name is misspelled.

THE INTERVIEW. The intent of both cover letter and résumé is to get you an interview. The act of getting an interview itself means you're probably in the top 10–15% of candidates. Once you're into an interview, a different set of skills is needed.

You need to look clean and well-groomed, of course. Richard Bolles suggests you also need to say what distinguishes you from the 20 other people the employer is interviewing. "If you say you are a very thorough person, don't just say it," suggests Bolles. "Demonstrate it by telling them what you know about their company, which you learned beforehand by doing your homework."[29]

Onward

PREVIEW Life is an endless process of self-discovery.

Life isn't a mountain that has a summit . . .," says John Gardner, the founder of the public-interest lobby Common Cause. "Nor a game that has a final score." Rather, "Life is an endless unfolding and—if we wish it to be—an endless process of self-discovery, an endless and unpredictable dialogue between our own potentialities and the life situations in which we find ourselves." A person's potentialities, Gardner says, include not just intellectual gifts. They cover "the full range of one's capacities for learning, sensing, wondering, understanding, loving, and aspiring."[30]

This, then, is not the end. It is the beginning.

HOW CAN YOU BUILD AN IMPRESSIVE RÉSUMÉ?

For this exercise, it doesn't matter whether you're of traditional college age or are a returning adult student. Its purpose is to get you accustomed to thinking about one important question: *What kinds of things might you be doing throughout your college years in order to produce a high-quality résumé?*

Fill in the lines below with your *present* experience. Then add ideas about *experience you might acquire* that would help you in the next few years.

■ 1. MY PRESENT EDUCATION:

_____
_____
_____
_____
_____

Highlights of my present education (your most impressive accomplishments):

_____
_____
_____
_____
_____

■ MY FUTURE EDUCATION:

_____
_____
_____
_____

Highlights of my education (impressive accomplishments you would like to be able to list):

_____
_____
_____
_____

■ 2. MY PRESENT WORK EXPERIENCE:

_____
_____

_____
_____

Highlights of my present work experience (your most impressive accomplishments):

_____
_____
_____
_____
_____

■ MY FUTURE WORK EXPERIENCE:

_____
_____
_____
_____

Highlights of my work experience (impressive accomplishments you would like to be able to list):

_____
_____
_____
_____

■ 3. MY PRESENT CO-CURRICULAR ACTIVITIES:

_____
_____
_____
_____

Highlights of my present co-curricular activities (your most impressive accomplishments):

_____
_____
_____
_____

■ MY FUTURE CO-CURRICULAR ACTIVITIES:

_____
_____
_____
_____

Highlights of my co-curricular activities (impressive accomplishments you would like to be able to list):

_____
_____
_____
_____

■ 4. MY PRESENT HONORS AND AWARDS:

_____
_____
_____
_____

■ MY FUTURE HONORS AND AWARDS:

_____
_____
_____
_____

1. Dominguez, J., & Robin, V. (1992). *Your money or your life*. Bergenfield, NJ: Penguin.

2. Gallup Organization October 1989 survey for National Occupational Information Coordinating Committee. Reported in: Associated Press (1990, January 12). Working at the wrong job. *San Francisco Chronicle*, p. C1.

3. Falvey, J. (1986). *After college: The business of getting jobs*. Charlotte, VT: Williamson.

4. Yate, M. J. Quoted in: McIntosh, C. (1991, May). Giving good answers to tough questions. *McCall's*, pp. 38, 40.

5. Falvey, 1986.

6. Shertzer, B. (1985). *Career planning* (3rd ed.). Boston: Houghton Mifflin.

7. Deci, E. L., & Flaste, R. (1995). *Why we do what we do: The dynamics of personal autonomy*. New York: Grosset/Putnam.

8. Holland, J. (1975). *Vocational preference inventory*. Palo Alto, CA: Consulting Psychologists Press.

9. Bolles, R. N. Quoted in: Rubin, S. (1994, February 24). How to open your job 'parachute' after college. *San Francisco Chronicle*, p. E9.

10. Bolles, R. N. (1994). *What color is your parachute?* Berkeley, CA: Ten Speed Press.

11. Bolles, R. N. (1990). *The 1990 quick job-hunting (and career-changing) map: How to create a picture of your ideal job or next career*. Berkeley, CA: Ten Speed Press.

12. Bolles, R. N. Cited in: Minton, T. (January 25, 1991). Job-hunting requires eyes and ears of friends. *San Francisco Chronicle*, p. D5.

13. Falvey, 1986.

14. Palladino, B. (1992, Winter). Job hunting online. *Online Access*, pp. 20–23.

15. Anonymous. (1992, October). Online information. *PC Today*, p. 41.

16. Strauss, J. (1993, October 17). Online database helps job seekers. *San Francisco Sunday Examiner & Chronicle*, Help wanted section, p. 29.

17. Murray, K. (1994, January 2). Plug in. Log on. Find a job. *New York Times*, sec. 3, p. 23.

18. Mannix, M. (1992, October 26). Writing a computer-friendly résumé. *U.S. News & World Report*, pp. 90–93.

19. Bulkeley, W. M. (1992, June 16). Job-hunters turn to software for an edge. *Wall Street Journal*, p. B13.

20. Anonymous. (1992, June). Pounding the pavement. *PC Novice*, p. 10.

21. Anonymous. (1993, September 13). Personal: Individual software ships ResumeMaker with career planning. *EDGE: Work-Group Computing Report*, p. 3.

22. Mossberg, W. S. (1994, May 5). Four programs to ease PC users into a job search. *Wall Street Journal*, p. B1.

23. Kennedy, J. L., & Morrow, T. J. (1994). *Electronic job search revolution: Win with the new technology that's reshaping today's job market*. New York: Wiley.

24. Pender, K. (1994, May 16). Jobseekers urged to pack lots of 'keywords' into résumés. *San Francisco Chronicle*, pp. B1, B4.

25. Howe, K. (1992, September 19). Firm turns hiring into a science. *San Francisco Chronicle*, pp. B1, B2.

26. Bulkeley, W. M. (1992, June 23). Employers use software to track résumés. *Wall Street Journal*, p. B6.

27. Kennedy, J. L., & Morrow, T. J. (1994). *Electronic résumé revolution: Create a winning résumé for the new world of job seeking*. New York: Wiley.

28. Bennett, H., & McFadden, C. (1993, October 17). How to stand out in a crowd. *San Francisco Sunday Examiner & Chronicle*, help wanted section, p. 29.

29. Bolles. Quoted in: Rubin, 1994.

30. Gardner, J. W. 1991 commencement address, Stanford University, June 16, 1991. Quoted in: Gardner, J. W. (1991, May-June). You are what you commit to achieve. *Stanford Observer*, pp. 10–11.

1. *What would you like to spend your life doing?* Ask students to write down on a sheet of paper three things that (whether working or not working) they would like to spend their lives doing if they had a reasonably modest income and didn't have to work. (These are supposed to express their dreams, so tell students to make them as detailed as possible.)

    Now ask them to write down three more things they would like to do for their work or career if money were no object.

    In a small group or classroom setting, have students discuss their choices. Questions to consider: Why would you choose these directions? Do you think you could achieve any of these? How might you go about it?

2. *What interests and skills are you attracted to?* Ask students to complete Personal Exploration #13.1, "The 'Career Video.'" When everyone is done, ask each student to join with others in a group that corresponds to his or her first choice of career video. (If a student turns out to be the only one in a group, he or she should join the second-choice group.)

    Within each group, students should discuss the following questions: What qualities led you to this choice? What kinds of occupations mentioned above seem attractive to you? Does the major (or majors) you're contemplating lead in this direction?

    Now ask each student to join with others in his or her second choice of career video. Discuss the same questions. If there's time, have students join the group of their third choice. Questions to consider: Do you find yourself assembling with most of the same people as before? If not, what seems to account for the differences? What information of personal value to you can you take away from this?

3. *Visiting the career counseling and job placement office.* Have students complete (out of class) Personal Exploration #13.2, "What Can You Learn from a Visit to the Career Counseling & Job Placement Office?" Have them discuss the results of their investigations in class. Then ask them to make an appointment to follow up on one of the components (such as taking a vocational test). Suggest students write a one-page report on their follow-up investigation to turn into the instructor.

4. *How can you build a great résumé?* In small groups have students complete Personal Exploration #13.3, "How Can You Build an Impressive Résumé?" Brainstorming may help in putting together a résumé. Have students talk through their responses to the Personal Exploration and take turns asking for feedback and suggestions.

5. *The informational interview.* Have students look back at the heading "Ways of Looking for Jobs" and the discussion of informational interviews. Instruct them to obtain an informational interview with someone (preferably an executive or administrator) in an organization for which they might be interested in working, either as an intern or in a possible career capacity. Have them prepare a list of questions to ask the person they'll be interviewing.

    After the interview, the student should write a one-page paper reporting on his or her experience for submission to the instructor.

JOURNAL ENTRY #13.1: DREAMING WHAT YOU'D LIKE TO STUDY The best way to start thinking about your prospective major is to dream your dreams. Your journal is the place to do this. Take 15 minutes to free-associate, and write as quickly (but legibly) as you can all your desires about things you're curious about or enjoy and would like to study. Then state what majors might best serve your wishes.

_____

_____

_____

_____

_____

_____

_____

_____

JOURNAL ENTRY #13.2: DREAMING YOUR CAREERS You go through life only once. Yet it's possible to have more than one career—be a physician/musician, a writer/attorney, a social worker/social activist, for example. Or you might have successive careers, each one different. When you "dream the impossible dream," what careers come to mind?

_____

_____

_____

_____

_____

_____

_____

JOURNAL ENTRY #13.3: GETTING GOOD AT JOB INTERVIEWS Interviewing for jobs is a skill all by itself. This book did not have space to give this subject the coverage it deserves. What kinds of skills do you think are needed for interviewing? What books can you find in the library that might help you refine your interviewing techniques?

_____

_____

_____

_____

_____

_____

_____

sources & credits

CHAP. 1: **Pers Expl #1.1** adapted from Nowicki-Strickland Scale and results from Nowicki, S. Jr. & Strickland, B. R. (1973, February). A locus of control scale for children. *Journal of Consulting & Clinical Psychology, 40*(1), 148 – 54. Copyright © 1973 by the American Psychological Association. Adapted by permission. **Panel 1.1** adapted from McGinnis, A. L. (1990). *The power of optimism.* San Francisco: Harper & Row, p. xiv.

CHAP. 3: **Panel 3.1** courtesy Genesee Community College. **Panel 3.3** adapted from San Jose State University Police Department (1989). Safety and security at San Jose State. San Jose, CA: San Jose State University, Police Department, Investigations/Crime Prevention Unit.

SPECIAL SECTION: Special section adapted from Williams, B. K., Sawyer, S. C., & Hutchinson, S. E. (1995). *Using information technology: A practical introduction to computers & communications.* Burr Ridge, IL: Irwin. Used with permission of Richard D. Irwin, a Times Mirror Higher Education Group, Inc., company. **Panel SS.1** adapted from the Editors of *PC World Magazine* (1992, November 13). Mobile computing, special pullout section sponsored by Intel. *Newsweek,* p. N26. **Panel SS.2** from Williams, Richard. (1993, April 10). On the hunt for a used computer. *The Globe & Mail* (Toronto), p. B13.

CHAP. 5: **Panel 5.1** from Weiten, W. (1989). *Psychology: Themes and variations.* Pacific Grove, CA: Brooks/Cole, p. 254. Used with permission. Based on material from D. van Guilford, Van Nostrand, 1939. **Pers Expl #5.1** adapted from "Modality Inventory" by Ducharme, A., & Watford, L., Middle Grades Department, Valdosta State University, Valdosta, GA 31698. Reprinted with the kind permission of Dr. Adele Ducharme and Dr. Luck Watford. **Page 99**, material beginning "A Rustler . . .; from Weiten, W., Lloyd, M. A., & Lashley, R. L. (1990). *Psychology applied to modern life: Adjustment in the 90s* (3rd ed.). Pacific Grove, CA: Brooks/Cole, p. 24. Adapted from Bower, G. H., & Clark, M. C. (1969). Narrative stories as mediators for social learning. *Psychonomic Science, 14,* 181 – 82. Copyright © 1969 by the Psychonomic Society. Adapted by permission of the Psychonomic Society.

CHAP. 6: **Pers Expl #6.1** adapted from "Modality Inventory" by Ducharme, A., & Watford, L., Middle Grades Department, Valdosta State University, Valdosta, GA 31698. Reprinted with the kind permission of Dr. Adele Ducharme and Dr. Luck Watford. **Panel 6.1** adapted from Lindgren, H. C. (1969). *The psychology of college success: A dynamic approach.* New York: Wiley.

CHAP. 7: **Pers Expl #7.1** adapted from Cortina, J., Elder, J., & Gonnet, K. (1992). *Comprehending college textbooks: Steps to understanding and remembering what you read* (2nd ed.). New York: McGraw-Hill, pp. 3 – 4. **Panel 7.1** reproduced from Weeks, J. R. (1992). *Population: An introduction to concepts and issues* (5th ed.). Belmont, CA: Wadsworth. **Panel 7.2,** page reproduced from Biagi, S. (1994). *Media/Impact: An introduction to mass media,* updated second edition. Belmont, CA: Wadsworth, p. 180.

SPECIAL SECTION: Portions of special section adapted from Williams, B. K., & Knight, S. M. (1994). *Healthy for life: Wellness and the art of living* (Pacific Grove, CA: Brooks/Cole), pp. 12.16 – 12.20. Used with permission.

CHAP. 10: Portions of chapter adapted from Williams, B. K., & Knight, S. M. (1994). *Healthy for life: Wellness and the art of living* (Pacific Grove, CA: Brooks/Cole), especially Unit 2. Used with permission. **Pers Expl #10.1** from Mullen, Cathleen, & Costello, Gerald. (1981). *Health awareness through self-discovery.* Edina, MN: Burgess International Group. **Panel 10.2** from Benson, H. (1989). Editorial: Hypnosis and the relaxation response. *Gastroenterology, 96,* 1610.

CHAP. 11: Portions of chapter adapted from Williams, B. K., & Knight, S. M. (1994). *Healthy for life: Wellness and the art of living* (Pacific Grove, CA: Brooks/Cole), especially Units 8, 9, 11. Used by permission. **Pers Expl #11.1** from Sternberg, R. J., & Soriano, L. J. (1984). Styles of conflict resolution. *Journal of Personality & Social Psychology, 47,* 115 – 26; Weiten, W., Lloyd, M. A., & Lashley, R. L. (1991). *Psychology applied to modern life: Adjustment in the 90s* (3rd ed.). Pacific Grove: CA: Brooks/Cole; Williams, B. K., & Knight, S. M. (1994). *Healthy for life: Wellness and the art of living* (Pacific Grove, CA: Brooks/Cole), pp. 8.36 – 8.39. **Pers Expl #11.2** from Lazarus, A. A. (1971). Assertiveness questionnaire, in *Behavior theory and beyond.* New York: McGraw-Hill. (Reissued by JasonAronson, Northvale, NJ, 1996.) By permission of Arnold A. Lazarus, Ph.D. **Pers Expl #11.3** adapted from: Anderson, D. M., & Christenson, G. M. (1991). Ethnic breakdown of AIDS related knowledge and attitudes from the National Adolescent Student Health Survey. *Journal of Health Education, 22,* 30 – 34; Timoshok, L., Sweet, D. M., & Zich, J. (1987). A three city comparison of the public's knowledge and attitudes about AIDS. *Psychology & Health, 1*(1), 43 – 60; Weiten, W., Lloyd, M. A., & Lashley, R. L. (1991). *Psychology applied to modern life: Adjustment in the 90s* (3rd ed.). Pacific Grove, CA: Brooks/Cole, p. 408. **Panel 11.3** from Williams, B. K., & Knight, S. M.

(1994). *Healthy for life: Wellness and the art of living.* Pacific Grove, CA: Brooks/Cole, pp. 9.8 – 9.9. Used with permission. Based on data from Centers for Disease Control (1990). *Contraceptive options: Increasing your awareness.* Washington, DC: NAACOG. Hatcher, R., Guest, F., Stewart, F. et al. (1990). *Contraceptive technology, 1990 – 1992.* New York: Irvington. Leads from the MMWR (1988). Condoms for prevention of sexually transmitted diseases. *Journal of the American Medical Association, 259,* 1925 – 27. Harlap, S., Kost, K., & Forrest, D. (1991). *Preventing pregnancy, protecting health: A new look at birth control choices in the United States.* New York: Alan Guttmacher Institute. Anonymous (1991, December). Deconstructing the condom. *Self,* pp. 122 – 23. Consumers Union (1989, March). Can you rely on condoms? *Consumer Reports,* pp. 135 – 41. Consumers Union (1995, May). How reliable are condoms? *Consumer Reports,* pp. 320 – 25.

CHAP. 13: Portions of chapter adapted from Williams, B. K., & Knight, S. M. (1994). *Healthy for life: Wellness and the art of living* (Pacific Grove, CA: Brooks/Cole), especially pp. 2.32, 16.31. Used with permission. Parts of chapter also adapted from Williams, B. K., Sawyer, S. C., & Hutchinson, S. E. (1995). *Using information technology: A practical introduction to computers & communications.* Burr Ridge, IL: Irwin, pp. 589 – 92. Used with permission of Richard D. Irwin, a Times Mirror Higher Education Group, Inc., company. **Pers Expl #13.1** adapted and reproduced by special permission of the Publisher, Psychological Assessment Resources Inc., Odessa, FL 33556, from the *Self-Directed Search Assessment Booklet* by John L. Holland, Ph.D. Copyright 1970, 1977, 1985, 1990, 1994 by PAR, Inc. Further reproduction is prohibited without permission from PAR, Inc. The Self-Directed Search materials are available for purchase through PAR, Inc. by calling 1-800-331-8378. **Panel 13.1** from Falvey, J. (1986). *After college: The business of getting jobs.* Charlotte, VT: Williamson Publishing, p. 37. **Panel 13.3** from Pender, K. (1994, May 16). Resume dos and don'ts. *San Francisco Chronicle,* p. B4. © San Francisco Chronicle. Reprinted by permission.

glossary/ index

balancing with school and work, 7
making friends on campus and, 5–6
stress of, 215, 222–223
time needed for, 77, 79
Comparison charts are useful for studying several concepts and the relationships between them, 153, 154
Compromise, 239
CompuServe, 102
Computer-friendly résumés, 286–287
Computers
communications tools for, 101–105
desktop vs. portable, 90–91
job-hunting with, 289–290
power needed in, 91–92
purchasing, 93–95, 267
software available for, 95–101
styles of, 90
writing term papers on, 188, 200, 205, 206
Concept maps are visual diagrams of concepts, 153, 154
Condoms are thin sheaths made of latex rubber or lamb intestine, 250
buying, 250–251
using, 249, 250–252
Conflict
personal exploration on, 238
styles of dealing with, 239–240
Congressional Methodology formula, 271
Control, personal sense of, 10–13
Conversation starters and stoppers, 242
Cooperative education programs allow you to improve your marketability upon graduation by giving you work experience in your major, 272
Coping is a way of dealing with stress where you change the stressor or your reaction to it, 226
Copyright page (on the back of the title page) gives the date the book was published, 140, 141, 143
Cornell method of note taking, 127
Counseling center, 46
Counselors, 228

Course list is a list of the courses being taught in the current school term, 37
Courses
identifying for goal-achievement, 67, 68
syllabus for, 70
Cover letter, 290
Cramming is defined as preparing hastily for an examination, 109
problems with, 84, 108, 114
Crash-avoidance techniques, 215
Creativity refers to the human capacity to express ourselves in original or imaginative ways, 14
Credentials, teacher, 43
Credit cards are those that allow the charges to be paid off in installments plus interest, provided you make a minimum payment every month, 269
Crisis is an especially strong source of stress, 224
Crisis intervention services, 228
Crying, 228
Curriculum worksheet is a list of courses required for the major and the semesters in which it is recommended the students take them, 42
Cut and paste feature, 97

Daily expense record, 264
Daily "to do" lists, 76
Database, 98
Database management system (DBMS), 98, 99
Dean of Students office, 45
Debit cards enable you to pay for purchases by withdrawing funds electronically directly from your savings or checking account, 269
Debts, 269
Dedicated fax machines, 101
Defensive driving, 216
Degree program is a list of courses a student must take to obtain a college degree in a specific field, 41
Delaying tactics, 81
Demonstrated financial need means that you have proven you need financial aid according to a certain formula, 271

Deposition Test, 180
Depth-of-processing principle states that how shallowly or deeply you hold a thought depends on how much you think about it and how many associations you form with it, 115
Desktop accessories, 96, 98
Desktop personal computers, 90
Developmental classes, 5
Diagrams, study, 152
Dictionaries, 196, 197
Disabled students, 54, 224
Disarming technique, 242
Discipline, 31
Dishonesty, academic, 177–181
Distractions, 82–83
Distress is the effect when stress occurs owing to a negative event, 224
Distressor is the result when the source of stress is a negative event, 224
Distributed practice is when the student distributes study time over several days. It is more effective for retaining information, 114
Diversion, 241
Diversity means variety–in race, gender, ethnicity, age, physical abilities, and sexual orientation, 51
age, 52–53
gender, 51–52
physical disabilities, 54
racial/cultural, 53–54
sexual orientation, 52
Doctorate degree, 43
Documentation, 205–206
Domination, 239
Driving safety, 214–217
Dropping out
reasons for, 9–10, 42
statistics on, 9
Drugs, 226

Earnings, lifetime, 26
Eating
driving and, 217
stress-release through, 227
time needed for, 77
Edwards Personal Preference Schedule (EPPS), 282
Eidetic imagery, 108

Hardware, computer, 92
Hassles are simply frustrating irritants, 224
Health
    effect of humor and hope on, 228
    sexually transmitted diseases and, 244–248
    stress and, 224, 226, 229, 231
Health insurance, 269
Health service, 46
High school vs. college, 4–5
Hispanic-Americans, 53–54
HIV (Human Immunodeficiency Virus) is the virus causing AIDS. It brings about a variety of ills, the most important of which is the breakdown of the immune system, which leads to the development of certain infections and cancers, 244–248
    testing for, 247–248
Holmes-Rahe Life Events Scale, 224
Homework. *See also* Study
    keeping up with, 133
    scheduling time for, 74
Homophobia is fear of, or resistance to, the idea of homosexuality or of homosexuals, 52
Homosexuality
    HIV/AIDS and, 247, 248
    school policies on, 52
Honesty
    academic, 177–181
    personal exploration on, 179
Hopelessness, 240
Housing expenses, 265, 267
Housing office is a campus office to help students find housing either on or off campus, 48
Humor, 228

IBM-style computers, 90
Idea cards, 199
Immediate perceptual memory is defined as a reflex memory in which an impression is immediately replaced by a new one, 109
Income
    of college graduates, 25–26, 258
    managing, 258–259, 260
    sources of, 259
Index is an alphabetically arranged list of names and subjects that appear in the text, giving the

page numbers on which they appear, 142, 143
    of periodicals, 196, 197
Information
    high-tech ways of collecting, 200
    low-tech ways of collecting, 198–199
    online, 104–105, 197, 198
Informational interview, 284–285
Information cards, 198–199
Information technology
    communications tools, 101–105
    computer software, 95–101
    personal computers, 90–95
Inner voice, 149, 151, 228
Instructor evaluations consider how fairly instructors grade and how effectively they present their lectures, 37
Instructors
    academic help from, 43–44
    negotiating with, 181
    psyching out, 160–161
Insurance, 269–270
Integrated software packages, 100–101
Integration
    conflict, 239–240
    daily life, 212
"Integrators," 212
Interference is the competition among related memories, 115
Interlibrary loan is a service that enables you to borrow books from other libraries, 193
Intermediate-range goals, 64–66
Internal locus of control is the belief that rewards and punishments are due to one's own behavior, character, or efforts, 11
International students, 54
Internet, 51, 100, 103, 104–105
InterNIC, 105
Internships, 285
Interviews
    employment, 290
    informational, 284–285
Intravenous drug use, 247, 249
Italic type, 97, 144

Job placement office is a campus office that provides job listings from local or campus employees looking for student help, 48

services provided by, 279–280
    visiting, 282–283
Jobs. *See* Career; Employment; Work
Journal entries, 17
Journal research, 196

Keywords are important terms or names that you are expected to understand and be able to define, 194
Kinesthetic learners learn best when they touch and are physically involved in what they are studying, 113

Laboratory assignments
    career skills and, 27
    usefulness of, 152
Laptop computers, 91
Laughter, 228
Learning
    demonstrating, 187
    difficult subjects, 149–154
    reading for, 138–139
    tools for aiding, 152–153
Learning center is a special center where students go to learn a specific subject or skill, 45
    academic help from, 38, 45
Learning lab. *See* Learning center
Learning objectives are topics the student is expected to learn, which are listed at the beginning of each chapter, 143–144
    Learning skills, 28
Learning styles are the ways in which people acquire knowledge, 111
    lectures and, 122
    personal exploration of, 111–112
    types of, 112–113
Lectures, 121–135
    career skills and, 27
    classroom participation and, 125–126, 132–133
    fighting boredom and fatigue in, 130–133
    learning styles and, 122
    note-taking and reviewing system for, 126–130
    taping, 84, 133, 154
Legal services, 49
Lesbians. *See* Homosexuality

Narrative story method is a memory technique that involves making up a narrative, or story. It helps students recall unrelated lists of words by giving them meaning and linking them in a specific order, 117

Native Americans, 53, 54

Need-based financial aid requires you and your parents to fill out forms stating your resources. The college then determines how much aid needs to be made up from somewhere else, 270

Needs analysis document is a form for helping people prove their financial need to colleges, 271

Negative thoughts, 149–150, 151, 165

Negotiation, instructor, 181

Networking, 41

Newsgroups, 105

Newspaper research, 196

Nonassertive behavior means consistently giving in to others on points of difference. It means agreeing with others regardless of your feelings, not expressing your opinions, hurting yourself to avoid hurting others, 243

Nonoxynol-9 is a spermicide that kills STD organisms, 249

Nontraditional students are post-secondary students who are older than 24 years, 52

Notebook computers, 91, 93

Note-taking system, 126–130

Objective questions are those that are true-false, multiple-choice, matching, and fill-in, 166
    fill-in-the-blank questions, 170
    matching questions, 169–170
    multiple-choice questions, 168–169
    strategies applicable to, 167–168
    true-false questions, 168

Obstacles
    identifying, 65, 66
    strategies for overcoming, 67, 69

Online computerized catalogs require that you use a computer terminal or microcomputer that has a wired connection to a database, 194

Online information services, 100, 102–103, 197

Optimism, 13

Orientation program, 37

Outgo, financial, 258, 259–260

Outline processor, 97

Outlines
    for long-answer essays, 172, 174
    for term papers, 191–192, 202

Overlearning is defined as continued rehearsal of material after you first appeared to have mastered it, 114, 162

Papers. *See* Term papers

Parent Loans for Undergraduate Students (PLUS), 272

Parents, living with, 7–8

Passive aggression, 240

Passive behavior means consistently giving in to others on points of difference. It means agreeing with others regardless of your feelings, not expressing your opinions, hurting yourself to avoid hurting others, 243

Passive reading, 145

Pell Grants, 271

People distractions, 83

Performance anxiety, 163

Periodical research, 196, 197

Perkins Loans, 272

Personal associations, 130

Personal best, 23

Personal computers. *See* Computers

Personal development, 26

Personal Finance for Dummies (Tyson), 213

Personal information managers (PIMs), 96, 98

Personal word-processor, 96

Personal writing, 186

Photocopiers, 200

Photographic memory, 108

Physical disability is a health-related condition that prevents a person from participating fully in daily activities, 54

Plagiarism means presenting another person's ideas as one's own, 178
    of term papers, 187

Planning process
    actions based on, 66–69
    intermediate-range goals and, 64–66

long-range goals and, 28–29, 64

Poetry, memorizing, 109, 110

Police, campus, 46–47

Portable computers, 90–91, 93, 200

Positive self-talk consists of giving yourself positive messages, 150, 151
    coping with stress through, 228
    test taking and, 165

Posters, 38

Power of Optimism, The (McGinnis), 13

Preface tells the reader the intended audience for the book, the author's purpose and approach, why the book is different, and perhaps an overview of the organization, 141, 143

Presentation graphics, 100

Priority setting, 70, 76

Proactive interference, 115

Process diagrams are useful for representing the steps in a process and thus are useful in such subjects as biology, geology, or environmental science, 152, 153

Procrastination is defined as putting off things intentionally and habitually, 80
    fighting, 80–81

Prodigy (online service), 102

Professors. *See* Instructors

Progressive muscular relaxation consists of reducing stress by tightening and relaxing major muscle groups throughout your body, 229

Projects, 28

Proofreading
    term papers, 206
    test answers, 167, 176

Provocation, driver, 214

Psychological risks, 14–15

Psychological services, 46

Publications, college, 37–38

Public transportation, 213, 265–266

Questioning process
    SQ3R reading method and, 145–146
    3Rs reading method and, 147–148

Questions on tests or exams
    objective, 166, 167–170
    subjective, 166

Thinking
multiple-choice questions and, 168–169
positive, 150, 151, 165
as study, 84
3Rs reading system has three steps for mastering textbooks: Read, Record, Recite, 147–148
Time
log-keeping exercise, 78
required for study, 6–7, 62, 79, 150–152
weekly use of, 77–79
for writing term papers, 200
Time lines are sketches representing a particular historical development, 153, 154
Time management, 61–88
action plan for, 66–69
boosting performance through, 83–84
as career skill, 28
distractions and, 82–83
life goals and, 28–29, 62
master timetable and, 70–72
planning process and, 64–66
procrastination and, 80–81
scheduling study time as, 79–80
six-step program for, 29, 62–77
test taking and, 162, 177
time wasters and, 77–84
"to do" lists and, 76–77
weekly timetable and, 73–75
Timetables
master, 70–72
weekly, 73–75
Title page gives the title, edition number (if later than the first edition), author, and publisher, 140, 141
"To do" lists, 76–77
Topics, term paper, 188–190
Traditional students are post-secondary students between the ages of 18 and 24 years, 52
Transitions, daily, 212
Transportation expenses, 213, 265, 267
Transportation office is the office that issues permits for parking on campus and gives out information on public transportation and car pools, 48

Troubleshooting, 41
True-false questions are statements that you must indicate are either correct or incorrect, 168
Tutor is a private teacher or coach to help an individual student improve a particular skill, 45

Underlining key information, 147–148
Unloading means taking 2–3 minutes to jot down on the back of the exam sheet any keywords, concepts, and ideas that are in your mind, 165–166
Upgradability, computer, 92
Used computers, 93–94
Usenet, 105

Values are principles by which you lead your life. They are important beliefs or attitudes that you think "ought to be" (or "ought not to be"). Moreover, they are beliefs that you feel strongly enough about to take action on, and which have been consciously chosen, 20
on achieving your personal best, 23
characteristics of, 20–21
on higher education, 21–22
Vehicles. *See* Cars
Venereal disease. *See* Sexually transmitted diseases
Verbal memory aids, 116
Visualization is a procedure in which you essentially daydream an image or desired change, anticipating that your body will respond as if the image were real, 230
Visual learners like to see pictures of things described or words written down, 113
Visual memory aids, 117
Vocational Preference Inventory, 280
Vocational testing, 279–280
Voice mail, 101–102
Voice Of Judgment, 149, 151

Weekly timetable, 73–75
Wellness services, 47
What Color Is Your Parachute? (Bolles), 284
What-Would-Your-Parents-Say Test, 180
When Smart People Fail (Hyatt & Gottlieb), 14
Word processing software, 96, 97
Word processing typewriter, 95–96
Work. *See also* Career; Employment
average commute to, 2
balancing study with, 7
process of looking for, 284–290
stress related to, 223
time needed for, 79
Working title is a tentative title for your paper, 202
Work-Study programs, 272
World economy, 51
World Wide Web, 100, 103, 105
Writing
as career skill, 27
documentation and, 205–206
environment for, 200
essays on tests, 170–177
fine tuning, 205
first drafts, 202–203
outlines, 174, 191–192
paragraphs in essays, 175–177
proofreading, 206
reorganizing, 205
revising, 204–205
term papers, 185–210
tips on, 203–204
using computer, 188, 200, 205, 206
Written examinations require the student to write essays, either short or long, 170–177

Yearly money plan, 262, 263
Your Maximum Mind (Benson), 231
Your Money or Your Life (Dominguez & Robin), 278
Your Perfect Right (Alberti & Emmons), 243

Zen driving technique, 215